Music by William Henry Havergal

The edition of *The Complete Works of Frances Ridley Havergal* has five parts:

Volume I *Behold Your King: The Complete Poetical Works of Frances Ridley Havergal*

Volume II *Whose I Am and Whom I Serve: Prose Works of Frances Ridley Havergal*

Volume III *Loving Messages for the Little Ones: Works for Children by Frances Ridley Havergal*

Volume IV *Love for Love: Frances Ridley Havergal: Memorials, Letters and Biographical Works*

Volume V *Songs of Truth and Love: Music by Frances Ridley Havergal and William Henry Havergal*

David L. Chalkley, Editor   Dr. Glen T. Wegge, Music Editor

Frances Ridley Havergal's formal education ended when she was 17, with one term at a young women's school in Düsseldorf, Germany, yet she was a true scholar all her life. Fluent in German and French and nearly so in Italian, she read and loved the Reformers in Latin, German, and French. Knowledge was never an end in itself, only a means to know better her Lord and Saviour and to help to bring others to know Him. The Bible was her only Book, and she studied the Hebrew and Greek texts of Scripture, memorized nearly all the New Testament and large portions of the Old Testament, and loved the Author with all her being.

Frances was brought to a saving knowledge of Christ when she was 14, and the rest of her life was consecrated to her Saviour, the Lord Jesus. Keenly aware of her own sinfulness and inability, her sole desire was to please and glorify Him alone. Very finely gifted, she was truly diligent with her gifts: her poetry is among the finest in the English language, after George Herbert; her prose works are deeply beneficial; a musician to the core, she left behind important compositions. Like her works, her life richly touched the ones near her and countless many who met or heard her. The Lord Jesus Christ was her alone, only beauty, and she glowed Him and His truth. Never wanting attention to herself, Frances' desire of her heart was for herself and for others to know her King, the Lord Jesus Christ. Her works are a gold-mine of help and enrichment. There is life in these pages: her works truly glorify the Lord, truly benefit His people, and powerfully reach those who do not yet know Him.

The Music of Frances Ridley Havergal by Glen T. Wegge, Ph.D.

This Companion Volume to the Havergal edition is a valuable presentation of F.R.H.'s scores, most or nearly all of F.R.H.'s scores very little if any at all seen, or even known of, for nearly a century. What a valuable body of music has been unknown for so long and is now made available to many. Dr. Wegge completed his Ph.D. in Music Theory at Indiana University at Bloomington, and his diligence and thoroughness in this volume are obvious. First an analysis of F.R.H.'s compositions is given, an essay that both addresses the most advanced musicians and also reaches those who are untrained in music; then all the extant scores that have been found are newly typeset, with complete texts for each score and extensive indices at the end of the book. This volume presents F.R.H.'s music in newly typeset scores diligently prepared by Dr. Wegge, and Volume V of the Havergal edition presents the scores in facsimile, the original 19th century scores. (The essay—a dissertation—analysing her scores is given the same both in this Companion Volume and in Volume V of the Havergal edition.)

Dr. Wegge is also preparing all of these scores for publication in performance folio editions.

The Havergal Trust   P.O. Box 649   Kirksville, Missouri 63501

William Henry Havergal (1793–1870) was the foremost church musician and composer of sacred music in England in his generation. A finely gifted performer and music leader, he composed and published important music, and was a leading reformer of church music practice. He was offered a professorship in music at Oxford University, but he declined that for his first calling, to be a minister and pastor. Though rarely gifted to write music, he preferred to prepare a sermon than to compose a score. Music was a very important part of his ministry, and always a pleasure and rest to him, but he concentrated on music only when his physical health prevented him from his pastoral work. His Sermons, printed in four volumes, are gold. He was the most important musical mentor to his daughter, Frances Ridley Havergal.

Music by William Henry Havergal.

A Collection of Various Scores

Not Contained in Havergal's Psalmody and Century of Chants

Taken from the New Edition of
The Complete Works of Frances Ridley Havergal.

"Knowing her intense desire that Christ should be magnified, whether
by her life or in her death, may it be to His glory
that in these pages she, being dead,
'Yet speaketh!'"

MUSIC BY WILLIAM HENRY HAVERGAL.
A Collection of Various Scores not Contained in Havergal's Psalmody and Century of Chants
Copyright © 2017 by the Havergal Trust.

ISBN 978-1-937236-57-1   Library of Congress Control Number: 2016919858

Printed in the United States of America   *This book is printed on acid-free paper.*

Cover Design by Glen T. Wegge.

Havergal, William Henry
Music by William Henry Havergal: prose, poetry, and music taken from the edition of the complete works of Frances Ridley Havergal / William Henry Havergal.
1. Havergal, William Henry, 1793–1870. 2. Christian Life. 3. Christian Poetry, English. 4. Music. I. Title

This is taken from *The Complete Works of Frances Ridley Havergal.*
David L. Chalkley, General Editor.   Dr. Glen T. Wegge, Music Editor.

Notice of Copyright: © 2017 The Havergal Trust. All rights are reserved by the Havergal Trust. Only with permission from the Havergal Trust, a portion or portions of this edition may be copied and used by others so long as these three requirements are met: 1. No commercial purposes, monetary profit, or financial gain should be involved. 2. No alteration, transformation, development, nor any derivative works, should be done in any way with any of these materials, so that further use should be presented precisely as done in this edition. 3. The user should clearly state this: Copied without changes, and with permission, from the edition of *The Complete Works of Frances Ridley Havergal*, copyright The Havergal Trust.

The purpose of this work is ministry, and any money received by the Havergal Trust from sales of these books is to be applied to continue the work of the Trust, all revenues being applied to cover true costs of production and distribution and then to publish and distribute more books more widely, with very affordable prices, with no financial profit to any involved beyond fair market compensation for time and labor. The purpose of the Trust is to preserve far into the future (if our Lord does not return sooner) works by and about F.R.H., to make available to many these works, and to publish works by other authors similar to Havergal.

While most of the Havergal edition is made of public domain works published before 1923, throughout the edition are numerous items of new work in 2003–2011.

Frances Ridley Havergal used language clearly, specifically, powerfully, precisely, and beautifully, and no alteration of any of her works should be done. At the beginning of the 21st century her words are as simple and fresh as they were when she was here, and they should be left precisely as she wrote them without any change.

Many valuable, important works have been gutted with a pretence of improving or clarifying the language, when the language of Bonar, Spurgeon, Chambers, and others should be left alone in its original clarity, beauty, and power. F.R.H.'s sentences—and very words—have a special power, clarity, beauty, sweetness, and precision which cannot be improved nor even matched—only harmed and distorted—by any changes. Similarly, C. H. Spurgeon, J. C. Ryle, John Owen, John Flavel, Thomas Watson, George Whitefield, Jonathan Edwards, Robert Murray M'Cheyne, and many other similar authors should be left alone in their precise words they originally wrote: any "improvement" of their precise words improves nothing, harms and distorts what they really said, and very often if not always guts what they meant and invites things they never meant. This is far worse than "improving" paintings by Rembrandt, Vermeer, Monet (which would be derided by anyone serious about art), or "improving" scores by Bach, Beethoven, or Rachmaninoff (any true musician cleaves to the original scores with absolute fidelity to the tiniest notated details), and serious people would not accept such against Shakespeare, Nathaniel Hawthorne, Goethe, nor such secular authors. It is a remarkable distortion for an editor to impose "trust me, I know better" rather than the original author.

The photographs and illustrations should also be left just as they are, not "updated," "enhanced," nor changed in any way. ("Improving" Frances does not improve her.)

Many pieces such as "One Hour with Jesus," any of the poems, or other parts of this edition would be very beneficial to print in bulletins, periodicals, and other formats.

The Havergal Trust   P.O. Box 649   Kirksville, Missouri 63501

In all that she did, and in all that she wrote, Frances Ridley Havergal's one overriding desire was—as Colossians 1:18 says—"that in all things he [*her Lord*] might have the pre-eminence." She saw herself as an instrument in her Saviour's hand, writing for His sake, His glory alone. Indeed the words of Psalm 45:1 were true of her: "My heart is inditing a good matter: I speak of the things which I have made touching the King: my tongue is the pen of a ready writer."

The truth of Christ, which she so loved, and which He used her to present to others, is what is relevant and important, not Frances herself. Understanding the truth of this, you don't first of all think "what a wonderful, fine lady she was" but "what a Saviour ! she had." Jesus Christ alone was changing her from what she was, to become daily more like Himself. Frances would not want anyone to look solely or primarily at her, but she would want all to see her Lord and Saviour. He was her only beauty, righteousness, wisdom, her all. So as you embark on reading, may you too see the Lord Jesus Christ. To see her King is what she would have wanted, the true conclusion of her works and life, and of any genuine disciple's works and life. The Lamb is all the glory in Emmanuel's land, the kingdom of God.

A NOTE TO THE READER

Serious effort has been made to publish this edition of *The Complete Works of Frances Ridley Havergal* very closely to the original texts of F.R.H. When clear mistakes had been made in the original books, they were corrected without comment, and other, exceptional changes were made only when there was very good reason. Details of spelling and punctuation were preserved as they were found in the original works.

There were many inconsistencies in the original texts. For example, among different books, or even within the same book on occasion, "labour" and "endeavour" might also be spelled "labor" and "endeavor." Even among the original 19th century Havergal books published by James Nisbet & Co. (F.R.H.'s primary publisher), there is much inconsistency in the way quotation marks were done, consistent within the same book but different from one Nisbet book to another. The British way is to place quotations within single quotation marks, and to place quotations in quotations within double quotation marks: 'Jesus says, and says to you, "Come, oh come, to Me."' The American way is the reverse: "Jesus says, and says to you, 'Come, oh come, to Me.'" As this edition was typeset in 2004, the British way of quotation marks was used for the first item, the definitive, remarkably fine Nisbet edition of *The Poetical Works of Frances Ridley Havergal*, because this original volume used the British style of quotation marks. As we proceeded beyond Nisbet's *Poetical Works*, we saw that various original books alternated between the British and American styles, both among different books by the same publisher Nisbet, and also among other contemporary publishers of F.R.H. in the United Kingdom (Home Words Publishing Co. in London, Marcus Ward in Belfast, and others). Even a manuscript in Frances' own handwriting used the American way of quotation marks. Because there was a need for consistency (not an appearance of randomness or chaos), and because comparatively few are likely to see the pages of the original books, all the quotation marks in this edition are given in the American way, except for Nisbet's *Poetical Works*. Besides quotation marks, there were several other details that we would have done differently ourselves now in the 21st century, which we left the same as we found them in the original books.

If, in reading through these volumes, there is an *appearance* of randomness in the way the various works appear printed on the pages, we would ask that the reader please bear in mind that this edition was typeset using the *original* works: numerous volumes of poetry, prose (including biographies, sermons by Frances' father and others, etc.), and music by a number of different authors and publishers. As much as was practicable, considerable effort was made to make these works in this new edition "mirror" the original works—title pages, contents pages, etc.—even though we knew it is unlikely that the vast majority of readers will ever actually *see* these original works.

The desire and earnest effort was that this edition be an "urtext" edition, cleaving very closely to the original text. Exceptions were made when there was good reason, but these were rare. Perhaps the careful reader will also notice that most of the punctuation marks within the text of the Havergal edition have spacing inserted between them and adjacent letters and/or additional punctuation marks, reflecting typesetting practices of the 19th century. Significant effort was expended to accomplish this, the reason being, again, to cleave as closely as possible to the original text, as well as to give the finished version as much of an authentic look as practicable.

The important matter is, that we sought not to "improve" Frances (and her father, her sisters, and the others in this edition) but to present her as she originally wrote.

David Chalkley, Thomas Sadowski, Dr. Glen Wegge

For more than twelve years, Dr. Glen T. Wegge has been involved in the work to complete the Havergal edition. Without payment of money, with remarkable diligence, patience, persistence, and hard work, he has labored to prepare for publication all of the music in the Havergal edition, and also to complete and publish his own book, *The Music of Frances Ridley Havergal*, a Companion Volume to this edition of *The Complete Works of Frances Ridley Havergal*. He has also done so much to bring to completion (in countless hours of work) <u>all</u> of the other books in the Havergal edition. The patience and support of his wife, Denise, are also appreciated. So much thought, diligence, hard work, countless hours, a servant's heart, a labor of love. My estimate or guess is that Glen has worked approximately 1,500 hours on the Havergal edition, without pay. His work is remarkable both in quantity and in quality, first-rate, sterling work. How many times ? (the Lord knows how many times) has he gone back again and again to fix a text or an illustration until it was just right. Most of the details of his work were known only to Glen and me, much now forgotten, but God sees and knows every trace. How compassionately and richly He has blessed us in all of this.

    For much or most of the past 100 years, few if any have realized the value of Frances' music, and Glen (who completed his Ph.D. in music theory at Indiana University at Bloomington and is so finely gifted and prepared to do this work) is the first one to analyze and present her music in such a scholarly way. He began his work on this in very difficult circumstances, and his diligence, persistence, and servant's heart are a true example for believers. Glen is worthy of strong gratitude from all those who will be encouraged and enriched by F.R.H.'s poetry, prose, and music.

    The Lord reward him as I cannot, as no man can reward.

    This is all the Lord's doing. Thanks be to God for His indescribable gift to us in Christ.

David Chalkley

The Complete Works of Frances Ridley Havergal is dedicated to the glory of the Lord Jesus Christ, laying this at His feet and asking Him to bless to others what He has provided,

"for Jesus' sake only"

and is gratefully inscribed to two people:

    Miss Janet Grierson,
    Mr. Stanley Ward.

Miss Grierson's Biography and her other work on F.R.H. are the most important work on Frances since Maria V. G. Havergal, and she has been invaluably helpful in the preparation of this edition.

Mr. Stanley Ward has been deeply interested in Frances since the 1960's, and his kindness, insights, and help have been truly and profoundly important to this edition.

Thanks be to God for His indescribable gift to us in Christ.

CONTENTS

	PAGE
Preface to music by William Henry Havergal	xv
Music by William Henry Havergal	1

    i. "Just as I am, without one plea" Op. 48 (words by Charlotte Elliott) 1

    ii. "O Thou Dread Power" Op. 42 (words by Burns) 4

    iii. "Poland" Op. 50 (words by William Henry Havergal) 11

    iv. "Gentle Dew" (words by W.H.H.) 17

    v. "Lord, Build Thy House Speedily" Op. 5 (apparently an English translation of a Hebrew hymn, Adir Hu Yivne veito b'karov, with a Hebrew melody notated and arranged by W.H.H.) 24

    vi. Three Hymns by Reginald Heber Op.10 27

        1. "Who shall separate us from the love of Christ?" 28

        2. "Lord! if Thou wilt Thou canst make me clean." 30

        3. "Joy in Heaven." 31

    vii. "From Greenland's Icy Mountains " (words by Reginald Heber) the Robert Cocks score for solo voice and piano published by Robert Cocks & Co.. 34

    viii. "From Greenland's Icy Mountains" (words by Reginald Heber) the score for voices with organ or piano published by Novello 44

    ix. *Original Airs and Harmonized Tunes Adapted to Hymns of Various Measures*, Op. 2. . . . 55

        Note: The words in Numbers 4, 21, and 26 are by W.H.H.; the others are by various authors.

        Preface by W.H.H. 56

        1. "Messiah! At Thy Glad Approach." 58

        2. "Hapless Child of Desolation!" 60

        3. "Desponding Spirit, Rise!" 62

        4. "O Saviour! When with Raptur'd Eye." 63

        5. "When We Pass Thro' Yonder River." 64

        6. "How Sweet to Know the Saviour's Name." 65

        7. "How Sweet the Name of Jesus Sounds." 66

        8. "Day of Vengeance!" 67

        9. "Ere Time Her Circling Course Began." 68

        10. "Come Thou Source of Ev'ry Blessing!" 69

        11. "Saviour! I Thy Word Believe." 70

        12. "How Sweet to Seamen Tempest Toss'd." 72

13. "Eternal God! Our Wand'ring Souls." 73

14. "Sweet the Moments" 74

15. "Jesus! Calm My Troubled Heart." 76

16. "The Dying Believer to His Soul." 78

17. "O God of Abram!" 80

18. "The Lord Jehovah Reigns." 81

19. "O That I Might Walk with God!" 82

20. "The Martyrs' Hymn." 83

21. "Soon the Trumpet of Salvation." 86

22. "Hark! What Mean Those Lamentations." 87

23. "Whence Those Sounds Symphonious?" 88

24. "O God! Mine Inmost Soul Convert." 90

25. "Jesus! Didst Thou Bleed." 92

26. "Calm the Scene." 94

27. " Israel, See the Lord's Salvation!" 96

28. "Rise to Arms!" 97

29. "Awake My Soul!" 98

30. Psalm 27. 100

x. *An Evening Service, and a Hundred Antiphonal Chants*, Op. 35 (the Novello edition) . . . 103

    Remarks on Chants and Chanting 105

    Cantate Domino 114

    Deus Misereatur 126

    Double Antiphonal Chants 140

xi. *An Evening Service*, Op. 37 166

    Magnificat 167

    Nunc Dimittis 173

xii. "Acquaint thee with God" Op. 38 (a paraphrase of Job 22:21) 177

xiii. *Te Deum and Jubilate*, with Chants, Op. 39 183

    Te Deum 185

    Jubilate 204

    Antiphonal Chants, Chants in Later Style, Single Chants. 212

xiv. *An Anthem*, "Give Thanks" Op. 40 (I Chronicles 16:8–10) 214

xv.	Excerpts from *Lyra Ecclesiastica*	228
	2 title pages and inscription page	228
	"Introduction" by Joshua Fawcett, the editor of *Lyra Ecclesiastica*	231
	"Preface" by William Henry Havergal, and Sonnet by Rev. C. Hoyle	233
	Lists of Patrons and Subscribers, Index, List of Authors, and correspondents by W.H.H.	250
	Scores composed by W.H.H., and a score by William Crotch	259
xvi.	*The Grand Chant in Forty Different Forms*, Op. 52	286
xvii.	The Chant and the Psalm Tune, for September 6, 1848	294
xviii.	The Chants and the Psalm Tune, for August 26, 1851	295
xix.	Two Chants, for September 5, 1854	296
xx.	Four Double Chants (No. 1 Recte et Retro, No. 2 Double Counterpoint, No. 3 Recte et Retro, No. 4 Double Counterpoint and Retrogradation).	297
xxi.	Veni Creator	298
xxii.	No. 209 "Venite Adoremus"	299
xxiii.	No. 210 "Winterdyne"	300
xxiv.	No. 211 "Zared"	301
xxv.	No. 212 "Zeboim"	302
xxvi.	"Non Nobis, Domine" (the first part of Psalm 115:1)	303
xxvii.	"God Save the Queen" (In Memoriam December 14, 1861) for four voices (words by W.H.H.)	304
xxviii.	"God Save the Queen" for solo, duet, and trio	305
xxix.	"A New National Hymn" for March 10, 1863 (words by W.H.H.)	308
xxx.	"Fireside Music" by the Rev. W. H. Havergal, M.A.	309

Note: The words for these 16 scores are by W.H.H. unless otherwise noted.

"Harverst Choral."	310
"The Fireside Good Night."	311
"The First 'Fireside' Anniversary of Christmas."	312
"The Fireside Good Morning."	313
" 'Fireside' Grace Before and After Meat."	314
"The Child's 'Fireside' Morning Hymn." (words by Miss Jane Taylor)	315
"The 'Fireside' Hour of Sorrow." (words by Rev. J. D. Burns)	316
"Spring-Tide" and "Loyalty" Two "Fireside" Rounds.	317
"Summer-Tide Is Coming."	318
"Children's 'Fireside' Evening Hymn." (words by Miss Jane Taylor)	319

A Collection of Various Scores not Contained in Havergal's Psalmody and Century of Chants

	"The Pilgrim 'Fireside' Invitation." (words, anonymous)	320
	"A 'Fireside' Hymn of Praise."	321
	"A 'Fireside' Invitation."	322
	"A 'Fireside' View of Sunset."	323
	"A 'Fireside' Christmas Carol." (A-major, words by W.H.H.)	324
	"A 'Fireside' Christmas Carol." (B-flat major, words by Rev. Thos. Davis)	325
xxxi.	"A Christmas Carol" (words by W.H.H.)	327
xxxii.	"The Bethlehem Shepherd-Boy's Tale" (words by W.H.H.)	330
xxiii.	"Christmas Carol" (words by W.H.H.)	332
xxxiv.	"Mementote Vinctorum" ("A Musical Inverse Palindrome, Composed for Three Voices")	333
xxxv.	Enigma No. 23 (words by W.H.H.)	334
xxxvi.	Manuscript "A Gloucester Cry" (Double Antiphonal Chant from a subject "Hot cross buns")	336
xxxvii.	Manuscript "Child's Morning Hymn" August 5, 1843 (words likely by W.H.H.)	338
xxxviii.	Manuscript "Saviour, when from realms above" ("Each Part in Each Strain Per Recte et Retro") Bonn January 18, 1866 (words by W.H.H.)	341
xxxix.	Manuscript "Tunes for grandchildren"	343
xl.	Manuscripts "Hark my mother's voice I hear" and "Sleep baby sleep Our cottage vale is deep" for his granddaughter, Frances Anna Shaw (words likely by W.H.H.)	346
xli.	Manuscript "Mighty Father! Blessed Son!" (words by Dr. John S. B. Monsell)	350
xlii.	Manuscript "An Identical Inverse Palindrome (to a Missionary Hymnette)"	352
xliii.	A Reprint of *All the Tunes in Ravenscroft's Book of Psalms* with Introductory Remarks by W.H.H. (London: Novello, 1845)	356
xliv.	*A History of the Old Hundredth Psalm Tune*, with Specimens by W.H.H. (New York: Mason Brothers, 1854)	472
Words of missionary hymns by W.H.H., sung at meetings on behalf of the Church Missionary Society		547
xlv.	"Nuptial Grace" words by W.H.H., to be sung to his score "Eden"	566
xlvi.	the score entitled "from 'Glory to Glory.'" words by F.R.H. set to music by W.H.H.	567
Manuscript letter to W.H.H. from a friend, Rev. Jarratt, about a poor woman's support of missionaries		568–570
Three Sermons on true, holy music in the true, holy worship of God		571
i.	Holy Praise Offered by Means of Holy Music II Chronicles 5:13	572
ii.	The Union of Sacrifice and Song II Chronicles 29:27	577
iii.	Elisha and the Minstrel II Kings 3:15	584

ILLUSTRATIONS

	PAGE
William Henry Havergal, photograph portrait and signature, undated	ii
Dr. Glen T. Wegge	vi
Miss Janet Grierson, and Mr. and Mrs. Stanley Ward	vii
Dr. William Crotch, undated portrait	xiii
W.H.H., undated portrait	xiv
Lowell Mason, undated portrait	xxiii
W.H.H., manuscript score, "Saviour, when from realms above"	xxvii
Title page of *Havergal's Psalmody and Century of Chants*	xxviii
Advertisement page of *Havergal's Psalmody and Century of Chants* and *Songs of Grace and Glory*	xxix
William Henry Havergal, painted by Solomon Cole in 1845	xxx
Jane Head Havergal, F.R.H.'s mother, painted by Solomon Cole in 1845	xxxi
W.H.H., portrait in pen or charcoal by Edwin Cocking, 1855, with signature and partial score by W.H.H.	10
W.H.H., manuscript of poem "Softly the dew" December 13, 1869	16
Pages from W.H.H.'s Sermon Record Book	23
Advertisement of Miriam Crane's *Records of the Life of the Rev. William Henry Havergal, M.A.*	26
Advertisement page of published music by W.H.H.	54
W.H.H., undated photograph portrait	101
Astley Church and Rectory, published print by Jane Miriam (Havergal) Crane	104
St. Nicholas Church, Worcester, photograph from the 19th century	165
Worcester Cathedral, exterior and interior photographs	278
W.H.H., manuscript first page of sermon on Hebrews 13:17	355
George Herbert, portrait	360
A published copy of the Consecration Hymn, words by Frances Ridley Havergal set to W.H.H.'s score "Patmos"	480
W.H.H., sculpture bust of W.H.H. by Robert Pauer of Creuznach in 1868	524
W.H.H., print based on oil portrait by Solomon Cole in 1845, with signature	542
W.H.H., manuscript first page of sermon on Acts 14:27	547
A photograph of W.H.H. in 1869	569

A Collection of Various Scores not Contained in Havergal's Psalmody and Century of Chants   xiii

Published leaflet score, "From 'Glory to Glory'"   567

Manuscript letter to W.H.H. from a friend, Rev. Jarratt, about
a poor woman's support of missionaries   568–570

Dr. William Crotch (1775–1847). A brilliant composer and performer, Dr. Crotch was a true friend to William Henry Havergal, and a profoundly valuable influence on W.H.H.'s music.

Found among Havergal manuscripts and papers, unsigned and undated, this is almost certainly a portrait of William Henry Havergal, likely done by one of his children (very possibly by his eldest child, Miriam, a fine artist, or his daughter Ellen, also a exceptionally fine artist). See also the portraits of W.H.H. on pages ii, 1520, 1605, 1984, 2028, and 2046 of Volume V of the Havergal edition.

MUSIC BY WILLIAM HENRY HAVERGAL

William Henry Havergal (1793–1870) was a pastor, musician, scholar, and an example of the believer. His sermons are true gold, so good, fully at the level of rich benefit of sermons by J. C. Ryle, Charles Spurgeon, and D. Martyn Lloyd-Jones. Accounts of his pastoral ministry are true examples, glowing the Lord and His truth.

Born at High Wycombe, Buckinghamshire, on January 18, 1793, he was sent at age eight to a school at Princes Risborough, and later to Merchant Taylors' School in London. He matriculated at St. Edmund's Hall, Oxford, in 1813, receiving his B.A. on February 24, 1816, and an M.A. from Oxford on June 25, 1819.

On May 2, 1816, he married Jane Head. They had six children: Jane Miriam (Havergal) Crane (1817–1898), Henry East Havergal (1819–1875), Maria Vernon Graham Havergal (1821–1887), Ellen Prestage (Havergal) Shaw (1823–1886), Francis Tebbs Havergal (1829–1890), and Frances Ridley Havergal (1836–1879).

Ordained in 1816, he became Curate (assistant pastor) under Rev. Thomas Tregenna Biddulph, Vicar of St. James's Church, Bristol, and Rector of Durtons and Lyng, working in churches in Somersetshire. He was Curate at Coaley, Gloucestershire, 1819–1822. He moved to Astley, Worcestershire, where he served as Curate 1822–1829, and then Rector of Astley 1829–1842. On June 14, 1829, when driving alone, he had a very dangerous accident, throwing him out of the carriage, nearly killing him, causing a brain concussion, a gravely serious injury that caused him very poor health and bad eyesight (at times near blindness) for much or most of the rest of his life. He was Rector of St. Nicholas Church, Worcester, 1845–1860. His wife Jane died on July 5, 1848, aged 54. In July, 1851, he married Caroline Ann Cooke, who survived him, living till 1878. Poor health caused him to resign as Rector of St. Nicholas, and to move to Staffordshire, where he was Vicar of Shareshill Church 1860–1870. His youngest daughter, Frances Ridley Havergal, said that his last conscious day (Saturday before Easter) was "a very climax of peace and brightness in all respects." The next morning apoplexy rendered him unconscious, and he remained unconscious till he died two days later, April 19, 1870.

Like his daughter Frances Ridley Havergal, W.H.H. was a musician to the core, a rarely and finely gifted one. He was a master at the keyboard (his improvisations were profoundly rich), he had a fine, beautiful voice, and he composed valuable scores. Early in his life, he was offered a professorship in music at Oxford University, a very high honor in that day, but he declined that and a career in music to be a pastor. Few could so well compose music, yet he preferred to write a sermon than to compose a score. Though music was so very important to him, and he used music to enrich his ministry and benefit his hearers (he was the music leader in the churches he pastored), yet music was a secondary pursuit to him, and an enjoyment and relaxation, not his priority, unless his physical health precluded pastoral work. Though his priority was pastoral work, he was the foremost church musician in England in his generation (Dr. William Crotch was the generation before W.H.H., and William Sterndale Bennett was not primarily a church musician), and was very highly regarded by knowledgeable people for his compositions and his knowledge of music. The American music leader Lowell Mason wrote concerning his second trip to England, in 1850, that W.H.H.'s church music was the best that he heard, "excellent in all particulars and far in advance of anything that he heard" in England. (See footnote 8 given later in this essay.) W.H.H. led the reform of church music, and few today realize the value of his efforts and publications to improve the practice of music in church worship. A generous—though not nearly complete—number of his published scores, his edition of Thomas Ravenscroft's Psalter (London: Novello, 1845), and his musicological treatise *A History of the Old Hundredth Psalm Tune* (New York: Mason Brothers, 1854) are given in Volume V of the Havergal edition (*Songs of Truth and Love: Music by Frances Ridley Havergal and William Henry Havergal*). He was a remarkably gifted organist and pianist, a beautiful singer, a valuable composer, and a true scholar of music.

He was also a finely gifted poet, leaving richly edifying poems and hymns, and a generous—though not complete—number of his poems are given in Volume I of *The Complete Works of Frances Ridley Havergal*.

William Henry Havergal preached more than 2,000 sermons over more than five decades (likely approaching or exceeding 3,000 sermons, based on his handwritten record of his sermons from 1816 to 1869), each sermon a true labor of love, a heart work, sermons searched from the Scriptures and taught to him by God, diligently prepared, preached to parish congregations and other audiences. Only four volumes of his sermons were published, all given in Volume IV of the Havergal edition; he very likely was ready to publish many more if an opportunity were given, but these that we have are very rich, full of treasure.

Writing about William Henry Havergal's practice of preparation to preach his sermons, his daughter Maria V. G. Havergal wrote these comments at the bottom of an announcement sheet of Two Sermons on behalf of the Church Missionary Society preached on Sunday, October 21, 1860 in the Parish Church of Shareshill:

One Sermon always written by Wednesday p.m. – the 2nd by Saturday before breakfast. ! (No "hours of darkness" work! N.B. It was my fathers rule to carefully look over all the Scripture, for each Sunday's service, & select his text from these. (Exceptions – also). He generally did so after each Sunday's work over. So getting a clean week to meditate on his texts ! ! [This transcription leaves Maria's precise text as she wrote this, not correcting her mistakes, which are minor.]

Remember that he was a true Anglican, and thus would have been mindful of the Scripture lessons to be read in church each Sunday morning and evening through the calendar year.

His daughter Miriam (the first-born of the six children, and the last one to die, 1817–1898) wrote a richly valuable account, *Records of the Life of the Rev. William Henry Havergal, M.A.* (London: Home Words Publishing Office, 1882). In this biography (original book page 29, page 593 of Volume IV of the Havergal edition), Miriam quoted this part from a letter dated October 23, 1821, early in his ministry:

My parish has called me out a good deal, while my indoor hours have been fully occupied in attending to my pupil and in preparing sermons. In this latter employment my thoughts have little rest. I am an *anxious* sermon writer. Few things are more painful to me than to be obliged to preach a sermon I have used before, and it is so for two reasons: first, every old sermon skeleton rather pains me by its defects; and secondly, I love to preach that which I have felt and desire, and desire to feel that which I preach, and these things are only effected when the heart and the head and the hand have been engaged in the work of preparation.

In the same biography (*Records*, original book page 330, page 662 of Volume IV of the Havergal edition), Miriam wrote this of him near the end of his ministry:

My father was again alarmingly ill early in January, 1869, and expressed himself as distressed at not being able to preach at Christ Church for Dr. Bickmore, as arranged for the very day after his illness began. He frequently preached for his friends in Leamington when at all able to do so, especially at Milverton and Holy Trinity, in which district he resided. He used in his study a folio Bible on a lectern, and having looked out his text would ruminate on it for a day or two, and then write down the heads of the subject; but in the pulpit delivering the sermon without notes, and enlarging upon it extemporaneously.

One very important part of William Henry Havergal's work was his strong desire and advocacy to promote and advance the work of the Church Missionary Society, to raise awareness and support—by money and by prayer—for the missionaries bringing the good news of Christ to foreign lands. Over several decades he travelled and preached in many churches, presenting the need and the work of the C.M.S. His daughter Maria, in 1886 before she died in 1887, gave to the Church Missionary Society an invaluable collection of manuscripts and other items by F.R.H. and W.H.H. (now kept in the C.M.S. Archives at the University of Birmingham in England). Among these items was a travelling case with this label handwritten by Maria: "Revd W. H. Havergal's travelling case for C.M.S. in 1824–1828. Many C.M.S. papers & outlines of his speeches were kept in this till his rest from labours. April 19, 1870 Bequeathed to the C.M.S. M.V.G.H. 1886." This case contains handwritten notes, letters, and other manuscripts and items. There was also a bound volume (of pages originally blank, like a bound diary) of W.H.H.'s handwritten notes for sermons, and Maria wrote this on a label on the front cover:

"One of my beloved father's (Revd W. H. Havergal's) Sermon cases, about 1817. Outlines of his C.M.S. sermons herein, bequeathed to that Society. My father extemporized his carefully prepared thoughts. Bequeathed to the C.M.S. 1886. M.V.G.H."

Maria also bequeathed to the C.M.S. another bound volume with this label handwritten by her on the front cover:

"Rev. W. H. Havergal's life prints. 'A faithful minister in the Lord.' — The Record of texts & sermons – from March 31.1816. to Janry 3.1869. Sermons from June 5. to Sept 12.1869. not entered'. The last text 'The Lord Jesus Christ be with thy spirit.' Preached at Pyrmont – Waldeck Sep 1.1869 Bequeathed to the C.M.S. 1886. (M.V.G.H."

This is a golden volume of W.H.H.'s handwritten record of sermons he preached: the first sermon recorded was dated March 31, 1816, preached at Durston on Acts 4:12, and the last sermon recorded was dated January 3, 1869, preached at Milverton in Leamington on Deuteronomy 33:16. This volume is his handwritten record of 160 pages of recorded entries of sermons he preached, recording the place, date, and Scripture text for each sermon. At the end, one of his children wrote this entry:

> My father's last Sermon was preached at Pyrmont Waldeck [in Germany] C.C.C.S.) Sept 12 1869. text "The Lord Jesus Christ be with thy spirit." 2 Timothy IV.22.

See pages 689, 719, and 1433 of Volume IV of the Havergal edition. All these items were copied in the research on the Havergal edition, but now after years of effort, the lack of time, means, and energy preclude for now the transcription and publication of the true gold in these manuscripts of W.H.H. The bound volume of his handwritten record of his sermons (bequeathed by Maria V. G. Havergal to the Church Missionary Society) had another part: the record of the sermons filled 160 pages, but did not take nearly all of the pages of the volume, and W.H.H. turned over the volume and wrote from the back side forward (inversely from the front, effectively making two books of the single bound volume) 19 pages of handwritten notes on a book entitled *The Art of Logic, on Simple Terms*. This was apparently his notes and reacting comments to John Milton's Latin treatise *Artis Logicae* published in 1672. W.H.H. was a wonderfully brilliant man, and a true scholar with wide interests. This and indeed all of these comments are only a brief, very incomplete description of him, his life, and his work.

Among the Havergal manuscripts and papers was found a copy of *The Work of Jesus Christ, as an Advocate, Clearly Explain'd, and Largely Improv'd, for the Benefit of All Believers. From I John ii.1.* by John Bunyan, this copy printed in London for John Marshall, 1725. In the front of the book this is signed: W. H. Havergal. St Nicholas, Worcester 1847. Below his signature, his widow Caroline Ann Havergal wrote "Last book finished by my blessed husband 1870."

Given next are four quotations from Miriam's biography of William Henry Havergal.

This was written by his second wife, Caroline Ann, on September 23, 1857, concerning a period of W.H.H.'s very severe illness:

> "Wednesday, 23rd.—He was fully dressed for the first time. A kind message from his curate (the Rev. S. B. James) elicited, 'I thank him from the depths of my heart, and pray the Lord to sustain and comfort him.' Poor Fanny had had an alarming attack of erysipelas, brought on by imprudence, but as she was recovering he said, 'God is better than our fears.' I have omitted one little thing: as Fanny one evening bent over him to bid him good-night, saying to him, 'What a gem you are!' he said, 'Hush, hush, my child, your father is unworthy, unworthy—a worm and no man.' " [1]

His wife Caroline also recorded,

> . . . . A lady calling, expressing her thanks to him for his sweet and comforting sermon, he meekly answered, "The Lord make it profitable, and then take all the praise." Another thanking him said it was a precious sermon. "Nothing in itself," he said, "all nothing; but the Lord can make it precious, and may He do so." [2]

His former curate and later successor as Rector of St. Nicholas' Church, Worcester, England, Charles Bullock, wrote,

> Yes, he knew and groaned under the "plague of his own heart." He felt cause enough to lie low before God, whilst he was conscious of his integrity before man; and it was this combination of integrity and humility which gave such power to his testimony to the Gospel of God's grace, and made him not only a

---

[1] Jane Miriam (Havergal) Crane, *Records of the Life of the Rev. William Henry Havergal, M. A.* (London: Home Words Publishing Office, 1882), original book page 244, page 420 of this book.

[2] Crane, *Records*, original book page 239; page 419 of this book.

preacher in the pulpit, but a preacher in the world—a preacher of what Herbert has beautifully styled 'the visible rhetoric of a holy life.'" 3

Next is a larger quotation of Charles Bullock's memorial sermon on W.H.H. Note especially the first sentence of the second paragraph, "In all that he did he was emphatically 'real.' "

> Not, indeed, that he was without faults or failings, for "there is not a just man upon earth that doeth good and sinneth not;" but Gospel grace wrought so manifestly in him "the fruits of the Spirit," that, to a remarkable degree, he "adorned the doctrine of God his Saviour:" so that it would be difficult for those who knew him best to specify what those faults and failings were.
>
> In all that he did he was emphatically "real." There was harmony in his character; the counterpart of that harmony of musical genius which gave him a world-wide reputation. [W.H.H. as a church musician was very highly regarded on both sides of the Atlantic.] None could fail to recognize his "godly sincerity." He preached and said what he felt: and from the heart he spoke to the heart, as if he really had a message from God to deliver. He was always the pastor. His was not the ministry of official routine: it was the ministry of the life. His testimony respecting his friend, the Rev. John East, of Bath, when preaching his funeral sermon, applies most truly to himself:—
>
>> The livery of his Divine Master was always and everywhere visibly upon him. Whether in the desk or the pulpit, the committee-room or the platform, the cottage or the mansion, the schoolroom or the sick chamber, the street or the railway, he was always the recognized but unostentatious servant of the Saviour whom he loved. He was not ashamed of his Master, or of His Name, or to speak a word for Him, or to do an act for Him whenever a favourable or fitting opportunity presented itself.
>
> He advised, he admonished, he sympathized; and, to the utmost of his means, he aided those who stood in need of aid. And throughout his ministry he was eminently "faithful." He did not hesitate, though he well knew the cost, to battle manfully with the vices and frivolities of the day. None could hearken to his conversation and think it possible to "serve God and mammon." 4

Andrew James Symington wrote this in his "Biographical Sketch" of W.H.H.:

> As genial as he was gentlemanly, refined in his tastes, high-souled, and gifted, his own immediate home circle, relatives, and numerous friends, were all perfectly devoted to him; and no one could possibly approach him, even in a casual way, without feeling the radiation of Christian light and warmth from his heart and beaming face; for to the core he was a true man: true to God, and true to his fellow men.5

". . . to the core he was a true man: true to God, and true to his fellow men." This is reminiscent of Matthew 22:37–40, the two commandments. Only Jesus Christ alone can do that in a person.

These comments are only brief, very incomplete glimpses of W.H.H. Much more can be said of this genuine disciple of the Lord Jesus Christ. He was a true example, as Paul wrote, "Be ye followers of me even as I also am of Christ." I Corinthians 11:1

Before the first score by William Henry Havergal (his setting of "Just as I am" by Charlotte Elliott), this is a set of quotations of correspondence between Lowell Mason and W.H.H., and other quotations and details concerning them.

---

 3 Crane, *Records*, original book pages 380–381; page 483 of this book.
 4 Crane, *Records*, original book pages 373–375; pages 448–449 of this book.
 5 *The Pastor Remembered, and the Brethren Entreated A Memorial of the Rev. W. H. Havergal, M.A.* by Charles Bullock, with the "Biographical Sketch" by Andrew James Symington (London: W. Hunt & Co., S. W. Partridge & Co., and The Christian Book Society, no date, likely 1870), original book pages 52–53, page 492 of this book.

A Collection of Various Scores not Contained in Havergal's Psalmody and Century of Chants

Dr. Lowell Mason (1792–1872), the American composer and publisher of hymns and very prominent, important, influential leader and reformer of church music in the United States, wrote this in a letter dated "London, Jan. 9th, 1852:"

> On Sunday morning, at 11 o'clock, we attended divine service in the parish church of St. Nicholas [Worcester], Rev. Mr. Havergal, rector. The exercises commenced by a few measures as a voluntary, or rather prelude, and the "giving out" the tune on the organ, after which all the congregation united in a single stanza sung to the old tune called "Tallis's Evening Hymn." The hymn was not read nor named, but it appeared to be a common thing for the worship to commence in the use of a stanza well known, always the same, and to the same tune. It was a hearty commencement, for every one seemed to join with full voice. The service was read by the curate. The chanting was done by the whole congregation, and the responding was between the occupants of the lower floor and those of the gallery—but the song was universal—men, women and children uniting harmonious voices. The Venite and the Te Deum were chanted responsively; the psalms were not chanted but, read in the usual manner. Two metrical hymns were sung during the service. The tunes were both of the old ecclesiastical class, and were in the same rhythmic form as St. Ann's, York, &c. appear in the *Cantica Laudis*. The first and last words of each line being long, and all the rest short. They were sung by all the people, and in very quick time; as fast as propriety would allow the enunciation of the words. They were somewhat quicker than the writer has taught this class of tunes in musical conventions and singing classes in America. Let the tune Uxbridge, for example, be sung in quick time, somewhat quicker than usual, and the crotchets will give the time of the minims in the above-named class of tunes. There were one or two organ interludes introduced in a psalm of five stanzas; but these were very short, not more than about two measures, or the length of the last line of a common metre tune. "These tunes would be popular in America," said the lady who was with me, who, though not a singer, has been accustomed for many years to give close attention to the Psalmody, and to hear criticisms and remarks concerning it. And indeed, they are as far from being dull and heavy as need be; I doubt not that many good people, with us, would think it almost irreverent to sing a hymn through with such rapidity. Yet all the people, old and young, joined—all seemed to know the tunes perfectly, and all kept well together.
>
> Mr. Havergal is himself, as is well known, much of a musical man and an excellent composer. He has once or twice obtained the Gresham prize medal for the best composition of a church service or anthem; and he is well-known by numerous sacred songs, published with pianoforte accompaniment. But it is metrical psalmody and the chant in which he is most interested, and in which he has produced some very fine specimens. He only devotes odds and ends of time to music, and never writes music when he is able to write sermons; but it has been, when weary with the labors of the day, or when travelling, that he has composed most of his popular and excellent tunes. He has many curious and valuable old books of psalmody, and is now himself writing, as he can find time, some historical notice of the "Old Hundredth Psalm Tune."[6]

He later wrote:

> .... The St. Nicholas Church, in Worcester, England, has the true Congregational style, and when that, which we have heretofore described, shall universally prevail, Congregational singing will be excellent and effective.[7]

This next quotation refers to Lowell Mason's second trip to England in 1850, when he visited St. Nicholas' Church, Worcester, in which William Henry Havergal both was the pastor and led the music. In the periodical *Music*, Volume IV, May, 1893 to November, 1893, in an essay entitled "Lowell Mason, American Congregational Musician" (pages 527–530), this was written:

> Mason went to Europe twice, in 1837, the year of the accession of Queen Victoria, and in 1850. In England he interested himself in church music and congregational singing. He found the musical service, in Rev. W. H. Havergal's church, Worcester, England, "excellent in all particulars and far in advance of anything that he heard."[8]

---

[6] *Musical Letters from Abroad* ("Including Detailed Accounts of the Birmingham, Norwich, and Dusseldorf Musical Festivals of 1852") by Lowell Mason (New York: Mason Brothers, 1854), pages 13–14.

[7] *Musical Letters from Abroad* by Mason, pages 163–164.

[8] *Music* ("A Monthly Magazine Devoted to the Art, Science, Technic and Literature"), Volume IV, May, 1893 to November, 1893, W. S. B. Mathews, Editor and Publisher (Chicago: Published at 240 Wabash Avenue, 1893), page 529. This ending sentence was found in two other places: In *Education* ("A Monthly Magazine, Devoted to the Science, Art, Philosophy, and Literature of Education"), Frank H. Kasson and Frank H. Palmer, Editors, Volume XIV, September, 1893—June, 1894 (Boston: Kasson and Palmer, 50 Bromfield Street, 1894), in an essay on Lowell Mason entitled "Lowell Mason, American Musician" by Rev. James H. Ross, Somerville, Massachusetts (pages 411–416), Ross wrote this same quotation (on page 415): "He found the musical service, in Rev. W. H. Havergal's church, Worcester, England, 'excellent in all particulars and far in advance of anything that he heard.'" In *The Poets of the Church* A Series of Biographical Sketches of Hymn-Writers with Notes on Their Hymns by Edwin F. Hatfield, D.D. (New York: Anson D. F. Randolph & Company, 1884), page 302, in his entry on William Henry Havergal, Dr. Hatfield wrote this same statement (only without the same quotation marks in Dr. Hatfield's text): "He [Dr. Lowell Mason] describes the musical service in Mr. Havergal's church as excellent in all particulars, and far in advance of anything that he heard in England."

In the July 16, 1870 issue of *The Musical World*, in a memorial notice of "The Late Rev. W. H. Havergal" (which apparently was a quotation from another periodical, the *Tonic Sol-fa Reporter*), this was written:

> When Dr. Lowell Mason visited this country, one of his first and most sacred pilgrimages was to Mr. Havergal's house in Worcester, and we well remember the heartiness and earnestness with which Dr. Mason acknowledged the obligations of American psalmodists to this good man.[9]

Next are quotations from a number of letters between Mason and W.H.H.

Frances Ridley Havergal wrote this in her "Supplementary Remarks" in *Havergal's Psalmody and Century of Chants*: "The selections from 'Havergal's Psalmody' will be found, as experience has proved them to be, easily learnt, greatly liked, and practically adapted for congregational singing. Of one of these, Dr. Lowell Mason, the great American promoter of choral singing, wrote as follows:—"

> I have lately introduced into my choir, and sung with admirable effect, your tune "St. Nicholas" [now called "Eden," No. 38 in this volume]. The effect of it was truly magnificent. My choir consists of about sixty singers; the different parts are well sustained, and about equally balanced. I have never heard anything come nearer to my *beau ideal* of Church Music than did the singing of this tune, on a fine Sabbath morning, in a church filled with people. It made a deep impression; and the next day one and another was asking, "What tune did you sing yesterday morning?" "Where did you get that tune?" etc. The performance of "St. Nicholas" ["Eden"] makes one feel as did Jacob at Luz, and involuntarily exclaim, "This is none other but the house of God, and this is the gate of heaven." Wonderful would be the effect of Psalmody were all the people to unite in such lofty and majestic strains.—April 30, 1847.[10]

Miss Grierson wrote that Mason described "Eden" (the hymn score that had earlier been named "St. Nicholas") as "sublime."[11]

The next three quotations from letters by Lowell Mason were given in Miriam Crane's biography *Records of the Life of the Rev. William Henry Havergal, M.A.*:

> *(Letters from Dr. Lowell Mason)*
>
> I have lately introduced into my choir and sung with admirable effect your tunes of St. Nicholas and Glasshampton. The effect of St. Nicholas was truly magnificent; I have never heard anything come nearer to my *beau ideal* of Church music than did the singing of this tune on a fine Sabbath morning, in a church filled with people. It made a deep impression, and the next day one and another was asking, "What tune did you sing yesterday morning?" "Where did you get that tune?" etc.
> On the Sabbath following we sung Glasshampton; this is beautiful, but St. Nicholas is sublime. The performance makes one feel as Jacob did, "none other but the gate of heaven." Wonderful would be the effect of psalmody were all the people to unite in such lofty, majestic strains.
>
> November, 1848. My book the "National Psalmist" was completed about September last. I fear to send it you, for there is, I well know, much that you cannot approve. There is much indeed, I (who am not so orthodox as you are) do not like, but I was obliged to adapt myself to the state of things, and I introduce into my book quite as much of the real psalmody as the people are prepared for. But I have done something towards reformation. A few of your tunes which I took a little liberty with I have marked; forgive me, my dear sir, for the few instances in which I deviated a little from your copy, for the purpose of adapting them for more general use here. Much have you enriched my book. Your letters and remarks have much modified my book. For all this and much more I shall ever be truly grateful.
>
> March, 1862. I thank you for your kind note of February 2. It has gladdened my heart, and caused me to look upon your portrait, ever before me, with renewed interest, and, if possible, with a deeper respect and affection for its original,

---

[9] *The Musical World* Vol. XLVIII (London: Duncan Davison & Co., 244, Regent Street, 1870), page 483.

[10] F.R.H.'s "Supplementary Remarks" published in *Havergal's Psalmody and Century of Chants* (London: Robert Cocks & Co., 1871). She also quoted this same letter in her "Original Preface to the Musical Edition of Songs of Grace and Glory" published by Nisbet in 1876 and later re-published in the definitive "New and Enlarged Musical Edition" of *Songs of Grace and Glory* (London: James Nisbet & Co., 1880). See pages 163–164 and 528 of Volume V of the Havegal edition.

[11] *Frances Ridley Havergal Worcestershire Hymnwriter* by Janet Grierson (Bromsgrove, Worcestershire: The Havergal Society, 1979), page 63. See page 1159 of Volume IV of the Havergal edition. Miss Grierson wrote, ". . . . The tune "St. Nicholas," described as "sublime" by the American musician Dr. Lowell Mason of Boston, was appropriately re-named ' Eden ' in the posthumous publication of Havergal's Psalmody."

who has been so kind to me. Ten years ago, on January 3, I saw you at Worcester; dined with you on Saturday. On Sunday I attended divine service at your church; you preached from Jeremiah 50:5. I wish you had put that sermon into your printed volumes. In the evening you preached again on Psalm 23:4. It is most pleasant to recall the remembrance of kind friends. I shall never cease to hold them dear. Now, dear sir, may the blessing of our heavenly Father ever rest upon you and yours, and at last, when you shall be called home, may an abundant entrance be ministered to you into everlasting habitations.
  Yours most truly,
    Lowell Mason.[12]

Miriam later quotes two letters by W.H.H. to Lowell Mason: "After an illness in the summer my father gives a short account of his autumn holiday in a letter to Dr. Lowell Mason."

                       Killarney, Oct. 22, 1856.
My dear Sir,
  Your kind letter of the 29th ult. has overtaken me in this charming locality. An attack of poor or suppressed gout left me in an enfeebled state. As, too, I had had no holiday for fifteen months, I felt obliged as soon as practicable to take a long rest. With Mrs. Havergal and our neighbours, the Misses Nott, I have been in Ireland for more than a month, and hope to reach home again next week. The main attraction to Ireland was the new home of my dear daughter Ellen; we are thankful to say we found everything equal to our fondest wishes. We spent three weeks at Kilkee, a wild but noble spot on the western coast, where the waves and breezes of the Atlantic greatly refreshed and delighted us. I am, thank God, much benefited by the change.
  While out I have been catching an hour now and then to arrange and copy a selection of my own psalm and hymn tunes, which have either never been published or are scattered in the publications of others. My children are urgent for me to do this, but it is a difficult task with my imperfect vision. I have had some very large music paper ruled on purpose for the occasion. If the accompanying MSS. will be of any service to you, all is yours ad lib. The sacred round was hit off sortie years ago. The recto et retro chant was picked by Fanny, my scribe, out of a lot of such articles. I never have time for greater things, but scraps of weary hours will lead my thoughts to some little contrivances of a short description. My dear wife joins me in very best remembrances to Mrs. Mason.
    Believe me,
      Most faithfully yours,
      W. H. Havergal.[13]

(*To Dr. Lowell Mason, of Boston, U.S.*)

                       Poppelsdorfer Allée, Bonn,
                        March 5, 1866.
My dear Friend,
  Your letter has just been welcomed. I hasten to reply to it as well as my eyes will allow. I can hope only for less dimness of vision at the most. At this distance I dare not advise you; possibly an operation may restore you to perfect sight spite of advancing years; I have known many such instances. The good Lord favour you. I can keenly sympathize with you. I feel that I write worse than I did, and can read only large church print for a few minutes; but all these things, though trying, are but light afflictions compared with what might be. Then our great standing mercies in Christ Jesus, how precious are they! May they abound to you. Only my dear wife is now with me and one of our home servants. My parish is left in good hands. I regret to hear of the popularity of Robertson's sermons in America. There is much of splendid trifling in them, with "fair speeches" on behalf of erroneous novelties.
  As to music I do but little, although I cannot keep from nibbling at chants and metrical tunes. I have fifty varied forms of the Grand Chant,* and have one hundred other chants, mostly single, ready for publication.
  All that has been passing in America has engaged my anxious attention. In dear old England Church matters are perilous, though I hope for the best by reason of the Bishops having spoken out well on ultra-ritual movement.
  Here, as in England, we have had no winter yet. My own parish is still mercifully preserved from cattle-plague. My old friend Dr. Hodges is gradually failing at Bristol. My dear wife is better, and joins me in best regards.
    Ever faithfully yours,
      W. H. Havergal.[14]

* Early in 1867 J. Shepherd published "The Grand Chant in Forty Different Forms." By the Rev. W. H. Havergal, M.A., Op. 52.

---

[12] *Records of the Life of the Rev. William Henry Havergal, M.A.* by his daughter Jane Miriam Crane (London: Home Words Publishing Office, 1882), pages 188–190. See pages 630–631 of Volume IV of the Havergal edition.

[13] *Records*, pages 188–190. See page 636 of Volume IV of the Havergal edition.

[14] *Records of the Life of the Rev. William Henry Havergal, M.A.* by his daughter Jane Miriam Crane (London: Home Words Publishing Office, 1882), pages 313–314. See page 659 of Volume IV of the Havergal edition.

This next quotation is taken from a "Biographical Sketch" by Andrew James Symington:

> Mr. Havergal's severe and classical music is often to be heard in our cathedrals; and in Scotland and America no Psalm tune is oftener sung than "Evan." The history of this tune is somewhat peculiar, and, as its authorship has been questioned, it may be well to mention the matter here, as the writer can do so authoritatively from Mr. Havergal's own words, as well as from written statements. In 1847 Mr. Havergal published an original air (a sacred song) to Burns's words, "O Thou dread Power." Dr. Lowell Mason, of New York, arranged the first half of that air as a psalm tune, altering both the time and key, and called it "Evan." Hence it is frequently given in collections with Mason's name, and at other times simply with the letter H, under which initial it first appeared, because Dr. Mason did not wish to attribute the liberty he had taken in arranging the part of a melody to the composer of the original air. This is Dr. Lowell Mason's own explanation, which we have seen. Mr. Havergal has since arranged it as it should be, and within the last month played over the tune, and gave a MS. copy of it to the writer, with its curious history noted on the sheet. It has travelled far and wide, and been claimed for many composers, and even been called an old Celtic air. We have here stated the true origin of this unprecedentedly popular tune. [15]

F.R.H. wrote this in a letter to Charles Busbridge Snepp:

> Ascension Day 1871.
> Do you know my father's tune "Evan"? It has been claimed as a Celtic air by some of those Celts who want to appropriate anything that can add to Celtic glory! The Andersonian Professor of Music at Glasgow has recently inserted a challenge to all Highlanders on the subject in the Scotch papers, and the result is, that it is finally and incontestably proved to be my father's own, entirely and only, and neither Celtic nor Lowell Mason's, to whom he once played and sang the melody,—which the Doctor much admired, and took it with him to America,—reducing it to a commometre tune, with only my father's initial "H." All my dear father's own tunes are wonderfully suited to large congregations. [16]

His daughter Maria wrote this in her *Autobiography*:

> It was during this visit to Scotland that my father became acquainted with Dr. Laurie, of Monckton Manse, to whom he dedicated a lovely melody to "Burns's Prayer." This had a piano accompaniment, and is the original air from which the popular tune "Evan" was afterwards taken by Dr. Lowell Mason. When visiting my father, Dr. Mason was charmed with his singing it, and requested a copy. Turning to Frank, my father told him to give his copy to the Doctor, who took it to America. He wrote for permission to shorten the air to a C.M. hymn tune. My father did not think it in strict, ecclesiastical style, and would not allow his name to appear; hence it got published with his initial H. only, and, appearing in Dr. Mason's collection, soon got his name instead of my father's.
> Would that more had heard my father's exquisite touch and extemporized fugues and harmonies—waves of melody, now richest chords, then gentlest adagios. His voice was sweet and clear, and his long-sustained shake would hush us completely. [17]

These are only glimpses of the relation and communication between Mason and W.H.H., most of the details no longer extant. Finally, these are two more glimpses.

W.H.H.'s *A History of the Old Hundredth Psalm Tune* with Specimens was published by Mason Brothers, New York, in 1854. Mason Brothers was the publishing firm of Lowell Mason's sons Daniel Gregory Mason (1820–1869) and Lowell Mason (1823–1885), who began the publishing firm in 1853.

In the first Volume of *Sermons, Chiefly on Historical Subjects from the Old and New Testaments Preached in the Parish Church of St. Nicholas, Worcester* by W. H. Havergal, Volume I, Old Testament (London: Hamilton, Adams, and Co., and Hatchard, 1853), in the published list of subscribers of the books, this entry was given: "Mason, Lowell, Esq., Boston, U.S. Two copies." See page 1317 of Volume IV of the Havergal edition (page xiv of the original book).

---

[15] *The Pastor Remembered, and the Brethren Entreated A Memorial of the Rev. W. H. Havergal, M.A.* by Charles Bullock, with the "Biographical Sketch" by Andrew James Symington (London: W. Hunt & Co., S. W. Partridge & Co., and The Christian Book Society, no date, likely 1870), pages 51–52. See page 714 of Volume IV of the Havergal edition.

[16] *Letters by the Late Frances Ridley Havergal* edited by her sister, Maria V. G. Havergal (London: James Nisbet & Co., 1886), Appendix II, pages 388–390. See also page 257 of Volume IV of the Havergal edition.

[17] *The Autobiography of Maria Vernon Graham Havergal* edited by her sister Jane Miriam Crane (London: James Nisbet & Co., 1887), pages 50–51. See pages 506–507 of Volume IV of the Havergal edition. "Frank" was William Henry Havergal's fifth child, Francis Tebbs Havergal (1829–1890).

This is a final note in this section on Lowell Mason and William Henry Havergal: Few today realize how remarkably prominent and successful Lowell Mason was as a musician in the 19th century. He was very famous, highly regarded, and his many editions of hymnbooks were published in the millions. He became one of the wealthiest men of his generation in the United States, enormously wealthy from the sales of his hymnbooks and other publications. (This was the generation before the U.S. railroad "robber barons" and other extremely wealthy industrialists of the last half of the 19th century.) The mention of this is not at all meant to impugn nor question Dr. Mason's ethics or integrity. William Henry Havergal never sought any financial gain from his music, only a desire to glorify God and to serve others. For one example, his daughter Maria wrote in the first chapter of *Memorials of Frances Ridley Havergal* (see page 6 of Volume IV of the Havergal edition): "My father's first published musical composition was a setting of Bishop Heber's hymn, 'From Greenland's icy mountains.' The proceeds amounted to £180, and were devoted to the Church Missionary Society." Another very representative example of this is the statement "Profits to Various Charities" at the top of a list of published music scores composed by W.H.H., found on page 1558 of Volume V of the Havergal edition. Over and over he would assign any profits from published scores to a specific church or to another work of ministry, and he freely gave his music, knowledge of music, and advice to others without price. Beyond his intentionally declining any financial gain from his published scores, W.H.H. was notably not much honored formally or famously for his work that surely must have been realized and valued by many in his day (for one example, he was a fine musicologist, abundantly worthy of a doctorate in just that area alone, and that is not as important as other areas of his interest, prominently foreign missions and the work of the Church Missionary Society): though there is no proof of this, there is a temptation—after much research—to infer that he may have been offered an honorary doctorate, knighthood, or other honor, and declined them.

Lowell Mason (1792–1872)

One can rightly ask, In an edition of *The Complete Works of Frances Ridley Havergal*, why is music by her father William Henry Havergal (also music by her brother, Henry East Havergal) included? One can further ask, In an edition already so large, and in the already large Volume V, is the inclusion of hundreds of pages by another person appropriate? This is an attempt to answer that concern. F.R.H.'s own work on *Havergal's Psalmody and Century of Chants* and then *Songs of Grace and Glory*, a long, costly, remarkable labor of love so important to her, is very much connected to W.H.H.'s music. Beyond that, he was by far her most important teacher, mentor, influence in music, profoundly important in her own musical abilities and perspective. While they were both independent thinkers, and her musical personality was notably different from W.H.H.'s musical personality, he was profoundly important to her in music (and in many other ways). Completely apart from F.R.H., music by W.H.H. is very richly valuable in itself, but his profound influence and importance to F.R.H. in music is the strongest reason for the inclusion of this music by W.H.H. (Very similarly in Volume IV, the inclusion of 287 pages of Lectures and Sermons by W.H.H. was done for the same reasons: completely apart from F.R.H., the Sermons by W.H.H. are very richly valuable in themselves, but his profound influence and importance to F.R.H. was the strongest reason for the inclusion of those Sermons in Volume IV.) Remember that F.R.H. was the music leader at St. Paul's Church in Leamington, and was importantly involved in church music in a number of other places. That these scores by W.H.H. should be included in Volume V has been obvious to me since the fall of 2001, when the general structure of the Havergal edition was realized and written on paper. Though not at all unmindful of the large size both of the complete Havergal edition and of Volume V of the Havergal edition, and not at all indifferent to the cost and size of the books, I have included these scores by W.H.H. because I believe that they are valuable in themselves and also relevant to F.R.H. With the items by F.R.H., I have not included anything in this edition that I did not think to be 1. valuable in itself, apart from F.R.H., and 2. importantly relevant to F.R.H., to know or understand her better. That is true of every item in the Havergal edition, and that is why this music by W.H.H. (also the music by H.E.H.) is included in Volume V. I could double the size of Volume V with valuable things, but I am convinced that the things included in Volume V are truly valuable in themselves and relevant to F.R.H.

This selection of music by William Henry Havergal is not nearly complete: he composed and wrote far more (and his unwritten – never transcribed onto paper – improvisations must have been vast, rich, valuable, fine). Limitations of time, energy, resources, to say nothing of the already large size of Volume V (*Songs of Truth and Love Music by Frances Ridley Havergal and William Henry Havergal*) of the Havergal edition, explain at least partially why more scores by him are not given here. His music is a gold-mine for research, publication, study, performance. His eldest child's biography *Records of the Life of the Rev. William Henry Havergal, M.A.* and four volumes of his Sermons—true gold from the Lord—are given in Volume IV of the Havergal edition.

Next is an extensive quotation from a "Biographical Sketch" written by Andrew James Symington, describing details of W.H.H. as a musician.

> To hear Mr. Havergal improvise, seated at a good harmonium with many stops, given him by his parishioners, was a rare treat; something higher, deeper, and more than a pleasure—a thing, or rather a spiritual experience, which cannot be forgotten. Sweet-flowing melody, accompanied with strange, unexpected combinations of harmony full of mysterious chords and curious synchronous and successive felicities, each part capable of being resolved into a perfect and separate composition—fugues chasing each other, turning, meeting, and then passing through the theme in quite opposite directions, meeting again, then twining lovingly together, and, like the strands of a new cable, finding strength in unison—starry phrases of melody echoed from heavenly heights till lost in the distance; then vast galaxies of chords "swim into ken," dependent on and perfectly balanced by other galaxies, controlled even to the perturbation of a satellite, till all is light and motion; while Handelian shakes, like auroras, at intervals gleam and dart across the blue starlit dome. Yet with all this there is no hesitation, no confusion, no fear; ruled by the genius of a master, every phrase, chord, and movement progresses with stately grandeur and precision towards the evolution of the one idea which informs and pervades the whole marvellous performance. Sometimes we wander far away through wild intervals into weird discords; and then these, ere they become too painful, are resolved with consummate skill, and we mark "lines of different method" all meeting "in one full centre of delight," as we find ourselves led on and on, and ever by new and unexpected ways, home again at last to the key-note.

The firmness, precision, and delicacy of Mr. Havergal's touch were each and all remarkable, both in kind and degree. These several characteristics were strikingly brought out in his improvisations, which never by any chance contained anything approaching the commonplace. Instead of that, his every combination was original, often a surprise even to himself; many lovely transient effects thus flashed and faded that could not be repeated. Compositions of daring originality and perfect rounded beauty—now bold and strident, like the tramp of a giant army, and now ethereally delicate, like the dying cadences of an Æolian harp—streamed from the keys at the magic "touch" of that "vanished hand" we shall hear no more on earth.

Although Mr. Havergal's ecclesiastical music is of the very highest type and severe in style, he has also written many beautiful songs, rounds and catches for the young, which are full of childlike life and bird-like glee; also numberless carols, hymns, and sacred songs, composing both the words and the music.[18]

Symington wrote this in another place:

Mr. Havergal's severe and classical music is often to be heard in our cathedrals; and in Scotland and America no psalm tune is oftener sung than "Evan." . . . . [The rest of this paragraph is Symington's explanation of Lowell Mason's use of W.H.H.'s score "Evan," already quoted (on page 714 of Volume IV of the Havergal edition) in the previous section on Lowell Mason and W.H.H.]

Of the Hundred Tunes it is not too much to say that they are a monument of learning and industry; and are all, or nearly all, in entire agreement with the principles which its author so long and so successfully propounded.

Handel, Corelli, and our great Cathedralists, were his masters. His aim was to preserve purity of style, and put down musical vanities. Notoriously liberal to publishers of music, he has been equally willing to aid, by scientific criticism and research, all who applied to him.[19]

Dr. Glen T. Wegge, in his sterling essay or dissertation entitled "The Music of Frances Ridley Havergal," wrote this after quoting the first two paragraphs by Symington just given here: [20]

The above quotation asserts his consummate performance skill and facility. Typical for organists, W. H. Havergal was trained in improvisation. Two composers were named as influences—Handel and Corelli. Handel was an especially important composer to F.R.H. In Appendix V are lists of compositions that F.R.H. knew and probably performed. Handel is featured often on the list. Only one piece by Corelli is on the list. Mentioned in the quotation above was W.H.H.'s fine touch on the keyboard. His touch suggests that he was well-practiced and sensitive to the needs of the music. It is interesting that the writer of this quotation suggested that to hear his performance was close to a religious experience. Also, the writer noted that W.H.H.'s grasp of harmony was remarkable. All three of these last mentioned qualities were asserted about his daughter, Frances Ridley, by other writers. William Henry Havergal was also a composer of many pieces. He wrote airs, sacred songs, carols, psalms, duets, many hymns, many chants, services, as well as larger works such as a *Magnificat* and *Nunc Dimittis*. His compositions of church music were much valued by his contemporaries, and he was twice awarded the Gresham Prize for church music (in 1836 for an evening Service, *Magnificat* and *Nunc Dimittis* in A, Op. 37, and in 1841, for an anthem "Give Thanks unto the Lord," Op. 40), an important, notable honor. (After awarding this to W.H.H. twice, the judges

---

[18] *The Pastor Remembered, and the Brethren Entreated A Memorial of the Rev. W. H. Havergal, M.A.* by Charles Bullock, with a "Biographical Sketch" by Andrew James Symington (London: W. Hunt & Co., S. W. Partridge & Co., and The Christian Book Society, no date, likely 1870), Pages 48–51. See pages 713–714 of Volume IV of the Havergal edition.

[19] The same essay on W.H.H. by Symington was published largely the same in a number of books or periodicals, with a few paragraphs added or removed in different places. These three paragraphs were published in Miriam Crane's quotation of Symington in *Records of the Life of the Rev. William Henry Havergal, M.A.* by his daughter Jane Miriam (Havergal) Crane (London: Home Words Publishing Office, 1882), original book pages 337–338. See page 664 of Volume IV of the Havergal edition.

[20] *The Music of Frances Ridley Havergal An Analysis of Her Compositions, and All of Her Extant Scores.* by Glen T. Wegge, Ph.D. (Kirksville, Missouri: Frances Ridley Havergal Trust, 2008), pages 2–3. This book is the "Companion Volume" to the new edition of *The Complete Works of Frances Ridley Havergal*. The title of the book is also the title of Dr. Wegge's dissertation, which is pages 1–128 of the same book.

decided that no one should receive this Prize more than twice.[21]) In his two prefaces to the hymnals he created (*Old Church Psalmody* in 1847 and *A Hundred Psalm & Hymn Tunes* in 1859),[22] W.H.H. exhibits much specialized music theory and an exceptionally well-grounded understanding of music history, but obviously bent toward church music in the best way. His knowledge was quite deep and thorough. W.H.H. was a leading reformer of church music in his day, and did much to raise the level of singing in worship services. He was very highly regarded by his contemporary scholars as an authority on both past and present church music, and a number of other scholars in this field wrote to him for information or advice. His treatise A History of the Old Hundredth Psalm Tune[23] is remarkable and shows exceptional ability and musicological insight. [This is the end of the excerpt from *The Music of Frances Ridley Havergal* by Dr. Glen T. Wegge. See footnote 20.]

His ministry was a heart work, to God and to others. A brilliantly gifted musician, he declined a career in music (as a composer, organist, music director, or professor), and became a pastor. Fame or praise of men was no interest to him, but he greatly desired that others know his Saviour.

William Henry Havergal was a man truly blessed by God and used by Him to bless many others. Similarly to Robert Murray M'Cheyne, John Newton, J. C. Ryle, Horatius Bonar, Alexander Bonar, and other godly ministers of his time more widely known today, W.H.H. is a large, rich gold-mine full of true treasure from the Lord. Thanks be to God. The Lamb is all the glory in Emmanuel's land, the kingdom of God.   David Chalkley

Harvest Hymn.

"He will gather His wheat into the
garner."—Matthew 3:12.

Our faithful God hath sent us
    A fruitful harvest-tide;
He summer boons hath lent us,
    And winter wants supplied.

The fields, at His ordaining,
    Stand thick with golden sheaves;
And man, full oft complaining,
    New bounty now receives.

Though Mercy largely giveth,
    Is Justice pacified?
We live through Him who liveth,
    The "Corn of Wheat" that died.

Then full be our thanksgiving,
    And clear each note of joy;
While faith and holy living
    Our earnest thoughts employ.

And at the last great reaping,
    When Christ His sheaves will own,
May we, no longer weeping,
    Be garnered near His throne!

Praise we the Godhead-Union,
    The eternal Three in One;
With them may our communion
    For ever be begun.

W.H.H. 1863.

D ear Jesus, teach a little child,
A nd kindly hear me when I pray;
V ouchsafe to me Thy mercy mild,
I nstruct me early in Thy way.
D raw, dearest Lord, my heart to Thee.

C leanse it from every youthful sin,
L et not the least impurity
E ntwine itself for ill within.
M ake me as David was when young,
E nriched by grace, beloved by Heaven;
N or let my heart, or hand, or tongue,
T ransgress the precepts Thou hast given.

Wiliam Henry Haveragal

---

[21] Andrew James Symington, "Biographical Sketch" of W.H.H. in *The Pastor Remembered and the Brethren Entreated by Charles Bullock and Andrew James Symington* (London: W. Hunt & Co., S. W. Partridge & Co., and The Christian Book Society, undated, likely 1870 or 1871), p. 45. See Volume IV of the Havergal edition, pp. 692–693. This was also mentioned in articles on W.H.H. in *The Musical Amateur* for June 4, 1861, and in the *London Morning Advertiser* (unknown date, found among Havergal manuscripts and papers). See Volume IV of the Havergal edition, pp. 691–692 and p. 712.

[22] William Henry Havergal, *Old Church Psalmody: a Manual of Good and Useful Tunes, either Old or in Old Style, Selected, Harmonized, and Arranged, with Prefatory Remarks and Historical Notices* (London: J. Hart, 1847), and William Henry Havergal, *A Hundred Psalm and Hymn Tunes* (London: Addison, Hollier, and Lucas, 1859).

[23] William Henry Havergal, *A History of the Old Hundredth Psalm Tune* (New York: Mason Brothers, 1854; and London: Sampson Low Son, & Co., 1857). This is published in facsimile on pp. 1976–2050 of Volume V of the Havergal edition.

A Collection of Various Scores not Contained in Havergal's Psalmody and Century of Chants xxvii

"So shall we ever be with the Lord."

(I Thessalonians 4:17.)

Oh, thrilling thought ! that I shall be
With Him who shed His blood for me,
    Where naught from Him shall sever;
Where I, with sainted hosts above,
O'ershadowed by the Holy Dove,
Shall banquet on His boundless love,
    And know those words, "For ever."

Oh, thrilling thought! to see Him shine,
For evermore to call Him mine,
    With heaven, all heaven, before me!
To stand where angel myriads gaze,
Amid the illimitable blaze,
While He the Godhead full displays,
    To all the sons of glory!

                  Rev. W. H. Havergal.

This is the last page of F.R.H.'s signature Album (containing poems, verses, and other items by her friends, 1860–1868), a score written by her father.

Each part in each strain
  Per Recte et Retro
    On a ground bass
Saviour, when from realms above,
Thou shalt come with glory 'round
May the names of all we love,
In Thy Book of Life be found! Amen.
  In that Great Day,
  Lord, grant that I may
  With rapture say,
"Behold I, and the children which
    God hath given me." Heb. 2:13.
Bonn. January 18. 1866. W. H. Havergal.

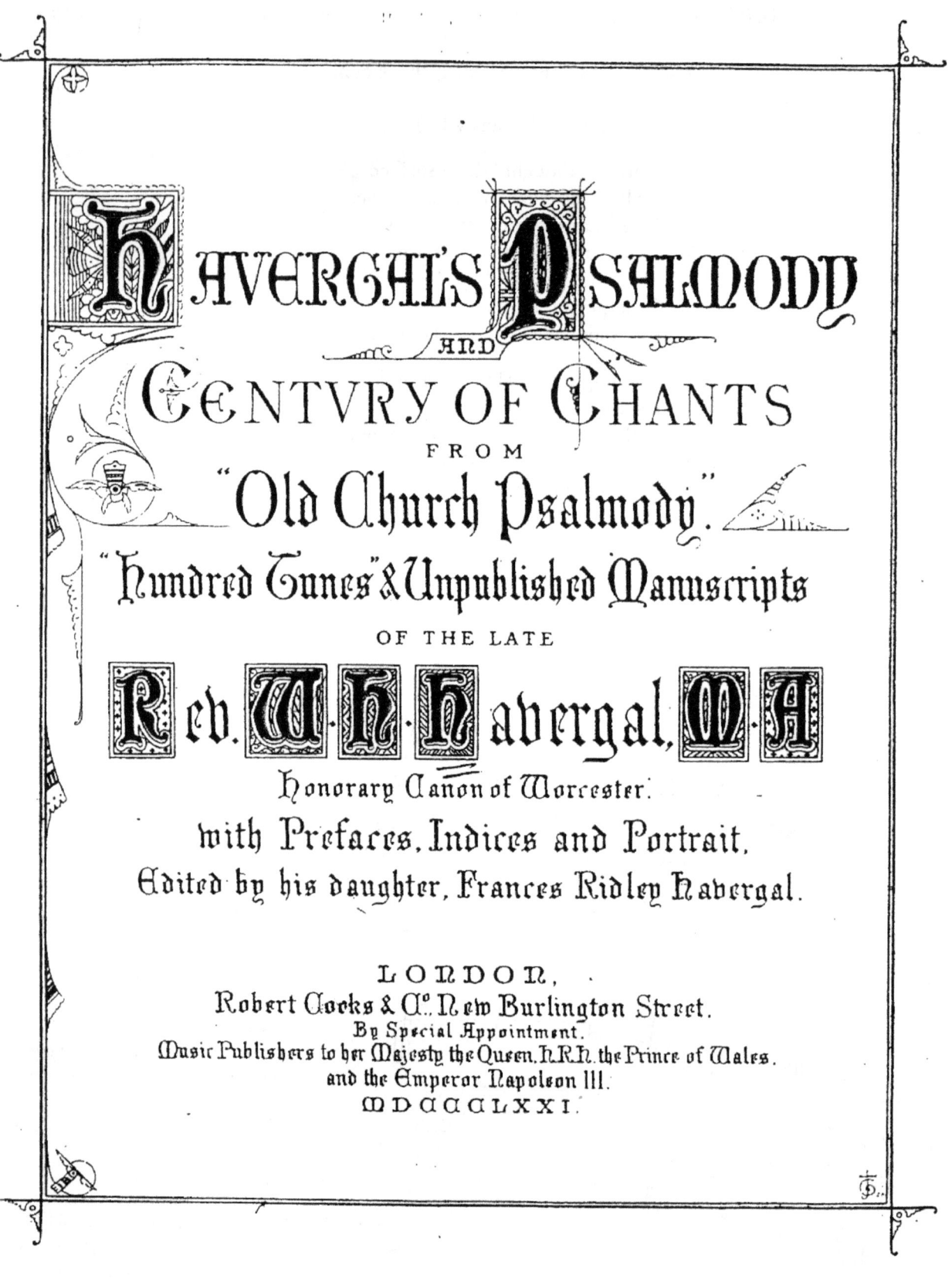

Havergal's Psalmody and Century of Chants *was the foundation for the music scores of the goldmine hymnbook* Songs of Grace and Glory *(a very valuable hymnbook though very obscure now, the texts edited by Charles Busbridge Snepp, the music edited by Frances Ridley Havergal).* William Henry Havergal was the foremost church musician and composer of sacred music in England in his generation. Called to be a pastor, he declined a career in music and used music as a benefit to his church ministry, and for rest and pleasure. He would rather write a sermon than compose a score, though few had his ability and love to write and perform music at that level. He was a true scholar both in the Bible, theology, and music, and his ministry to others was a true example of Matthew 22:37–40. When his physical health removed him from pastoral work, he concentrated more on composition of music. *See Volume V of the Havergal edition,* Songs of Truth and Love: Music by Frances Ridley Havergal and William Henry Havergal, *which has all of* Havergal's Psalmody and Century of Chants *and also all of* Songs of Grace and Glory.

FORMS AND PRICES
OF
HAVERGAL'S PSALMODY & CHANTS.
Companion Volume to Songs of Grace & Glory.

		s.	D.
A.	HAVERGAL'S PSALMODY AND CENTURY OF CHANTS, bound in cloth, gilt lettered, with full Prefaces, Indices, and Photographic Portrait	5	0
B.	Ditto, ditto, without Chants	3	6
C.	Chants and Preface alone	1	6

CHEAPER EDITIONS.

		s.	D.
D.	HAVERGAL'S PSALMODY AND CHANTS, without Prefaces and Portrait	1	6
E.	Ditto, Ditto, without Chants	1	0
F.	CHANTS alone, without Preface	0	9

London:
ROBERT COCKS & CO., NEW BURLINGTON STREET, W.
By Special Appointment
Music Publishers to Her Majesty the Queen, H.R.H. the Prince of Wales, and H.I.M. Napoleon III.,
AND THROUGH ALL MUSICSELLERS.

FORMS AND PRICES
OF
SONGS OF GRACE AND GLORY.

		s.	D.
A.	Extra large paper, very superior binding	10	0
B.	Large type, leather gilt	5	0
C.	Large type, cloth gilt and lettered	4	0
D.	Large type, cloth limp	3	6
E.	Small type, leather gilt	2	6
F.	Small type, cloth gilt and lettered	1	6
G.	Small type, cloth limp	1	0

For reduced terms on Editions A. to E., apply to Rev. C. B. Snepp, LL.M., Vicar of Perry Barr, near Birmingham.

"SONGS OF GRACE AND GLORY." A Hymnal, containing 1,025 Hymns for Private, Family, and Public Worship, Edited by the Rev. C. B. SNEPP, LLM., Vicar of Perry Barr. With copious Indices of Authors and Dates, Subjects, Texts, and Tunes; also a Table of Hymns for the Sundays and Holy Days of the Ecclesiastical Year.

London:
WILLIAM HUNT & CO., HOLLES ST., CAVENDISH SQUARE.

This is an advertisement page (after page xx) in the original Robert Cocks edition of Havergal's Psalmody and Century of Chants. *Cocks' publication of H.P.C.C. had the music for the hymns in* Songs of Grace and Glory, *and William Hunt's publication of* Songs of Grace and Glory *had the words only, without music. Later the words and music were printed together in a "Musical Edition" of S.G.G. This 1880 Nisbet edition of* Songs of Grace and Glory *is the definitive version, published approximately six months after F.R.H. died (June 3, 1879) and approximately six months before Charles Busbridge Snepp died (June 23, 1880).*

This is a black-and-white copy of the oil portrait of William Henry Havergal painted by Solomon Cole in 1845. W.H.H. had his 52nd birthday on January 18, 1845. See also page 2046 (a print copy of this oil portrait), and pages lxxiii and 1026 (oil portraits of Jane Head Havergal and F.R.H. painted by Solomon Cole in 1845) of Volume V of the Havergal edition.

Jane Head Havergal. This is her epitaph, on a marble plaque in St. Nicholas' Church, Worcester: "Jane, The Beloved Wife of The Revd W. H. Havergal, M.A. Rector of This Parish, and Honorary Canon of the Cathedral In This City. Died in Holy Peace July 9th 1848, Aged 54. 'I give unto them Eternal Life.' John x, 28." Her first child, Jane Miriam Crane, wrote this in her biography Records of the Life of the Rev. William Henry Havergal, M.A.*: "On . . . the 2nd of May, 1816, my father married, in the parish church of East Grimstead, Jane, the fifth daughter of William and Mary Head of that town. She was beautiful and graceful, and by her piety, energy, and practical ability was well fitted for a clergyman's wife." (See page 590 of Volume IV of the Havergal edition.) Her youngest child, F.R.H., was 11 when she died, though her true example, godly desire, and words remained profoundly important to Frances the rest of her life. This was a color portrait painted by Solomon Cole in 1845. See also pages 1026 and 1984 of Volume V of the Havergal edition.*

"Rest in the Lord."

"Rest in the Lord."—Psalm 37:7.

"Rest in the Lord!" Sweet word of truth,
A word for age, a word for youth,
A word for all the weary world,
A banner-word by love unfurled.

Then cease, ye wearied ones of earth,
To slave for pleasure, gain, or mirth;
Cast down your load of vanities,
And welcome God's realities.

"Rest in the Lord!" Sweet word of grace
To all the Saviour's new-born race;
'Tis music, light, and balm to them,
An hourly guiding apothegm.[1]

Then, Lord of rest, we rest in Thee,
For all our daily destiny;
Our mighty guilt, our grief, our care,
We cast (strange act!) on Thee to bear.

For Thou, dear Lamb of God, wast slain,
To bear each load, and ease each pain;
And now Thy blood and righteousness
Are rocks of rest in all distress.

And when at last we fall on sleep,
Nor heart shall throb, nor eye shall weep;
Then, blessèd Saviour, let it be,
That Thou shalt write, "They rest in Me!"

William Henry Havergal

[1] apothegm: a short, instructive saying or maxim.

"My Times are in Thy Hand."

Psalm 31:15.

"My times are in Thy hand,"
  Their best and fittest place;
I would not have them at command
  Without Thy guiding grace.

"My times," and yet not mine;
  I cannot them ordain;
Not one e'er waits from me a sign,
  Nor can I one detain.

"My times," O Lord, are Thine,
  And Thine their oversight:
Thy wisdom, love, and power combine
  To make them dark or bright.

I know not what shall be,
  When passing times are fled;
But all events I leave with Thee,
  And calmly bow my head.

Hence, Lord, in Thee I rest,
  And wait Thy holy will;
I lean upon my Saviour's breast,
  Or gladly go on still.

And when my "times" shall cease,
  And life shall fade away,
Then bid me, Lord, depart in peace
  To realms of endless day!

W.H.H. 1860.

"Heralds of the Lord of Glory."

"Say (Tell it out) among the heathen,
that the Lord reigneth."—Psalm 96:10.

Heralds of the Lord of glory!
  Lift your voices, lift them high;
Tell the Gospel's wondrous story,
  Tell it fully, faithfully;
Tell the heathen 'midst their woe,
Jesus reigns, above, below.

Haste the day, the bright, the glorious!
  When the sad and sin-bound slave
High shall laud in pealing chorus
  Him who reigns, and reigns to save.
Tempter, tremble! Idols, fall!
Jesus reigns, the Lord of all!

Christians! send to joyless regions
  Heralds of the gladdening word,
Let them, voiced like trumpet-legions,
  Preach the kingdom of the Lord:
Tell the heathen—Jesus died!
Reigns He now, though crucified.

Saviour, let Thy quickening Spirit
  Touch each herald-lip with fire,
Nations then shall own Thy merit,
  Hearts shall glow with Thy desire,
Earth in jubilee shall sing.
Jesus reigns, the eternal King.

W.H.H.

"O Cast on Christ your Mighty Care."

"Casting all your care upon Him for
He careth for you."—I Peter 5:7.

O cast on Christ your mighty care,
  However great it be;
He knows it well, and can prepare
  Some sure relief for thee.

Thy surging thoughts and spectral fears
  Thy boding dreams of ill,
Thy sighings, and Thy silent tears,
  Are all within His will.

Lay these upon His holy arm,
  For He can all sustain:
He'll end thy cares, as with a charm,
  And lift thee up again.

Sustaining grace waits His command,
  And He awaits thy call;
Then pray, and down within thine hand
  Shall strength and comfort fall.

I, Lord, would cast on Thee my care,
  And nothing anxious be;
Content if Thou, who hearest prayer,
  Wilt care, O Lord, for me.

W.H.H.

In *Records of the Life of the Rev. William Henry Havergal, M.A.*, this account is given (April 30, 1857): After seeing this verse pencilled on a train station wall,

"Love not, love not–what you love will die;
Love God–He will not die."

W.H.H. instantly said this:

"Love not too well–the dearest one will die;
Love Him who loves, and lives on high;
And then you'll love eternally."

"Just as I am,

without one plea,"

(A MUCH APPROVED HYMN.)

Set to Music

IN FOUR PARTS, & ALSO FOR A SINGLE VOICE,

WITH

Organ or Pianoforte Accompaniment,

and, with kind permission, Inscribed to The Right Honorable

LADY HATHERTON,

BY

The Revᵈ W. H. Havergal, M.A.

Honorary Canon of Worcester, & Incumbent of Shareshill, Staffordshire.

──── OP. 48. ────

Ent. Sta. Hall.   *Price 1/6*

PROFITS TOWARDS IMPROVING THE CHURCHYARD OF THE COMPOSER'S PARISH.

London,
JOHN SHEPHERD, 98, NEWGATE STREET.

"Just as I am, without one plea," Op. 48

2
Just as I am— and waiting not
To rid my soul of one dark blot,
To Thee, whose blood can cleanse each spot,
    O Lamb of God, I come!

3
Just as I am— though tossed about
With many a conflict— many a doubt,
Fightings within, and fears without,
    O Lamb of God, I come!

4
Just as I am— poor, wretched, blind,
Sight, riches, healing of the mind,
Yea, all I need in Thee to find,
    O Lamb of God, I come!

5
Just as I am— Thou wilt receive,
Wilt pardon, welcome, cleanse, relieve,
Because Thy promise I believe,
    O Lamb of God, I come!

6
Just as I am— Thy love unknown
Has broken every barrier down,
Now, to be Thine, yea, Thine alone,
    O Lamb of God, I come!

Just as I am.

O Thou Dread Power.

The Prayer of Burns,

For the Family of Revd G. Lawrie, D.D.:

Set to Music, & very respectfully Inscribed to

Mrs Lawrie of Monkton Manse,

By

W: H: Havergal · M: A

Honorary Canon,
& Rector of St Nicholas, Worcester.

Op. xlii.

Profits to the Monkton Industrial Schools.

Ent. Sta. Hall.   Price 2/6

LONDON SACRED MUSIC WAREHOUSE,
J. ALFRED NOVELLO,
Music Sellers (by Appointment) to Her Majesty,
69, Dean Str.^t Soho, & 24, Poultry.

[1847]

This portrait of William Henry Havergal was signed "Edwin Cocking 1855." The score and signature are W.H.H.'s handwriting. He was 62 on January 18, 1855.

POLAND,

A Song for the Times,

Composed, and by Permission Inscribed to

THE RIGHT HON^{BLE}

The Earl of Shaftesbury, K. G.

BY

W. H. HAVERGAL, M.A.

Honorary Canon of Worcester, and Incumbent of Shareshill, Staffordshire.

Op. 50.   PROFITS TO THE LADIES POLISH RELIEF FUND.   *Price 2^s/=*

London,

JOHN SHEPHERD, 98, NEWGATE STREET,

AND

ADDISON & LUCAS, 210, REGENT STREET.

POLAND

A Song for the Times.

For a Medium Voice. By W. H. Havergal, M.A.

This manuscript of William Henry Havergal's poem was written on the back of a sheet (apparently advertisement or promotion) on the importance of a good piano. This poem was selected by F.R.H. to be the poem for July in her 366-day book *Red Letter Days*. See pages 941 and 1008 of Volume I of this Havergal edition. This was published, set to his music, and is given on pages 1521–1526 of Volume V of the Havergal edition. A note at the end of Chapter IV of *Starlight Through the Shadows* indicates that this was his last hymn (see page 520 of Volume II of the Havergal edition).

Written impromptu 13th Decr 1869 at 9 P.M. for the little tune "Pussy cat" [written for his granddaughter, on pages 343–345 of this book]

Softly the dew in the evening descends,
    Cooling the sun-heated ground and the gale:
Flowerets all fainting it soothingly tends,
    Ere the consumings of mid-day prevail.
Sweet, gentle dewdrops, how mystic your fall;
Wisdom and mercy float down in you all.

Softer and sweeter by far is that Dew,
    Which from the Fountain of Comfort distils;
When the worn heart is created anew,
    And hallowèd pleasure its emptiness fills.
Lord, let Thy Spirit bedew my dry fleece;
Faith then shall triumph, and trouble shall cease.

GENTLE DEW.

Sacred Song

WORDS AND MUSIC

by the late

REV⁰ W. H. HAVERGAL, M.A.

(Hon: Canon of Worcester.)

Ent. Sta. Hall.　　　　　　　　　　　　　　　Price 3/=

London;
HUTCHINGS & ROMER,
9, CONDUIT STREET, REGENT STREET, W.

GENTLE DEW.

Words & Music by The Late Revᴅ W. H. HAVERGAL, M.A.

(H & R. 9448.)

SACRED SONGS & PIANOFORTE PIECES

SONGS.

XIV

Title	Composer	Price
ABIDE WITH ME	H. FOSTER	2/6
ABSALOM	J. F. DUGGAN	4/-
ADAM'S DREAM OF PARADISE	H. FOSTER	3/-
AFTER!	FRANCIS RIDLEY HAVERGAL	3/-
ASK ME NOT TO LEAVE THEE (RUTH)	H. FOSTER	2/-
AS PANTS THE HART (SOLO OR DUET)	SPOHR	2/6
AT THE GATE	K. L. WARD	2/6
A VOICE FROM HEAVEN	C. M. HEWKE	3/-
A VOICE FROM HEAVEN	ESTELLE	3/-
BEATITUDES THE	F. HASSE HODGES	
No 1. BLESSED ARE THE POOR IN SPIRIT		1/6
2. BLESSED ARE THEY THAT MOURN		1/6
3. BLESSED ARE THE MEEK		1/6
4. BLESSED ARE THEY THAT DO HUNGER		1/6
5. BLESSED ARE THE MERCIFUL		1/6
6. BLESSED ARE THE PURE IN HEART		1/6
BLESSED ARE THE MERCIFUL	E. LAND	3/-
BLESSED ARE THEY THAT MOURN	SIR H. R. BISHOP	3/-
BLESSED BE THY NAME FOR EVER	ANDREWS	2/6
BOW DOWN THINE EAR	RANDEGGER	3/-
BROKEN REEDS	GOUNOD	3/-
BY BABYLON'S WAVE	GOUNOD	3/-
CAUSE ME TO HEAR	MISS DAVIS	3/-
CHARITY (ARRANGED BY CALLCOTT)	ROSSINI	3/-
CHILD'S EVENING PRAYER	RANDEGGER	4/-
CHOSEN	BLUMENTHAL	4/-
COME UNTO ME	MISS DAVIS	3/-
CONSIDER THE LILIES	MISS DAVIS	3/-
DAVID'S PRAYER	COSTA	2/6
DREAM OF ST JEROME	BEETHOVEN	3/-
ENTREAT ME NOT TO LEAVE THEE (RUTH)	H. FOSTER	2/-
ESTHER'S PRAYER THE REV: H. F. THOMSON		3/-
FALLEN IS THY THRONE OH ISRAEL	T. MOORE	3/-
FAR LAND	E. ALMOND	2/6
FATHER, HALLOWED BE THY NAME	ANDREWS	3/-
FATHER OF ALL (WORDS BY POPE)	ANDREWS	2/6
FATHER WHOSE BLESSING (ST CECILIA)	SIR J. BENEDICT	3/-
GOD OF MERCY	MENDELSSOHN	2/-
HAGAR	J. F. DUGGAN	4/-
HAIL TO THEE JESUS OF NAZARETH	F. ROMER	3/-
HANDEL'S SONGS	(SEE CATALOGUE)	
HEAVENLY REST (IN E♭ & F)	CHOPIN	3/-
HE WILL GIVE YOU REST	S. GLOVER	3/-
HIS HOLY WORD	J. L. HATTON	2/6
HONOR THY FATHER	J. L. HATTON	2/6
HOW GLORIOUS IS OUR HEAVENLY HOME	Mrs McKINLAY	2/6
HYMN OF PEACE (GIVE PEACE IN OUR TIME O LORD)	CALLCOTT	1/6
I HEARD THE VOICE OF JESUS SAY	R. REYNOLDS	3/-
INFANT'S EVENING PRAYER	TULLY	3/-
IN THEE I TRUST	F. R. HAVERGAL	2/6
IS THERE NO BALM IN GILEAD	R. REYNOLDS	3/-
JESUS IS HERE	ASHE	3/-
JESUS OF NAZARETH PASSETH BY	F. ROMER	3/-
JOY CANNOT LAST FOR EVER	S. GLOVER	2/6
LEAD ME	COSTA	3/-
LORD IS MY SHEPHERD	E. F. HORSLEY	3/-
LOVE ONE ANOTHER	GOUNOD	3/-
MIRIAM AT HER HARP	COSTA	2/6
NEARER	COSTA	3/-
O JERUSALEM	TOPLIFF	3/-
O LORD HAVE MERCY UPON ME	PERGOLESI	2/6
O LORD IN THEE I PUT MY TRUST	COSTA	2/6
O LORD THY WILL BE DONE	E. ALMOND	2/6
O SEND OUT THY LIGHT	MOZART	2/-
OUR HEAVENLY HOME	S. GLOVER	2/6
PILGRIMS REST	GABRIEL	3/-
PRAYER	ESTELLE	3/-
ROCK OF AGES	CALLCOTT	3/-
SAVIOURS LOVE	GOUNOD	3/-
SENT TO HEAVEN	J. F. DUGGAN	3/-
SILENT NIGHT	DURRNER	2/6
SILENT NIGHT	CRAMPTON	2/6
SOLOMAN'S PRAYER	J. L. HATTON	2/6
SONG OF ST CECILIA	SIR JULIUS BENEDICT	3/-
SUN OF MY SOUL	KEBLE	1/6
TELL IT OUT	F. R. HAVERGAL	1/6
THE HEAVENS ABOVE US	DURRNER	1/6
THEY ARE NOT DEAD	BLUMENTHAL	3/-
THOU ART GONE TO THE GRAVE	MENDELSSOHN	2/6
THY CHURCH	VINCENT WALLACE	3/-
WHEN THOU PASSEST	F. R. HAVERGAL	3/-
YE CHILDREN OF JUDAH	COSTA	3/-

PIANO-FORTE.

Title	Solo	Duet
AGUILAR, O LORD REMEMBER	4/-	
ARNOLD, SABBATH HOURS IN TWO BOOKS. EA.	2/6	
BEETHOVEN, DREAM OF ST JEROME	3/-	
CALLCOTT, W.H. SACRED HALF HOURS WITH THE BEST COMPOSERS		
BEETHOVEN	4/-	5/-
MENDELSSOHN	4/-	5/-
MOZART	4/-	5/-
HAYDN	4/-	5/-
HANDEL	4/-	5/-
GOUNOD	4/-	5/-
WEBER	4/-	5/-
HYMN OF PEACE	3/-	3/-
MOZART'S 12TH MASS IN 3 BOOKS. EACH	5/-	6/-
KYRIE ELEISON	2/6	
GLORIA IN EXCELSIS	2/-	
DONA NOBIS	3/-	
GUOMAM TU SOLUS	2/6	
FRANKS, SIX SACRED MELODIES EACH	1/-	
GOODBAN, W.H. HOMAGE TO HANDEL		
No 1. MESSIAH	3/-	
2. DETTINGEN TE DEUM	3/-	
3. ISRAEL IN EGYPT	3/-	
HENAULT, F. SOUND THE LOUD TIMBREL	3/-	
WITH VERDURE CLAD	3/-	
BENEDICTUS MOZART	3/-	
LAYLAND, MOZART'S 12TH MASS IN 2 BOOKS EACH	3/-	5/-
ROSSINI'S STABAT MATER Do	3/-	5/-

Title	Solo
LAYLAND, CUJUS ANIMAM (ROSSINI)	3/-
SUN OF MY SOUL	3/-
AS PANTS THE HART (SPOHR)	3/-
SOUND THE LOUD TIMBREL	3/-
MASTERS, W.C. SANCTUS FROM GOUNOD'S MESSE SOLENELLE	3/-
MARSCHAN, A. BACH'S 12 HYMNS IN 3 BOOKS - EACH	3/-
MATTEI'S ENGLISH & RUSSIAN NATIONAL HYMNS	5/-
MONTGOMERY, W.H. SACRED HARMONIES OR POPULAR SACRED MELODIES, EASILY ARR IN 20 NUMBERS EACH	1/6
OSBORNE, G.A. WITH VERDURE CLAD	2/6
SEVEN LAST WORDS OF CHRIST	2/6
WAFT HER ANGELS	2/6
O THOU THAT TELLEST	2/6
JUDGE ME O LORD	1/6
AGNUS DEI	1/6
BENEDICTUS FROM MOZART REQUIEM	1/6
HE SHALL FEED HIS FLOCK	1/6
HOW BEAUTIFUL ARE THE FEET	1/6
RHODES. JERUSALEM THE GOLDEN (TRANSCRIBED)	3/-
HARK THE VESPER HYMN	3/6
RUMMELL. STABAT MATER	4/-
STEIN. GLORIA IN EXCELSIS	3/-
LET THE BRIGHT	3/-
AGNUS DEI	3/-
CUJUS ANIMAM	3/-
STONE, J.S. THE OLD HUNDREDTH (TRANSCRIBED)	3/-

PUBLISHED BY HUTCHINGS & ROMER, 9, CONDUIT STREET, REGENT ST. LONDON, W.

These are the first two pages of sermons recorded, and the last two pages of sermons recorded in W.H.H.'s handwriting, in his Sermon Record Book. He wrote in this book the date, place, and text of Scripture for each sermon, more than 150 pages of entries, from 1816 to 1869.

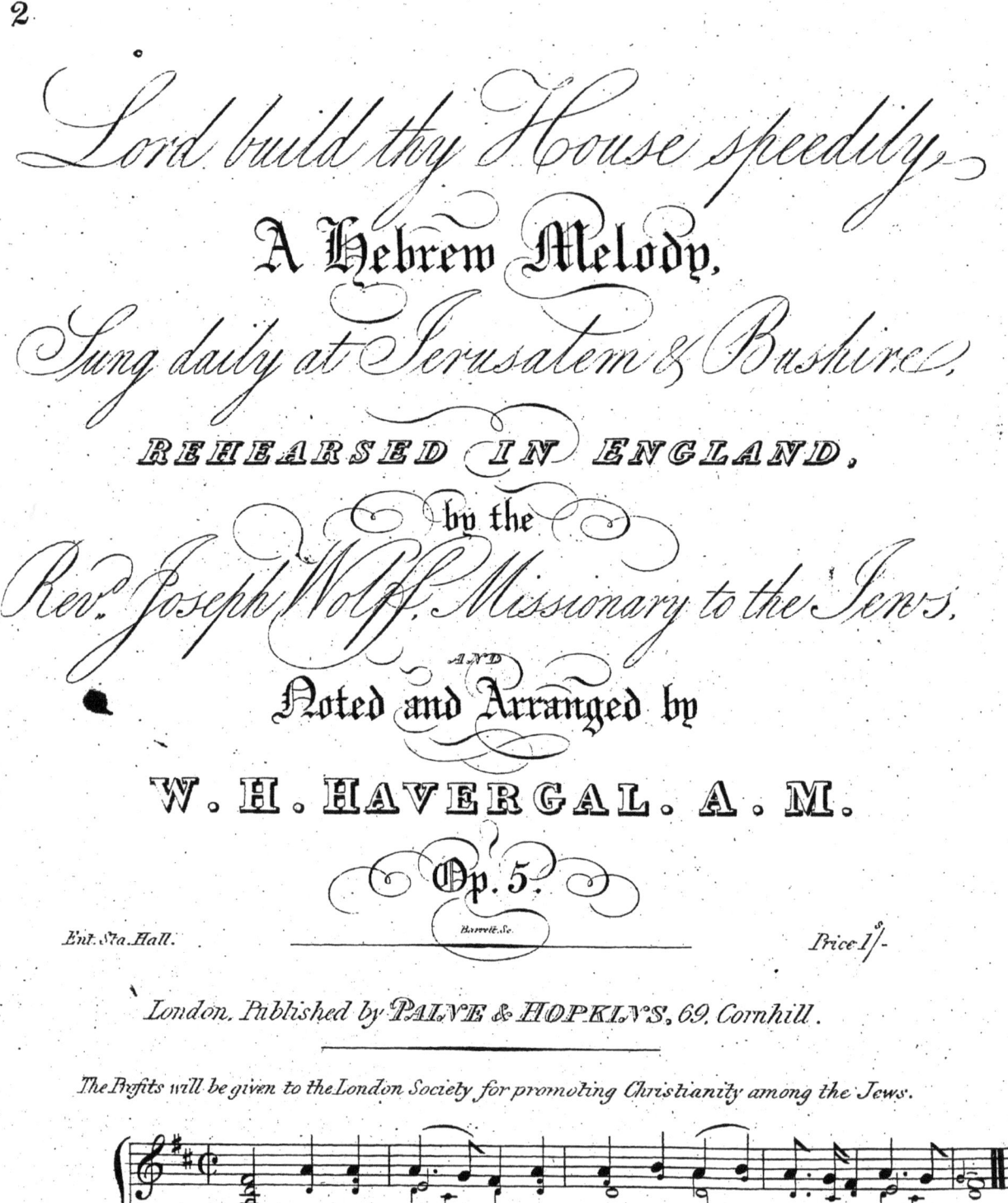

"Lord, Build Thy House Speedily," Op. 5

In rich cloth, bevelled, with Portrait and Illustrations, price 6s.,

RECORDS OF THE LIFE OF THE
REV. WM. H. HAVERGAL, M.A.

BY HIS DAUGHTER, JANE MIRIAM CRANE.

'"Yet speaketh!" In the memory of those
To whom he was indeed "a living song."'
—FRANCES RIDLEY HAVERGAL.

'Canon Havergal was no ordinary man. He was rich in grace as well as rich in gifts. "Who could see him and not love him?" asked a brother pastor, his friend for many years. The readers of "The Memorials of Frances Ridley Havergal" will remember how intense was her veneration for her loved father, and these pages will show how justly he held the highest place in the affections of all who knew him. This Biography is admirably written, and gives charming word-pictures of home and parish life. The illustrations include a portrait from a painting by S. Cole, and another from a bust taken by Robert Pauer, of Creuznach. Engravings are also given of Astley Church, and St. Nicholas' Church, Worcester.'—*Church Standard.*

'The Life of the Rev. W. H. Havergal (written by his daughter, J. Miriam Crane) deserves to take its place with the Memoirs of M'Cheyne. It has the same gracious interest, the same powerful unction, the same fervour, force, tender love and practical sympathy. It is written by a refined, skilful, and attractive pen. The reading of such a beautiful work as this is nothing short of a means of grace. Pastors will find in it much stimulus, inspiration, and many practical hints. Young Christians will be strengthened by its perusal, and the aged will read it with zest and delight. It is a biographical gem, and deserves a place in every Christian home.'—*Oldham Chronicle.*

'HOME WORDS' OFFICE, 1 PATERNOSTER BUILDINGS.

This advertisement was found at the back of a copy of Letters by the Late Frances Ridley Havergal *(James Nisbet & Co., "Third Thousand," 1885). This biography of W.H.H. is found on pages 581–675 of Volume IV of the Havergal edition. The Havergal edition also has four volumes of Sermons—true gold—by W.H.H., on pages 1301–1587 of Volume IV. Beyond his Sermons and the biography by his eldest child, Miriam Crane, Volume IV also has valuable accounts of W.H.H. written by others who knew him, on pages 677–725, as well as briefer references and accounts of him in many other places in Volume IV. A generous number of his poems are given on pages 1003–1081 in Volume I, and his valuable account of* A Wise and Holy Child *is given on pages 441–452 in Volume III.*

THREE HYMNS.

Written by Bishop Heber,

And Set to Music,

FOR VOICES & THE ORGAN OR PIANO FORTE,

by the

REVD. W. H. HAVERGAL, A.M.

Op. 10.

Ent. Sta. Hall.   Reduced Price 1/-

The Profits will be given to Native Female Schools in India.

London, J. Alfred Novello, 69, Dean Street, Soho.

Also, by the same Composer and Publishers.

Op. 1. From Greenland's icy mountains	2/6	for Hindoo Female Schools
2. A Volume of Original Psalm & Hymn Tunes to Words partly original	10/6	Do. Do.
3. Crown with freedom Afric's brows	1/6	Anti-Slavery Association.
4. Thou art gone to the Grave (Bp. Heber)	1/6	Hindoo Female Schools.
5. Lord build thy House speedily (Hebrew Melody)	1/0	London Jews' Society.
6. Let there be Light. (Revd. J. Marriott)	1/6	Newfoundland Schools.
7. Farewell (Bp. Heber)	1/6	Irish Reformation Societies.
8. The Lily & the Rose, or "By cool Siloam's shady rill" (Bp. Heber) an easy Duett.	1/6	Hindoo Female Schools.
9. Greek Hymn (translated by Bp. Heber)	1/6	Do. Do.

4.

2nd HYMN.
"LORD! IF THOU WILT THOU CANST MAKE ME CLEAN." 5. Luke 12.

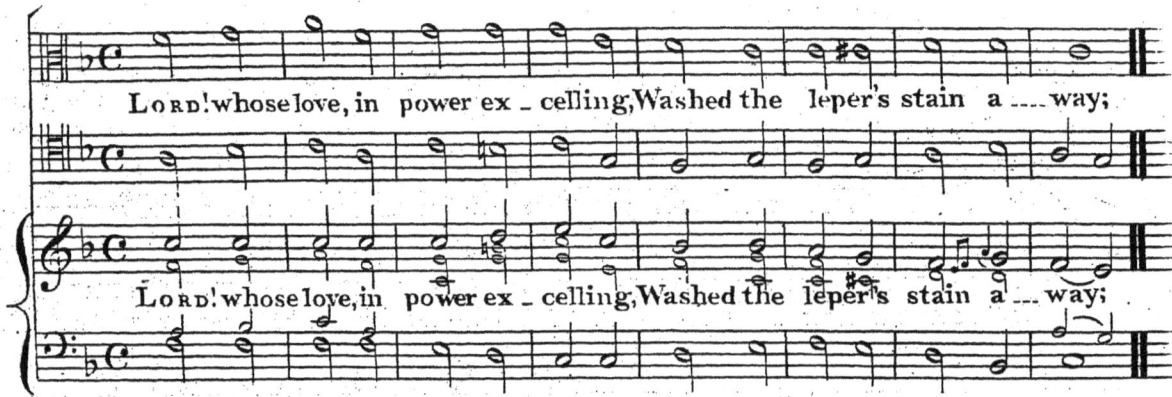

Lord! whose love, in power excelling, Washed the leper's stain away;

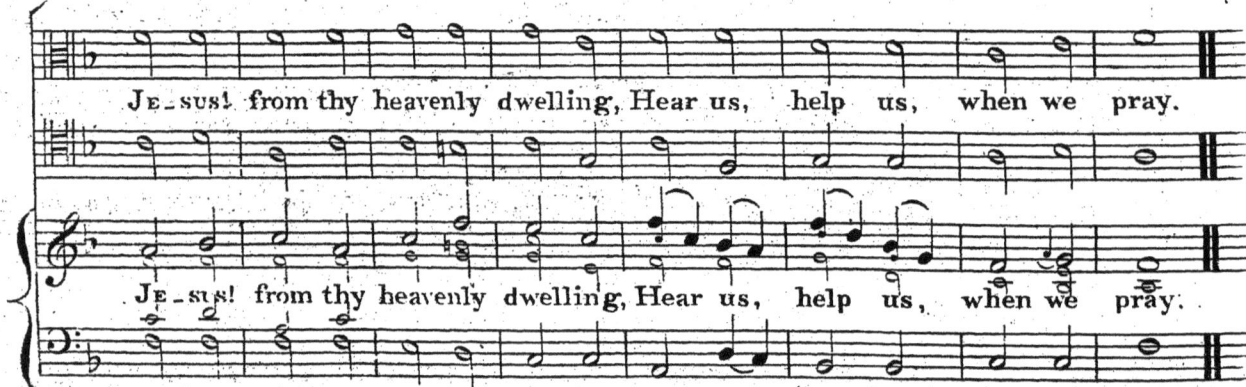

Jesus! from thy heavenly dwelling, Hear us, help us, when we pray.

—— 2 ——

From the filth of vice and folly,
From infuriate passion's rage,
Evil thoughts and hopes unholy,
Heedless youth and selfish age;

—— 3 ——

From the lusts whose deep pollutions
ADAM's ancient taint disclose,
From the Tempter's dark intrusions,
Restless doubt and blind repose;

—— 4 ——

From the miser's cursed treasure,
From the drunkard's jest obscene,
From the world, its pomp and pleasure;
JESUS! Master! make us clean!

— 2 —
There was joy in Heaven!
There was joy in Heaven!
When the billows, heaving dark,
Sank around the stranded ark,
And the rainbow's watery span
Spake of mercy, hope to man,
And peace with God in Heaven!

— 3 —
There was joy in Heaven!
There was joy in Heaven!
When of love the midnight beam
Dawn'd on the towers of Bethlehem;
And along the echoing hill
Angels sang "On Earth good will,
And glory in the Heaven!"

— 4 —
There is joy in Heaven!
There is joy in Heaven!
When the sheep that went astray
Turns again to virtue's way,
When the soul, by grace subdued,
Sobs its prayer of gratitude,
Then is there joy in Heaven!

FROM GREENLAND'S ICY MOUNTAINS,

Arranged as a

Sacred Song by M. Greville,

The Poetry by Bishop Heber,

The Music Composed by

THE LATE

REV: W. H. HAVERGAL.

Ent. Sta. Hall. — *Price 3s/=*

London,
ROBERT COCKS & Cº NEW BURLINGTON STREET, REGENT STREET, W.
by special Appointment
MUSIC PUBLISHERS TO HER MOST GRACIOUS MAJESTY QUEEN VICTORIA,
HIS ROYAL HIGHNESS THE PRINCE OF WALES,
and His Imperial Majesty The Emperor Napoleon III.

From Greenland's icy mountains. M. GREVILLE.   15,726.

"From Greenland's Icy Mountains"

From Greenland's icy mountains. M. GREVILLE.   15,726.

From Greenland's icy mountains. M. GREVILLE.

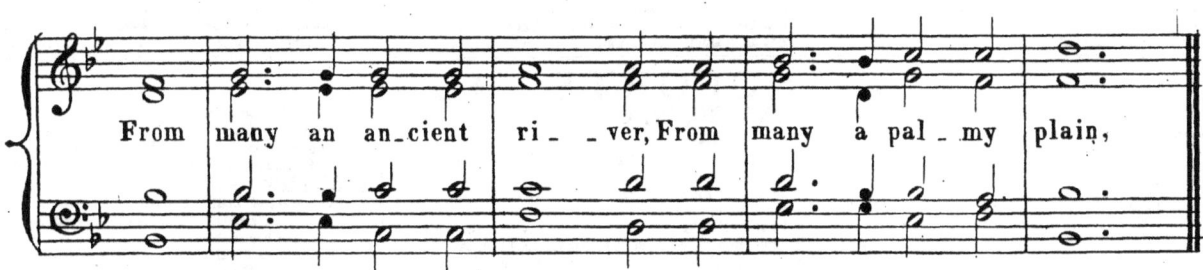
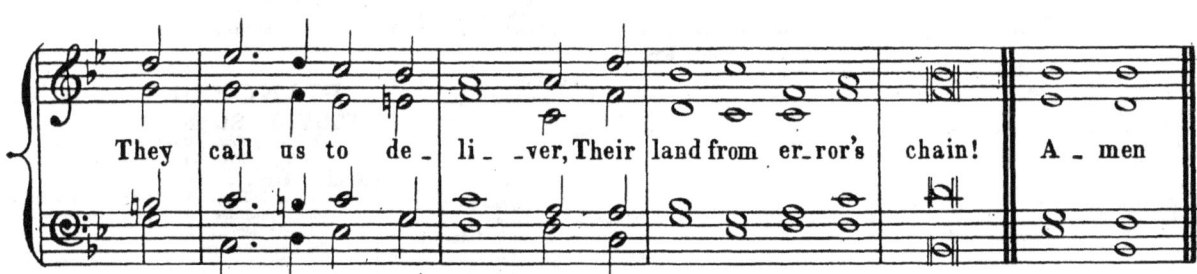

ROBERT COCKS & CO.'S LIST OF RECENT PUBLICATIONS,
VOCAL AND PIANOFORTE.

NOTE.—THIS LIST INCLUDES THE LATEST NOVELTIES. THOSE MARKED THUS (*) ARE ILLUSTRATED.
ALL MUSIC SUPPLIED AT HALF PRICE.

No. 29.

VOCAL MUSIC.

ABT, Franz.   S. D.
- Not a sparrow falleth. Sacred ... 3 0
- My mother's voice ... 3 0
- Our blessings on the daisies ... 3 0
- Almond Blossoms ... 3 0
- The Message of the Clouds ... 3 0
- Blissful Dreams come stealing o'er me ... 3 0
- Oh! ye Tears. (In C and D) ... each 4 0
- Kathleen Aroon ... 4 0
- Appendix to Hamilton's singing tutor ... 5 0
  "A work so comprehensive and at so moderate a price should command, and will doubtless experience, an extensive sale."—*Vide Cheltenham Looker-on.*

FRICKER, Anne.
- Mine eyes are to the Lord. Sacred ... 3 0 | Consolation ... 3 0
- Regret ... 3 0 | Two spirits plumed their wings ... 3 0
- I stood beneath the chestnut trees ... 3 0 | I built a bridge of fancies 4 0
- | *The Robin. Illus. ... 3 0

GATTY, A. S.
- The Mill Lad's Love ... 3 0
- Friend Sorrow ... 3 0
- Some future day ... 3 0
- *Brightrammargate-on-the-Sea. Comic. Illustrated ... 3 0
- *The three little pigs. Comic. Illus. ... 3 0
- *A sneezing song. Comic. Illus. ... 3 0
- *Cent. per Cent. Comic. Illus. ... 3 0
- *I really am so sleepy.' Comic ... 3 0
- Oh, doubting heart. No. 1 in C, No. 2 in E flat, each 3 0
- I'll not try it again. Comic ... 3 0
- Tell him I love him yet ... 3 0
- Songs for our little ones ... each 2 6
  1. Robin, robin.   4. Papa, I am weary.
  2. A Child's Fancy.   5. High and Low.
  3. A New Year's Carol.   6. Naughty Tom.
- Songs for children Nos. 1 to 6 ... each 3 0
  1. Rain drops patter.   4. Going to school.
  2. Child's good-night.   5. Burial of the linnet.
  3. The snow man.   6. Above the spire.
- O fair dove! O fond dove. Sung by Madame Patey ... 4 0
- Long, long ago ... 3 0
- The lights far out at sea ... 3 0
- I prithee send me back my heart ... 3 0

LINDSAY, Miss M.   S. D.
- Alone. Sacred ... 3 0
- *In this I hope—(In hoc spero). Sacred. Illus. ... 3 0
- Low at thy feet. Sacred song ... 3 0
- Far away ... 4 0
- Home they brought her warrior dead. In E flat and G ... each 4 0
- *The bridge ... 4 0
- *The snow lies white. Poetry by Miss Ingelow ... 3 0
- *When sparrows build. Illus. ... 3 0
- *Too late, too late ... 4 0
- Tired. No. 1 in D flat, No. 2 in D. ... 4 0
- Oh! when wilt thou come unto me. (Sacred) ... 3 0
- *Resignation. In B flat and E flat ... each 3 0
- *Rest. Sacred song ... 3 0
- Give us Thy rest. (Sacred) ... 3 0

SCHUMANN, R.
- Come when the soft twilight falls ... 3 0
- When gentle winds ... 3 0

SMART, HENRY.
- The face at the Window 3 0 | Bells ... 3 0

TUCKER, H.
- Do not heed her warning ... 3 0

WHITE, C. A.
- Put me in my little bed. (The cradle song of America) ... 2 6

WRIGHTON, W. T.
- The waking of the Flowers, No 1 in C, No. 2 in E flat ... 3 0
- Troubled, but not distressed. Sacred ... 3 0
- Speak well of the absent. Embossed ... 3 0
- The Song of the Bee. Embossed ... 3 0
- Bright star of eve arise. Embossed ... 3 0
- Morn in the Meadows. Embossed ... 3 0
- The Lily. Embossed ... 3 0
- *Norah, sweet Norah. (In D and F) ... each 3 0
- In the downhill of life. Embossed ... 3 0
- Memories. Illuminated ... 3 0
- Her bright smile haunts me still. Embossed ... 4 0
- She sang among the flowers. Embossed ... 3 0

WRIGHTON, W. T.—*continued.*   S. D.
- Shylie Bawn ... 3 0
- The liquid gem. Embossed ... 4 0
- *The wishing cap ... 4 0
- Thy voice is near. Embossed ... 4 0

NEW VOCAL DUETS.

ABT, F.
- Oh! ye tears ... 3 0 | Fairy Chimes ... 3 0
- Kathleen Aroon ... 3 0

GATTY, A. S.
- O that we two were Maying ... 4 0

GLOVER, S.
- Let us roam ... 4 0
- The beautiful and true ... 4 0
- The music of the birds ... 3 0
- Maids of the greenwood ... 3 0
- The fairy queen (in C and D) ... each 3 0
- Flowers of the Garden and Flowers of the Wildwood ... 4 0
- The silent Teachers. Sacred ... 3 0
- *The crystal cave ... 3 0

LINDSAY.
- Low at thy feet ... 4 0 | Too late, too late ... 4 0
- Tired ... 4 0 | Far away ... 4 0
- The Bridge ... 4 0

SMART, H.
- The twilight hour has come ... 4 0

SCHUMANN, R.
- When gentle winds ... 4 0

THOMAS, J. R.
- Happy be thy dreams ... 4 0

WRIGHTON, W. T.
- Liquid gem ... 4 0
- As one by one our friends depart ... 3 0
- Her bright smile ... 4 0

PIANOFORTE MUSIC.

ASCHER, J.   S. D.
- Vaillance. Polka militaire ... 2 6

BELLAK, J.
- Wild Flowers—Nos. 1 to 12 ... each 1 0
- Jewels—Nos 1 to 6 ... each 2 6
- Dewdrops, 25 easy pieces ... each 1 0
- Buds of melody, 31 Nos. Easy pieces ... each 1 0

CALLCOTT, W. H.
- *The Holy Family. Books, 10, 11, and 12 ... each 5 0
  This valuable work is now completed in 12 Books.

CASPAR, C. A.
- The Exile. (Schubert) 3 0 | "Aspen leaves," by
- Rosamunda. (Schubert) 4 0 | R. Schumann ... 3 0

DELASEURIE, A.
- *Petit Timbalier Polka. Illustrated ... 2 6
- *Fête au Chalet Valse. Illustrated ... 2 6

GLOVER, S.
- The Zouaves' Retreat March, Illus. ... 3 0
- The Royal Greek March, Illus. ... 3 0

KORNATZKI, F.
- Chiming May Bells 3 0 | Angelic Whispers ... 3 0
- The Hunter's Horn 4 0

LEE, Maurice.
- Fleur de L'ame. Op. 24 ... 3 0
- Azur. Nocturne sentimentale ... 4 0
- L'Electricite. Etude de salon ... 4 0
- Au bord de la Fontaine. Romance-Etude ... 4 0

LEMOINE, F.
- Une Cascade des Fleurs ... 4 0

LIEBICH, J.
- Musical box ... 4 0

LUINI, C.
- *Too late (Lindsay) 3 0 | Far away (Lindsay) ... 3 0
- O fair dove ... 3 0 | *Resignation (Lindsay) 3 0

MATTINI, F.
- Most useful Teaching Pieces, each ... 2 6
  Charming Polka | The bush aboon Traquair
  Bon Soir Schottische | The Waefu' heart
  The Matchless Schottische | The last time I came
  Golden leaf (Melody)   o'er the muir
  Wild Waves March | O, Bothwell Bank, thou
  The Striking Polka   bloomest fair!
  The Streamlet | For the sake of gold she left me
- Sunday Echoes. 12 easy pieces ... each 1 0
- Sweet Melodies 24 easy pieces, as duets ... each 1 0

ROCKSTRO, W. S.   S. D.
- Moonlit Waters
- Gavotte and Rondo. (From J. S. Bach's Sixth Violin Sonata) ... 3 0
- Jessie, the Flower of Dunblane ... 4 0
- Batti Batti ... 4 0
- Di tanti Palpiti ... 4 0
- Bourrée, from J. S. Bach's 4th Sonata for Violoncello 4 0
- *Echoes from the Rhine ... 4 0 | Echoes of Mont Blanc.
- Echoes from the High-   Fantasia ... 4 0
  lands ... 4 0 | Echoes of Zurich ... 4 0
- Echoes from the green isle 4 0 | Kelvin Grove ... 4 0
- Voices from the hill-side 4 0 | The flower gatherers ... 4 0
- Gems from the Emerald | Border legends ... 4 0
  isle ... 4 0 | La ci darem ... 4 0
- The Gipsy Countess ... 4 0 | Mountain echoes ... 4 0

WALPOLE, Frank.
- Adeste Fideles ... 2 6 | Hearts of Oak ... 2 6
- German Hymn ... 2 6 | The Roast Beef of Old
- O lovely Peace ... 2 6 | England ... 2 6
- La mia Letizia ... 2 6 | Cease your funning ... 2 6
- Ciascun lo dice ... 2 6

WEST, G. F.
- Favourite Waltzes, by Mozart, Nos. 1, 2, and 3, each 3 0
- Lieber Augustin. (Celebrated Bavarian air) ... 3 0
- Andante. (From Beethoven's Symphony in O minor) 3 0
- But Thou didst not leave ("Messiah") ... 3 0
- When the rosy morn. (From Shield's opera of "Rosina") ... 3 0
- March from Handel's Occasional Oratorio ... 3 0
- Favourite Waltzes of Labitzky, Lanner, and Strauss. Nos. 1 and 2, each ... 4 0
- "But the Lord is mindful," and "Sleepers awake" ... 3 0
- Gloria in Excelsis, from Haydn's Imperial Mass ... 3 0
- Ave Maria. (Cherubini) ... 3 0
- Der lustige Bauer (Schumann) ... 3 0
- Marcia Eroica. Extract from Mendelssohn's 1st rondo ... 3 0
- Paraphrase on Weber's Grand Mass in G ... 4 0
- I would that my love. (Mendelssohn) ... 3 0
- Benedictus Requiem. (Mozart) ... 3 0
- Menuetto e Trio. Symphony in D major. (Mozart) ... 3 0

WEST, G. F.—*continued.*   S. D.
- Welcome me Home 3 0 | La Marseillaise ... 4 0
- On mighty pens ... 3 0 | Freischütz ... 4 0
- Rule Britannia ... 4 0 | Stabat Mater Dolorosa 3 0

WRIGHT, A.
- The Maid of Lodi. Fantasia ... 4 0
- "Die Zauberflöte," Fantasia on airs from ... 4 0
- Hey, the bonnie breast knots ... 4 0
- Six Studies for the Piano ... 4 0
- Oft in the Stilly Night ... 4 0
- My ain Fireside ... 4 0
- I've been roaming ... 3 0
- My highland home. (Sir H. Bishop) ... 4 0
- Fantasia on "The Miller of the Dee" ... 4 0

WYMAN, A.
- Pictures of thought ... 4 0
- Silvery Waves ... 4 0

PIANOFORTE DUETS.

GLOVER, Stephen.
- The Happy Family Quadrille ... 4 0
- The Royal Greek March ... 4 0

LIEBICH, J.
- Woodland Trillings 4 0 | Her bright smile ... 3 0
- Brighton Quadrilles 4 0 | Sing me that song again 3 0
- The Liquid Gem ... 3 0
- The Opera Bouquet ... each 3 0
  1. Oberon.   7. Die Zauberflöte.
  2. Don Giovanni.   8. Guillaume Tell.
  3. Lucrezia Borgia.   9. Tancredi.
  4. Masaniello.   10. La Clemenza.
  5. Sonnambula.   11. La Gazza Ladra.
  6. Norma.   12. Zampa.

LUINI, Carl.
- Les Gardes du Roi ... 3 0

RICHARDS, B.
- The Carmarthen March ... 4 0

WEST, G. F.
PROGRESSIVE PIANOFORTE DUETS ARRANGED AND FINGERED.
First Stage.
1. Morceau de Robert le Diable (Meyerbeer) ... 4 0
2. Ah che assorta (Venzano) ... 3 0
3. Krieger's Lust March (Gung'l) ... 3 0

Second Stage.

PIANOFORTE MUSIC.

ASCHER, J. — s. d.
Vaillance. Polka militaire 2 6

BELLAK, J.
Wild Flowers—Nos. 1 to 12 ...... each 1 0
Jewels—Nos 1 to 6 ...... 2 6
Dewdrops, 25 easy pieces ...... each 1 0
Buds of melody, 31 Nos. Easy pieces ...... each 1 0

CALLCOTT, W. H.
*The Holy Family. Books, 10, 11, and 12 ...each 5 0
This valuable work is now completed in 12 Books.

CASPAR, C. A.
The Exile. (Schubert) 3 0 | "Aspen leaves," by
Rosamunda. (Schubert) 4 0 | R. Schumann 3 0

DELASEURIE, A.
*Petit Timbalier Polka. Illustrated 2 6
*Fête au Chalet Valse. Illustrated 2 6

GLOVER, S.
The Zouaves' Retreat March, Illus. 3 0
The Royal Greek March, Illus. 3 0

KORNATZKI, F.
Chiming May Bells 3 0 | Angelic Whispers ... 3 0
The Hunter's Horn 4 0 |

LEE, Maurice.
Fleur de L'ame. Op. 24 ...... 3 0
Azur. Nocturne sentimentale 4 0
L'Electricite. Etude de salon 4 0
Au bord de la Fontaine. Romance-Etude 3 0

LEMOINE, F.
Une Cascade des Fleurs 4 0

LIEBICH, J.
Musical box 4 0

LUINI, C.
*Too late (Lindsay) 3 0 | Far away (Lindsay)... 3 0
O fair dove ...... 3 0 | *Resignation (Lindsay) 3 0

MATTINI, F.
Most useful Teaching Pieces, each 2 6
Charming Polka | The bush aboon Traquair
Bon mot Schottische | The Waefu' heart
The Matchless Schottische | The last time I came
Golden leaf (Melody) | o'er the muir
Wild Waves March | O, Bothwell Bank, thou
The Striking Polka | bloomest fair!
The Streamlet | For the sake of gold she left me
Sunday Echoes. 12 easy pieces ...... each 1 0
Sweet Melodies 24 easy pieces, as duets ...... each 1 0

PRIDHAM. J.
The Soldier's Return. Descriptive Fantasia 4 0
*The sailor's dream 4 0
The soldier's farewell. Descriptive Fantasia 4 0

RICHARDS, Brinley.
Far away (Miss Lindsay) 4 0
Low at Thy feet (Miss Lindsay) 3 0
Excelsior (Miss Lindsay) 3 0
The Minstrel's Song 3 0
L'Etoile du Soir 3 0
The Morgan March 3 0
The new Welsh Fantasia, introducing "The
Morgan March" and "Come to Battle" 4 0
Tired (Melody by Miss Lindsay) 3 0
Warblings at Dawn, and Noon ...... each 3 0
Pianist's library ...... each 2s. 6d., 3s. and 3 0
The Carmarthen March 3 0
Thy voice is near... 3 0 | Warblings at Eve 4 0
The liquid gem ... 4 0 | Kathleen Mavourneen 4 0
Kathleen Aroon ... 3 0 | The wishing cap 3 0
I'll hang my harp... 4 0 | Happy be thy dreams 3 0

ROCKSTRO, W. S. — s. d.
Moonlit Waters
Gavotte and Ronde. (From J. S. Bach's Sixth
Violin Sonata) 3 0
Jessie, the Flower of Dunblane 4 0
Batti batti 4 0
Di tanti Palpiti 4 0
Bourrée, from J. S. Bach's 4th Sonata for Violoncello 4 0
*Echoes of the Rhine ...4 0 | Echoes of Mont Blanc.
Echoes from the High- | Fantasia 4 0
lands ...... 4 0 | Echoes of Zurich 4 0
Echoes from the green isle 4 0 | Kelvin Grove 4 0
Voices from the hill-side 4 0 | The flower gatherers... 4 0
Gems from the Emerald | Border legends 4 0
isle ...... 4 0 | La ci darem 4 0
The Gipsy Countess... 4 0 | Mountain echoes 4 0

WALPOLE, Frank.
Adeste Fideles ... 2 6 | Hearts of Oak 2 6
German Hymn ... 2 6 | The Roast Beef of Old
O lovely Peace ... 2 6 | England 2 6
La mia Letizia ... 2 6 | Cease your funning ... 2 6
Ciascun lo dice ... 2 6 |

WEST, G. F.
Favourite Waltzes, by Mozart, Nos. 1, 2, and 3, each 3 0
Lieber Augustin. (Celebrated Bavarian air) 3 0
Andante. (From Beethoven's Symphony in C minor) 3 0
But Thou didst not leave ("Messiah") 3 0
When the rosy morn. (From Shield's opera of
"Rosina") 3 0
March from Handel's Occasional Oratorio 3 0
Favourite Waltzes of Labitzky, Lanner, and Strauss.
Nos. 1 and 2, each 4 0
"But the Lord is mindful," and "Sleepers awake" 3 0
Gloria in Excelsis, from Haydn's Imperial Mass 3 0
Ave Maria. (Cherubini) 3 0
Der lustige Bauer (Schumann) 3 0
Marcia Eroica. Extract from Mendelssohn's 1st
rondo 3 0
Paraphrase on Weber's Grand Mass in G 4 0
I would that my love. (Mendelssohn) 3 0
Benedictus Requiem. (Mozart) 3 0
Menuetto e Trio. Symphony in D major.
(Mozart) 3 0
I waited for the Lord. Hymn of Praise.
(Mendelssohn) 3 0
Favourite Old English melodies. No. 1 ...... 4 0
Beethoven's Lebensglück 4 0
"   March in Fidelio 4 0
Appendix to Hamilton's piano tutor 5 0
Extract from Beethoven's choral fantasia 3 0
Extract from Beethoven's septet 3 0
Beethoven's waltzes, in 6 books ...... each 3 0
Haydn's Kyrie Eleison, from 2nd Mass 3 0
Extract from Mendelssohn's 1st concerto 3 0
Mendelssohn's Maid of the Ganges (Auf Flügeln) 3 0
Extract from Haydn's symphony, letter V 3 0
Scottish Melodies:
 1. Scots wha hae and Bonnie Dundee 4 0
 2. Logie o' Buchan and Wha wadna fecht for Charlie 4 0
 3. Auld Lang Syne and We're a' noddin' 4 0
 4. Comin' thro' the rye and The Campbells are comin' 4 0
Songs without words. No. 1—La ci darem 3 0
Songs without words, No. 2 (Placido e il mar) ... 3 0
Old English melodies. No. 2—containing Black
eyed Susan and The Girl I left beind me 3 0

WEST, G. F.—continued. — s. d.
Welcome me Home 3 0 | La Marseillaise 4 0
On mighty pens ... 3 0 | Freischütz 4 0
Rule Britannia ...... 4 0 | Stabat Mater Dolorosa 3 0

WRIGHT, A.
The Maid of Lodi. Fantasia 4 0
"Die Zauberflöte," Fantasia on airs from 4 0
Hey, the bonnie breast knots 4 0
Six Studies for the Piano 4 0
Oft in the Stilly Night 4 0
My ain Fireside 4 0
I've been roaming 3 0
My highland home. (Sir H. Bishop) 4 0
Fantasia on "The Miller of the Dee" 4 0

WYMAN, A.
Pictures of thought 4 0
Silvery Waves 4 0

PIANOFORTE DUETS.

GLOVER, Stephen.
The Happy Family Quadrille 4 0
The Royal Greek March 4 0

LIEBICH, J.
Woodland Trillings 4 0 | Her bright smile 3 0
Brighton Quadrilles 4 0 | Sing me that song again 3 0
The Liquid Gem ... 3 0 |
The Opera Bouquet ...... each 3 0
 1. Oberon.   7. Die Zauberflöte.
 2. Don Giovanni. 8. Guillaume Tell.
 3. Lucrezia Borgia. 9. Tancredi.
 4. Masaniello.   10. La Clemenza.
 5. Sonnambula.   11. La Gazza Ladra.
 6. Norma.   12. Zampa.

LUINI, Carl.
Les Gardes du Roi 3 0

RICHARDS, B.
The Carmarthen March 4 0

WEST, G. F.
PROGRESSIVE PIANOFORTE DUETS ARRANGED AND FINGERED.
First Stage.
 1. Morceau de Robert le Diable (Meyerbeer) 4 0
 2. Ah che assorta (Venzano) 3 0
 3. Krieger's Lust March (Gung'l) 3 0
Second Stage.
 4. Agnus Dei, from 12th Mass (Mozart) 4 0
 5. Gloria in Excelsis (Pergolesi) 4 0
 6. La Preghiera de Mose (Rossini) 4 0
 7. Gloria in Excelsis, from 1st Mass (Haydn) 4 0
 8. Sonata in D major (Mozart) 5 0
Third Stage.
 9. Gloria, from 12th Mass (Mozart) 4 0
10. Kyrie, from 12th Mass (Mozart) 4 0
11. Benedictus, from 12th Mass (Mozart) 4 0
12. Theme de Lucrezia Borgia (Czerny) 5 0
13. The Hallelujah chorus (Handel) 4 0
Fourth Stage.—(OVERTURES).
14. La Gazza Ladra (Rossini) 6 0
15. Zampa (Herold) 4 0
16. Le Cheval de Bronze (Auber) 6 0
17. Der Freischütz (Weber) 5 0
18. Fra Diavolo (Auber) 6 0
19. Masaniello (Auber) 6 0
Teacher and pupil (Home, sweet home) 4 0

VALENTINE, T.
Duets for little fingers, Nos. 1 to 12 ...... each 1 0

A *New Edition of "The History and Construction of the Organ,"* by E. J. Hopkins and E. F. Rimbault. 780 pp. Just Published, price £1 11s. 6d.
"The only authority upon this subject published in this country."

LONDON: ROBERT COCKS & CO., NEW BURLINGTON STREET, W.,

Music Publishers (by special appointment) to Her Majesty the Queen, H.R.H. the Prince of Wales, and the Emperor Napoleon III.

"From Greenland's icy Mountains"

WRITTEN BY

The Right Reverend Reginald Heber, D.D.

late Lord Bishop of Calcutta.

SET TO MUSIC.

for Voices and the Organ,

or

Piano Forte;

and

with Permission most Respectfully Dedicated to

Mrs HEBER.

By the Rev. W. H. Havergal, A.M.

(New Edition, Revised & Enlarged.)

Profits to Hindoo Female Schools.

Ent. Sta. Hall. — London. — Price 2/6

Published by J. Alfred Novello, 69, Dean Str. Soho.

"From Greenland's Icy Mountains," the Novello score for voices with organ or piano

N. B. As various editions of this Hymn are extant, it may be expedient to state that the present edition is taken from a copy in the Bishop's own hand, in the possession of the Rector of Whittington, Salop. In the Church of that Parish his Lordship, in April 1820, preached a Sermon on behalf of the Church-Missionary-Society, on which occasion the Hymn was for the first time printed. The net-profits of the former editions of this Publication were, up to May 1828, £120.

* The mode of notation which occurs in this and similar passages is adopted on the authority of Dr Crotch. ("Elements of Musical Composition." p 71.) "The flat seventh on Fa sharp, in the major key especially, after the sixth and fifth on Fa, is often written as an extreme sharp sixth and fifth, but is then always resolved into a sixth and fourth on Sol."

* See the Bishop's Journal prefixed to his Narrative. Page 42. date 21st September 1823. Quarto Edition.

"From Greenland's Icy Mountains," the Novello score for voices with organ or piano

"From Greenland's Icy Mountains," the Novello score for voices with organ or piano

MUSICAL COMPOSITIONS

BY

The Rev. W. H. HAVERGAL, A.M.

[PROFITS TO VARIOUS CHARITIES.]

WORDS BY BISHOP HEBER.

	s.	d.
"From Greenland's icy mountains," 2nd edit. (Hymn)	2	6
"Thou art gone to the grave" (Elegy) Op. 4	1	6
"Grant me, released from matter's chain," (Hymn) Translated from the Greek of Synesius, Op. 9	1	6
Farewell,—"When eyes are beaming," Op. 7.	1	6
The Lilly and the Rose,—"By cool Siloam's shady rill," Op. 8	1	6
"If thou wert by my side, my Love," Op. 12.	1	6
"Life nor Death shall us dissever" "Lord, whose love in power excelling" "There was joy in Heaven" (Three Hymns) Op. 10	2	0
"God that madest earth and Heaven" (Vesper Hymn) Op. 14	2	0
"Oh! green was the corn, as I rode on my way," Op. 15	2	0
"When Spring unlocks the flowers," Op. 20	1	6
"Jerusalem! Jerusalem! enthroned once on high," Op. 21	2	6
"The Son of God goes forth to war" (Hymn for St. Stephen's Day) Op. 22	2	0
Hope,—"Reflected on the lake I love, to see the stars of evening glow," Op. 23	1	6
The Loyal Englishman's Litany—"From foes that would the land devour," Op. 28	2	0
"I praised the earth in beauty seen," Op. 29	2	6
"Wake not, O Mother," Op. 32	2	0

WORDS BY OTHER AUTHORS.

	s.	d.
"Beloved Saviour! let not me," Hymn composed in Hindoostanee, by the Rev. Abdool Messeeh, Op. 19.	2	0
Protestant's Hymn—"Thou, whose uplifted arm," Op. 16	1	6
Newfoundlander's Petition	2	0
"Let there be light," Op. 6	1	6
"Lord, when our wayward feet," Op. 13	1	6
"Lord, build thy house speedily," (Hebrew Melody,) Op. 5.	1	0
Lay of the Persian Muleteer, Op. 17	1	6
A Cradle Hymn. Words by the daughter of a Clergyman, (Lithographic Vignette,) Op. 18	2	0
"Rest is not here." Words by Miss Emra, Op. 24	1	6
"How fair are the beauties of Nature arround." By Ditto, Op. 26	2	0
"O speak that gentle word once more." Words by the Rev. J. East, A.M. Op. 25	2	0
A Nursery Scene. Words by Miss Emra, (Lithographic Vignette,) Op. 27	2	6
Original Airs and Harmonized Tunes, adapted to Hymns of various measures	10	6
"Weep not for me"—from the Poems appended to "The Widow of Nain," Op. 30	2	0
"We will not weep for thee"—from "The Widow of Nain," Op. 31	2	6
"Fly ye hours." Words by the Rev. H.F. Lyte, A.M. Op. 33	2	6
"Hark! to the Old Bell's Chime"—by the Authoress of "Scenes in our Parish," Op. 34	2	6
"I love—I love the Morning," (Duett) Op. 36	2	0
An Evening Service, with 100 Antiphonal Chants, Op. 35.	12	0
Morning and Evening Hymn. An Inverse Palindrome on coloured card	1	0
Mementote Vinctorum . Ditto Ditto	1	0
Four Double Chants, (Recte et Retro, &c.) on coloured card	1	0

The Gresham Prize Composition, No. 6, by the Rev. W. Havergal, A.M. . . 5 0

ALSO

The Gresham Prize Composition, No. 1, "Jubilate"	by Charles Hart	8	6
—————— No. 2, "Turn thee again, O Lord"	Kellow J. Pye	5	0
—————— No. 3, "Have mercy upon me"	John Goss	3	6
—————— No. 4, "Bow down thine ear"	Elvey	5	0
—————— No. 5, "My Soul doth magnify the Lord"	Lucas	5	0

ARE ALL PUBLISHED BY

J. ALFRED NOVELLO,
MUSIC SELLER (BY SPECIAL APPOINTMENT) TO HER MAJESTY,
69, DEAN STREET, SOHO.

This advertisement list of music scores by William Henry Havergal is not nearly a complete list of his published music; much of his music was unpublished. Andrew James Symington, in his "Biographical Sketch" of W.H.H., wrote, "Notoriously liberal to publishers of music, he has been equally notorious in aiding, by scientific criticism and research, all who have applied to him. He has written and kept back far more than he has published." (This was found in the "Biographical Sketch of Rev. W. Havergal, A.M., Editor of Old Church Psalmody," *by his friend, Dr. Andrew James Symington, published in* The Musical Amateur *for June, 1861, also given on pages 691–692 of Volume IV of the Havergal edition.*

A Collection of

ORIGINAL AIRS & HARMONIZED TUNES

Adapted to

HYMNS OF VARIOUS MEASURES

with an ACCOMPANIMENT for the

Organ or Piano Forte

BY THE

Rev.d W. H. Havergal, A.M.

OP. 2.

Ent. Sta. Hall.   Price. 10/6.

London

Printed for the Author by Paine and Hopkins,
69, Cornhill.

PREFACE.

IN publishing the following Compositions, the Author is unwilling to allege any of those apologetical reasons, which, though they may be very true, are unpleasantly trite. The fact is this:—that most of the Tunes were written during seasons of indisposition, for mental recreation, some of them for private devotion, and others for parochial congregations. As they seem to have pleased the Author's musical friends, he hopes that they may please other individuals; and, therefore, though with much diffidence, he submits to the Christian Public the present Volume, as a very humble assistant of devotional Music. And, truly, should it, in any instance, excite or aid devotional feeling, by causing even one heart to vibrate in consonance with those who, without imperfection, are singing the Song of the atoning Lamb, his fervent wishes will be accomplished.

To positive originality of composition, no pretensions are advanced: but, while criticism is therefore deprecated, all consciousness of plagiarism is disavowed. That others may, in some passages, discern a similarity to what they have previously seen or heard, is, indeed, very possible. This, however, will not occasion any surprise, since so much vocal Music has been written, that coincidences, without the slightest breach of integrity, frequently occur in the best compositions. It is, perhaps, extremely difficult, if not impracticable, to write for the voice a short phrase, which, strictly speaking, shall be original. Composers, therefore, of metrical tunes especially, must hope to succeed, if not solely, yet chiefly, by a fresh combination, and a varied arrangement, of existing phrases.

In No. 15, will be found an attempt at *Double Counterpoint*, which, however humble its merits may be, is at least not likely to have been anticipated.

As it respects the words which have been selected, it is hoped that, while they are calculated to promote edification, they will in no case be deemed objectionable. Those which are distinguished by an asterisk are original. Really good Hymns, such as are at once spiritual and poetical, and well accentuated for singing, are still somewhat rare.

PREFACE.

It is greatly to be regretted, that congregational singing, though a most delightful part of Divine worship, should hitherto be in its infancy among us. Whatever means may be adopted to accelerate its growth, it is probable that by nothing will it be more speedily and effectually promoted, than by the diffusion of musical science, controlled by genuine piety, among the Clergy of our revered and apostolical Church. Availing himself, therefore, of the present opportunity, the Author would unhesitatingly commend the attainment of a moderate portion of musical knowledge, not only as a relaxation, but as an auxiliary, in the great and hallowed "*work of the Ministry.*" The utility of it in enabling a Clergyman to reform or regulate the singing, in either his Church or his Sunday-School, is very considerable. It invests him with an additional authority, to which the members of a choir will less reluctantly submit; and thus, independently of its other advantages, will probably prevent those unhappy differences which frequently occur between the wishes of the Minister and of the Singers.

In offering this recommendation, the Author begs that he may not be misunderstood; he would not countenance that inordinate attention to Music, which is likely to engender a light and worldly spirit: he would have musical science aid and adorn, and not impede and desecrate, the highest of all vocations: he would have whatever attention is devoted to it regulated by "the Law and the Testimony;" "All things are lawful for me, but I will not be brought *under the power of any.*" (1 Cor. 6, 12.) An individual habitually subjecting himself to this test, and taking for his models such men as Luther, Jones (of Nayland), and Cecil, may safely acquire that degree of proficiency which the Author has ventured to commend.

Astley, Worcestershire,
   1st March, 1826.

2
The hidden fountains at thy call,
Their sacred stores unlock;
Loud in the deserts, sudden streams
Burst living from the rock.

3
The incense of the spring ascends
Upon the morning gale;
Red o'er the hills the roses bloom,
The lilies in the vale.

4
Renew'd, the earth a robe of light,
A robe of beauty wears;
And in new heavens a brighter sun,
Leads on the promis'd years.

5
The kingdom of Messiah come,
Apointed times disclose;
And fairer in Emmanuel's land,
The new Creation glows.

6
Let Israel to the Prince of Peace,
The loud hosanna sing!
With hallelujahs, and with hymns,
O Zion, hail thy King!

Logan.

HAPLESS CHILD OF DESOLATION!

"*But Zion said, The Lord hath forsaken me, and my Lord hath forgotten me,*" 49. Isaiah. 14.

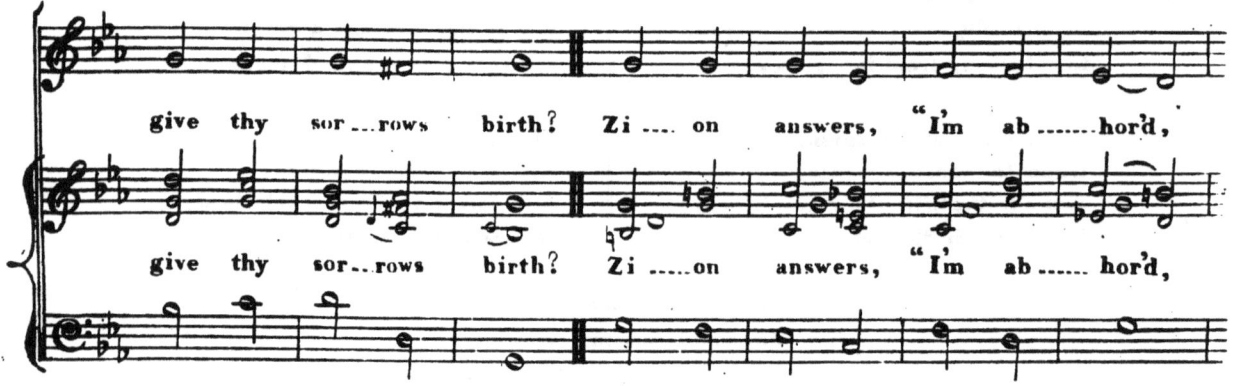

Original Airs and Harmonized Tunes Adapted to Hymns of Various Measures, Op. 2

*J.E.Riddle.

6. DESPONDING SPIRIT, RISE!

"*Come unto me all ye that are weary and heavy laden, and I will give you rest.*" 11 Matt: 28.

Nº 3. Aria. Espressivo Affettuoso.

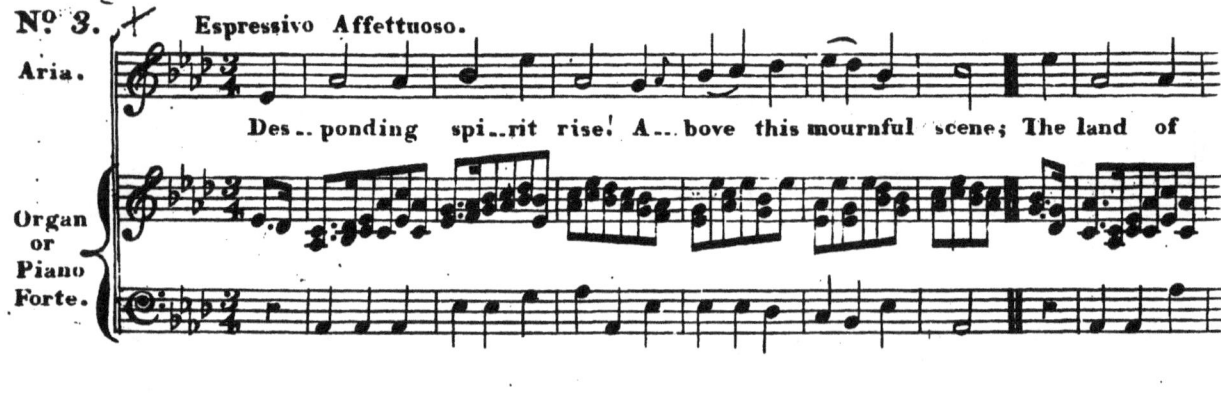

Des--ponding spi--rit rise! A--bove this mournful scene; The land of

pro--mise lies, In re--gions yet un--seen. Haste! Je--sus calls thee near, He

bids thy sor--rows cease, He dries the fall--ing tear, In--vi--ting thee to peace.

2
Beyond those suns of night,
  Far in the dark blue heaven,
Th' inheritance of light
  To thee, my soul, is given.
Nor distant is the hour
  Of ent'ring thine abode,
When messengers of power
  Shall bear thee home to God.

3
Then bid this world farewell,
  And speed thee on thy way,
With blessed souls to dwell
  In everlasting day.
To love, and joy, and rest,
  Where toil, and doubt, and woe
No more shall pain thy breast,
  Nor cause thy tears to flow.

* Revᵈ J. East.

O SAVIOUR! WHEN WITH RAPTUR'D EYE.

"*And I said, Oh that I had wings like a Dove! for then would I fly away, and be at rest.*" 55 Psalm. 6.

Nº 4. Andante Affettuoso.

Aria / Organ or Piano Forte.

O Sa..viour! when with rap-tur'd eye Thy glo..ries and thy grace I view; My trou..bled spir..it fain would fly And far from hence And far from hence her course pur...sue. And far from hence her course pur...sue.

2
Here darkness reigns, here grief and woe;
And foes within and foes without
Now rack my breast, now round me throw
The chains of fear, the toils of doubt.

3
But Saviour! raise thy mighty hand,
And o'er me cast thy fav'ring shield;
O crush each foe! O burst each band!
And conqu'ring lead me from the field.

4
Then Saviour! while on earth I stay
To suffer or to do thy will;
Each night, each morn, my grateful lay
Shall echo to thy holy hill.

* H.

WHEN WE PASS THRO' YONDER RIVER.

"Speak unto the children of Israel that they go forward". 14. Exodus 15.

No. 5.

When we pass thro' yonder river, When we reach the farther shore, Warfare then shall cease for ever, We shall see our foes no more; All our conflicts then shall cease, All our conflicts then shall cease, Follow'd by eternal peace.

2
When we enter yonder regions,
  When we touch the sacred shore,
Blessed thought! no hostile legions
  Can alarm or trouble more.
Far beyond the reach of foes,
We shall dwell in sweet repose.

3
O that hope, how bright, how glorious!
  'Tis his people's blest reward,
In the Saviour's strength victorious,
  They at length behold their Lord.
In his kingdom they shall rest,
In his love be fully blest.

4
When the sight of war alarms us,
  Let us call to mind our friend:
He who for the conflict arms us,
  Will be with us to the end.
'Tis enough, the war is his:
God our King, and Leader is!

Kelly.

2.
Then let a world of shadows go,
We fear not, while with joy we know
　Our treasure still is sure;
Tis firmly lodged where nothing fades,
Nor rust consumes nor thief invades,
　And there it is secure.

3.
How sweet to have our portion there,
Where sorrow never comes nor care;
　Whence nothing will remove!
We then may hear without a sigh,
The world's destruction to be nigh,
　Our treasure is above.

Kelly.

HOW SWEET THE NAME OF JESUS SOUNDS.
"*Thy name is as ointment poured forth*" 1 Canticles.3.

No. 7.

How sweet the name of Je...sus sounds, In a be...lie....ver's ears, It soothes his sor...rows heals his wounds, And ban...ish...es his fears And ban...ish...es his fears.

2
It makes the wounded spirit whole,
And calms the troubled breast,
'Tis manna to the hungering soul,
And to the weary, rest.

3
Jesus, my husband, shepherd, friend,
My prophet, priest, and king,
My Lord, my life, my way, my end,
Accept the praise I bring!

4
Weak is the effort of my heart,
And cold my warmest thought;
But when I see thee as thou art,
I'll praise thee as I ought.

5
Till then, I would thy love proclaim
With ev'ry fleeting breath,
And may the music of thy name
Refresh my soul in death!

Newton.

DAY OF VENGEANCE!

"*For the trumpet shall sound, and the dead shall be raised incorruptible*," 1 Cor: 15. 52.

Day of vengeance! loud resounding, Hark! the thrilling trumpet's swell, Peal on peal o'er earth rebounding, Nature's universal knell; Deeply echoing Deeply echoing Deeply echoing Bursts the bands of Death and Hell!

2
O'er the ruins of Creation,
 See! on high the crucified,
Mid the wid'ning devastation,
 On the wings of whirlwinds ride.
  Man before Him
Bows the spirit of his pride.

3
Lo! the dead in thronging numbers,
 Awe-struck at the stern command,
Springing from their iron slumbers,
 Round the dread tribunal stand,
  View with trembling,
Judgment in his red right hand.

4
O Immanuel! spirit broken,
 At thy pierced feet I lie,
What my hope? behold that token,
 See that bloodstained cross on high!
  Glorious symbol
Brightly beaming on my eye!

5
By thy life spring's purple fountain;
 By thine agonizing groan;
By thy cross on Calvary's mountain;
 By thy dark, sepulchral stone;
  O Immanuel!
Save me prostrate at thy throne!

*J. A. Latrobe, A. B.

COME THOU SOURCE OF EV'RY BLESSING!

Nº 10.

Come thou sourse of ev'..ry blessing! Tune my heart to sing thy grace, Streams of mer..cy nev..er ceasing, Call for songs of loudest praise. Teach me that de..light.ful sto..ry, Sung by flaming tongues a...bove, "To the Lamb be end..less glory, Fount of bliss and God of Love."

2
Here I raise my Eben. Ezer,
  Hither by thy help I'm come,
And I hope, by thy good pleasure,
  Safely to arrive at home.
Jesus sought me, when a stranger,
  Wand'ring from the fold of God,
He, to rescue me from danger,
  Interpos'd with precious blood.

3
O to grace how great a debtor,
  Daily I'm constrain'd to be,
Whilst redemption's golden fetter,
  Binds my wand'ring soul to thee.
Prone to wander, Lord, I feel it,
  Prone to leave the God I love,—
Here's my heart, O take and seal it,
  Seal it for thy courts above.

Send the wit...ness in my heart, The Ho.....ly Ghost re.....veal.

Send the wit...ness in my heart, The Ho.....ly Ghost re.....veal.

2

Blessed Comforter, come down
　And live, and move in me,
Make my every deed thine own,
　In all things led by thee.
Bid my sins and fears depart,
　And with me O vouchsafe to dwell,
Faithful witness, in my heart,
　Thy perfect light reveal.

3

Whom the world cannot receive,
　Lord, manifest in me;
Son of God, I cease to live,
　Unless I live to thee.
Make me choose the better part,
　Display thy love, my pardon seal;
Send the witness, in my heart,
　The Holy Ghost reveal.

Toplady.

16

HOW SWEET TO SEAMEN TEMPEST TOSS'D.

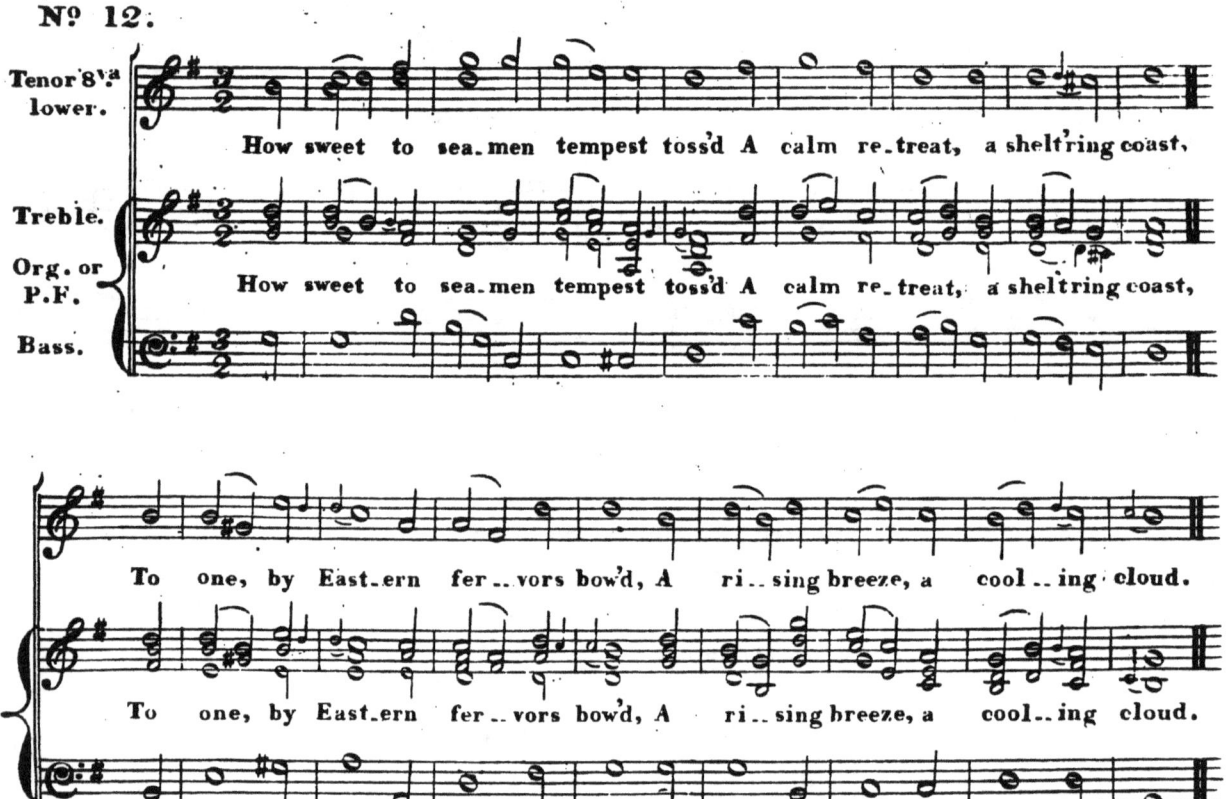

2
How sweet, upon the embattled field,
The sheen of a protecting shield,
A friend regained, a hope fulfilled,
The inward storm of passion stilled.

3
How sweet, yea sweeter far than aught
That wooes the eye, or springs the thought,
The feast of sainted hosts above,
The banquet of a Saviour's love.

4
'Tis this that soothes the racking breast,
And lulls the spirit to its rest,
That leaves, when past the fleeting breath,
Its impress on the face of death.

5
What reck I of the world's proud scorn,
The smitten cheek, or plaited thorn?
Give me but Christ; no tempest shock
Can rend me from the eternal rock!

*J. A. Latrobe A.B.

2
Cheer'd with thy converse I can trace
   The desert with delight;
Thro' all the gloom one smile of thine
   Can dissipate the night.

3
Nor shall I thro' eternal days
   A restless pilgrim roam,
Thy hand, that now directs my course,
   Shall soon convey me home..

4
I ask not Enoch's rapt'rous flight,
   To realms of heav'nly day,
Nor seek Elijah's fiery steeds
   To bear this flesh away

5
With joy my spirit will consent
   To drop its mortal load,
And hail the sharpest pangs of death
   That break its way to God.

Doddridge.

2

Truly blessed is the station,
  Low before his cross to lie;
While I see divine compassion
  Floating in his languid eye.
Here it is I find my heaven,
  Here the God of mercy trace,
"Loving much for much forgiven"
  Made a monument of Grace.

3

Love and grief my heart dividing,
  Fain with tears His feet I'd bathe,
Constant still "in Him abiding,"
  Life deriving from His death:
May I still enjoy this feeling,
  In all need to Jesus go;
Prove his wounds each day more healing,
  And Himself more deeply know!

<u>Robinson</u>.

22

THE DYING BELIEVER TO HIS SOUL.

No. 16.

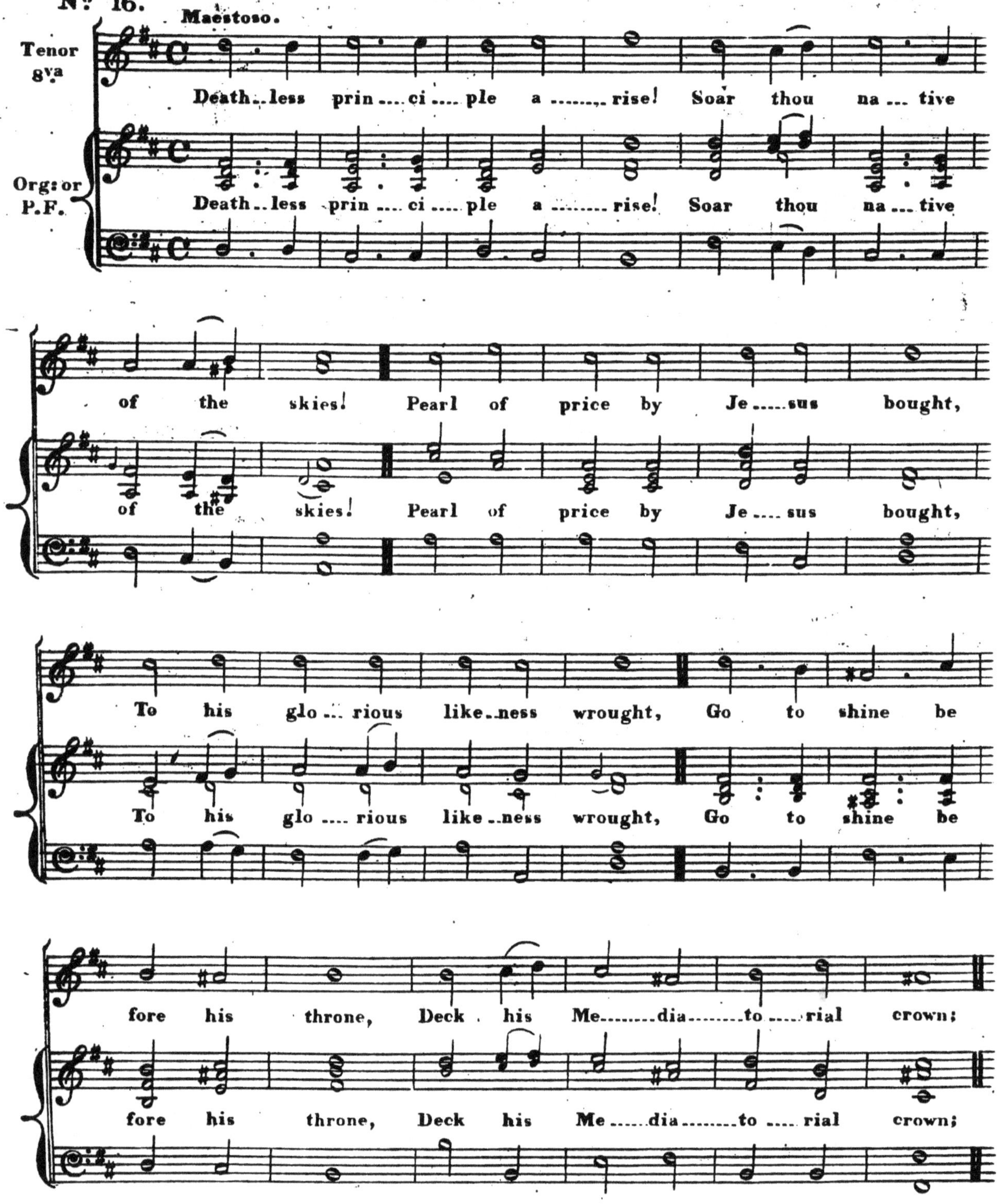
Maestoso.
Tenor 8va
Org: or P.F.
Death..less prin....ci....ple a........rise! Soar thou na...tive
of the skies! Pearl of price by Je.....sus bought,
To his glo...rious like..ness wrought, Go to shine be
fore his throne, Deck his Me.........dia.........to.....rial crown;

23

Go his tri-umphs to a......dorn, Made for God, to God re.....turn.

2
Lo, he beckons from on high!
Fearless to his presence fly,
Thine the merit of his blood,
Thine the righteousness of God!
Angels, joyful to attend,
Hov'ring round thy pillow bend,
Wait to catch the signal giv'n,
And escort thee swift to heav'n.

3
Is thy earthly house distrest?
Willing to retain its guest?
'Tis not thou, but it, must die,
Fly, celestial tenant fly!
Burst thy shackles, drop thy clay,
Sweetly breath thyself away,
Singing, to thy crown remove,
Swift of wing, and fir'd with love.

4
Shudder not to pass the stream,
Venture all thy care on Him,
Him, whose dying love and power,
Still'd its tossing, hush'd' its war:
Safe is the expanded wave,
Gentle as a summers eve,
Not one object of his care,
Ever suffer'd shipwreck there.

5
See the haven full in view!
Love divine shall bear thee through,
Trust to that propituous gale,
Weigh thy anchor, spread thy sail:
Saints in glory perfect made
Wait thy passage through the shade,
Ardent for thy coming o'er,
See, they throng the blissful shore!

6
Mount, their transports to improve,
Join the longing choir above,
Swiftly to their wish be given,
Kindle higher joy in heaven!
Such the prospects that arise
To the dying Christians eyes!
Such the glorious vista, faith
Opens through the shades of death!

Toplady.

O GOD OF ABRAM!

"And, He led them forth by the right way that they might go to a city of habitation." — 107. Psalm. 7.

2
Our vows, our prayers, we now present
   Before thy throne of grace,
God of our fathers, be the God
   Of their succeeding race.

3
Through each perplexing path of life,
   Our wandering footsteps guide,
Give us by day our daily bread,
   And raiment fit provide.

4
O spread thy covering wings abroad,
   Till all our wanderings cease,
And at our Father's lov'd abode,
   Our feet arrive in peace.

5
Now with the humble voice of prayer,
   Thy mercy we implore,
Then with the grateful voice of praise,
   Thy goodness we'll adore.

Logan.

25

THE LORD JEHOVAH REIGNS.

The Lord Jehovah is my strength and my song he also is become my salvation. 12 Isaiah. 2.

Nº 18.

2
This great Jehovah's mine,
The saint in rapture cries;
And to this everlasting rock
My joyful spirit flies

3
From this eternal spring
A full salvation flows;
And with the wonders of his love,
My grateful bosom glows.

4
His name shall be my song,
While life and breath are given,
And His unceasing praise resound
Eternally in heaven.

Original Airs and Harmonized Tunes Adapted to Hymns of Various Measures, Op. 2

THE MARTYRS' HYMN.

2
Hallelujah! King of Kings,
Now our spirits spread their wings
To the mansions of the blest,
To their everlasting rest.

3
Hallelujah! Lord of Lords,
Be our last and dying words,
Glory to our God above,
To our murd'rers peace and love!

Milman's Martyr of Antioch.

30. SOON THE TRUMPET OF SALVATION.

"And it shall come to pass in that day that the great trumpet shall be blown, and they shall come which were ready to perish." 27 Isaiah. 13.

2
Myriads, verging on perdition,
  Roused by its persuasive sound,
Shall with ardor and contrition,
  Come from earth's remotest bound.

3
Then the wounded and the fainting,
  Then the tortured idol-slave,
Then the captive exile panting,
  And the borderers of the grave;—

4
All shall haste and come believing
  To the refuge, of the cross;
And, the Saviour's grace receiving,
  Joyous count all else but loss.

5
Great Immanuel! send thy Spirit!
  Let the Gospel trump be blown;
May the heathen know thy merit,
  May they bow before thy throne!

*H

HARK! WHAT MEAN THOSE LAMENTATIONS.

"*Come over into Macedonia and help us*" 16 Acts. 9.

2
Lost, and helpless, and desponding,
Wrapt in error's night they lie:
To their cries your hearts responding,
"Haste to help them, ere they die!"

3
Hark, again! those lamentations
Rolling sadly through the sky:
Louder cry the Heathen nations
"Come and help us, ere we die!"

4
Hear the Heathens' sad complaining,
Christians! hear their dying cry;
And, the love of Christ constraining,
Join to help them ere they die!

*Revd. J. Cawood.

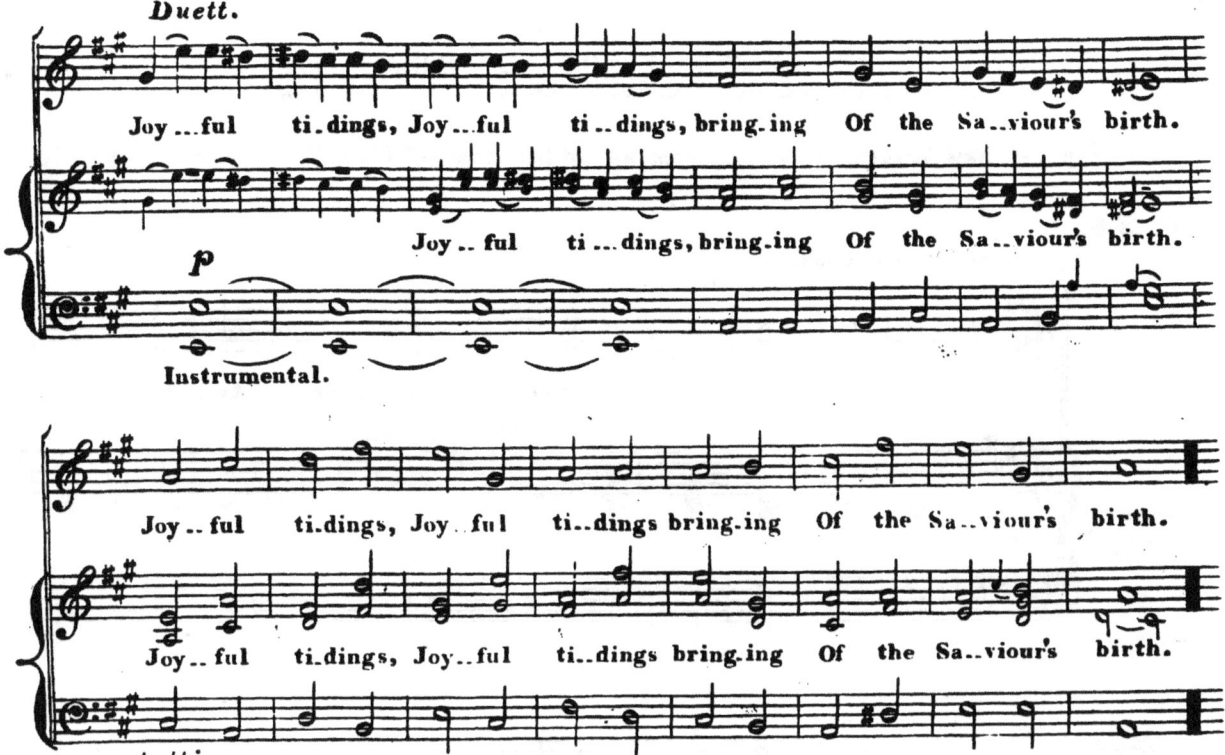

2
In that region yonder,
　Where the angels sing,
Bursts of joy and wonder,
　Make the air to ring.
Praise and adoration
　Be to Christ above,
Peace to ev'ry nation
　From the God of love!

3
Now ye heavens, sing ye;
　Earth break forth and cry;
O ye mountains, ring ye,
　With the sound of joy;
For the Lord has done it;
　His the victory;
His own arm hath won it;
　Israel shall be free.

Kelly.

O GOD! MINE INMOST SOUL CONVERT.

"Looking for and hasting unto the coming of the day of God." 2 Peter 3.12.

Nº 24.

on the brink of fate, And wake to righ...teous...ness. And wake to righ....teous.....ness.

2
Before me place in dread array
The pomp of that tremendous day,
  When thou with clouds shall come
To judge the nations at thy bar,
And tell me, Lord, shall I be there
  To meet a joyful doom?

3
Be this my one great business here
With serious industry and fear,
  Eternal bliss t'insure;
Thine utmost counsel to fulfil,
And suffer all thy righteous will,
  And to the end endure.

4
Then, Saviour, then my soul receive,
Transported from this vale to live,
  And reign with thee above;
Where faith is sweetly lost in sight,
And hope in full supreme delight,
  And everlasting love!

C. Wesley.

2
And when I no more shall number
Days and nights, but sweetly slumber
   In the grave which thou hast blest,
While my flesh in hope reposes,
Till thy day my tomb uncloses,
   With Thee, Saviour, I shall rest.

* Revd J. East.

2
Loudly sweet they hymn their chorus,
　"Glory be to God on high,
"Peace on earth, good will towards us"—
　See! they soar beyond the sky.
Did these Angels praise the Saviour,
　Who a Saviour do not need?
Let us not be silent ever,
　He for us was born indeed!

3
God Incarnate! Mighty Jesus!
　Lord of all above — below!
Thee we bless, who cam'st to free us
　From the chains of sin and woe.
Once a babe,— now King of Glory!
　Thee no Seraph's thought can scan,
But, dear Saviour, we adore Thee,
　Son of God, and Son of Man.

4
Let thy wond'rous Incarnation
　Soon throughout the world be sung;
Let the praise of Thy Salvation
　Dwell on evry Heathen tongue.
Oh! remember Abraham's Offspring,
　Joyless scattered o'er the earth!
Saviour God, we know rejoicing
　They shall celebrate thy Birth!

*H

ISRAEL SEE THE LORD'S SALVATION!

"*Fear ye not; stand still, and see the Salvation of the Lord.*" 14 Exodus.13.

No 27.

2
Shout for joy! our God hath spoken;
Earth before him melts away;
Hell's opposing bands are broken,
Backward borne in wild dismay;
And Messiah,
Conqu'ring reigns with boundless sway.

3
Victors rise! with joy and wonder,
Triumph o'er the Prince of air,
Snap your warrior arms asunder,
Crowns of promis'd glory wear:
Fir'd with rapture
Tune your harps, your hymns prepare.

4
Lord of Hosts! to Thee in Zion
Endless praises shall be sung;
Thou, the might of Judah's Lion,
Terror o'er our foes hast flung.
God our helper!
'Tis for thee our harps are strung.

5
Angels, saints! in adoration,
Fall before Jehovah's throne;
Him, whose arm hath wrought salvation,
Let your ceaseless praises own:
Blessing, honour,
Give to Him, and Him alone!

* J.E. Riddle.

41

RISE TO ARMS!

"Arise get thee down unto the host; for I have delivered it into thine hands."

7 Judges. 9.

Nº 28.

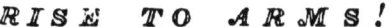

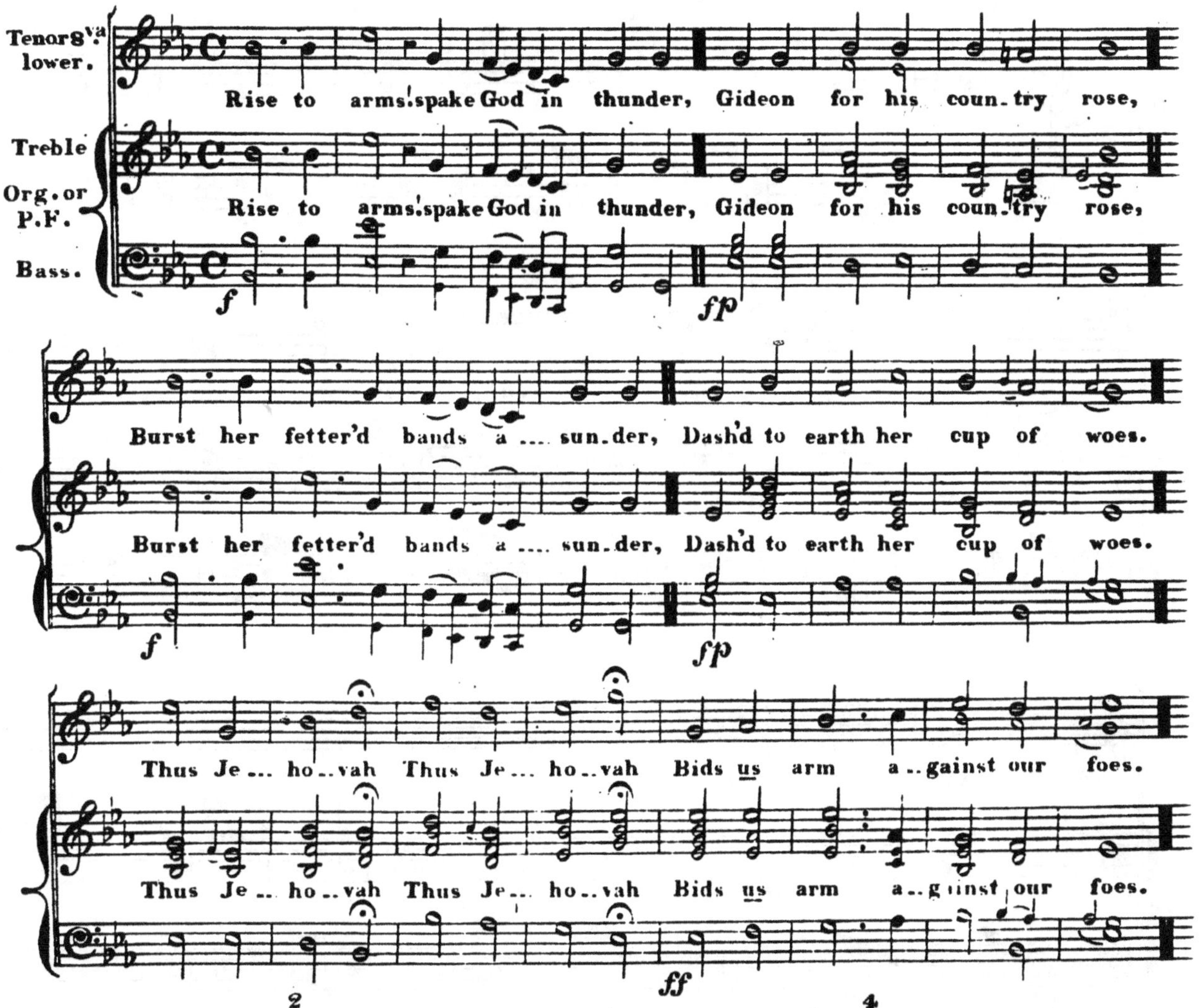
Tenor 8va lower.
Treble
Org. or P.F.
Bass.
Rise to arms! spake God in thunder, Gideon for his coun-try rose,
Burst her fetter'd bands a .... sun-der, Dash'd to earth her cup of woes.
Thus Je... ho..vah Thus Je... ho..vah Bids us arm a..gainst our foes.
f
fp
ff

2

Rise to arms! Hell's dreaded legions,
Throng with havoc in their train:
Rise to arms throughout all regions!
Break the Arch-apostate's chain!
Shall we slumber
While he spreads his iron reign?

3

Warriors, wake! o'er every nation
High the gospel standard bear;
Take the helmet of Salvation,
Shield of Faith, and lip of Prayer:
Girt with boldness,
Brave the Prince of earth and air!

4

Lord of Life! in fullest splendour
Beam upon a darkened world;
Be thy people's strong defender,
Be thy banner wide unfurled:
By thy power
Downward be the accuser hurled.

5

Hail the day! earth's sons and daughters,
Shall thy name in songs adore,
Like the sound of mighty waters,
Or the deep toned thunder's roar:
Alleluia,
God is King for evermore!

*J. A. Latrobe. A. B.

2

See where rebellious passions rage,
And fierce desires and lusts engage;
The meanest foe of all the train
Has thousands and ten thousands slain.

3

Thou tread'st upon enchanted ground,
Perils and snares beset thee round,
Beware of all, guard ev'ry part,
But most the traitor in thy heart.

4

Come then, my soul! now learn to wield
The weight of thine immortal shield;
Gird on thine arms, arms from above
Of heav'nly truth, and heav'nly love.

5

The terror and the charm repel,
The pow'rs of earth and pow'rs of hell;
The Son of God hath triumphed here,
Why should his faithful followers fear?

Mrs. Barbauld.

27. PSALM. N.V.

No. 30.

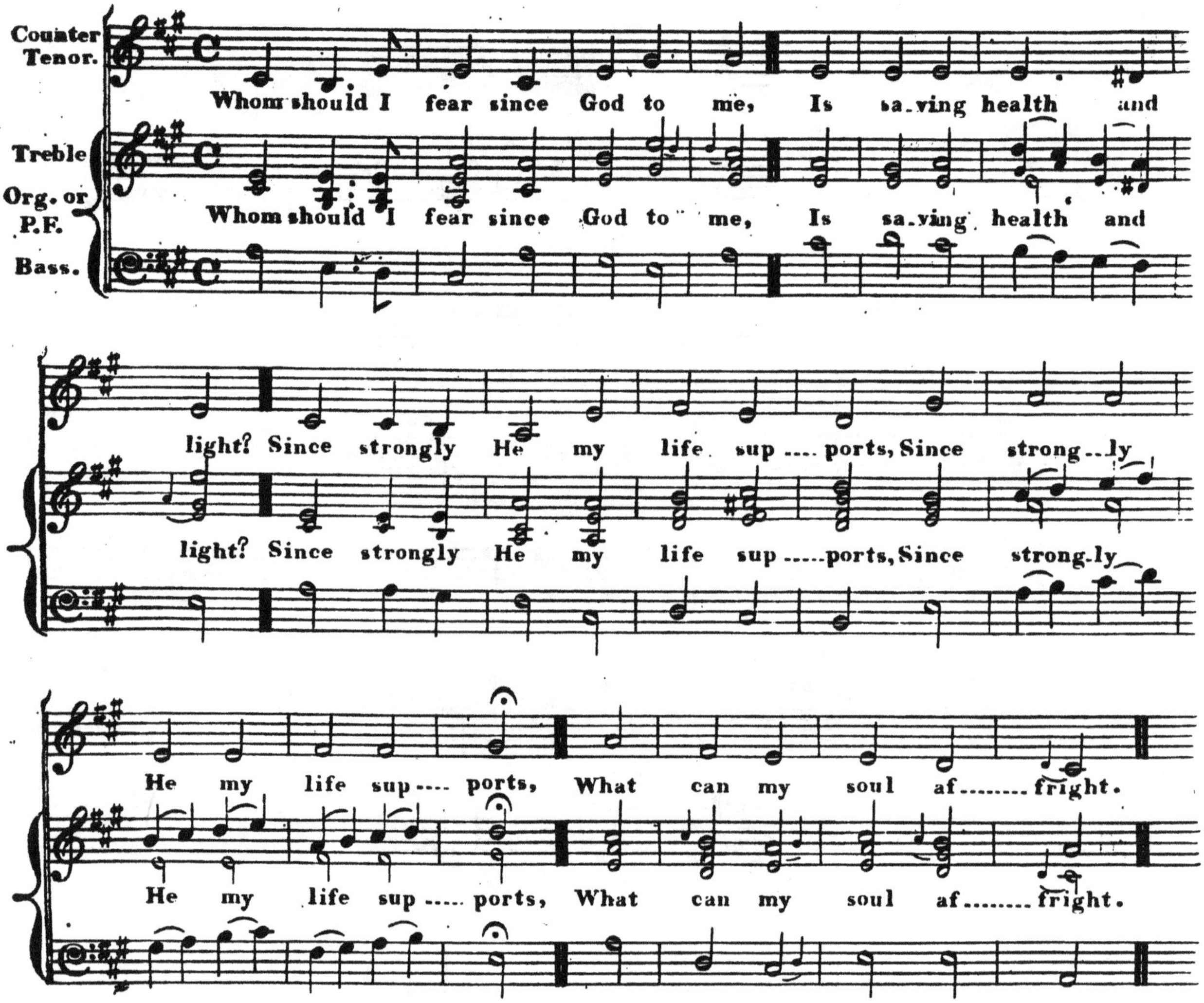
Counter Tenor.
Treble
Org. or P.F.
Bass.
Whom should I fear since God to me, Is sa-ving health and
Whom should I fear since God to me, Is sa-ving health and
light? Since strongly He my life sup-ports, Since strong-ly
light? Since strongly He my life sup-ports, Since strong-ly
He my life sup-ports, What can my soul af-fright.
He my life sup-ports, What can my soul af-fright.

2

Through Him my heart, undaunted, dares,
With num'rous hosts to cope:
Through Him, in doubtful straits of war
For good success I hope.

3

Henceforth, within His house to dwell,
I earnestly desire,
His wondrous beauty there to view,
And his blest will inquire.

4

For there may I with comfort rest
In times of deep distress;
And safe, as on a rock, abide
In that secure recess.

An undated photograph of William Henry Havergal.

This Review of music by W.H.H. (the composer's Op. 35) was found in the July, 1836 issue of the *Musical Library Monthly Supplement*.[1]

REVIEW.

An Evening Service, *and a* Hundred Antiphonal Chants, *with Remarks, &c., by the Rev.* W. H. Havergal, M.A. (Payne and Hopkins.)

Of all accomplishments, using the term in the sense of ornamental knowledge, none so well becomes a clergyman as music; and as an amusement, none is so entirely suited to the members of the sacred profession. If history is to be relied on, the first use to which music was applied was in the offices of religion; and when that improvement in the plan of education, which cannot be much longer retarded, shall take place,—when the system of music is simplified and freed from the perplexities that now deter so many from studying it,—which must soon happen,—our conviction is, that the art will become an almost necessary part of clerical education.

The author of the work before us is a proof that a very deep knowledge of music is not incompatible with that learning now required in him who aspires to holy orders, or with those studies which, if a conscientious man, form part of his duty. The Evening Service,—a *Cantate Domino*, and *Deus Misereatur*,—which occupy half the pages of this volume, are compositions that would do credit to any name in the musical history of our protestant church; it exhibits as much of what is called science as good sense permits, very superior taste, and the greatest judgment in setting the words, both as regards expression and accentuation. If this service be not speedily received into our cathedrals, it will lead to as suspicion that those establishments are governed by persons incompetent, from prejudice or want of discernment, to discharge their duties.

Of Mr. Havergal's hundred chants, some are very good, and all are, in every way, correct. To compose a really new chant is indeed a difficult task, for, as the late Dr. Beckwith of Norwich said, "the notes (of a chant) are too few, and those few are narrowed by beginnings and endings." But we must here observe that Mr. Havergal has not exactly understood Rousseau's remark; by *le chant*, the French writer means "song, melody," not what we denominate "a chant."

The preface to this work is not the least valuable part of it; every clergyman and organist ought to read it attentively: indeed it is generally interesting. In this is the following history, new to us and curious, of the origin of the double chant:—

> "The writer of these remarks (says Mr. Havergal) has been informed that the origin of double chants was somewhat accidental. It is stated that an apprentice of Mr. Hine* of Gloucester was one day playing the chant in time of Divine Service, and either from caprice or carelessness struck into another chant in the same key. This circumstance gave rise to the short-lived custom of linking two single chants together; whence the regular composition of double chants naturally followed."

The profits arising from the subscriptions to this volume are to be applied to the purchase of a church-clock for the parish of which the author is rector.

*Hine, a pupil of Jeremiah Clark, became organist of Gloucester about the year 1714. He was born in 1687, and died in 1730. [Footnote by the author of this Review of W.H.H.'s music.]

---

[1] *Musical Library Monthly Supplement* No. XXVIII, July, 1836, in the *Supplement to the Musical Library* November to July, 1836 (London: Charles Knight & Co., 72, Ludgate Street, 1836), pages 105–106. The reviewer was not named.

Ent. Sta. Hall. — OP. 35. — *Price* 12/-

The Profits will be applied to the purchase of a Church-Clock for the Composer's Parish.

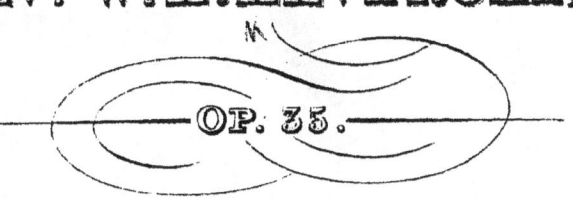

This is a print made from a drawing by W.H.H.'s eldest child, Jane Miriam Havergal (before she married Henry Crane on October 5, 1842, note her initials in the bottom right corner). Miriam may have had in mind herself and her youngest sister, little Fan, as she drew the two in the foreground. The statement "The profits will be devoted to further improvements to the Church" is reminiscent of how William Henry Havergal devoted profits from his published music to churches or other ministries.

REMARKS

ON

CHANTS AND CHANTING.

OF all modes of using the Psalms in Divine Worship, to chant them is unquestionably the most accordant with Hebrew custom, with apostolical injunction, and with primitive practice. When, therefore, the Reformers of our Church compiled the Book of Common Prayer in English, they were desirous that the Psalms should everywhere be chanted. In parish churches, the plain chant, similar to what is still prevalent in Yorkshire, was continued; but in cathedrals and collegiate choirs harmonized chants, accompanied by an organ, were used. These chants appear to have been extremely simple, so simple as seldom to be written down, but continued traditionally in the organ-loft and choir.

All the earlier chants were what we now denominate single chants. At what precise period double chants were introduced it is not easy to determine; but there is no evidence of their existence prior to the commencement of the last century *. Thomas Morley is said to have composed a double chant in D minor, about the year 1600; but that chant is, with greater probability, attributed to William Morley, a gentleman of the Chapel Royal, full a hundred years later.

The writer of these remarks has been informed that the origin of double chants was somewhat accidental. It is stated that an apprentice to Mr. Hine of Gloucester was one day playing the chant in time of divine service, and either from caprice or carelessness struck into another chant in the same key †. This incidental circumstance gave rise to the short-lived custom of linking two single chants together; from whence the regular composition of double chants naturally followed. Their introduction, however, was very gradual, as the older organists considered them an innovation. Without doubt they were rather uncommon before the middle of the last century; and did not come into general use till some time after that period. At the end of Dr. Boyce's first volume of Cathedral Music, published in 1760, is "A Double Chant," inserted apparently as somewhat of a rarity, and as one of the earliest and best of its kind ‡. It is usually attributed to Mr. Robinson, who was organist of Westminster Abbey, in 1740. In after years, it was a peculiar favourite with George the Third.

During the era in which Dr. Boyce was the first cathedral-musician in the kingdom, many good double chants were composed. His own are excellent, as also are some by Doctors Cooke §, Dupuis, and Randall, and by Messrs. Langdon and Jones. It is,

---

* There is no instance of a double chant in the Aldrichian MSS. at Oxford.
† The two chants are said to be these:—

The former is attributed to Dr. Turner, and the latter to Dr. Aldrich. They were certainly used as a double chant at Gloucester by Mr. Maverley, a talented pupil of Mr. Hine.

‡ Sundry chants are attributed to Handel; but they are merely adaptations from his works, and not compositions of his. He was too indifferent to cathedral-music to condescend to write a chant.

§ Some, however, of Dr. Cooke's chants are anything but satisfactory to the ear; e. g. No. 56, Bennett and Marshall's Collection. Reference is made to this Collection, merely because of its extensive circulation.

however, remarkable that the average number of really good and beautiful chants, composed by any one individual, does not exceed two. So accurate is the remark of Rousseau;—" To invent *new* chants requires a man of *genius*: to compose *beautiful* ones, a man of *taste*." "Those who can string a few chords together (says Dr. Beckwith) ought not to say—*We can make a chant!* It is by no means easy to produce a new and striking instance of this species of composition; the tones are too few, and those few narrowed by beginnings and endings."

In 1785 Mr. Jones, organist of St. Paul's Cathedral, published "Sixty Chants, Single and Double." No individual had previously published so many chants of his own composition, nor were the chants of any composer so extensively used as his. One of them, his octave chant in D, became pre-eminently popular, and still promises to perpetuate his name. (No. 18, in Dr. Beckwith's Collection, and No. 73, in Bennett and Marshall's.) This chant is remarkable on sundry accounts. It was the first of its kind, since singing in unison became obsolete, and presently gave rise to many octave chants of dubious merit. It was selected for performance on the memorable day, (23rd April, 1789,) when George the Third, like another Hezekiah, went, in becoming state, to St. Paul's Cathedral to return thanks to his God for deliverance from a most afflictive visitation. From its striking simplicity it was constantly used at the meeting of the charity-schools in that cathedral, on which occasion, in 1791, it was heard by Haydn, and gave him, as he said, "*the greatest pleasure* he ever derived from the performance of music." So pleased, indeed, was he with it, that he noted it down, and suggested an elegant improvement of the antepenultimate bar*.

The present century has hitherto been prolific in chants; but unhappily the quality of them bears an inverse proportion to their number. Very few first-rate chants have appeared; and scarcely any which, like Lord Mornington's, Battishill's, and Jones's, at once satisfy the musician, and fascinate the public ear. Invidious and inopportune as the remark may appear, it nevertheless is palpably true, that chants of the most trite and trashy description have insinuated themselves into some cathedrals, and into sundry collections, to the exclusion of older and incomparably better compositions.

In this age of innovation†, the best and highest style of music is either coldly approved, or flippantly despised. The fact is particularly observable in the chants of the day. Those which are airy and ballad-like are patronised and called "*pretty*" (an epithet quite out of place in cathedral-music): while such as are, what they ought to be, sober and dignified, are discarded as "*stupid and dull*." In even some good chants, we may discern phrases of that sort which should be pruned in time, and not suffered to luxuriate into levity. Gracefulness of melody may very properly be cultivated, but a transplantation of style must not be allowed. "Must we then have no new church-music?" "Yes, (replies Dr. Crotch,) but no new style; nothing which recommends itself for its novelty, or reminds us of what we hear at the parade, the concert, and the theatre." (*Lectures on Music*, p. 83.)

---

* Viz:—

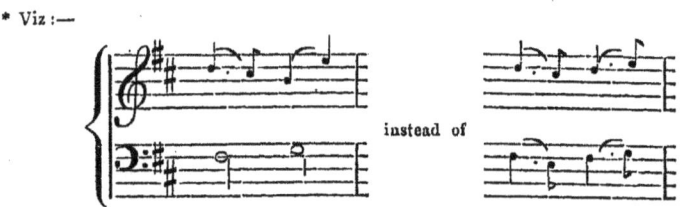

instead of

† Who, however, is to define the limits of genuine taste? Hitherto it has occurred that that which was an innovation in one age has become an established excellency in another. Three centuries ago, the key of C was thought so licentiously lively, as to be called "*the wanton key*." Even so late as 1784 the first philosophical musician of his time, the Rev. W. Jones, of Nayland, described the immortal Haydn as "*a wild warbler of the woods*." (Treatise on the Art of Music, p. 50.)

As to the construction of a chant, the rules laid down by Dr. W. Hayes, and quoted by Dr. Beckwith, are excellent. "The melody and harmony should be solemn and impressive; not trite, but elevating. The ear must not be surprised by harsh discords, though discords are not forbidden, except on the reciting notes." It is added, that "Dr. Boyce disliked every degree of volatility, either in the melody or harmony." Thus far well: but there is room for additional remark. It is desirable that the reciting notes in the treble should never be higher than E * in the fourth space, nor lower than C in the first line below the staff. The nearer they are to the middle of these extremes the better. In the contra-tenor the reciting notes should not exceed A; nor in the tenor F. In the bass they should not be lower than G. It is also expedient that these highest and lowest reciting notes should occur only once in the same half of the chant; and that the reciting notes of the treble, or at least of the harmonies to them, should be as diverse as practicable. The effect, too, is pleasing when the first reciting note is not the same as the final note. In a word, variety and smoothness, combined with good compass and "*good keeping*," are the essential qualities of a chant. Those chants, however, which, in the treble, scream above F are intolerable. Crotchets should be sparingly used, except as passing notes. The rule which forbids a discord on a reciting note may be a little relaxed; but not so as to tolerate crude and startling combinations. The dominant seventh and two of its inversions, the chord of the sixth and fifth, and that of the fourth and second, will perhaps be deemed sufficiently liberal. In some very modern chants there is a seemingly intentional departure from an established rule.† As that rule is founded in nature and good sense, it ought not to be wantonly transgressed. The rule, as stated by Dr. Crotch, is this :—"A passage must never begin, and never terminate with the sixth and fourth." (Elements of Musical Composition, p. 35.) In Bennett and Marshall's Collection of Chants, this rule is strangely and disadvantageously violated. (Ex. gr.: No. 52, 127, 180, 191, 195, 213, &c.) Since the publication of their collection, other composers of chants have followed or copied their error. Possibly this notice of it will help to check it.

The irregularity of the rhythm of our chants is, by custom, so familiarized to both the eye and the ear, that it would be fruitless, and almost pedantic, to attempt its improvement.

Of ingeniously constructed chants, few specimens of any worth are extant. There are none of an early date.† Dr. Crotch's retrograde chant in G (No. 73, Beckwith; 99, Bennett and Marshall) is an admirable instance of ingenuity combined with other good qualities. There are, however, sundry versions of this chant; the latest and best is that which the Doctor arranged for Bennett and Marshall. Dr. Chard's double counterpoint chant in G minor (No. 60, Beckwith; 112, Bennett and Marshall) is intrinsically good, but it has rarely been used. There is a superior specimen of a double counterpoint chant by Mr. Isaac Pring, in Bennett and Marshall's Collection,

---

* None of the oldest chants recite higher than D, and few of them so high.

† "The Grand Chant," so called from its noble simplicity, *may* be an exception, for it is an instance of double counterpoint in the fifteenth. Whether it was so constructed by accident or design does not appear; and, probably, it was never noticed before. Jones of St. Paul's turned it into a double chant, by assigning the tenor and counter-tenor to two trebles; but this process only spoiled it. An excellent single chant was formerly used at New College every 22nd morning of the month; but it is omitted both in Dr. Beckwith's Collection and in Bennett and Marshall's. Its exquisite simplicity, and its ingenious structure, render it worthy of preservation. The treble is composed chiefly of semitones, while the bass is a descending octave. It is attributed to Mr. Savage, and is altogether an elegant old chant.

No. 91. It was long a favourite at New College, without, perhaps, any suspicion of the skill with which it is constructed. Compositions of this class are practically valuable only when their movements are so natural and pleasing, that the labour of their contrivance requires to be pointed out‡.

Chants formed upon a tonic pedal-note are not common, nor is it desirable that they should be. They are said to have originated with Mr. Jackson of Exeter, whose well-known chant in B♭ is the best he ever wrote, and the chief of its kind. (No. 83, Bennett and Marshall.)

Chants in triple time have occasionally been attempted, but never with much approbation. Dr. Kemp composed a few in that measure; and one of them, long since forgotten, was in use at Christ-Church, Oxford. Triple measure, independently of its elongation of the chant, may be deemed objectionable on the score of its opposition to the style of the old Canto Fermo, in which triple time was never used.

Of late years the double chant has nearly superseded the single. There can be no objection to this, provided double chants are so constructed as not to destroy, what is too much overlooked, the antiphonal, or responsive, character of chanting itself. This antiphonal character is of no small moment. It is the special beauty, and almost the life, of Cathedral-Psalmody. For proofs of its Scriptural antiquity, and for irrefragable arguments in favour of its continuance, the reader is earnestly referred to an able and interesting volume, " The Music of the Church, by the Rev. J. A. La Trobe*."

That the Hebrew Psalmody was antiphonal, one half of the temple-choir responding to the other half, is beyond a doubt. That the early Christians adopted a similar mode of singing is equally certain; and it is quite plain that the compilers of our evangelical Liturgy intended the Psalmody of the church to accord with primitive custom. Their intention was eminently discreet; because no method of singing is either so lively in itself, or so animating to all who engage in it, as antiphonal singing†.

---

‡ " To subdue difficulties has ever been esteemed a merit of a certain kind in all arts, and treated with respect by artists. However contemptuously these harmonised contrivances may be treated by the lazy lovers of more airy and simple compositions, the study of them is still of such use to musical students, that a profound and good contrapuntist has, perhaps, never been made by other means. In the church they preclude levity, and in the chamber snatches ingenuity."—Dr. Burney's Hist. Mus., vol. ii. pp. 588, 589.

* " The Instructions of Chenaniah," by the same respected author, ought to be read by every churchman, and especially by every church-musician, in the kingdom. Too many efforts cannot be made to rouse Christians from their criminal apathy respecting the praises of the Triune God " in the great congregation." Want of voice and want of ear are very convenient excuses for *want of heart*. At all events those equivocal defects are, generally speaking, not misfortunes, but faults;—faults of either the parties themselves, or of their parents. Wherever there is a capability of articulation and hearing, there is also, at least in earlier life, a capability of singing. Were it otherwise there would, speaking with reverence, be an unreasonableness in the command to *sing* psalms and hymns and spiritual songs. For, be it well observed, that command is not a whit less binding than those injunctions which direct us to " search the Scriptures," to " pray without ceasing," and not to forsake the assembling of ourselves together. Many an individual who would blush to say, " I never read the Scriptures," feels no hesitation in saying, " Oh, I do not *sing*!"

† Only let it be tried, for instance, by a company of Christian friends in a drawing-room, and the truth of the remark will soon be felt. If the custom were revived in our churches; and we were to sing as Moses and Miriam, and as Deborah and Barak sang, how noble and how exhilarating would congregational singing be, and how much more of it might be enjoyed! " It was (says Bingham) a method of singing so taking and delightful, that they (the primitive Christians) sometimes used it where two or three were met together for private devotion. As Socrates particularly remarks of the Emperor Theodosius junior, and his sisters, that they used to sing alternate hymns together every morning, in the Royal Palace."

In some cathedrals antiphonal psalmody is duly kept up; but in others it is practically abolished, if not wholly forgotten. Instead of each entire side of the choir chanting a verse in turn, the two sides in some way or other unite: either the men of one side cross voices with the boys of the other side, or the boys of both sides chant together. In either case the prime object of the division of the choir is defeated, and the beauty of chanting is marred. Occasionally, as for instance at Bristol, each side of the choir sings two verses to the whole of a double chant. This practice, though it preserves antiphony, is extremely objectionable, if for no other reason, yet because it *needlessly* violates the ancient and authorised custom. It would be a far preferable deviation from the established rule, to recur to the original Hebrew method of dividing each verse between the two halves of the choir; as that would secure increased attention, and greater spiritedness of effect. The versicles which follow shortly after the Creed in the daily service of the church are instances of this method of division. One cause, and probably the main cause, of the evil alluded to, is the desultory and defective nature of most double chants. The majority of them, as many an intelligent organist must have felt, are composed not only without reference to antiphonal propriety, but with very little regard to even musical "keeping." Such chants naturally tend to vitiate the true responsive mode of chanting: for when the latter half of a double chant bears no resemblance to the former half, both sides of the choir must gradually cease to think of antiphony. If, therefore, antiphonal chanting is worth preservation, the nature of it should be better understood by our choirs; and, in addition to good single chants, only such double chants used as are antiphonal in their construction, or, at least, tolerably congruous in their phrases. For assuredly no reasonable person will dispute the truth or consistincy of the proposition:—*That if the Psalms are chanted antiphonally, the chant itself should be antiphonal.* The single chant by repetition becomes antiphonal: the double chant, therefore, ought to be so constructed as not to destroy what the single chant is designed to cherish.

As double chants of the kind proposed are by no means abundant, the chants in this volume are expressly intended to add to their number. If it be asked,—Wherein consists their peculiarity? the reply is,—They are each formed upon a subject, and all are more or less antiphonal. That subject is frequently very simple, and never, it is hoped, very "*pretty*." In many instances it is contained in the bass of the first strain, and taken up in the treble of the second: while in every chant the latter half is a response to the former half. The response is made by either double counterpoint ‡; retrogradation, or some other species of imitation.

There are, as was intimated, a few, and but a few, chants constructed upon this principle. They seem, however, to have been so constructed more from accident than design, or, at least, more from an intuitive consciousness of the naturalness and propriety of such a construction, than from any clear conception of the principle itself. Almost all the oldest double chants contain traces of this principle; and they are generally in excellent keeping. In some of them there is an evident correspondence between the first strains of each half, but it is not kept up in the other parts. There are also many double chants which are identically the same in the first strain of each half, while the other strains are only varied a little. They consequently are merely single chants diversified in their cadences. Mr. Langdon, organist, first, of Bristol and then of Exeter Cathedral, in 1760, is said to have elicited this species of chant. He was followed by Dr. Dupuis, and then by Mr. Battishill, whose very popular chant in E ♮ gave rise to many of the same sort.

The chanting of the Psalms, when devoutly performed, is, from its simplicity and

---

‡ Double counterpoint is the invention and coupling of two such phrases as will make good melody and correct harmony, when their relative position is changed, i. e. when the lower part is made the upper, and the upper the lower. It is not always easy or desirable for double counterpoint to be strictly observed at the close of a chant. A reasonable licence is, therefore, claimed for some instances in this volume.

liveliness, one of the most interesting parts of cathedral service. There are few persons who are not pleased with it. Many, however, complain of difficulty in adapting the words of the Psalm to the melody of the chant. The difficulty arises from want of facility in scanning at sight; the habit of which is attainable by a little attention, since choristers of nine or ten years of age acquire it with ease.

It is plain that no *precise* rule for chanting can be laid down; because there are many verses and half verses of the Psalms, which may be correctly scanned in two or three different ways. Ex. gr.

>   For the Lord is | a great | God. (Oxford.)
>   For the Lord | is a | great God. (Exeter.)
>   For the Lord | is a great | God. (Canterbury.)
>   For the Lord is a | great | God. (M. H. in the *Harmonicon*.)

Much depends on the melody of the chant, and the smoothness of the sentence. Occasionally, also, the structure of a verse will require a little sacrifice of rhythmical propriety; and particles and expletives must be accentuated beyond their intrinsic importance.

Upon these topics some excellent remarks have recently appeared from the pen of Jonathan Gray, Esq. of York*. That gentleman has been at the pains to collect and compare the different methods of chanting at several cathedrals. His comments on those methods, and on other subjects connected with chanting, are worthy of attention. As many remarks which would have been made in these pages have been anticipated in Mr. Gray's publication, the reader is referred, for the full benefit of them, to the publication itself. A few supplementary observations, however, may be added.

Of all methods of chanting, that must be the best which is most accordant with a natural and an easy pronunciation of the words. The old rule, which required all notes besides the reciting notes to be sung to a single syllable, often induced an awkward and a very feeble enunciation of emphatic words. Ex. gr.

>   Let us heartily rejoice in the strength | of our | salva | n ||
>   Let us come before his presence with | thanksgiv | ing||.   (Norwich and Lincoln method.)

There cannot be any necessity to consider the non-reciting notes as indivisible. They may be divided with perfect ease and good effect. Ex. gr.

>   Thou shalt not be afraid for any | *terror* by | night ||
>   nor for the | *arrow* that | *flieth* by | day. || (Canterbury method.)

To preserve emphasis and accent, an emphatic monosyllable, or an accented part of a word, may be chanted to two or more notes. Ex. gr.

>   O sing unto the Lord a | *new* | song ||
>   for he hath | *done* | marvellous | things ; ||
>   And he shall re | *deem* | Israel ||
>   from a | — | —ll his | sins.|| (Method recommended by M. H. in the *Harmonicon*.)

As a general rule it will be well to bring emphatic words, and accented syllables, on the first note of those bars or measures which follow the reciting notes. Whenever, also, the last word of either half of a verse is a dissyllable, or a trisyllable, or even a quadrisyllable, provided the first syllable only is accented, it is far more natural and elegant to pronounce the entire word on the final note of the passage, than feebly to divide it between that note and its penultimate. Ex. gr.

>   Then shall the earth bring | forth her | in'crease ||
>   God hath spoken | in his | ho'liness ||
>   Judah | was his | sanc'tuary ||
>   Blessed are they that | keep his | tes'timonies ||

---

* " Twenty-four Chants: to which are prefixed Remarks on Chanting, by Mr. J. Gray, of York."

The same rule may be observed when the last two words form a trochee or dactyl,
i. e. when in pronunciation they so coalesce as to sound like a dissyllable or a trisyllable
accented on the first syllable:

>The sea is his and | he | mad'e it||
>He sendeth forth his | word and | mel'teth them.||

In like manner, also, with the last two or three syllables of a final word:

>Let us come before his presence | with thanks | givi'ng||
>If I forget thee | O Je | ru'salem||

Or even when an emphatic word, with a strongly accented penultimate syllable, precedes a final short syllable; as

>My zeal hath | even con | su'med me.||

The Bangorian method, as described by Mr. Gray, is the freest of all methods in dividing the non-reciting notes. The principle is good, but the *indiscriminate* practice of it is ill. According to that method, two of the foregoing passages would be divided thus:

>Let us come before his | presence with thanks | giving.||
>God hath | spoken in his | holiness.||

In such instances, and many must occur, the effect is clattering, and rather indevotional; because emphatic or important words are too closely blended, and the whole too hurriedly pronounced. When, however, two or three minute words, or unaccented syllables, are preceded by an emphatic word or a strongly accented part of a word, the method answers very well. Ex. gr.

>O come let us | sing unto the | Lord||
>There brake he the | arrows of the | bow||

After all, till an accurately "*pointed*" Psalter is published, good sense and good taste must, in a great variety of instances, determine what method to adopt, or what rule to follow. A little good practice, however, in company with those who are familiar with the art of chanting, will be found more serviceable than the mere knowledge of any rules.

In the present day it is almost forgotten that, by " singing Psalms," both the Bible and our Liturgy mean, not singing a *metrical version* of the Psalms, but *chanting* a literal *prose* translation of them; such as the Septuagint translation provided for the Grecian Jews, and the translation in the Book of Common Prayer for the members of our church. Hence it follows that, by the disuse of chanting, the great body of christian worshippers rarely *sing Psalms*. We are strangely content, not merely with feeble paraphrases, and imperfect imitations of them, but with even scanty portions of those very substitutes: for instead of spiritedly chanting an entire Psalm of ordinary length, we spend as long time as that would require, in drawling over four or five verses in metre. Upon these topics the remarks of both Mr. La Trobe and Mr. Gray are forcible and interesting. Even the excellent and amiable Dr. Watts acknowledged the tedium and inefficiency of metrical Psalmody. " If," said he, in the preface to his Psalms, " the method of singing were but reformed to *a greater speed of pronunciation**, we might often enjoy the pleasure of a longer Psalm with less expense of time and breath; and our Psalmody would be *more agreeable to that of the ancient churches, more intelligible to others, and more delightful to ourselves.*" Nothing, truly, but a prose translation of a Psalm, and a good chant " to sound it withal," could ever come up to the Doctor's very correct notions of what Psalmody ought to be. But Dr. Watts, though one of the best of men, was a dissenter, and therefore, perhaps, did not recom-

---

* Nothing would effect this so well as actually *chanting* a hymn or metrical version of a Psalm. A double chant, especially to a long-metre hymn, would secure "a greater speed of pronunciation," would save "time and breath," and be both " more intelligible to others, and more delightful to ourselves." It would also be an easy introduction to the art of chanting our prose translation.

mend Psalm-chanting. With singular forgetfulness as a divine and an historian, he ventured to decide that " the Hebrew Psalter is *very improper* to be the precise matter and style of our songs in a Christian church!" Against this decision, and in support of genuine Psalmody, it may not be useless to quote the remarks of an author whose testimony is likely to be of most weight where it is most needed. In " An Essay on Psalmody, by the Rev. W. Romaine," among many notable observations are these:— " There is nothing little in divine worship. The majesty of God ennobles and exalts every part of it. He has commanded us to sing Psalms; and whatever he has been pleased to command has his authority to enforce it; and whatever he has engaged to bless, has his promise to make it the means of blessing. The first Christians would not sit down to meat, or rise up from it, without a Psalm. Jerome says, you might have heard the ploughmen and reapers in the fields singing Psalms; yea, several of them could repeat the whole book of Psalms in Hebrew. Church history relates many particulars on this subject: but the divine record is decisive. The Psalms are rejected in many congregations, as if there were no such hymns given by inspiration of God, and as if they were not left for the use of the church, and *to be sung* in the congregation. Human compositions are preferred to divine. Man's poetry is exalted above the poetry of the Holy Ghost. It is not difficult to account for this strange practice. Our people have lost sight of the meaning of the Psalms; they do not see their relation to Jesus Christ; although the design of all those hymns is to describe the love of God to sinners in Christ Jesus. They all treat of him in some view or other. I blame nobody, however, for singing human compositions. I do not think it sinful or unlawful, so the matter be scriptural. My complaint is against preferring men's poems to the good word of God, and preferring them to it in the church. I have no quarrel with Dr. Watts, or any living or dead versifier. My concern is to see Christian congregations shut out divinely inspired Psalms, and take in Dr. Watts's flights of fancy; as if the words of a poet were better than the words of a prophet, or as if the wit of a man was to be preferred to the wisdom of God. When the church is met together in one place, the Lord has made a provision for their songs of praise,—a large collection and great variety— and why should not these be used according to God's express appointment? What poetry is to be compared with the Psalms of God? Who can make the singing of any human verses an ordinance, or give a blessing to them, such as is promised and is given to the singing of Psalms? Singing of Psalms is commanded by divine authority, and commanded too as a part of divine worship; not left to man's wisdom how to provide for it, but it is expressly provided for in the good word of God."

It is acknowledged on all hands, that a really good metrical version of the Psalms has not yet been produced. Nor is it likely that such a version ever will be produced. It is a hopeless, and, perhaps, a needless task. That man must be a more mighty master of poesy than the world has ever yet seen, who, fettered by rhyme and verse, can accurately and neatly express all that the Hebrew Psalms contain, and no more than they contain.

The old Psalter in the Book of Common Prayer is, notwithstanding its imperfections, well adapted for chanting " the high praises of God*" As this translation was made by Protestant martyrs and confessors, it was highly esteemed by our pious forefathers. To the true British Christian it must ever be dear, not only for its hallowed antiquity, but for its genuine Saxon-English. He who dutifully loves his mother-tongue must devoutly love it: for so genuine and sweet is its English, that, apparently without any intention on the part of the translators, some verses are purely rhythmical; while others

---

* All organists, however, are not uniformly happy in their adaptation of chants to Psalms. Some excuse may be found from the fact of their often being requested to play a particular chant, though that chant may very ill suit the psalms for the day. It is singular that most organists are unwilling to use more than one chant to a set of four or five Psalms, however diverse the character of those Psalms may be. It is otherwise at musical festivals. " We want," says an individual well acquainted with these things, " organists *who have souls!* "

are either extremely spirited, or most musically plaintive*. The nervous simplicity of its phrases, the manly harmony of its periods, and the fine rich flow of language which pervades almost every part of it, may well, indeed, exalt it in our affections to a height which no classical refinements can ever attain. If its defective translations were but duly remedied, and the whole of it devoutly and antiphonally chanted, we should enjoy the perfection of Psalmody in the most Apostolical Church on earth.

Astley Rectory, Worcestershire, January, 1836.

CANTATE DOMINO, &c.

In the composition of the service, the following objects have been attempted; viz., to adopt a style which, without any unmeaning changes of time and key, should be somewhat fluent, and yet strictly accordant with the dignity and sobriety of cathedral-music; to observe an uniformly correct accentuation of words; to give a characteristic expression to the sentiments of each Psalm; and to adapt the whole for those seasons of cathedral or collegiate worship, *when it is wished that the musical portion of it should be extended*. The chants, for the sake of easier reference, are arranged in the order of their respective keys. -Those which contain any peculiarity of structure are noticed accordingly. Such as best admit of change into the major or minor key, are simply marked "major" or "minor;" and the change of notation indicated by the corresponding number of flats, sharps, or naturals. To the majority of performers this method will suffice, without the cost or the parade of what is but little more than a reprint of the chant in its original form.

---

* For these reasons it was exceedingly admired by the illustrious Robert Hall. This fact, communicated by a friend, is corroborated by the tenor of a conversation recorded by Dr. Gregory, in his edition of the works of the Rev. Robert Hall. Vol. vi., Memoir, p. 50.

SUBSEQUENT NOTE.

THE Chants in this volume, obtained much favor shortly after their publication, in 1836. But the Author, now in 1849, utterly repudiates the great mass of them. He would gladly consign at least ninety of them to the fire, and willingly halve the remaining ten. In some respects, they were, doubtless, an advance upon the trash which had for some time preceded them; but, compared with better models, which the Author has learned to appreciate, they now appear to him to be too light, "PRETTY," and secular to merit ecclesiastical use.

Worcester, March 14th, 1849.

An Evening Service, and a Hundred Antiphonal Chants, Op. 35 (the Novello edition)

An Evening Service, and a Hundred Antiphonal Chants, Op. 35 (the Novello edition)

An Evening Service, and a Hundred Antiphonal Chants, Op. 35 (the Novello edition) 119

An Evening Service, and a Hundred Antiphonal Chants, Op. 35 (the Novello edition) 125

An Evening Service, and a Hundred Antiphonal Chants, Op. 35 (the Novello edition)   129

An Evening Service, and a Hundred Antiphonal Chants, Op. 35 (the Novello edition)

An Evening Service, and a Hundred Antiphonal Chants, Op. 35 (the Novello edition) 133

22

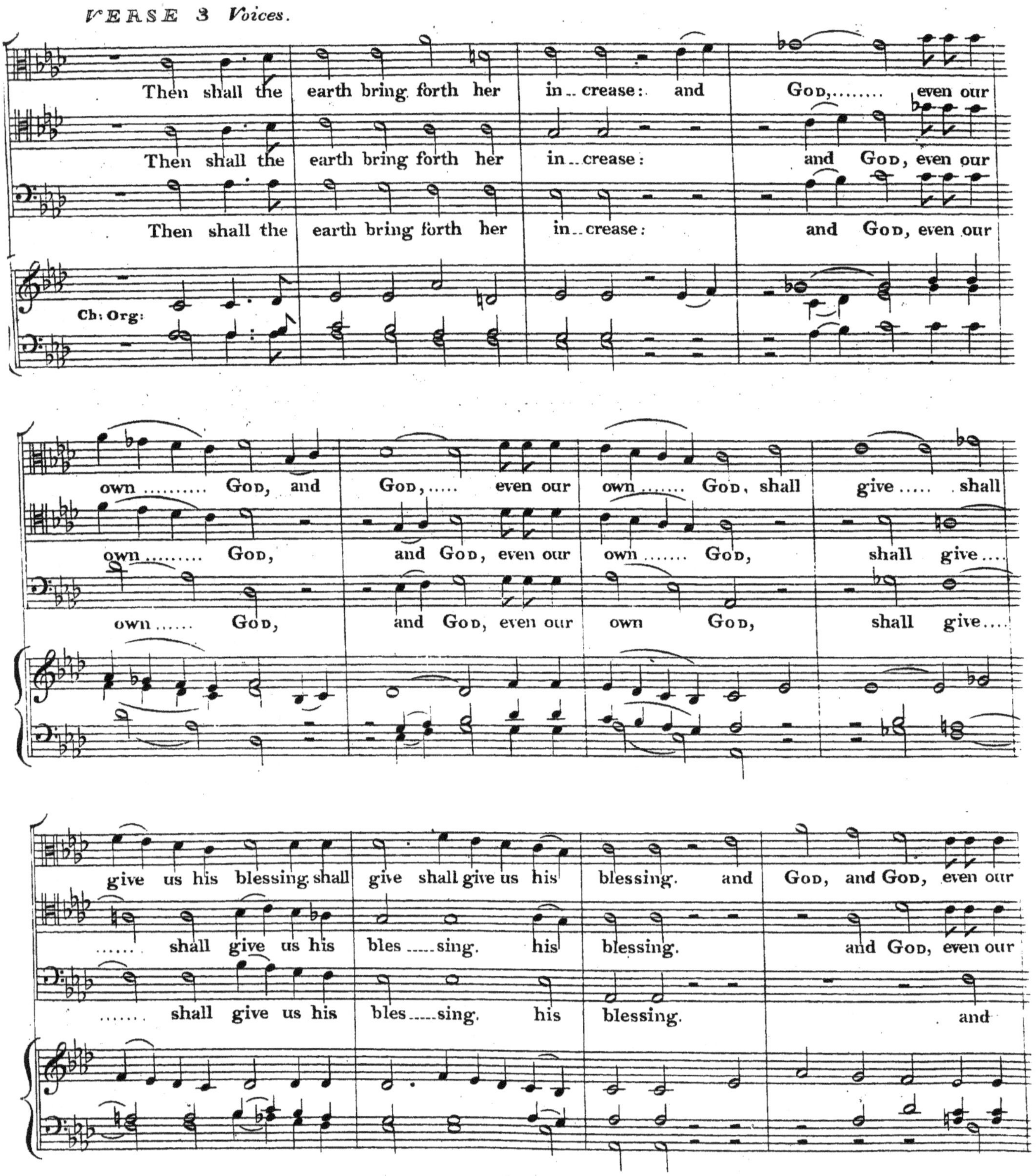
VERSE 3 Voices.
Then shall the earth bring forth her in.. crease: and God,........ even our
Then shall the earth bring forth her in.. crease: and God, even our
Then shall the earth bring forth her in.. crease: and God, even our
Ch: Org:
own .... God, and God,..... even our own....... God, shall give..... shall
own......... God, and God, even our own....... God, shall give....
own...... God, and God, even our own God, shall give....
give us his blessing. shall give shall give us his blessing. and God, and God, even our
...... shall give us his bles..... sing. his blessing. and God, even our
...... shall give us his bles..... sing. his blessing. and

An Evening Service, and a Hundred Antiphonal Chants, Op. 35 (the Novello edition)

An Evening Service, and a Hundred Antiphonal Chants, Op. 35 (the Novello edition)

An Evening Service, and a Hundred Antiphonal Chants, Op. 35 (the Novello edition)

An Evening Service, and a Hundred Antiphonal Chants, Op. 35 (the Novello edition) 141

An Evening Service, and a Hundred Antiphonal Chants, Op. 35 (the Novello edition)

An Evening Service, and a Hundred Antiphonal Chants, Op. 35 (the Novello edition) 145

An Evening Service, and a Hundred Antiphonal Chants, Op. 35 (the Novello edition)

35.

An Evening Service, and a Hundred Antiphonal Chants, Op. 35 (the Novello edition) 149

An Evening Service, and a Hundred Antiphonal Chants, Op. 35 (the Novello edition)

An Evening Service, and a Hundred Antiphonal Chants, Op. 35 (the Novello edition)

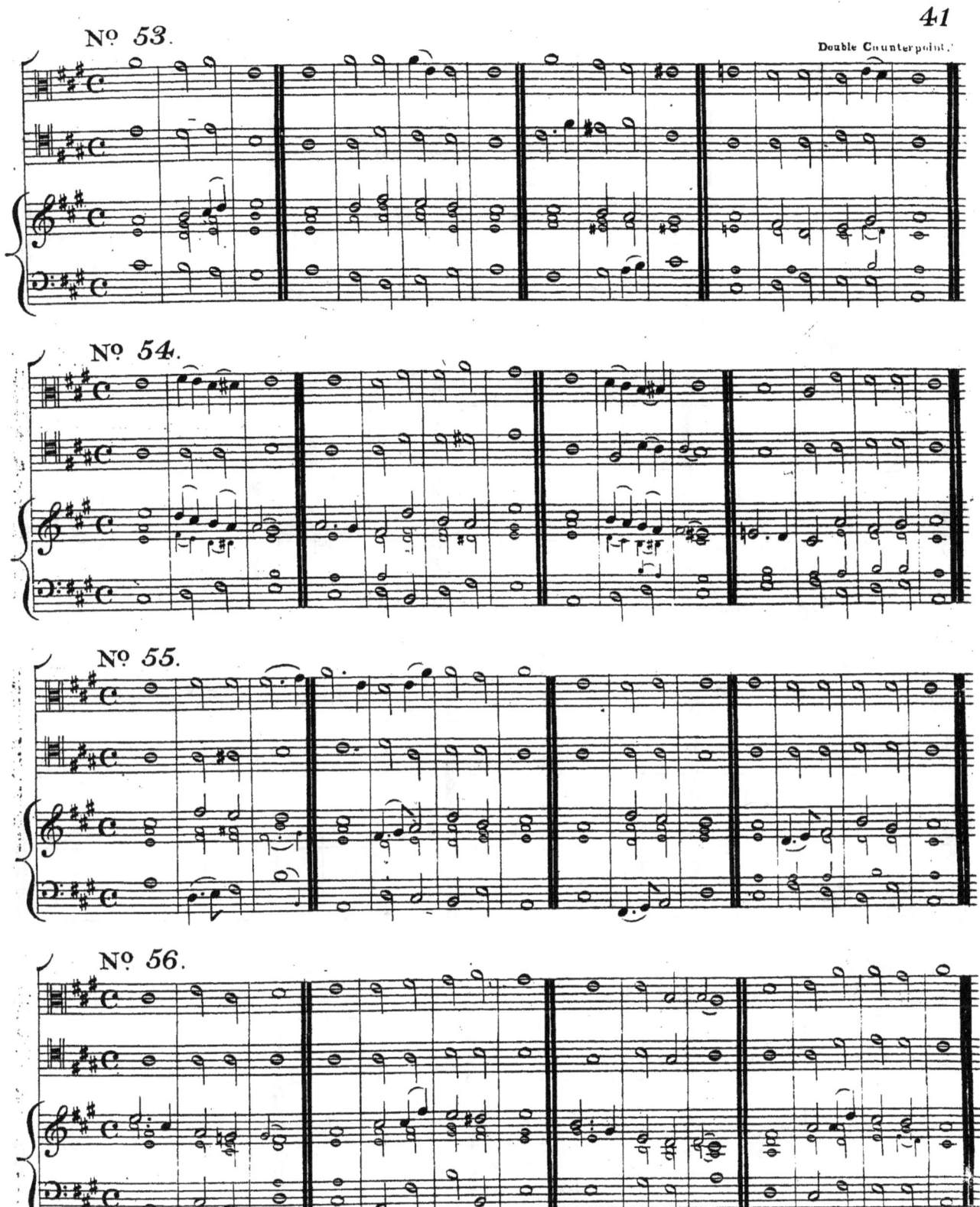

An Evening Service, and a Hundred Antiphonal Chants, Op. 35 (the Novello edition)

43

An Evening Service, and a Hundred Antiphonal Chants, Op. 35 (the Novello edition)

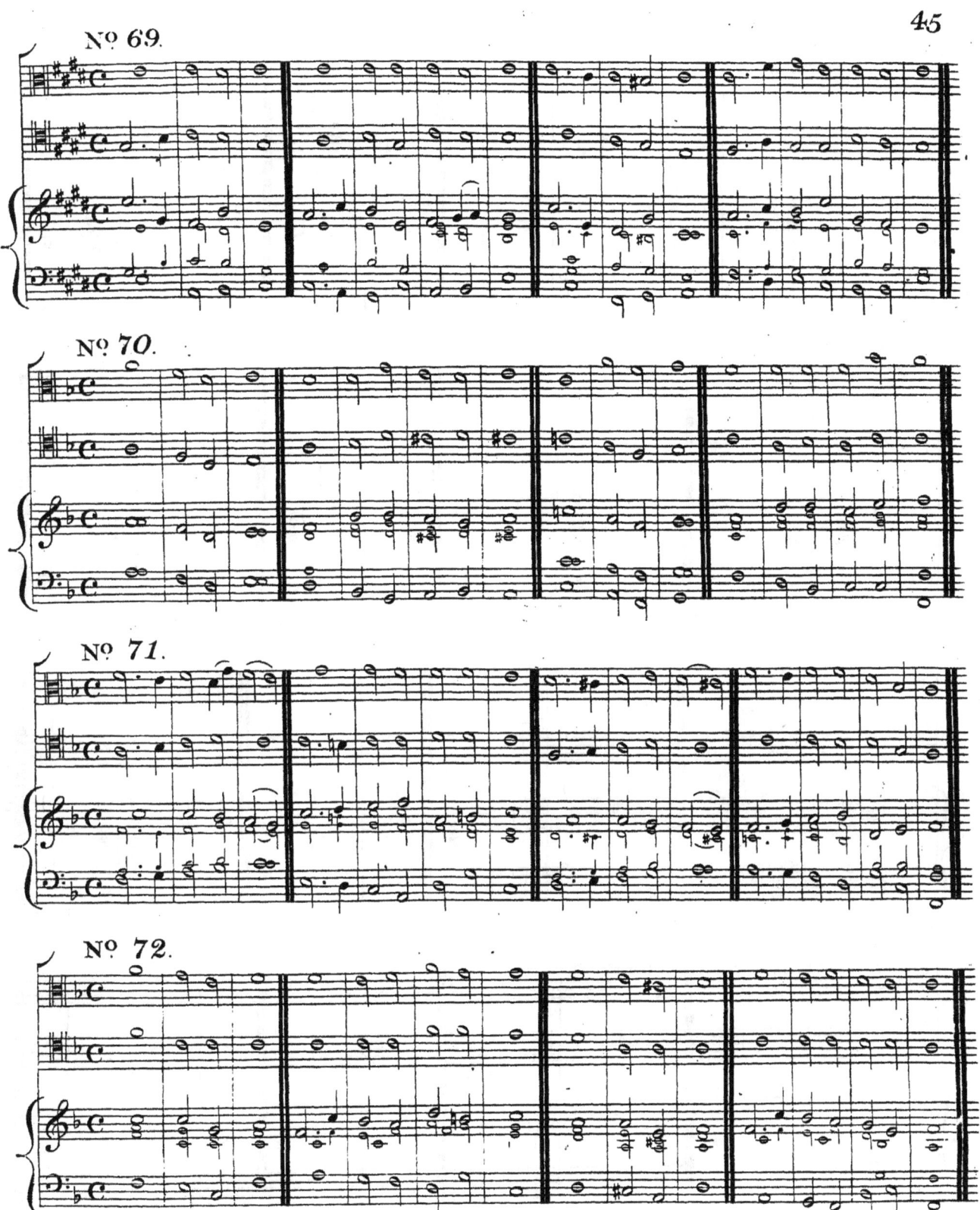

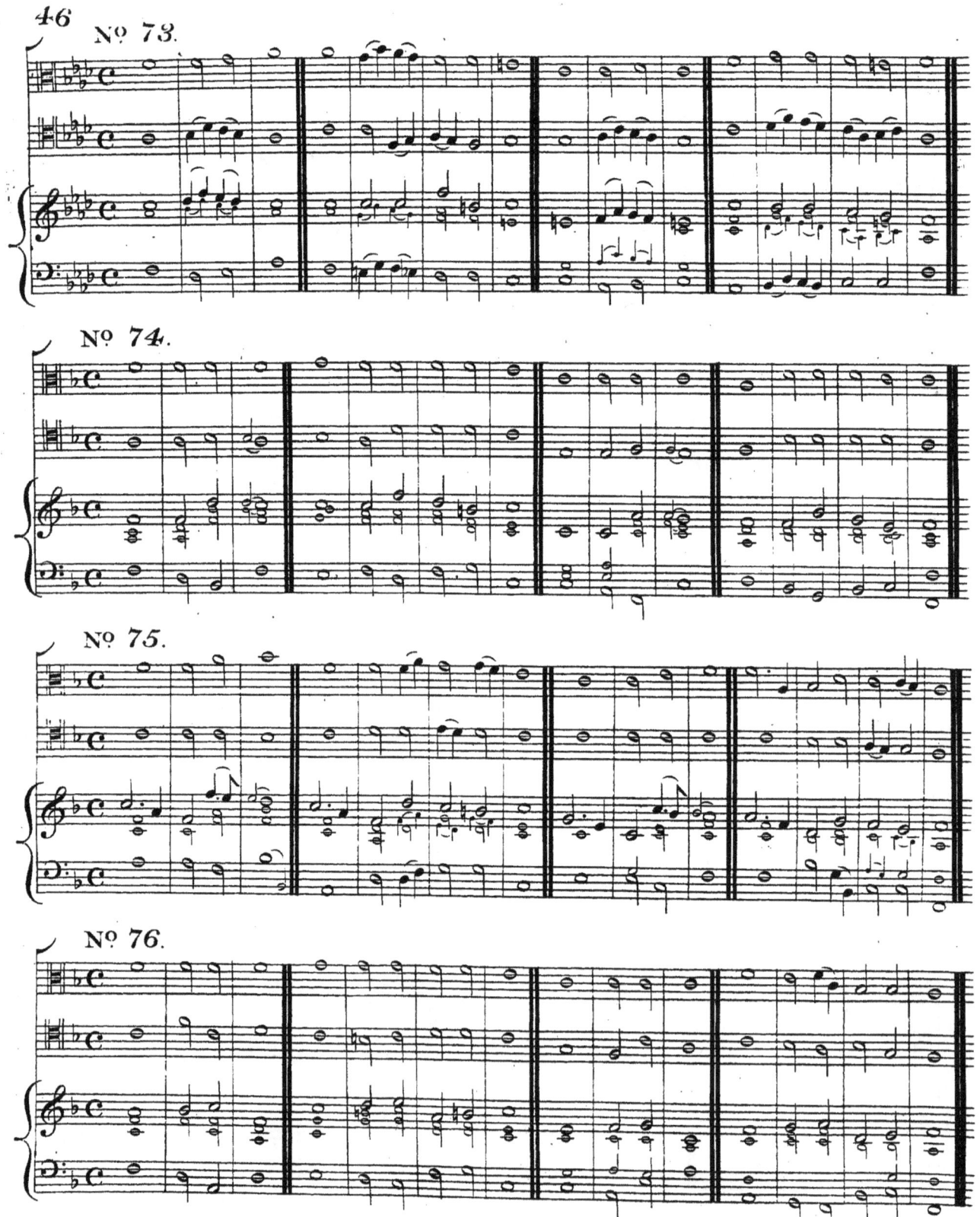

An Evening Service, and a Hundred Antiphonal Chants, Op. 35 (the Novello edition)

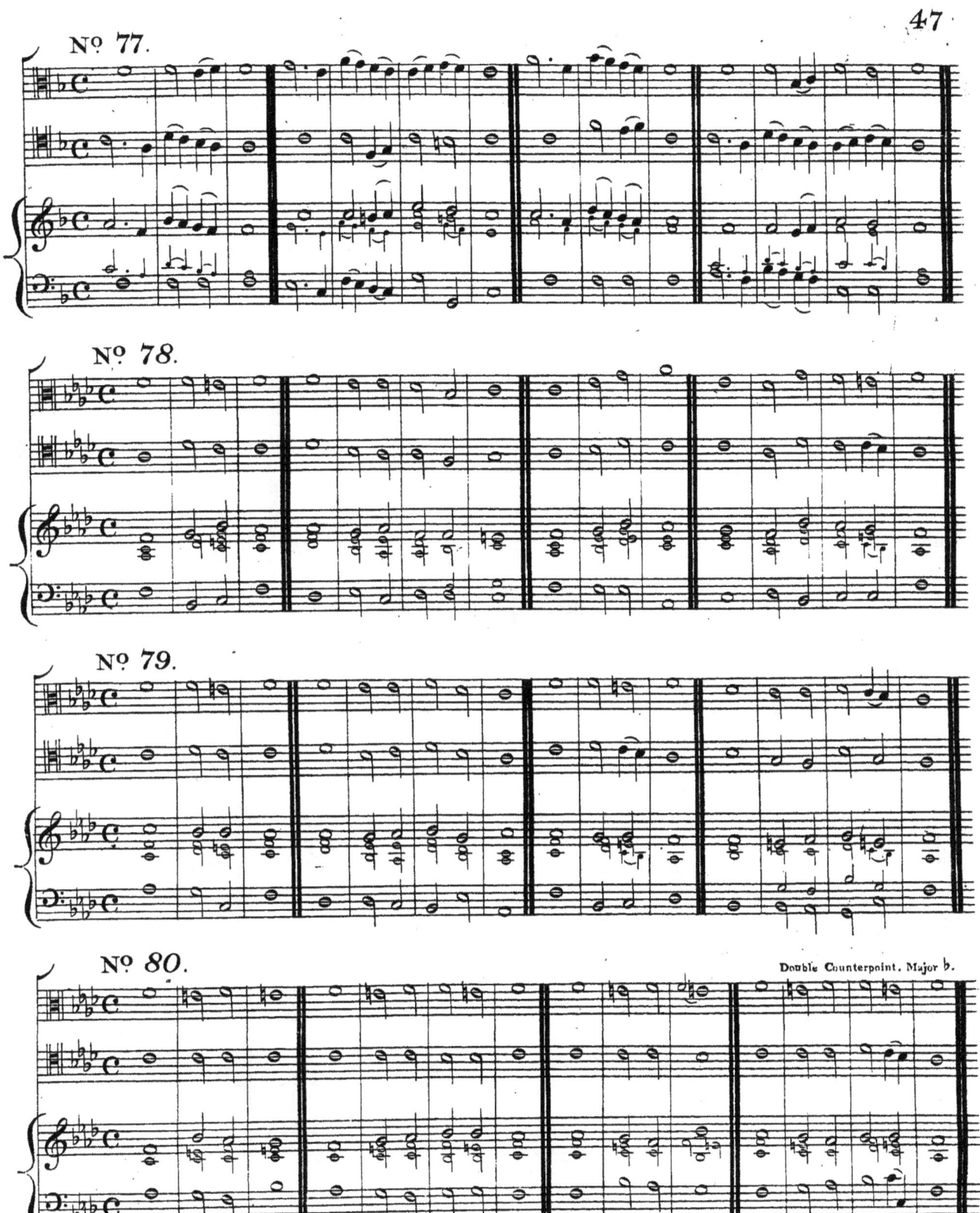

An Evening Service, and a Hundred Antiphonal Chants, Op. 35 (the Novello edition)

161

An Evening Service, and a Hundred Antiphonal Chants, Op. 35 (the Novello edition)

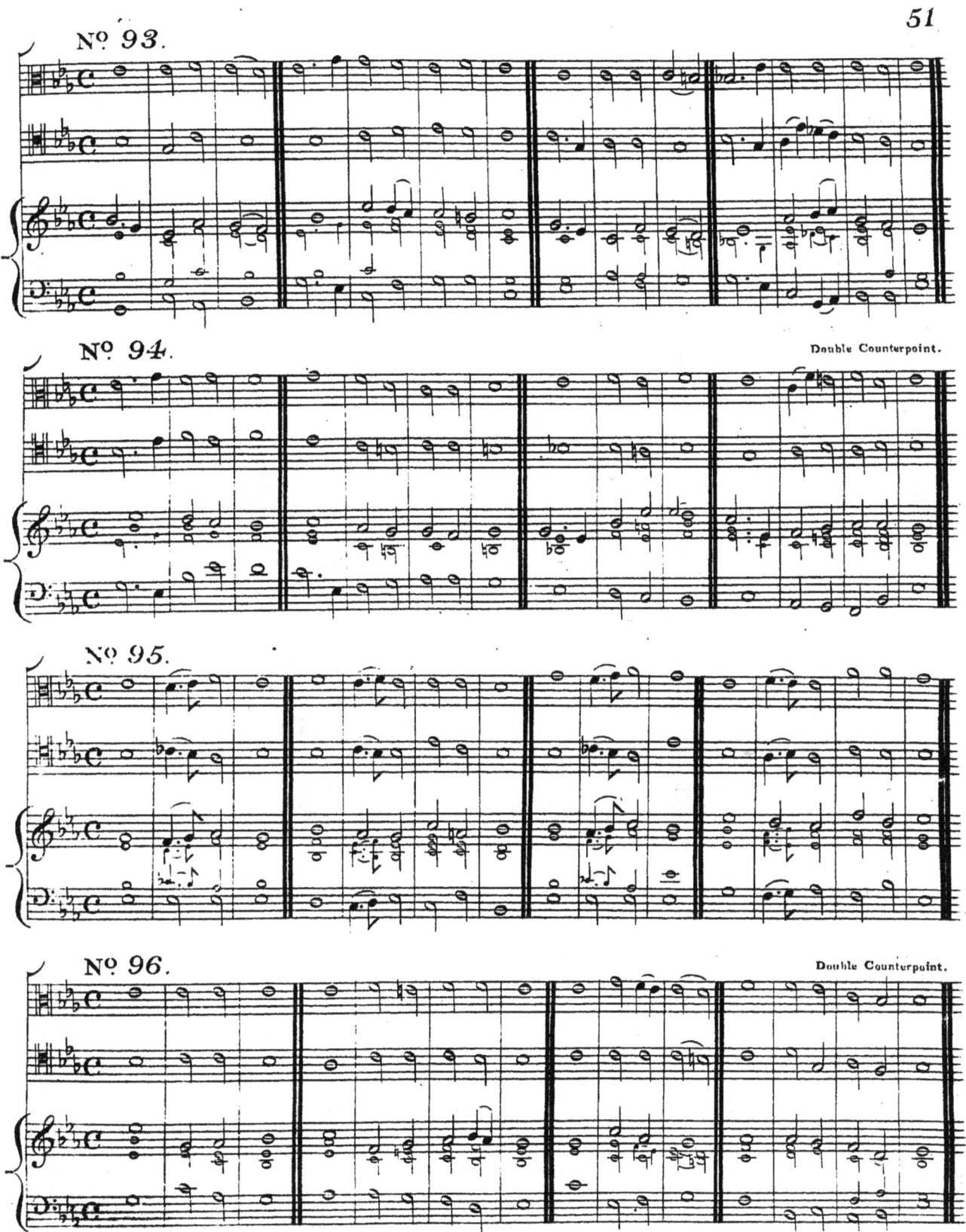

A 19th century photograph of St. Nicholas Church, Worcester, with the surrounding buildings. William Henry Havergal pastored here from 1845 to 1860. He truly loved the parishioners entrusted to his care, laboring to bring them to the truth and to strengthen them in their faith. He was also the music leader, and this was the church where Lowell Mason heard the music worship that so moved him (see page 1491 of Volume V of the Havergal edition).

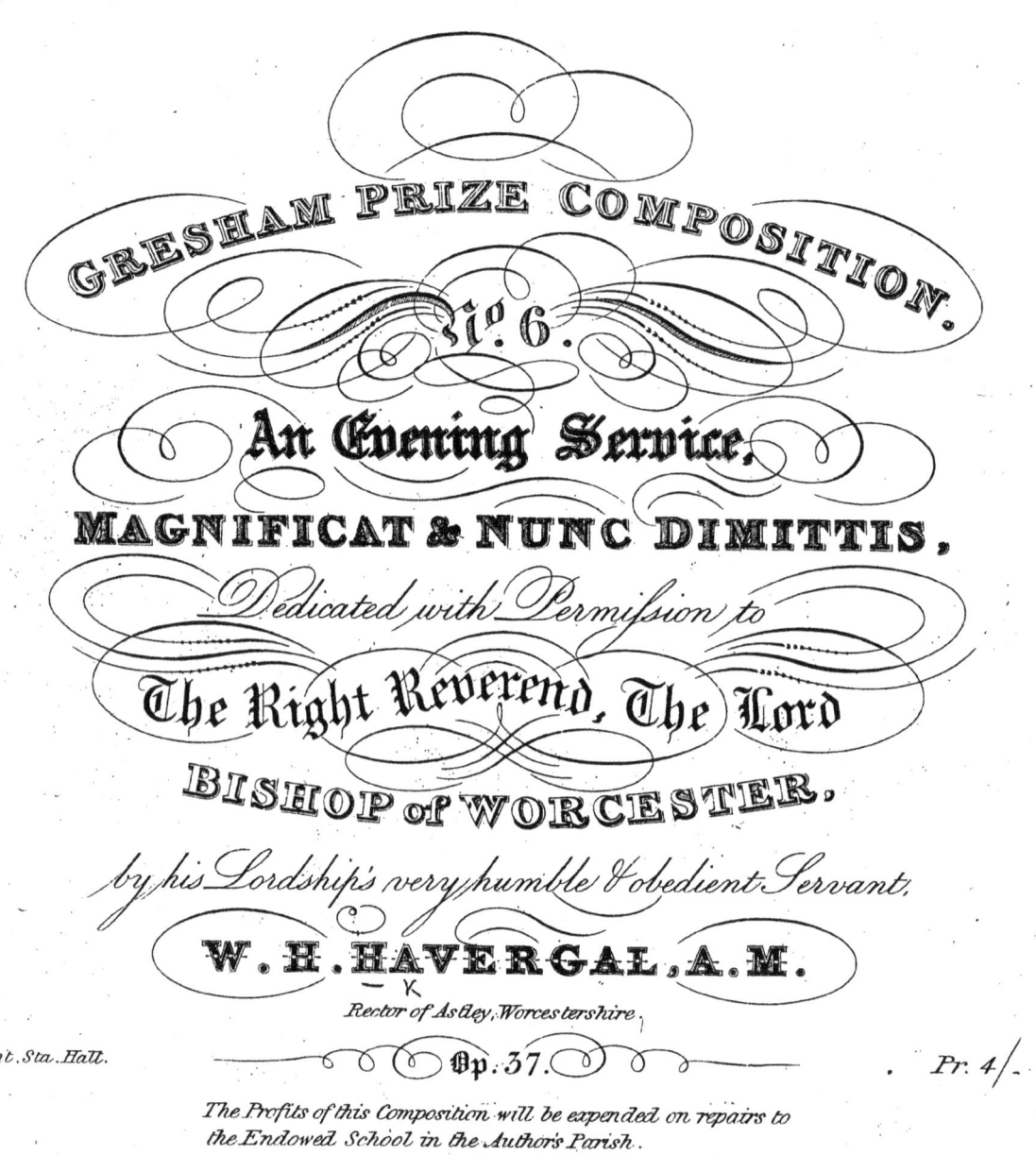

The Gresham Prize was awarded for this in 1836.

An Evening Service, Op. 37

An Evening Service, Op. 37

An Evening Service 175

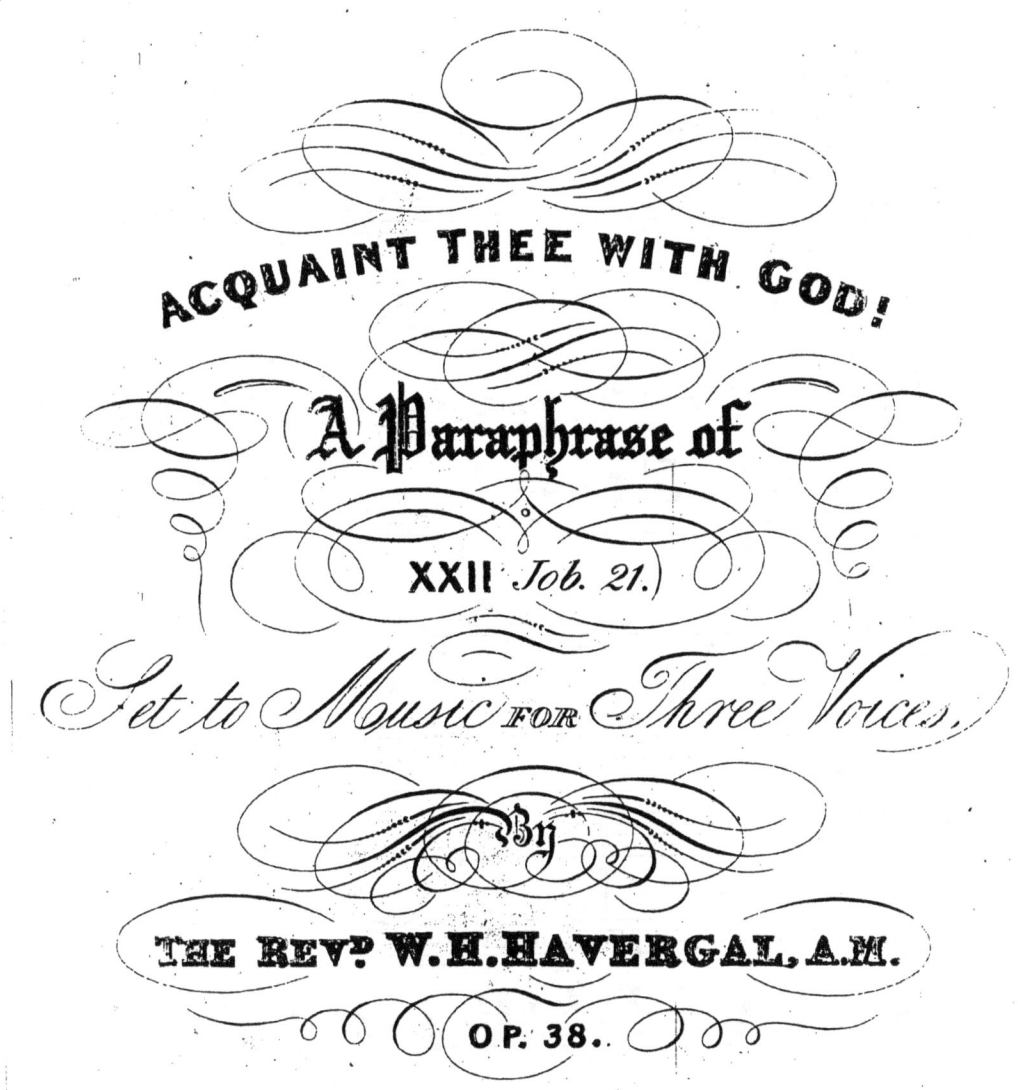

"Acquaint thee with God," Op. 38 (a paraphrase of Job 22:21) 179

"Acquaint thee with God," Op. 38 (a paraphrase of Job 22:21)

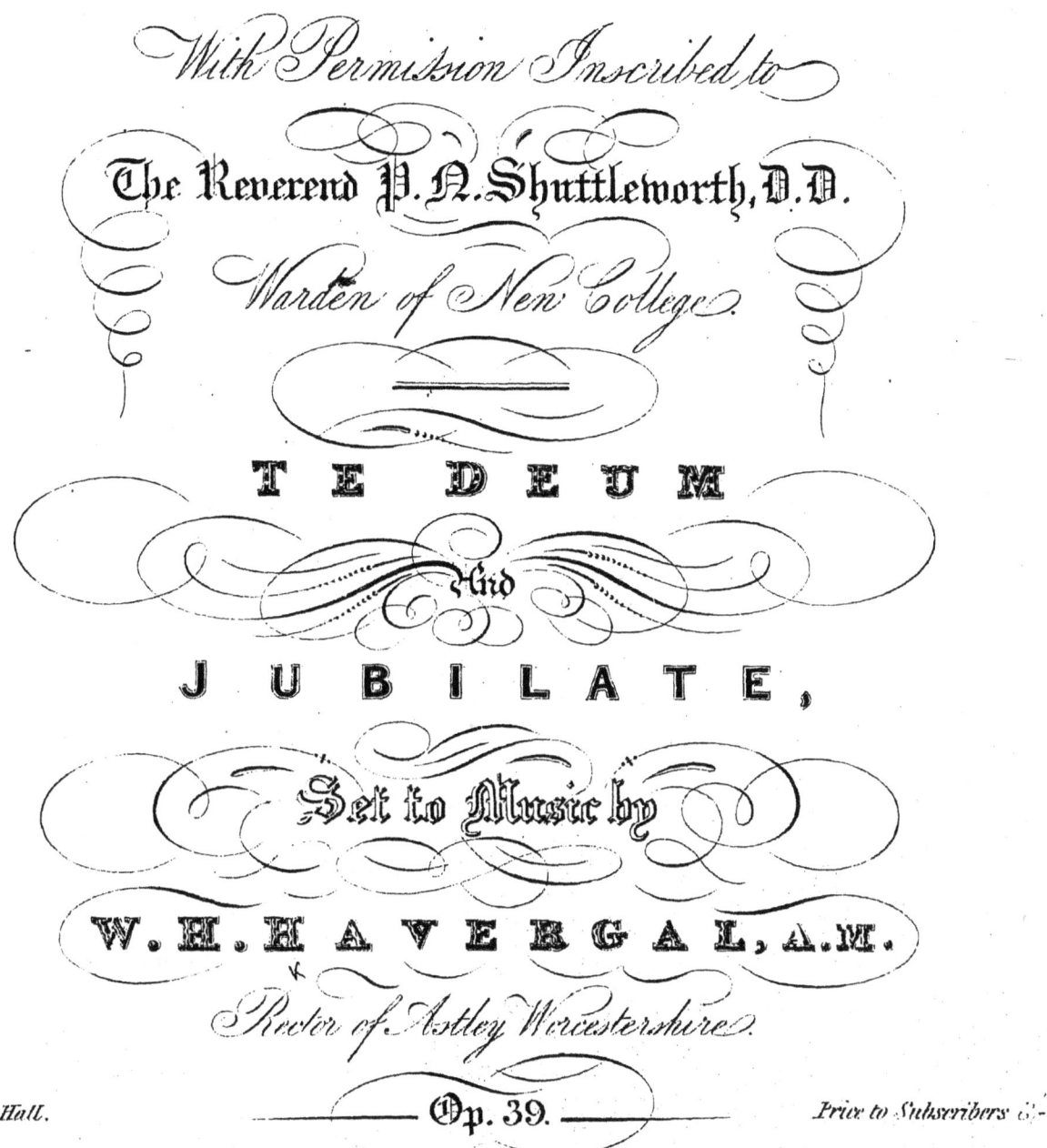

SUBSCRIBERS.

THE RIGHT REVEREND THE LORD BISHOP OF WORCESTER.   2 copies
THE RIGHT REVEREND THE DEAN and THE REVEREND THE CHAPTER OF CANTERBURY, 6 copies
THE RIGHT REVEREND THE DEAN and THE REVEREND THE CHAPTER OF WORCESTER, 10 copies
THE VERY REVEREND THE DEAN and THE REVEREND THE CHAPTER OF WINCHESTER, 6 copies

---

ATHLONE, THE EARL OF
Atkins, R. A. Esq. Organist of the Cathedral, &c. St. Asaph
Atkinson, Rev. T. D. Vicar of Rugaley

BANGOR, THE VERY REV. THE DEAN
Baldwyn, Mr. C. Organist of St. George's, Kidderminster   2 copies
Battersby, Rev. W. Minister of Heckmondwicke, near Leeds
Baxter, Rev. J. A. Churchill, Stourbridge
Bicknell, H. E. Esq. Blackheath
Boissier, Mrs. Malvern Wells   2 copies
Bull, Rev. J. G. Vicar of Godalming   3 copies

Cartwright, Rev. W. F. Vicar of Dudley
Clarke, C. Esq. Organist of the Cathedral, Worcester
Coldwell, Rev. W. E. Rector of Stafford
Corfe, A. T. Esq. Organist of the Cathedral, Salisbury   2 copies
Cotton, Rev. C. W. Windsor
Couchman, Mr. W. Cranbrook
Crook, Mr. T. H. Organist of Clifton and St. James's, Bristol
Crotch, W. Esq. Mus Doc. Professor, &c. Oxon.

Darling, Lady, Cheltenham   2 copies
Day, Alfred, Esq. L.L.D. Bristol
D'Egville, Mr. J. H. Worcester
Delafield, John, Esq. New York
Done, Mr. W. Assistant Organist of the Cathedral, Worcester
Driffield, Rev. G. T. Fellow of Brazennose College, Oxford

Ellacombe, Rev. H. T. Vicar of Bitton, near Bristol   3 copies
Elvey, G. I. Esq. Mus. Doc. Organist of St. George's Chapel, Windsor.
Emra, Miss, St. George's Vicarage, Bristol
Essex, Mr. T. Bristol

Fisher, Rev. T. Rector of Luccombe
Fletcher, Rev. I. Rector of Dowles, Bewdley
Fox, Rev. Octavius, College Green, Worcester
Tripp, E. B. Esq. Westbury-on-Trim
Fuller, Maitland, Mrs. Park Place, Henley-on-Thames
Fuller, Maitland, Miss   2 copies

Goss, I. Esq. Organist of St. Paul's Cathedral, &c. &c.
Greaves, Rev. A. Ancaster
Greig, Rev. G. Barford, near Warwick

Hackett, Miss, Crosby Hall, London
Hackett, C. D. Esq. Rotherham
Hancocks, W. Esq. Wolverley   2 copies
Hancocks, W. Jun. Esq. Wolverley   3 copies
Hay, G. E. Esq. Organist of the Collegiate Church, &c. Wolverhampton

Haydon, Mrs. T. Guilford
Hayward, H. Esq. Wolverhampton
Hodges, E. Esq. Mus. Doc. New York
Hooper, Rev. W. N. Precentor of the Cathedral, Winchester
Hopkins, Mr. E. I. 16, North Street, Westminster
Horsley, W. Esq. Mus. Bac. &c. &c. Kensington

Irving, John, Esq. Trinity College, Cambridge
Janes, R. Esq. Organist of the Cathedral, Ely
Jones, Edward, Esq. Langstone Court, Ross

King, Rev. S. Highbury
King, — Esq. Windsor
Kingdon, Miss C. Pyworthy, Devon

Latrobe, Rev. I. A. Minister of St. Thomas's, Kendal
Lee, Rev. Samuel, D.D. Professor, &c. &c. Cambridge

Mansfield, E. Esq. Exeter College, Oxford
Mathews, Mr. F. Organist of Preston
Marshall, W. Esq. Mus. Doc. &c. Oxford
Maurice, Rev. P. Chaplain of New College, Oxford
Moore, Clement, C. Esq. L.L.D. New York

Novello, Miss Clara, London
Novello, Vincent, Esq. London
Novello, Mr. Alfred, Music-seller, London

Palmer, Mr. B. Organist of St. James's, Clapham
Peurson, Rev. W. H. Rector of St. Nicholas, Guildford
Powell, Mr. H. I. Cathedral, Worcester

Ridley, Rev. W. H. Student of Christ Church, Oxford
Ridley, N. I. Esq. Christ Church, Oxford
Rogers, Mr. E. Cathedral, Worcester
Rouch, Rev. F. Minor Canon, &c. Canterbury

Shelton, Mr. H. Tything, Worcester
Stratton, Rev. I. Precentor of the Cathedral, &c. Canterbury
Sudlow, I. I. Esq. Compton Terrace, Islington
Spry, Rev. Dr. Prebendary of Canterbury, &c.

Wainwright, Rev. Dr. New York
Walmisley, T. A. Esq. Mus. Doc. Professor, &c. Cambridge
Wharton, Rev. C. Stourport
Wheeler, Rev. A. Precentor of the Cathedral, &c. Worcester
Wilkins, Mr. G. Organist of Guilford
Williams, Rev. Dr. Prebendary of Winchester
Wilson, Rev. W. Vicar of Walthamstow   3 copies
Wright, Miss, Northampton

Young, Mrs. Ossett   3 copies

Mem.—The Te Deum and Jubilate were sent in for the Gresham Medal of 1838. They were returned under testimony of having "stood *second* in the judgment of the umpires." The Chants in short score are supplementary to the author's prospectus. They are unpretending specimens of what may yet be done in the severe but incomparably excellent style of the sixteenth century. In framing a Chant, however, it is now all but impossible to invent a positively original phrase. Originality of combination or adaptation is the utmost in which a composer of Chants can hope to succeed: still it will be better to cease altogether from modern Chants than to favor that style which is suited only for the Concert Room or the Parade.

Astley Rectory, Worcestershire, June 1, 1840.

Te Deum and Jubilate, with Chants, Op. 39

TE DEUM.

Te Deum and Jubilate, with Chants, Op. 39

Te Deum and Jubilate, with Chants, Op. 39

Te Deum and Jubilate, with Chants, Op. 39

191

Te Deum and Jubilate, with Chants, Op. 39

Te Deum and Jubilate, with Chants, Op. 39

Te Deum and Jubilate, with Chants, Op. 39

Te Deum and Jubilate, with Chants, Op. 39

201

18

Te Deum and Jubilate, with Chants, Op. 39

Te Deum and Jubilate, with Chants, Op. 39

Te Deum and Jubilate, with Chants, Op. 39

211

27

GRESHAM PRIZE-COMPOSITION,

Nº XI.

An Anthem.

"Give Thanks:"

BY

THE REVD. W. H. HAVERGAL, M.A.

RECTOR OF ASTLEY, WORCESTERSHIRE.

Ent. Sta. Hall. — Op. 40. — Pr: 5/.

LONDON,
JOHN SHEPHERD, 98, NEWGATE STREET.

The Gresham Prize was awarded for this in 1841.

An Anthem, "Give Thanks," Op. 40 (I Chronicles 16:8–10)

An Anthem, "Give Thanks," Op. 40 (I Chronicles 16:8–10)

An Anthem, "Give Thanks," Op. 40 (I Chronicles 16:8–10)

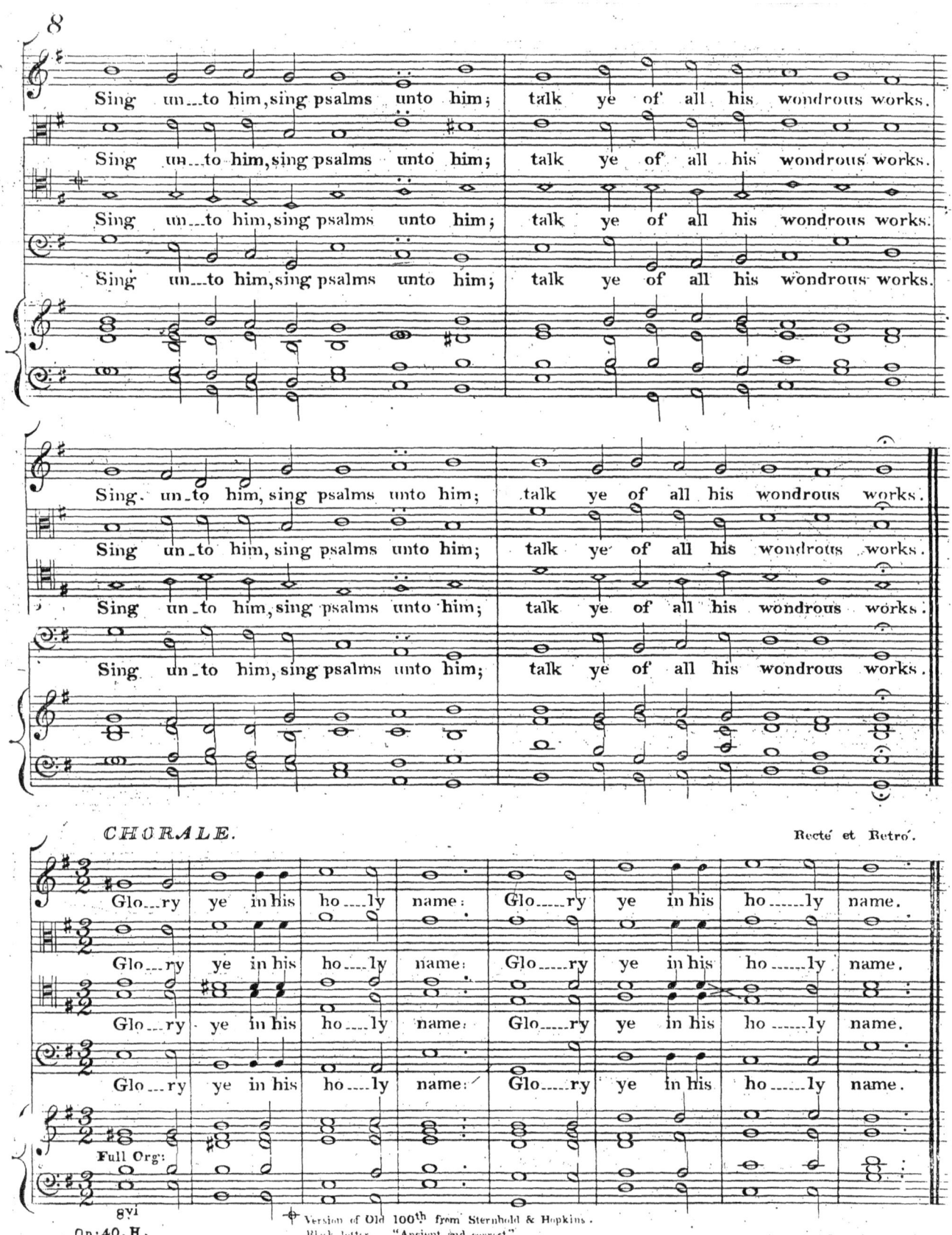

An Anthem, "Give Thanks," Op. 40 (I Chronicles 16:8–10)

An Anthem, "Give Thanks," Op. 40 (I Chronicles 16:8–10)

An Anthem, "Give Thanks," Op. 40 (I Chronicles 16:8–10)

THE
LYRA ECCLESIASTICA

CONSISTING OF

Voluntaries,   *Introits,*   *Chants,*

SERVICES, ANTHEMS, SANCTUSES, &c.,

BY

EMINENT LIVING COMPOSERS.

EDITED BY

The Rev.d Joshua Fawcett, M.A., Incumbent of Winsey

AND DOMESTIC CHAPLAIN TO
THE RIGHT HONOURABLE LORD DUNSANY.

E. A. W. TAYLOR, KIRKGATE;
LONDON: J. G. F. & J. RIVINGTON.

TO

Her Majesty

QUEEN ADELAIDE

This Volume

IS

(WITH PERMISSION)

INSCRIBED

By Her Majesty's most grateful

AND MOST DEVOTED SERVANT

The Editor

Introduction.

"Religious harmony must be moving, but noble withal; grave, solemn, seraphic; fit for a martyr to play, and an angel to hear."—*Jeremy Collier.*

IN presenting this Volume of Church Music to the public, the Editor thinks it necessary briefly to state its origin and object. The Church of which he is the Incumbent Minister, has recently been much enlarged, and completely repaired, at a cost of £2000., the whole of which, with the exception of £100 has been paid. To procure this £100, the Editor, who was responsible for the entire cost, formed the idea of publishing the present Work. Of its pecuniary success he feels very sanguine; but he is quite sure that a much higher object will be achieved, viz. the contribution of a Volume of rare and varied excellence to the stock of Sacred Music.

The distinguished and accomplished Contributors would feel no gratification in indiscriminate encomium, and it would indicate both presumption and deficiency in good taste for the Editor to point out particular authors. Nevertheless, the services rendered by the Rev. W. H. Havergal, M.A., are so numerous and so important, that the Editor must be pardoned in singling him out for special and individual

Introduction

thanks.—This gentleman besides being a liberal contributor himself, undertook the laborious task of examining any composition sent, at the same time offering his friendly suggestions towards making an impartial and discriminating selection, so that in fact all the excellencies of the editorial arrangements are justly due to him, though it is but right to add, that in a very few instances, which a cursory glance will suffice to discover, Mr. Havergal's judgment must not be held responsible.

The Editor will further venture to gratify his own feelings by also mentioning the Rev. G. S. Faber, B.D., Master of Sherburn Hospital, and Prebendary of Salisbury. He thinks himself peculiarly fortunate in being the means of drawing forth from their recesses contributions at once so beautiful and original, and of introducing to the public the pious and learned Divine as a Musical Composer. To the Earl of Westmoreland, the Earl of Wilton, and the other distinguished Contributors, he can but say that he feels deeply grateful for the interest and trouble they have taken in the Work. He believes that they will all be pleased with the compositions of their coadjutors, and ventures to hope that they will find some reward in the gratification thus derived from this united production of the living eminent genius of our country.

JOSHUA FAWCETT.

ANCIENT ORGAN—CIRCA 1450

PREFACE.

The Church of God, it is probable, was never without music. As creation was rapturously celebrated by angels, it is hard to suppose that our first parents were silent. Their vocal powers must have been perfect; and, therefore, as holy beings, admiring their Creator's work, and grateful for his goodness, they would naturally give those powers the most joyous scope. If, too, they had, as holy beings, praised their Creator for his goodness, they would consistently, as penitent believers, after their fall, praise Him for his mercy. Hence, it is not likely that, between the first typical sacrifice and the first eucharistic song, there was any lengthened interval.

But, of antediluvian music, we are told nothing, beyond the fact of its existence as a well-known art. "Jubal was *the father* of all such as "handle the harp and organ." The mention of these instruments, and of a few others equally indefinite, is all that is revealed upon the subject, till the time of Moses. Though he may have learned music from the Egyptians, and Philo and Clemens Alexandrinus assert that he did learn it in Egypt, yet there is reason to suppose that the Hebrews, as worshippers of the true God, were familiar with music before they went down into Egypt. Jacob, at least, was acquainted with it, while sojourn-

PREFACE.

ing for twenty years with Laban: (Gen. xxxi. 27.) and the Hebrews, while in Egypt, must have practised it, apart from their contemptuous oppressors, otherwise they could not have been qualified, immediately after the passage of the Red Sea, to sing *antiphonally* a magnificent chorus composed for the occasion. (Exod. xv. 1—20.)

Throughout, indeed, the whole of the Hebrew Scriptures, very scanty information is afforded as to particulars. We read of singers and musical instruments, and of splendid arrangements made, under David and Solomon, for the choral services of the Temple: but we apprehend nothing as to *the mode* of singing or playing.* And, as to Hebrew musical notation, the Old Testament is absolutely silent; while the Talmudists and other pseudo-sages are either so extravagant, or so inconsistent, that no certain conclusion can be formed. Still, the great principle of God's approbation of vocal and instrumental music for worship or praise, is everywhere recognized. Music was a standing art in the old Church. It was habitually practised and loved. Hence, sacrifice and song, battle and hallelujah, providences and psalms, were all but inseparable.

After the day of Pentecost, holy song was abundant in the Church. That it should have been abundant was reasonable and likely; because the very announcement of THE INCARNATION was audibly accompanied by a burst of angelic song.

What really was the character of the music, which the Apostles and their immediate converts used, is nowhere described. It does not, however, appear that any new or inspired style was introduced. In all probability, Jewish converts used Jewish chants, and Gentile converts

---

* Kircher supposes that the Hebrew musicians were inspired with the knowledge of vocal and instrumental music, and that their performance was equal to their skill. Hence their wondrous powers.

PREFACE. 3

used Gentile hymns. Subsequently, no doubt, they both used both, in proportion as "hymns and spiritual songs" were appended to the psalms.* But primitive music, most likely, was very primitive indeed. Judging from even later specimens, (as late as the sixth and seventh centuries) it seems to have been so simple and artless, that illiterate converts readily joined it. And yet, its earnestness and fervor must have been attractive and commanding. Pagan soldiers listened, with delight, to the christian hymn of dungeoned prisoners. Heathen idolaters were drawn to the company of believers, by the holy loveliness of their singing ; and believers themselves were soothed and animated, by their own spiritual strains.

Antioch, where the Disciples were first called Christians, was very fitly the place at which the music of the church received its first organisation. Choirs were formed there, and singing schools were established. These were followed by the framing of a rather elaborate choral service, and the observance of antiphony† in singing psalms and hymns. Ambrose, Augustine, and Chrysostom kindled their musical fervor in the choirs at Antioch ; and carried it with them to their respective sees. But Ambrose, as Bishop of Milan, surpassed his cotemporaries in extent of efforts to promote ecclesiastical music. He introduced, as stated by Eusebius, the Antioch-method of chanting and singing ; using the same melodies, but giving a more rythmical and systematic character to the whole.

---

* It is probable that the music of the hymns which were first received into the Church, wherever Paganism had prevailed, resembled that which had been many ages used in the temple-worship of the Greeks and Romans. Of this the versification of those hymns affords an indisputable proof, as it by no means resembles that of the psalms. In all the Breviaries, &c. examples may be found of every species of versification practised by the Greek and Roman poets.—*Dr. Burney's Hist. Music. vol.* ii. *p.* 8.

† It is asserted that antiphony was revealed to St. Ignatius in a vision, wherein he beheld choirs of angels singing *alternately,* to the praise of the Holy Trinity. Be this as it may, it is certain that antiphonal singing is older than Ignatius, or even the christian dispensation. (Is. vi. 3.) Antiphony at Antioch, was merely a revival of a very ancient custom.—*Hooker's Ecclesiastical Polity, Bk.* v. *ch.* 39, 3.

4   PREFACE.

What were the distinctive peculiarities of the music at Milan, little else is known, beyond the generally reported fact that the modes, or scales, were only four. The system of Ambrose was absorbed by later systems; so that such musical phrases as are said to be fragments of it, are but of dubious authority. Still, the name of Ambrose stands the earliest on the list of musical reformers; and "The Ambrosian Chant" goes down the course of the choir, with that of the more clearly defined "Gregorian."

At the close of the sixth century, Gregory the first, Bishop of Rome, outstripped his predecessors in the regulation and furtherance of church music. For simplifying crudities, extending the vocal compass, adding to the modes or scales, adopting an easier notation, and for collecting* and remodeling chants and melodies, he has well been called "the great father of the christian choir." For some time prior to his episcopate, serious irregularities had prevailed in the Roman choir. These he banished; and although a man of feeble health, and a Bishop of many cares; he nevertheless made time to compile his Antiphonary, and to take measures for its being sung in a dignified, sweet, and edifying† manner. He instituted a singing-school, erected houses for the residence of the scholars, taught them principally himself,‡ and left ample revenues for their support. Gregory is, also, deservedly memorable for reviving music in the Church of our own Island. The music of the ancient British Church had been dispersed or silenced by the Saxons.

---

* Gregory was not so much the author, as the collector and compiler, of the music of the church in his day. Hence, "the Gregorian music," as it is called, is the common property of the universal church, and not the exclusive right of the Romanists, as they are apt to boast.

† "To sing sweetly and devoutly, (says Maimbourg) is, according to St. Isidore, not to be obtained but by fasting and abstinence; for, says he, the ancients fasted the day before they were to sing, and lived, for their ordinary diet, on pulse, to make their voices clearer and finer; whence it is that the heathen called those singers 'bean-eaters'!!"—*Sir J. Hawkins's Hist. Mus. Vol. I. p.* 346.

‡ For many ages after his death, the bed on which he modulated as he lay, and *the whip with which he used to terrify the younger scholars,* were preserved with a becoming veneration, together with the authentic antiphonary, above said to have been compiled by him."—*Johannes Diaconus, in Sir J. Hawkins. ibid.*

PREFACE.

Moved by the sight of some British captives at Rome, Gregory generously sent missionaries to Britain. The leader of them was Augustine the monk. They landed in Kent; and, chanting, as they went, a solemn litany, approached the Saxon King at Canterbury. Had everything which they introduced been as good as their music, posterity would have been relieved from many regrets. But, apart from that topic, it may be remarked that, through the masterly discipline of Gregory, Rome soon became the great music-school of the Church. Precentors were sent from that city not only to Britain, but to most parts of Christendom. Wearmouth, in the County of Durham, subsequently became, among our Anglo-Saxon forefathers, the chief seat of musical proficiency. There the venerable Bede not only wrote history, but learned music and taught it.

From the death of Gregory in 604,[*] till the tenth century, no real progress was made in music. Instrumental music became more general; but corruptions of the grave and dignified simplicity of the Gregorian music so much prevailed, that disputes, complaints, and appeals originated in almost every quarter.

In the tenth century, Guido, a monk of Aretium in Tuscany, sedulously applied himself to simplifying notation. He so far succeeded as to banish the Gregorian method, and to attract almost universal attention. The most rapturous epithets were applied to his system; and all the world was expected soon to learn music. Gregory had retained, though with many extensions and improvements, the alphabetical

---

[*] Mrs. Elstob, in her translation of the Anglo-Saxon Homily on the death of Gregory, in allusion to his injunctions for *singing* the litany, remarks, "Singing the service was so much in practice in these times, that we find the same word *singan* to signify both to pray and sing." Among the ecclesiastical laws of Canute is one requiring the people to learn the Lord's Prayer and the Creed, because says the law, "Christ himself first *sang* paternoster, and taught that prayer to his disciples." Hence, perhaps, our liturgical use of the phrase "*sing or say*."—*Sir J. Hawkins, in loco.*

method of notation, indicating the lowest octave by capitals, the octave next above by small letters, and the highest of three octaves by either a dash under those small letters, or by their duplication. Guido adopted, for he may not have invented, lines, clefs, and musical characters. At all events, he is justly celebrated for laying the foundation of whatever is essential to the modern system of notation.

From the time of Guido to the opening of the fifteenth century, church-music was somewhat chaotic. There were struggles, indeed, towards shape and form, but the results would now be regarded as rather grotesque. Limited and meagre harmonies began to be tried; and descant, a sort of extemporaneous flourishing, or off-hand formation of parts by the voice, was the dandyism of church-choirs. Architecture, and not music, was the ascendant art in the Church. But, when architecture began to wane, music approached the zenith. Jusquin alias Josquin des Prez, (Latinè, Jodocus Pratensis, as though he were a native of Prato in Tuscany) generally believed to be a Belgian, has been called "the father of pure church-harmony." But strong claims for that honor are advanced, even by foreigners, on behalf of our countryman, John Dunstable. He lived at the same period as Josquin, and was buried in St. Stephen's, Walbrook, A.D. 1458. Be this question settled as it may, facts evince that, just before the Reformation, church-music had made, so far at least as respects harmonisation, even vast and rapid progress. Composers seem first to have tried their skill in fitting parts to Canto Fermo or Plain Song; and then to have taken phrases or short passages from those parts, as subjects for motetts or masses. In this art* no one excelled more than Palestrina, who surprised

---

* Modern Piano Forte music abounds with vitiated specimens of this art. All sorts of things are taken up under the dignified title of THEMAS, and turned into finger-flights without sense or soul. Properly applied the art is both profound and commendable. No great master has ever been formed without it, because it requires thought, and exercises ingenuity, beyond ordinary composition.

PREFACE.

and delighted the dignitaries of the Italian church, by his novel and interesting application of old and thread-worn strains. All our own masters simultaneously followed the same practice.

At this period, the highest personages cultivated church-music, and were emulous to be considered its patrons. Emperors, Kings, Princes, and Officers of State, not unfrequently put on a surplice, entered the singing-desk, and joined the choir. Our own Henry the Eighth, who was a very fair composer, and his Chancellor, Sir Thomas More, occasionally, if not habitually, did thus.

But, as is not unusual in all rapid strides towards perfection, abuses of the most grievous kind speedily followed. The Sanctuary, already defiled with superstitions, was engrossed with singing. Excess was the suicidal fault of the choir. Almost every thing was sung; and the whole service interrupted by a ceaseless multitude of "Anthems, Responds, Invitatories and such like things."* At the same time, the music most in vogue was full of pedantries and conceits. All was dry, intricate and curious, to a degree which few could understand, and which none but the initiated could follow. Even Papal authorities became alarmed at the magnitude of existing abuses. The Council of Trent took them into consideration: and under our own Reformers, in the reign of Edward the Sixth, an Ecclesiastical Court of Convocation presented a Report concerning the extravagances and abuses of church-choirs.† Enormity of abuse well nigh led to an extremity of reformation. Cranmer and his noble com-

---

* See Cranmer's Article "Concerning the Service of the Church," in the Preface to the Book of Common Prayer."

† One thing which added to the outcry against church-music, was the use of very unjustifiable methods for supplying choirs with good treble voices. So late as the reign of the eighth Henry, a writ was issued to authorize the seizure of any boys of the poorer class, who had good voices. Sir John Hawkins (vol. iii. p. 465) gives a curious and interesting account of one Tusser, who was thus kidnapped from Wallingford, and finally lodged at St. Paul's Cathedral.

pany of devout men, seriously thought of prohibiting all music in the Church, but the very plainest and simplest, such as the Gregorian had been. Latimer went so far as to forbid singing altogether, in the cathedral-choir at Worcester: and Bishop Burnett states that even organs* were saved from banishment by only a single vote, and that vote given by the proxy of an absentee.

Happily the end of these struggles, awed a little by "the pressure from without", was worthy of that pure and peaceful wisdom which characterized our English Reformers. Archbishop Cranmer himself adjusted the translation of the Litany to a species of chant, and took much pains to adapt the English translation of the Liturgical hymns to the Latin note.

In 1550, John Marbeck, Mus. Bac., Organist of St. George's, Windsor, and a most earnest Protestant, arranged and published the whole Cathedral Service of the English Church. For his extraordinary knowledge of the Holy Bible, he was, during the Marian persecutions, condemned to the stake. The interest of friends spared his execution; but three of his companions in the true faith were sacrificed to the Mother of Abominations. One of the three was Robert Testwood, confessedly a superior singer in the choir of St. George's Chapel. Seeing some superstitious pilgrims, from Cornwall, worshipping musty relicks, he remonstrated with them, and, with a large key which he happened to be holding, rather accidentally mutilated the ornaments of an image of the Virgin, and demolished her nose. On one occasion,

---

* Till just before the Reformation there were no organs of any size or efficiency. Those of Vitellius's time (the seventh century) and long after, were either feeble or clumsy inventions. The one at Munich, celebrated throughout Christendom, was little better than a monster-bag-pipe, having an elephant's hide for the bellows, and fifteen hollowed box-trees for pipes. St. Dunstan was the patron of organs in England. Besides others, he presented one of superior excellence to the splendid parish church of Wrexham.

PREFACE. 9

also, when singing a hymn to the Virgin, and his part required him to say, "O Redemptrix et Salvatrix", he emphatically sang, "*Non* redemptrix *nec* salvatrix." Principally for these alarming offences Testwood was burned to death. Thus Protestant musicians are in "the noble army of martyrs."

The reign of Elizabeth witnessed the settlement of our church-music after that simple and modest, but devout and dignified style, which choir-books still retain, and which choir-practice has not wholly relinquished. The compositions especially of Tye, Tallis, Byrd, Farrant, and Orlando Gibbons, are monuments of that sort, to which musicians of the present age may look back, with the same interest and profit, as architects revert to the structures of the thirteenth century and the fourteenth. In the choral music of those worthies and their cotemporaries, there is somewhat so spiritually majestic, so serenely noble, and so warmly devout, that few composers in the present day can produce even a tolerable imitation. To analyze that choral music, and point out its peculiarities, as contradistinct from modern secular music, would require more space than a Preface is wont to allow. It must suffice to state that the Elizabethan composers were men of profound erudition and excellent judgment. They clearly discerned the requisites of divine worship, and self-denyingly aimed to fulfil them. Instead of indulging a wanton fancy, or allowing their genius such scope as would fire passions, captivate imaginations, or turn auditors into applauders, they confined themselves to a style which of all styles contains the most art with the least ostentation. Their style accorded with the solemnities of holy service, and with the character of the edifices in which it was performed. "Awe, reverence, tenderness and devotion" were the feelings which that style tended to inspire. Consequently, our genuine cathedral-music contains nothing of the cataractal, the startling, the ornamental, or even the picturesque; but more appropriately abounds with the sublime and beautiful, the chastely fervid, and the touchingly devout. Too many modern composers for the church overlook, what the Elizabethan composers kept steadfastly in view. They do not regard *consistency of style*. So that they can present something novel, *pretty* or striking, they are content. The secular and the sacred are not separated by them. Like the architects of the last centuries, they spurn older models, and thus produce debased specimens of a noble art. Under the guise of enlarged developement, some affect Germanisms, while others run into levities of a nondescript character. Enlarged developement of musical skill there certainly is; but then it is a developement of instrumental power, not of vocally harmonious beauty. The perfection of such harmony still rests with the Elizabethan composers. That being the case, and as instrumental music is greatly subordinate to vocal in the church, modern ecclesiastical composers can hope to excel only by doing as modern ecclesiastical architects are doing,—studying older productions, discriminating styles, and keeping consistently to them. That the music of the church should be broadly distinguished from the music of the world, is a sentiment which, happily, is fast regaining lost ground. If we readily concede to the Church a peculiar style of architecture, vesture, and phraseology, why should she not have a style of music all her own? Let this rightful concession once be made, and followed out, and all that is trashy and secular in Services and Anthems, Chants, and Metrical Tunes, will speedily meet with the banishment which it has long deserved.

But, not only was church-music, of the higher species, perfected in the reign of Elizabeth.* Psalmody, also, as music of an humbler

---

* Archbishop Parker had "a great affection to music." He founded a school at Stoke in Suffolk, "in which the scholars were taught to sing and play on the organ and other instruments." He made provision, also, for eight or ten choristers; of whom "the most apt of wit and capacity" were to be sent as exhibitioners to Cambridge.

PREFACE. 11

grade, was so aptly arranged as to furnish a model for after ages. The first Psalm-tunes were, for want of better compositions, modifications of songs and ballads. Subsequently, other tunes of a more suitable character were brought from the Reformed Churches on the continent, especially after the death of Mary, when the exiled reformers returned to England. To the tunes which they had learned abroad, and introduced at home, many more, of a corresponding style, were added by native composers. These tunes were collected and published by Thomas Ravenscroft, Mus. Bac., in 1623. Other editors had previously published less complete collections. Ravenscroft's superseded them, and, being published again in 1633, became the standard repository of genuine English Psalmody.*

Through the extravagant claims, and pedantic, not to say disloyal, excesses of the anti-church party, metrical Psalmody was at first regarded with some distaste by sober authorities. Eventually, however, under the pious discretion of those authorities, Psalmody became a recognised part of public worship,† though not formally appended to the Liturgy. Hymns or Spiritual Songs, of no very polished description, had long been used in the vernacular tongue. At length both Psalms

---

* For a more elaborate account of the origin and progress of metrical Psalmody, the reader is referred to the Preface of HACKETT's NATIONAL PSALMIST. The writer of that Preface has now what he had not then, a copy of Ravenscroft's book. It was a rarity, said Sir John Hawkins, even a century ago.

† Strype states that the singing of metrical psalms commenced at St. Antholin's, London. "Immediately," says Bishop Jewell, in a letter to Peter Martyr, 1560, "not only the churches in the neighbourhood, but the towns far distant, began to vie with each other in the same practice. You may now sometimes see at St. Paul's Cross, after the service, six thousand persons, old and young, of both sexes, all singing together and praising God. This sadly annoys the mass-priests and the devil. For they perceive that by these means the sacred discourses sink more deeply into the minds of men, and that their kingdom is weakened and shaken at almost every note." Hence, it is evident that Bishop Jewell approved the practice of "singing *after* the service"; which, a few years ago, was more common in the Church than it now is.

PREFACE.

and Hymns were ordinarily used, in even Cathedrals and Collegiate Churches, whenever a sermon was preached. This is evident from the title of Ravenscroft's volume, from Clifford's collection of words "usually sung in all Cathedrals and Collegiate Choirs," (1664) and from Master Thomas Mace's statement respecting the super-excellency of the style in which Psalms were sung, by immense congregations, in York Minster, aided by its "large, plump, lusty, full-speaking organ, which cost a thousand pounds," during the siege of York, in 1644.*

Subsequently to the Elizabethan worthies, and prior to the Great Rebellion, Dr. Child was the most distinguished musician of his day. Charles the First was fond of his compositions, and frequently selected them for the Chapel Service at Windsor, where the Doctor was organist. But the overthrow of episcopacy and monarchy, by the atrocious execution of King Charles, silenced both organs and choirs. During the Cromwellian interregnum, organists and choir-men were little better than exiles. Their art was proscribed, their books were destroyed, and themselves scarcely ventured to be seen in public. Amidst, however, the virulence of the puritan-party, truth and nature very remarkably prevailed over two of its leading abettors. Oliver Cromwell was thoroughly fond of organs,† and his Latin Secretary, the immortal Milton, could not dissemble his religious admiration of cathedral-music, spite of his joining in its abolition.

At the Restoration in 1660, it was with difficulty that cathedral-choirs could be made up. Where they were revived, a sadly altered

---

* See Sir John Hawkins, vol. iv. p. 453.

† During the rage for organ-destruction, when the organ at Magdalen College, Oxford, was being pulled down, Cromwell, with consistent hypocrisy, ordered it to be removed to Hampton Court, where he used privately to indulge himself by hearing it played upon. After the Restoration it was carried back to the College.

PREFACE. 13

character was visible. It was the will of the Court that the music of the Church should be accommodated to the taste of the Sovereign. That taste had been fostered amidst the levities of the French choirs. The older composers, such as Dr. Child who lived to a very great age, stoutly resisted the unhallowed innovation. The younger aspirants, Lawes, Lock, Wise, Humphries, and Blow were more compliant. Still, their compositions were not destitute of the best qualities of church-music; though in many of them a sad falling off from the sobriety of the preceding century is very discernible. At this crisis, no individual did better or did worse than, that pride and paragon of British music, Henry Purcell. Rising at an early age to the summit of his profession, he had opportunities, by dint of his genius and station, for introducing the current style of the stage into the anthems of the church. Hence there are passages in some of his anthems which ought not to be heard in the Sanctuary.

For many years, till, indeed, towards the middle of the last century, our church-music, with occasional exceptions, maintained its character for dignity and sobriety. To the support of that character, Dr. Aldrich, Dean of Christ Church, contributed not a little.

About the commencement of the last century, Dr. Croft rose into notice as a composer of superior merit. He is inferior only when he turns from earlier models to later styles. He is described as "a grave and decent man," of most benevolent aspect, and of truly religious devotion. After him, Dr. Greene, who was cotemporary with Handel, and Organist of St. Paul's, became the arbiter of our choirs. Though the author of many excellent anthems, he was, unhappily, influenced by the prevailing taste for Operatic and Oratorial music. Somewhat like Purcell before him, he too well succeeded in introducing many of the peculiarities of that music into the church.

14 PREFACE.

Successor to Dr. Greene, as taking the lead in ecclesiastical music, was the amiable Dr. Boyce. He is worthy of all commendation, and is too well known to need any formal expression of it. A long series of superior musicians, might be added, both prior to Dr. Boyce, and, in more modern times, from Dr. Nares to the last, but living, and by no means the least, our own estimable Professor, Dr. Crotch.

It cannot, however, be dissembled that many a composer, who has been capable of better things, has accelerated the downward course of music, by pandering to a vitiated taste. Few authors are more chargeable with this fault than Mr. James Kent. His anthems have been extremely popular, and therefore, (to come at once to a conclusion) they have been extremely mischievous. Light, easy, and *pretty*, with here and there a good phrase, they have kept out better music, and opened the way for worse.*

Estimated by good sense, sound scholarship, and old-fashioned piety, the music which long has been current in the church, is of a debased and unworthy sort. Not that good music, or even some of the best music, is wholly banished, but light, gaudy, voluptuous music is too frequently introduced. Ballad-like Chants† sing-song Services, and

---

* Miss Hawkins, describing her father's interview with George the third, on presenting a copy of "The History of Music," says thus: "The King professed his decided taste for what is called *the old school;* and jocularly complained of his inability to persuade the Queen to prefer it to the modern style. There was a point, however, in which my father could subscribe to Her Majesty's opinion, without the sacrifice of his own. This was in condemning the light airs to which modern composers have set sacred words for choral service. She said she was extremely displeased with many anthems which she had heard at the Chapel-royal, for their want of devotion; and, to bring one to his recollection, she sang the first few bars of it. I think it was Kent's 'O Lord our Governor;' an anthem so much a favorite with some fashionable *amateurs,* that half-a-guinea was often given, by a musical man of rank, to a chapel-boy for singing it."—*Memoirs, Anecdotes, &c., collected by Miss Hawkins. Vol. II., pp.* 44 & 45.

† The prevailing style of modern Chants forms a perfect contrast to the style of former centuries. Chants were of old remarkably simple in melody, short in compass, full and plain in harmony, and

PREFACE.

trashy operatic Anthems, may almost everywhere be heard. A writer in "The Christian Remembrancer" has stated that in one of the metropolitan choirs, they actually sing adaptations from Weber's hobgoblin Opera, Der Freischütz, in which are crashing discords to represent the screams and yells of demons, and other monstrous personifications. Nearly as bad are such Anthems as " Plead thou my cause," an arrangement to English words from one of Mozart's Masses. The music certainly is beautiful of its sort, but that sort is neither devotional nor ecclesiastical.* Added to these debasing circumstances is the fact, that too many Organists adopt a style of Voluntary, which is more suited for the parade or the concert-room, than for the House of God.

With few exceptions, our parochial churches are conversant with a style of Psalm and Hymn tune, which would have shocked our pious forefathers. Instead of the severe but masculine melody of their day, with a syllabic utterance, and a fine rich harmony, all moving in stately yet easy and *un*drawling precision, our church-population are habituated to either a dronish, whining, or an effeminate class of tunes, in which noise is mistaken for harmony, and secularity for devotion. In fact, most of these tunes are made up of snatches from songs, glees, ballads, marches, and even more indecorous productions, and are as incapable of good harmonisation, as they are of inspiring either warm or elevated feelings. But, happily, there is hope of a return to a better and more becoming state of things, in both Cathedrals and Parish Churches. Public attention is awake; periodicals are on the alert;

---

always *single*. Now, they are airy, expansive, thin, chromatic, and *double*, without regard to the true nature of chanting, or the antiphonal character of that part of divine service. That Double Chants should be *antiphonal* in their structure, was first argued and urged by the Rev. W. H. Havergal, about eight years ago, in "Remarks on Chants and Chanting." (Novello) The monition has been pretty generally noticed, and many composers have been induced to *think*.

* At the risk of incurring wholesale wrath, from many who have yet to learn what *church*-music is,

PREFACE.

prize societies are encouraging native talent; and individuals as well as committees are republishing the good music of old times.*

But, may it never be forgotten, that the revival of the very best music will bring little profit to the church without a revival of the very best affections to accompany it. To "sing with the spirit," as well as "with the understanding," is the only singing which is tuneful in the ear of Him who says to every singer upon earth, "My son, give me thy heart." The great enemy of the church has turned, and still can turn, the music of the Sanctuary into a powerful auxiliary for the furtherance of his own dark purposes. He knows that there is nothing so good, but what may be converted into an evil. Hence, music, as well as architecture, must not be idolized, but held in subserviency to pure doctrine, and holy affections.

W. H. H.

May, 1844.

---

the writer ventures to assert that it is an anomaly which would have horrified the Elizabethan worthies, for a noble organ, a good choir, and a large congregation, to be represented by first, *one little* boy, and then, *two little* boys, in such Services as Arnold in B., and such Anthems as "My song shall be of mercy," and "Hear my prayer," Kent. Things of this sort may be very *pretty*, but, "in the great congregation," they are sadly out of place.

* The London Motett Society has begun a good object in admirable style. Rimbault's reprint of Dr. Arnold's Collection of Cathedral Music is a splendid undertaking. Hackett's National Psalmist, and Hullah's Psalter, are the best publications of their sort in the present day. Dr. Boyce's Cathedral Music is reprinting, by Mr. Warren; and a new edition of Ravenscroft is in the press. (Novello.)

Cathedral Service.

O melody divine, (for not of earth
   Art thou, nor wilt with ought of earth divide
   The full dominion of the soul) thy birth
Was from the song that welcomed, like a bride,
   The new-formed world, or hymned in Bethlehem's ear
   Glory and peace.   How awful rolls the tide
Of sound, and blends in harmony austere,
   (For human sense too mystical and high)
   The deep grave thunder, and the descant clear.
Down throbbing heart! what darkness veils the sky:
   How fade the shrines and altars from my sight.
   Oh could I listen, till mortality
Be swallowed up in vision, and take flight
Into the minstrelsies of endless light!

                      Rev. C. Hoyle,
                          Vicar of Overton, near Marlborough.

Patrons and Subscribers.

HIS GRACE THE LORD ARCHBISHOP OF YORK
THE RIGHT REVEREND THE LORD BISHOP OF BANGOR
THE RIGHT REVEREND THE LORD BISHOP OF DURHAM
THE RIGHT REVEREND THE LORD BISHOP OF HEREFORD
THE RIGHT REVEREND THE LORD BISHOP OF RIPON
THE RIGHT REVEREND THE LORD BISHOP OF KILDARE
THE RIGHT REVEREND THE BISHOP OF GLASGOW
THE MOST HONOURABLE THE MARCHIONESS OF LONDONDERRY. 2 COPIES
THE RIGHT HONOURABLE LORD BEXLEY
THE RIGHT HONOURABLE LORD RAVENSWORTH
THE RIGHT HONOURABLE LADY STANLEY
LORD ASHLEY, M.P.
THE HONOURABLE JOHN STUART WORTLEY, M.P.
THE HONOURABLE AND REVEREND F. DE GREY, M.A.
THE HONOURABLE AND REVEREND G. V. WELLESLEY, D.D., PREBENDARY OF DURHAM
THE HONOURABLE AND REVEREND THE DEAN OF ST PATRICK'S, DUBLIN
SIR MORGAN G. CROFTON, BART., M.P.
SIR ROBERT H. INGLIS, BART., M.P.
SIR THOMAS BARING, BART.
SIR F. LINDLEY WOOD, BART.
LADY BARING
THE REVEREND SIR CHARLES JOHN ANDERSON, BART., M.A.
SIR ROBERT FRANKLAND RUSSELL, BART.
SIR GEORGE SMART, ORGANIST TO HER MAJESTY'S CHAPEL ROYAL
THE HONOURABLE MRS. PACKENHAM
THE HONOURABLE MRS. HARCOURT
THE VERY REVEREND THE DEAN OF ELY
THE VERY REVEREND THE DEAN OF WESTMINSTER
THE DEAN AND CHAPTER OF SALISBURY. 2 COPIES
THE VENERABLE ARCHDEACON MUSGRAVE, D.D.
THE VENERABLE ARCHDEACON T. THORPE, B.D.
THE WORSHIPFUL THE CHANCELLOR RAIKES, M.A.
THE PRESIDENT OF MAGDALEN COLLEGE, OXFORD
THE WARDEN OF NEW COLLEGE, OXFORD
THE MASTER OF UNIVERSITY COLLEGE, OXFORD
THE RECTOR OF LINCOLN COLLEGE, OXFORD
THE REV. W. F. HOOK, D.D., PREBENDARY OF LINCOLN
THE REV. G. STANLEY FABER, B.D., MASTER OF SHERBURN HOSPITAL, AND
  PREBENDARY OF SALISBURY
THE REV. EDWARD ELLERTON, D.D.
THE REV. G. D. KENT, M.A., PREBENDARY OF LINCOLN
THE REV. G. TOWNSEND, M.A., PREBENDARY OF DURHAM
THE REV. W. S. GILLY, D.D., CANON OF DURHAM
THE REV. H. JENKYNS, M.A. CANON OF DURHAM
THE REV. H. DOUGLAS, M.A., CANON OF DURHAM
THE LATE REV. J. TATE, M.A., CANON RESIDENTIARY OF ST. PAUL'S
REV. J. JAMESON, B.D., PRECENTOR OF RIPON CATHEDRAL
JOHN HARDY, ESQ, M.P.
C. H. ELSLEY, ESQ., RECORDER OF YORK

SUBSCRIBERS.

Ackroyd, R.S., Bradford
Adam, Thomas, Halifax
Akers, Mrs. Charlotte, Halifax
Alderson, Mrs., Aston Rectory, near Sheffield
Anderdon, Miss, Farley Hill, Reading
Andrews, William, Bradford
Argent, E. A., Liverpool
Ash, Jarvis Holland, Cotham House, Bristol
Ashlin, W. C., Bank of Liverpool
Aspden, Richard, Mosley Street, Manchester
Atkinson, Charles, Lower Woodsford, Dorset
Atkinson, J. Robert, Elmwood House, Leeds
Atkinson, John, Solicitor, Little Woodhouse, Leeds
Attree, F. T., University College, Durham

Baddeley, Capt. Charles Holland, Wigston Hall, Leicester
Baker, Mrs. Whitburn Rectory, Sunderland
Baker, Miss, High Street, Bridgnorth
Barmby, Rev. J., M.A., Melsonby, Richmond
Barton, Rev. Miles, M.A., Rector of Hoole, Preston
Bayley, Rev. W. H. R., M.A., Stapleton, Bristol
Beale, J. E., Surgeon, Plaistow, Essex
Beasley, Rev. Henry Francis, A.M., Great Budworth
Beaufort, Miss L., Dublin
Beckett, C., Low Moor, near Bradford
Bellett, Rev. G., A.M., St. Leonard's, Bridgnorth
Benson, Miss, Whitby
Bentley, Rev. R. H., M.A., Cobridge
Beresford, Miss, Charles Street, St. James' Square, [London
Beresford Miss L., Dublin
Berry, James, Manchester
Bickerdyke, Rev. J., M.A., Bradford
Blackburn, John, Bradford
Blackburn, W. H., Bradford. 6 copies
Booth, William, Halifax
Borrer, Miss, Lewes
Boyd, Rev. W., M.A., Arncliffe, Skipton
Bracebridge, W. H., Moreville, Warwick. 3 copies
Bradshaw, Job, Nottingham
Bramley, Laurence, Halifax
Brindley, John, Tarvin Hall, Cheshire
Brook, Joseph, Huddersfield
Brooks, Rev. J. W., M.A., Vicar of St. Mary's, Nottingham
Brown, Richard, Ardwick, Manchester
Browning, A. H., Eton College
Buck, Z., Organist of Norwich Cathedral

Buckley, W. H. G., Bradford

Camm, Alfred, Well Holme, Brighouse
Cann, Abraham, Solicitor, Nottingham
Carus, Rev. W., M.A., Cambridge
Carr, Rev. Elliot E., M.A., Trawden, Colne
Carr, (the late) Rev. W., B.D., Bolton Abbey
Carpenter, John, Mount Tavy, Tavistock
Carter, Peter, Aston Park, Great Budworth
Chadwick, W., Leeds
Child, Charles, Sowerby Bridge
Chivers, Mrs., Belle Vue, Doncaster
Churchwardens of St. Matthew's, Birmingham
Clark, Rev. H., M.A., Harmston, Lincoln
Claye, Charles, Halifax
Coates, Mrs. G., The Square, Ripon
Cole, Edward, Turnhurst, near Burslem
Conington, Rev. John, M.A., Navenby, Lincolnshire
Cook, Rev. R. K., B.A., Smallbridge, Rochdale
Cooper, Rev. J., M.A., St. Jude's, Bradford
Cox, Samuel, Beaminster
Crabtree, Rev. W., M.A., Checkendon Rectory
Crabtree, ———, Henley-on-Thames
Crofts, Rev. H., M.A., Linton, near Skipton
Currer, Miss, Eshton Hall. 2 copies
Currie, R., Newcastle

Dale, Daniel, Liverpool
Darling, Ralph, Esq., Hampton Lodge, Brighton
Darlington, John, Bradford
Dean, Abel, Halifax
Dewe, John, Leamington
Dikes, W. H., Wakefield
Dimsdale, John, 5, Regent's Place, Regent's Park, London
Douglas, Rev. H., M.A., Rector, Whickham, Durham
Duesbery, W. D. T., Skelton Lodge, York
Duncan, Leonard, Halifax
Dyke, Rev. J. H., M.A., Long Newton, Stockton-upon-[Tees
Dyson, Samuel, Sowerby Bridge

Edge, J. G., Chipping Camden
Edis, R., Huntingdon
Edwards, Henry, Craven Lodge, Halifax
Elsley, Miss, Skipton Bridge, Thirsk
Elsley, Miss M., Skipton Bridge, Thirsk
Evans, Rev. Watkin, M.A., Astley Abbotts
Ewbank, W., Redcar

SUBSCRIBERS.

Faber, C. D., Bridlington Quay
Faber, Rev. F. A., A.M., Fellow of Mag. Coll., Oxford
Faber, Rev. J. C., M.A., Chicklade Hindon, Wiltshire
Faber, Mrs., Sherburn Hospital
Fairbank, Wm., Woodcroft, Otley
Faulkner, Isaac, Bloomsbury, Manchester
Fawcett, R., Shipley Hall
Fawcett, R. Jun., Bradford
Fearnley, John, Stanley Grove, Manchester
Fletcher, C., Organist, Kidderminster
Foulger, Wm., Norwich
Fountain, Mrs., Beaufort Buildings, Bath
Fox, George, Durham
Frobisher, J. H., Organist of Parish Church, Halifax
Fry, Rev. T., M.A., Emberton, Newport Pagnell

Garlick, J. W., M.D., F.R.C.S., Halifax
Gilpin, (late) Rev., J., B.D., Sedbury Park, Richmond,
Gilpin, Mrs., Sedbury Park, Richmond [Yorks
Goodall, Wm., The Heath, Halifax
Gott, John, Organist, Christ Church, Bradford
Gott, John, Esq., Wyther, Leeds
Gott, Miss, Armley House, Leeds
Gray, Wm., Wheatfield, near Bolton
Greame, Mrs., Redcar
Gundry, Mrs., Hyde
Gutch, Mrs., Oxford

Hackett, C. D., Bradford
Hailstone, Edward, Bradford
Hamilton, Henry, Fitzwilliam Square, West Dublin
Harcourt, Rev. L. V., M.A., West Dean, Chichester
Hardy, Mrs. C., Odsall, near Bradford
Harris Henry, Bradford
Harris, A., Bradford
Harris, W. Masterman, Bradford
Hartley, Joseph, Halifax
Hartley, Miss, Ashfield, near Otley, 3 copies
Harvey, Charles, Kidderminster
Hatsell, Miss, Acton House, Acton, Middlesex
Havergal, Rev. W. H., M.A., Henwick House, Worcester
Hawkins, E., 9, Tillotson Place, Waterloo Bridge, London
Hayward, J. Curtis, Quedgley House, near Gloucester
Hervey, James, Halifax
Hey, Wm., Albion Place, Leeds
Heywood, John, Manchester

Hopkins, Edward, London
Hopkinson, J. & J., Leeds,
Holden, G., Seymour Street, Liverpool
Hollings, Joseph, Bradford
Hoyland, Wm., Halifax
Hulme, Miss, Shirfield, Reading
Hulme, Rev. A., M.A., Reading

Illingworth, J. A., Surgeon, Bradford

Jackson, George, Sowerby Bridge
Jones, R. Deschamps, Spring Gardens, Manchester
Joyce, Jesse, Yeovil
Jowett, Rev. J., M.A., Rector of Silk Willoughby,
Jubb, Abraham, Halifax   [Lincolnshire

Lace, F. Ingthorp Grange, near Skipton
Lewis, Mrs., Kingston, Dublin
Lewthwaite, Rev. G., B.D., Rector of Adel, near Leeds
Lupton, Rev. John, M.A., St. Paul's Cathedral

Mallinson, J., Brighouse, near Halifax
Marsden, Rev. W. B., M.A., Vicar of St. John's, Chester
Marsden, W., Bradford
Marsland, Rev. George, M.A., Rectory, Beckingham,
Mangan, —— Esq., Dublin   [6 copies
Milne, Thomas, Warley House, Halifax
Mitchell, E. J., Bradford
Mitchell, J. H., Solicitor, Halifax
Mottram, Rev. C. J. M., Kidderminster
Munby, Joseph, York
Muskett, C., Norwich

Nelson, William, Fulneck, near Leeds
Newbery, Rev. T., M.A., Shipley
Newbery, Henry, Manchester
Newman, Edwin, Solicitor, Yeovil
Newton, R. A., Fifield House, Bensington, Oxon
Norris Charles, St. John's House, Halifax
Norris, F. W. N., Halifax

Ogden, B. C., Uppingham
Okes, Rev. R., Eton College
Oldham, Rev. John, M.A., St. Paul's, Huddersfield
Orr, J., Oxford
Orr, Miss, Brighton
Osborn, W. H., Bradford

SUBSCRIBERS.

Outhwaite, Miss, Bradford
Oxley, R. D., Ripon

Paine, Cornelius, Jun., Mountfort House, Islington
Painter, W. F., 342, Strand, London
Paley, Rev. George, M.A., Freckingham
Parke, Rev. J. A., M.A., Elwick Hall, Stockton-upon-Tees
Phibbs, Miss, 28, Merrion Square, South Dublin
Plumer, Rev. C., M.A., Norton, Stockton-upon-Tees
Poppleton, R., Moor Cottage, Wakefield
Powell, Rev. B., M.A., Wigan
Pratt, John, Bradford
Prescott, Miss, Everton, Liverpool
Pritchard, Rev. R., M.A., Kidderminster

Quarmby, John, Scammonden. 2 copies

Raper, Henry, London
Randell, Miss, Greenwich
Rawson, John, Jun., Brockwell, near Halifax
Rawson, T. W., Bradford
Reade, Miss, Ipsden House, Wallingford
Redhead, R., Marylebone, London
Rogerson, Michael, Bradford
Rothwell, Richard, Rookfield, Kells, Co. Meath, Ireland
Routh, Mrs. J., Tilehurst, Reading
Rowley, Rev. T., D.D., Head Master of the Grammar School, Bridgnorth
Russell, Mrs. R., Reading

Scholefield, Mrs., Doncaster
Schuster, S., Bradford
Scoresby, Rev. W., D.D., Vicar of Bradford. 2 copies
Schlesinger, Martin, Bradford
Serjeantson, Rev. R. J., M.A., Vicar of Snaith
Sharp, Samuel, Leeds
Shearman, Dr., Rotherham
Sheepshanks, Miss, Reading
Sidebottom, Edward, Wakefield
Simpson, Rev. R., M.A., Newark
Smith, Edward William, Routh, near Beverley
Smith, G., Leeds
Smith, Henry, Leeds
Smith, Samuel, Bradford
Smith, Solomon, Surgeon, Halifax
Stephens, Mrs., Prospect Hill, Reading

Stokes, J. G., Hoddesdon, Herts.
Stokes, Rev. W. R., M.A., Sherburn Hospital
Stott, F. S., Bowling
Stott, Miss, Bradford
Strong, W., Bristol. 2 copies
Styring, Thomas, Halifax
Sutcliffe, John, Halifax
Suter, Miss, Organist, Greenwich

Thoyts, Mrs., Emma, Seelhampstead House, Reading
Topham, Richard, Wortley, near Leeds
Townend, Simeon, Thornton, near Bradford
Townshend, Henry, Esq., Stoney Stanton, near Hinckley
Tucker, Abraham, Bridport
Turner, Ralph, Esq., Manchester

Vining, J. T., Solicitor, Yeovil

Wainhouse, Robert, Solicitor, Leeds
Waldy, Thomas, Egglescliffe, Yarm
Waldy, Mrs., Egglescliffe, Yarm
Walker, Charles, Bradford
Walton, James, Sowerby Bridge
Wase, Miss, High Street, Bridgenorth
Waterhouse, John, Well Head, Halifax
Wells, William, Bradford
Wheatley, John, Liverpool
White, Edward, Organist, Parish Church, Wakefield
White, John, Woodhouse, Apperley-Bridge
White, Mrs., Acton House, Acton, Middlesex
White, Rev. Richard, Perpetual Curate of Ribby-cum-Wrea
Whitley and Booth, Halifax
Whitmore, Thomas, Esq., Apley Park
Whitworth, Rev. W. H., M.A., Dedham, Essex
Whyman, Robert, Halifax
Wickham, L. W., Esq., Kirklees Hall, near Huddersfield
Wilkinson, James, Sheffield
Williamson, T., Cleckheaton, near Leeds, 2 copies
Wilson, Rev. W. C., M.A., Casterton House, Kirby Lonsdale
Winter, R. R., Durham
Wood, Miss Louisa, 31, Seymour Street, Liverpool
Wood, Rev. Peter, M.A., Broadwater, Shoreham, Sussex
Woodcock, Joseph, Bradford
Wyrill, William, Bradford. 2 copies

Yeadon, Rev. W., M.A., Waddington Rectory, near Lincoln

Patrons and Subscribers.

ADDITIONAL LIST.

HIS ROYAL HIGHNESS PRINCE ALBERT
HER ROYAL HIGHNESS THE DUCHESS OF KENT
THE RIGHT HONOURABLE THE LORD DUNSANY
SIR ROBERT PIGOT, BART.
SIR CHARLES DES VŒUX, BART.
THE HONOURABLE AND REVEREND F. GREY, M.A.
C. H. LOWTHER, ESQ.
REVEREND W. MARSH, D.D., PRINCIPAL OFFICIAL OF THE ROYAL PECULIAR, BRIDGNORTH
VALENTINE VICKERS, ESQ., ELLERTON GRANGE

Birdsworth, W. Carr, Lytham
Bruce, W. D., York

Crotch, William, Mus. Doc., Oxford
Couchman, William, Cranbrook

Ellacombe, Rev. H. I., M.A. Bitton Vicarage, Bristol
Ellison, Rev. N. T., M.A., Rector of Huntspill
Elvey, E. J., Mus. Doc., Windsor

Hart, Charles, Organist, London
Hey, Rev. S., M.A., Sawley, Derby

Macturk, William, M.D., Bradford
Misdale, Richard, Bradford
Mitchell, T. G. P., Oldbury, Birmingham

Morgan, Rev. W., B.D., Bradford
Morris, Joseph, Bradford,

Patchett, ———, Halifax
Pye, Kellow J., Mus. Bac., Exeter

Rhodes, Charles, Bradford
Roberts, Rev. H., Evesham
Robinson, Rev. R. B., M.A., Lytham   (2 copies)

Smith, John, Mus. Doc., Organist of St. Patrick's, Dublin
Stow, Mrs., Leeds

Whitmore, Rev. George, Rector of Kimberton, Salop

Yeoman, Rev. H. W., M.A., Vicar of Marske

Index.

INTRODUCTION	i.
PREFACE	iii.
Voluntaries	1
Introit	7
Chants	9
Services	17
Anthems	38
Sanctuses	82
Kyrie Eleeson, or Responses to the Commandments	98
Psalm and Hymn Tunes	111
Miscellanea	149

These are excerpts of letters written by W.H.H. to Rev. Joshua Fawcett, the editor of this book:[1]

Henwick House, Worcester,
Dec. 8, 1842.

Dear Sir,

As I told you, there is trouble enough in your undertaking. And you have not done yet. You want a competent hand to edit every piece that is sent you. I have done it only cursorily and generally. The fact is that most of the articles sent you are got up hastily, as their authors sometimes acknowledge, and as other cases plainly show. Some also are sent you at random without care or concern, *ex. gr.*, dear ———. Hence one half of the pieces, though more or less decent, are hardly fit for publication. Lots of little things want seeing to, altering, amending, correcting : otherwise, when the volume is out and has slept a little, it will be found full of oversights and imperfections. Bear, too, in mind that many of your contributors are not *Church* musicians, as ——— and ———, etc. Consequently they make a mess when they attempt a style they really do not understand. There is as much difference between styles in music as in architecture. Many a man who can manage a Grecian or an Italian structure well, is at sea in Gothic buildings. And this is a fact which I want to ding-dong in everybody's ears till they see and *feel* it.

Again, too, many of our cathedral, collegiate, and large parish-church organists are but poorly educated men, in music as well as in letters. They can play and, as they think, compose; but really they do not know what they are about. They have had

[This letter is continued and completed on page 1762.]

[1] These excerpts were found in *Records of the Life of the Rev. William Henry Havergal, M.A.* by his daughter Miriam Crane (London: Home Words Publishing Office, 1882), original book pages 169–172, pages 626–627 of Volume IV of the Havergal edition.

List of

NAMES OF COMPOSERS.	VOLUNTARIES.	INTROIT.	CHANTS.
Adams, Thomas	1	....	....
Anonymous	....	....	....
Barnett, John	....	....	....
Bayley, W.	....	....	....
Beckett, C.	....	....	....
Camidge, Matthew	....	....	....
Camidge, Dr.	....	....	10
Cartledge, J.	....	....	....
Chard, Dr.	....	....	....
Churchill, J.	....	....	....
Couchman, W.	....	....	10
Crook, T. H.	....	....	11
Crotch, Dr.	....	....	....
Elvey, Dr. G. J.	3	....	....
Faber, Rev. G. S., B.D.	....	....	....
Forster, A. V.	....	....	11
Goss, John	....	....	11
Hackett, Chas. D.	5	7	....
Hart. C.	....	....	11
Havergal, Rev. W. H., M.A.	....	....	9, 12, 13
Hird, Miss J.	....	....	14
Hopkins, Edward	....	....	....
Hoyle, Rev. C.	6	....	13, 14
Ingram, Thomas	....	....	14
Jones, R. D.	....	....	9
Jowett, Rev. J., M.A.	....	....	14
Knyvett, W.	....	....	14
Matthews, F.	....	....	14, 15
Novello, Vincent	....	....	....
Pye Kellow, J., Mus. Bac.	....	....	15
Pyne, J. K.	....	....	15, 16
Smith, Dr.	....	....	16
Taylor, Edward, Gres. Prof. Mus.	....	....	....
Walmisley, Dr.	....	....	....
Westmoreland, Earl of	....	....	9
Whitnall, G. B.	....	....	16
Wilkins, G.	....	....	16
Wilton, Earl of	....	....	9

Authors.

SERVICES.	ANTHEMS.	SANCTUSES.	RESPONSES.	PSALMS AND HYMNS.	MISCELLANEA
....	....	....	....	111	....
....	....	....	....	140	....
....	....	....	....	112	....
....	....	82, 83	98, 99	....	....
....	....	....	....	114, 115, 116	....
....	....	85	100	....	....
....	....	....	....	....	....
....	....	86	....	....	....
....	....	....	....	117	....
....	....	88	101, 102	118,119,120,121,122,123,124,125	....
17, 29	....	....	....	126, 127, 128, 129	143, 144
....	....	....	....	....	....
....	....	....	103	....	....
....	38	90	104	....	....
34	42	....	....	....	141
....	....	....	....	....	....
....	....	....	....	130	....
....	....	....	....	....	....
....	51	....	....	....	....
....	58, 63, 68	....	105	131,132,133,134,135	144
....	....	....	....	....	....
....	....	....	106	136	....
....	....	....	....	....	....
....	....	....	....	....	....
....	....	....	....	....	....
....	....	....	....	....	....
....	....	....	....	....	....
....	....	....	108	....	....
....	73	....	....	....	....
....	....	....	....	....	....
....	....	92	....	....	....
....	....	....	....	....	148
....	....	94	....	....	....
....	....	....	....	....	....
....	....	....	....	....	....
....	....	96	110	137, 138, 139	145
....	....	....	....	....	....

[This letter from W.H.H. to Rev. Joshua Fawcett is here continued from page 1759.]

no theoretical education, and in after life are too busy with teaching or performing to allow them to study, read, write, and *think*. Consequently many of them, ——, and even —— and —— pen trash, nonsense, and that in a thoroughly secular style. In truth they do not understand *style*; they do not discriminate.

Hence while many of your contributors show latent *power*, very few evince practical *skill*. They could compose Church music if they knew how. The consequence is they send you a lot of stuff, all very pretty and taking with the musical commonalty, but utterly unfit for Church service. Instead of music of a stately, dignified, majestically plaintive or devotionally warm character, they write things in the style of the tavern or concert-room—things which would have horrified the worthies of Queen Elizabeth's days.

All this applies to all the sorts of music you intend to comprise in your volume. Therefore, dear sir, keep a sharp lookout. Chants, for instance, are among the most meretricious doings of the present day. "Everybody thinks he can write a chant," and yet to write a good chant is *now* one of the most difficult things in the musical world.

One other general remark, and then to particulars. Most of your greater contributors are accustomed to send their contributions for a little pecuniary consideration. When they send gratis they send careless things. See Dr. C.'s shrewd hint at the end of his chants.

* * * * *

Further, I send for your inspection an introit anthem, " Arise, O Lord." It wants a little furbishing, which I will see to *if* you wish to have it. And now I beg to send you my Evening Service in E flat and one hundred chants; *Te Deum* to match, with sixteen chants; and Gresham Prize No. 6—I won't say as a present, but in exchange for a copy of your forthcoming volume. Read my preface on chants, etc. Any of those chants are at your service; if you wish it I will tell you which I deem the best. Now I would willingly dock the hundred by fifty or more. We grow wiser by time. So you see I cut up myself as well as others. But a truce, for I am tired. God's blessing.

Ever yours,
W. H. H.

P.S.—I do not exactly like *our* collects set to music, so I am not solicitous for your having any.

(*To the same.*)

Dec. 23rd.

——'s Chants are not worth your notice. Mr. —— is a clever and a capable man, and a superior organ-player; but from what I hear of him I am very wary how I put myself in his way. I did venture to point out to —— the crudities and incongruities of certain pieces of his, in consequence of which he threw them out of the second edition and sacrificed the costs. How different is the style of all our great English composers—Handel, Greene, Arne, Boyce, Crotch, etc. With them all is natural, simple, beautiful.

Some persons seem always to be wanting brisk and lively tunes—just as though they can drink nothing but champagne.

Some composers, A. and G. to wit, cannot harmonize a tune without seeking for discords at every step. They keep the ear in torment, teasing it at every turn; like persons who, in laying out grounds, place stiles and gates at every step for mere whim.

I should like to see anything of Gibbons and Palestrina's. They most likely would do for you. I send you a Decalogue Response, which will give you my idea of what *such* a Response ought to be, simple, plaintive, masculine, devout, without prettiness or repetition.

Note: This page was not in the original book *The Lyra Ecclesiastica*, but—like many of the illustration pages in Volume V of the Havergal edition—was placed here to keep the original left-page and right-page orientation of original pages from the 19th century.

Single Chants.

Nº 1. EARL of WESTMORELAND

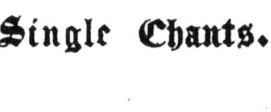

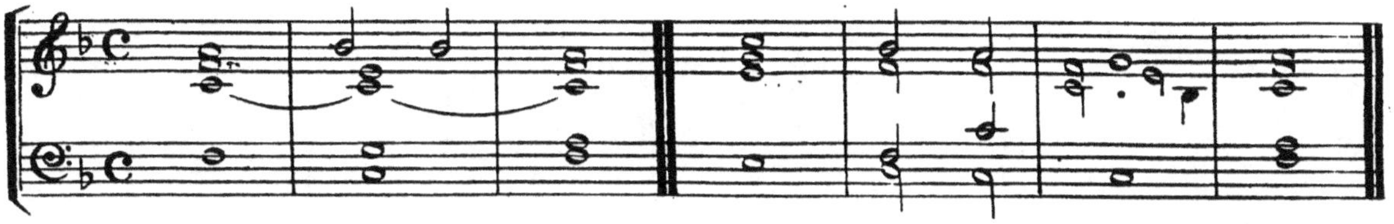

Nº 2. EARL of WILTON.

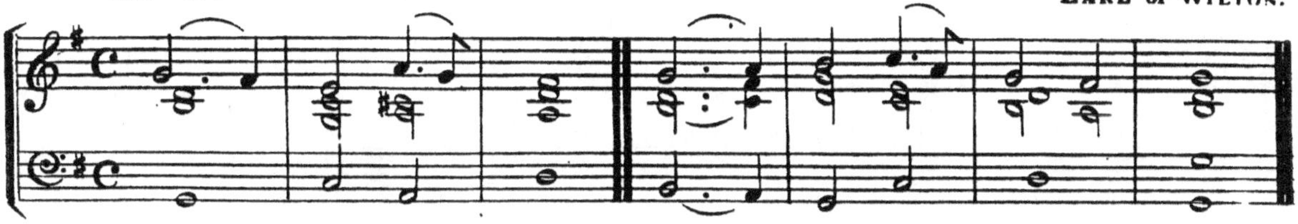

Nº 3. W. H. HAVERGAL. M.A.

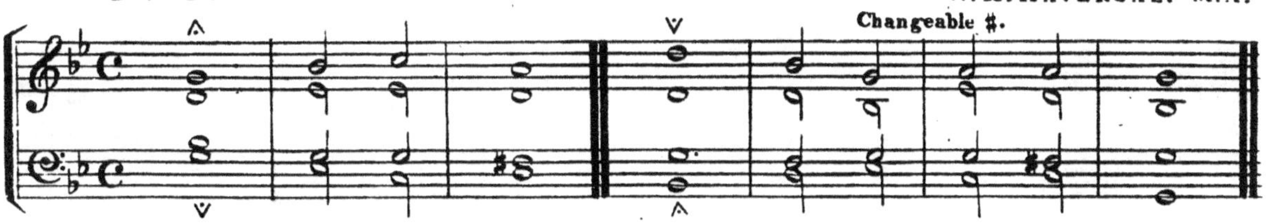

Nº 4. Dº

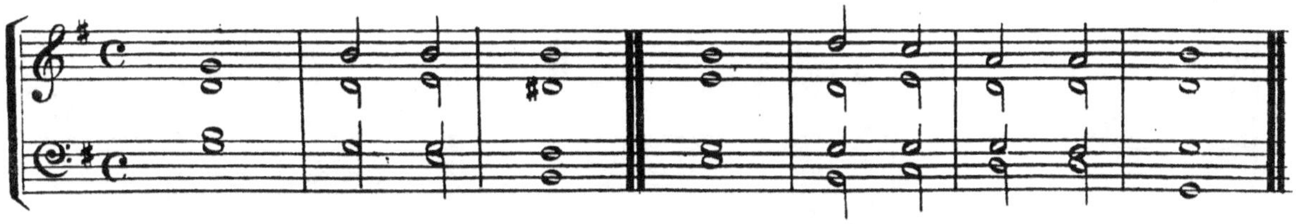

Nº 5. Dº

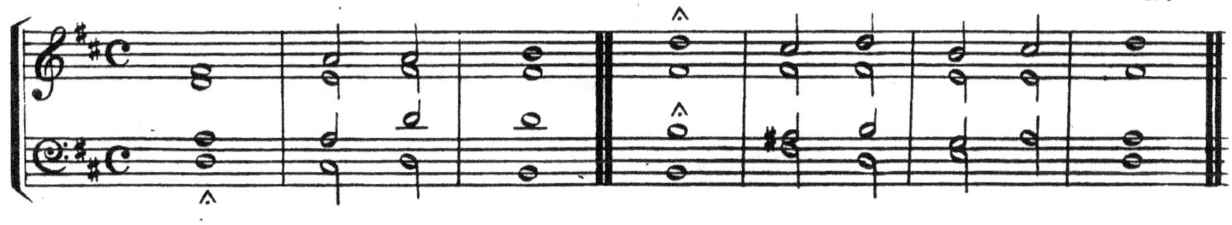

Nº 6. R. D. JONES.

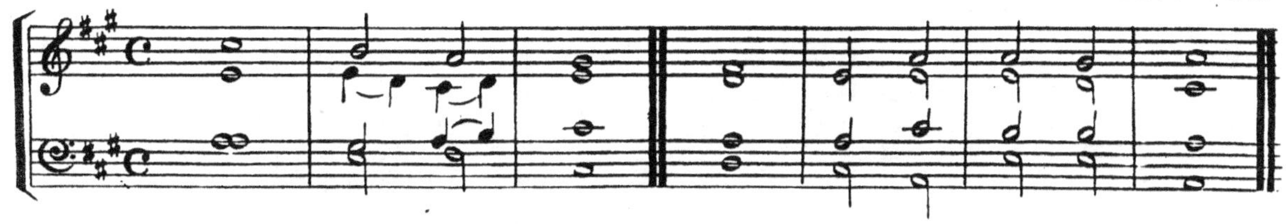

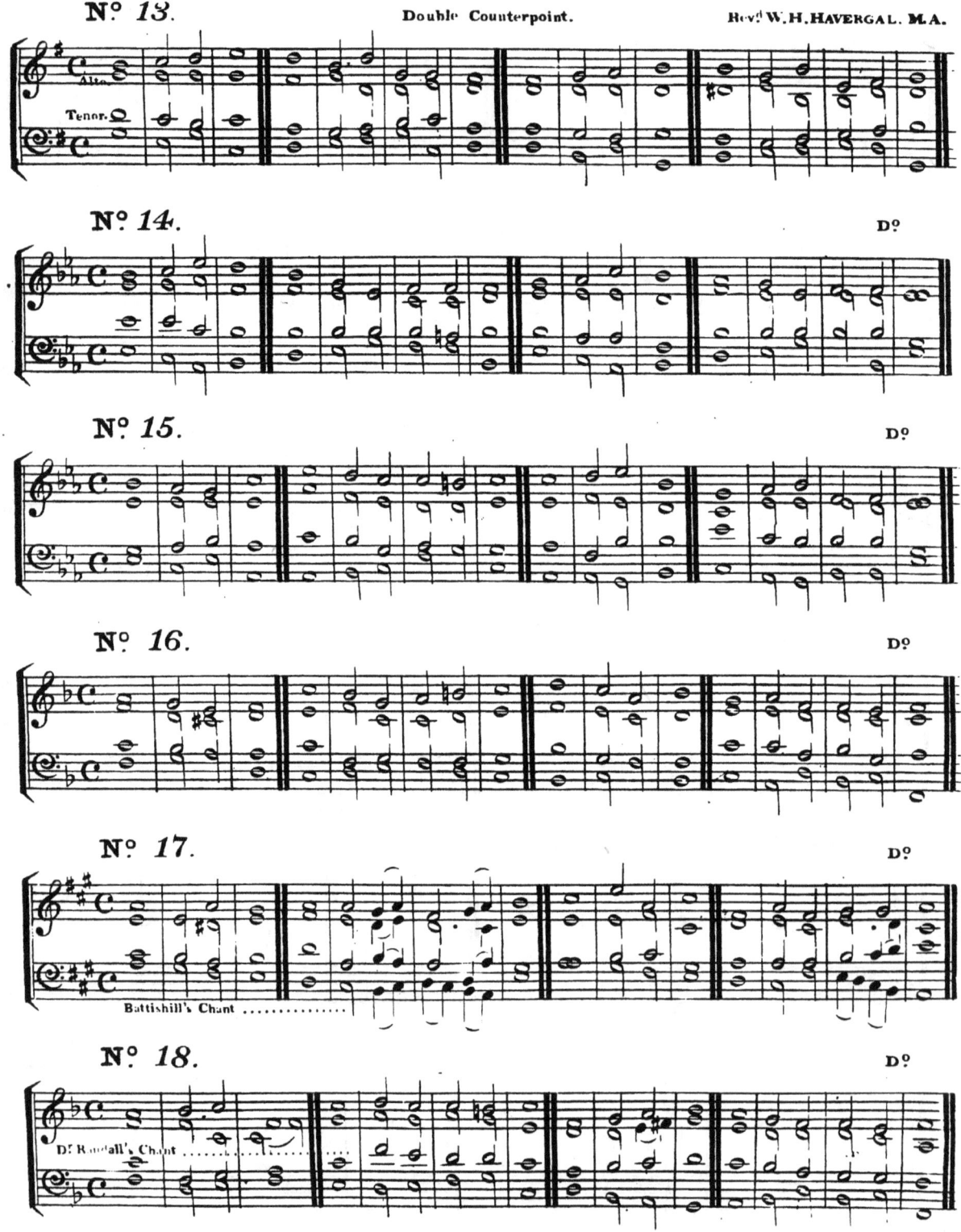

Excerpts from *Lyra Ecclesiastica*   261

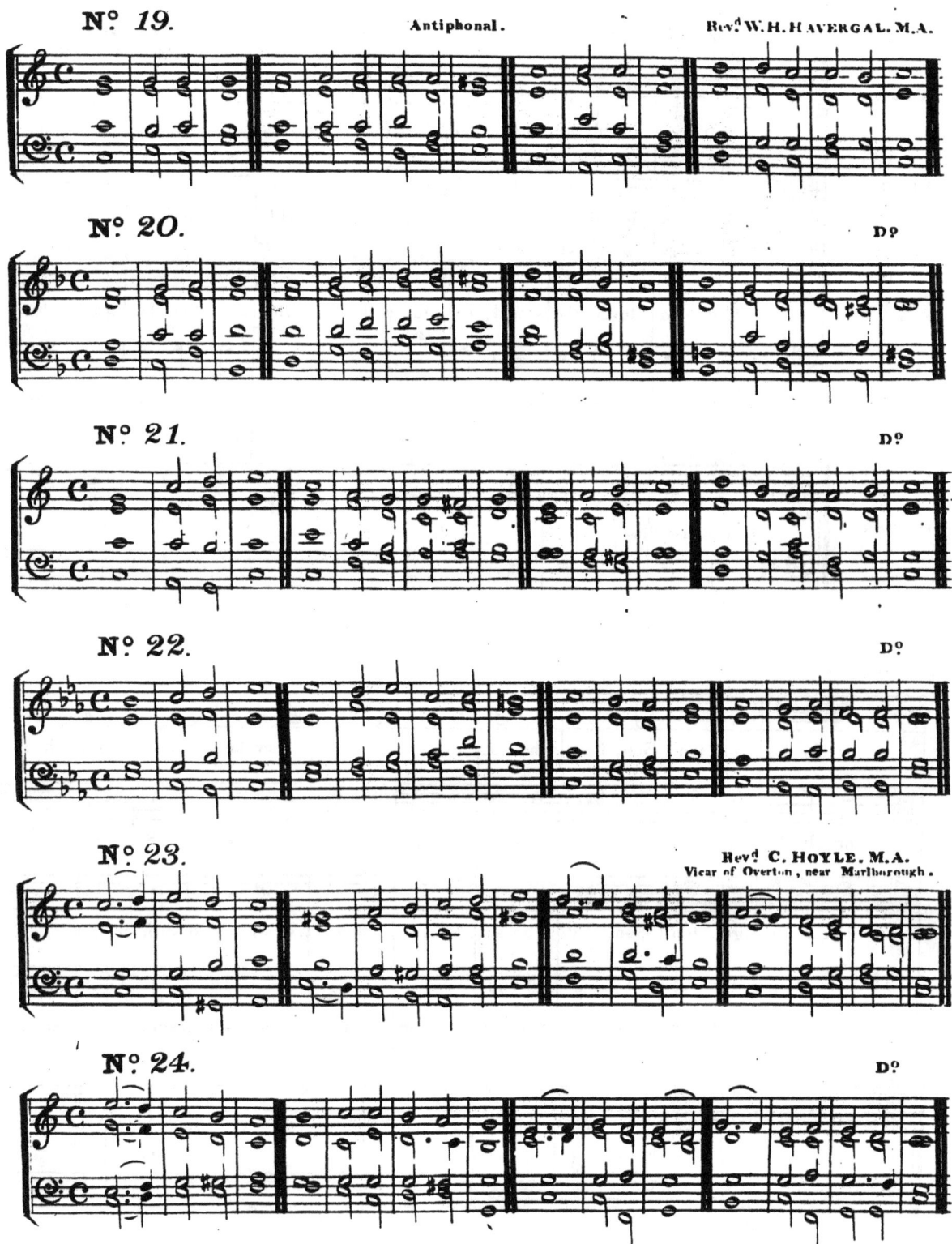

58 Anthem.

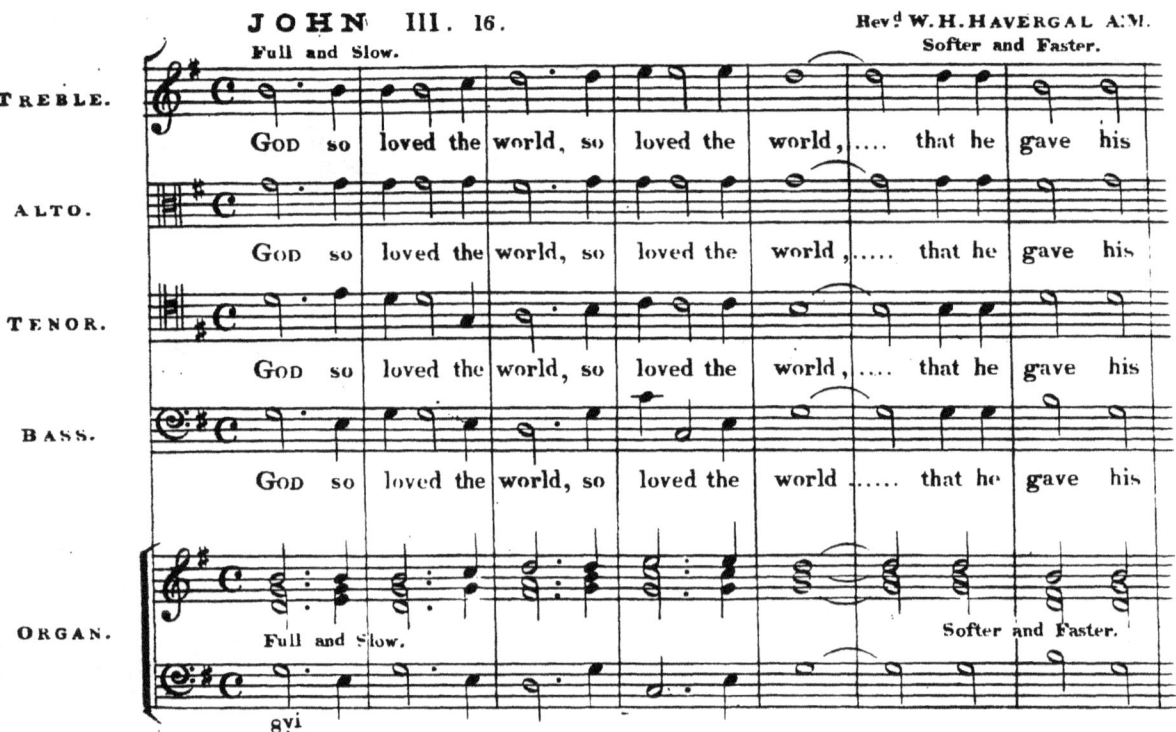

Excerpts from *Lyra Ecclesiastica* 263

59

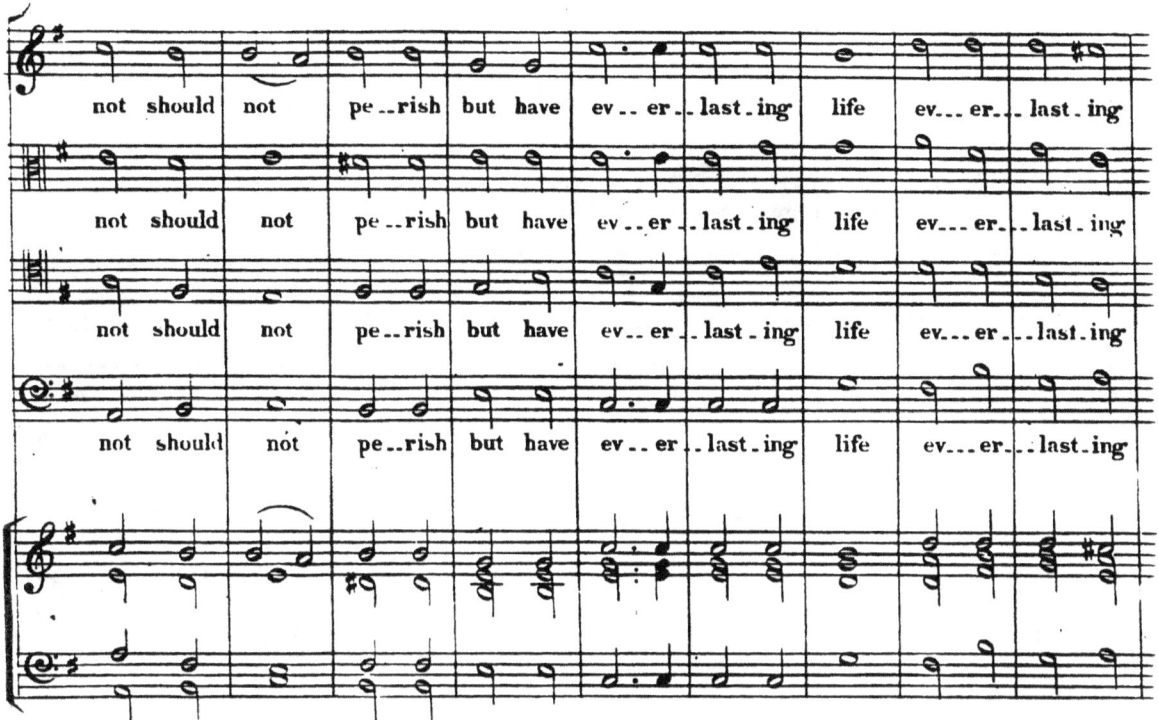

60

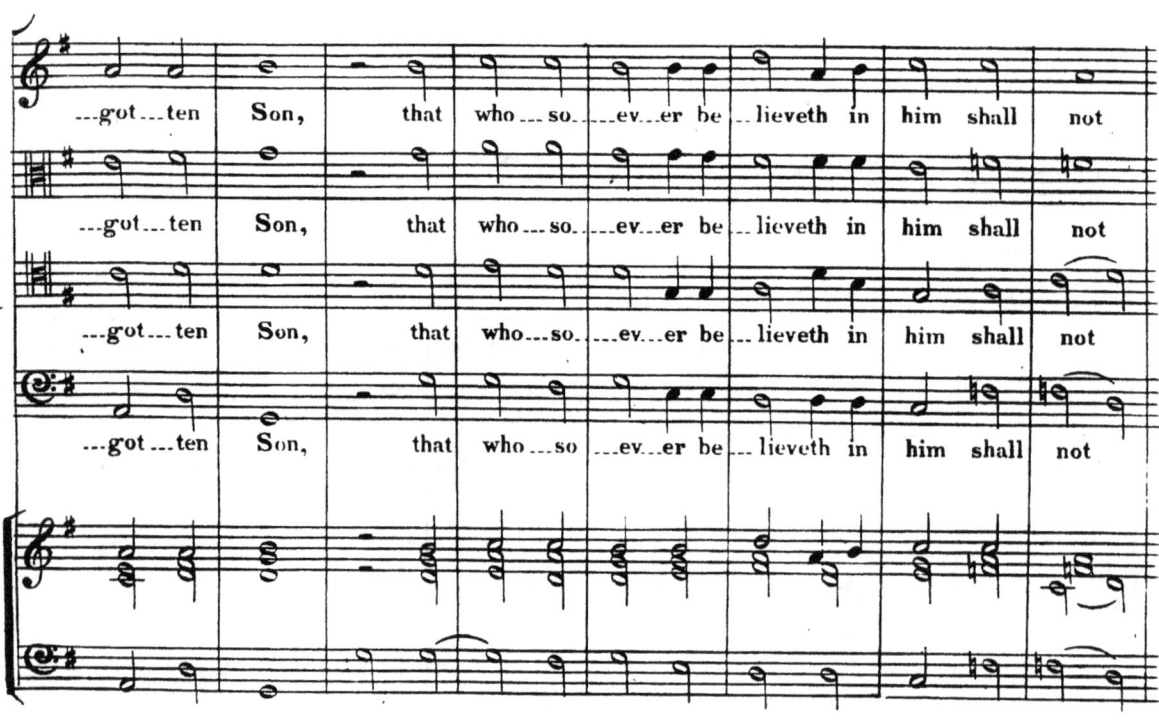

Excerpts from *Lyra Ecclesiastica* 265

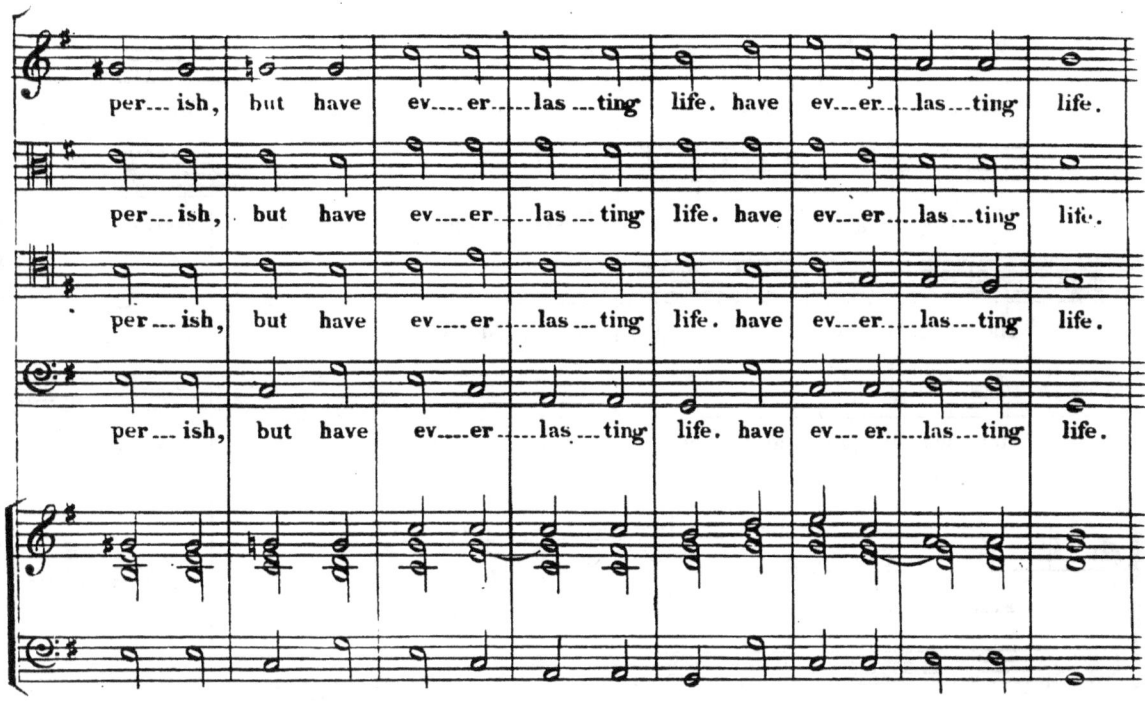

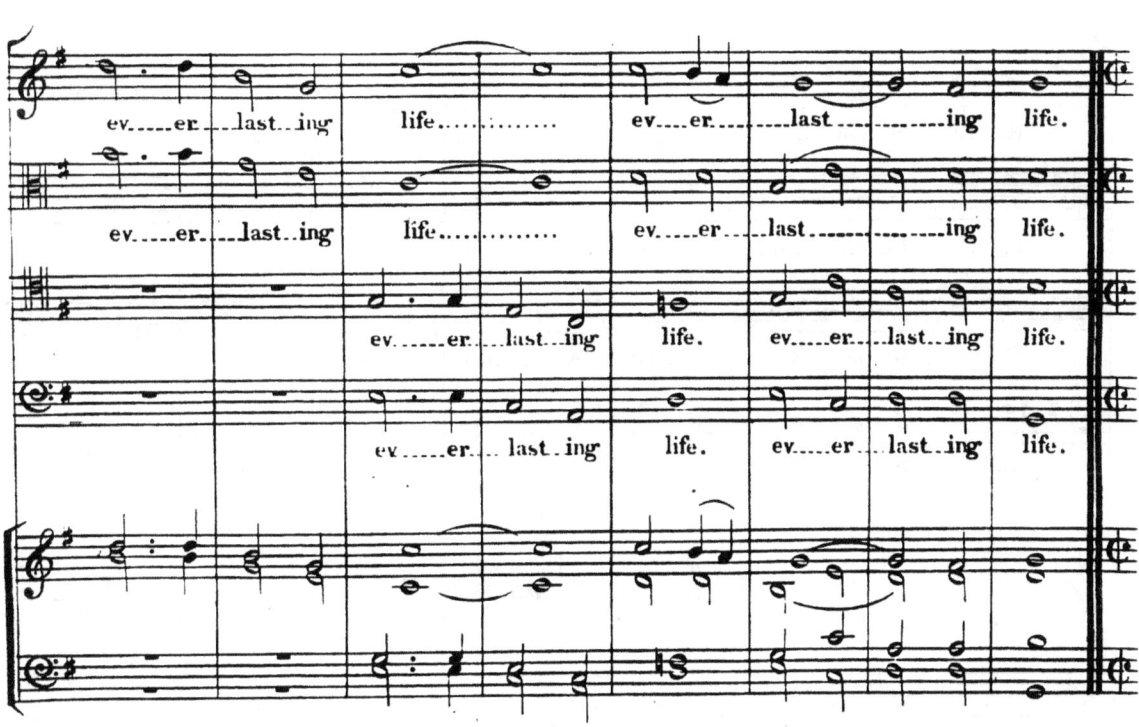

62

Anthem.
PSALM CXXXII. 8. 9. Ver:

Rev.d W. H. HAVERGAL. M.A.

64.

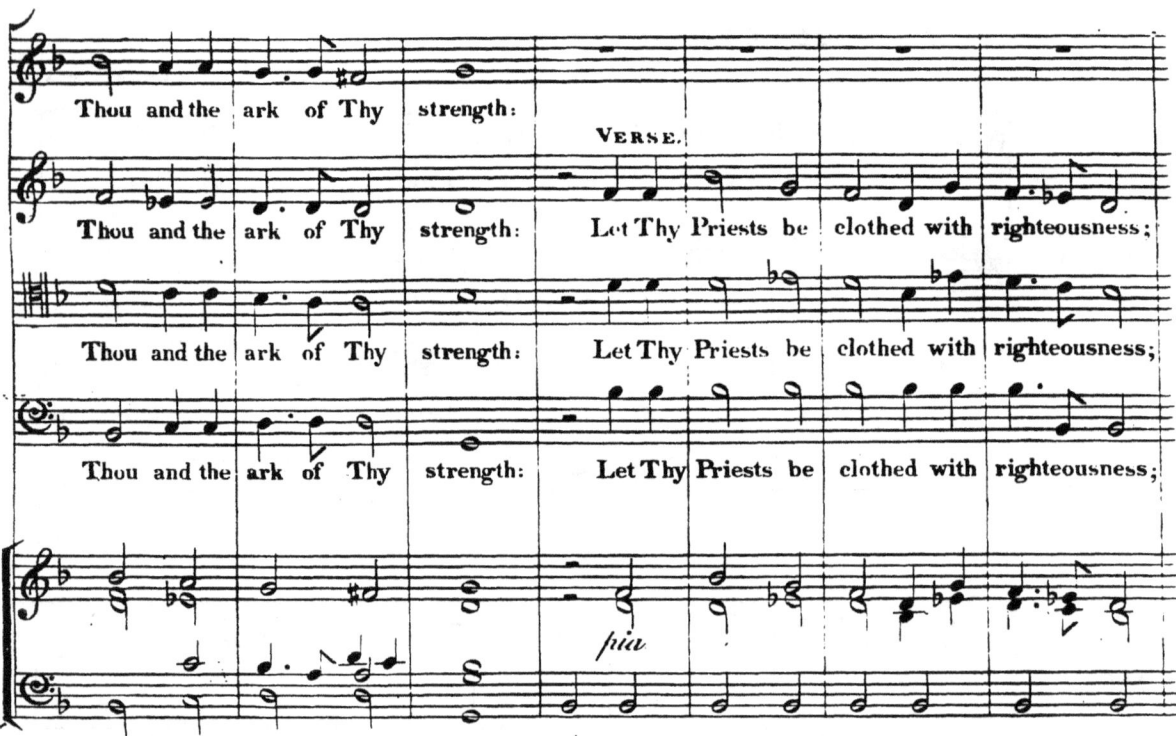

65

Excerpts from *Lyra Ecclesiastica* 271

67

69

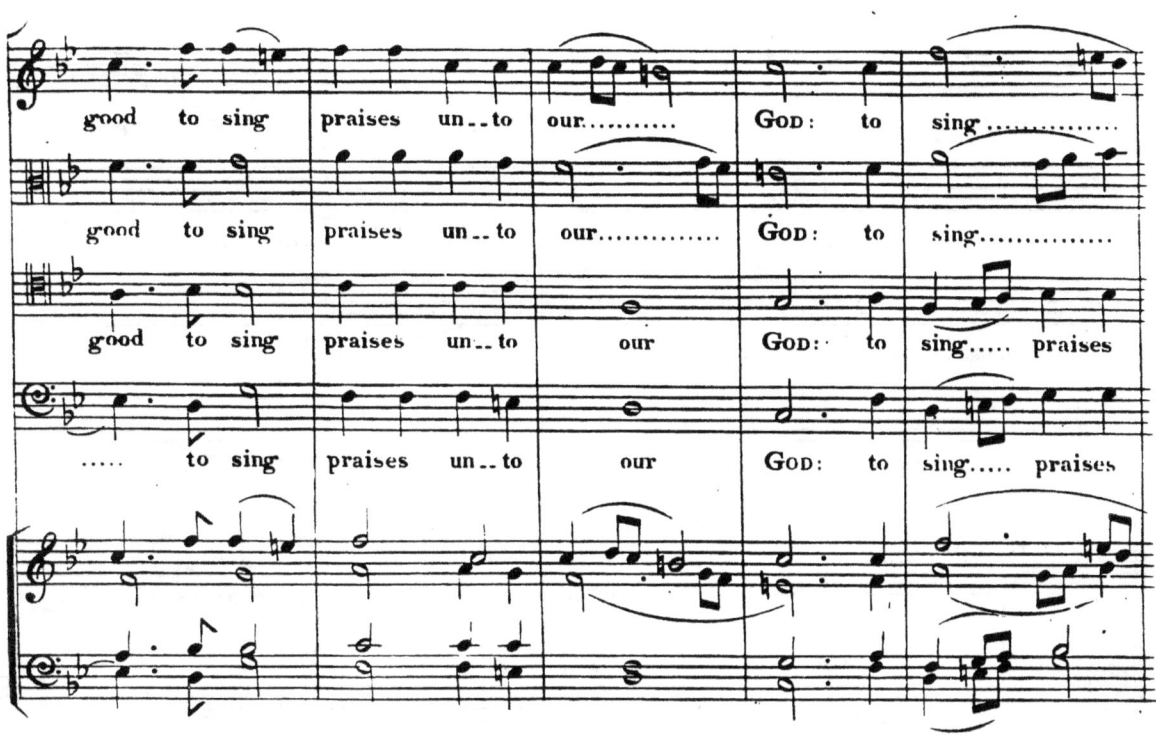
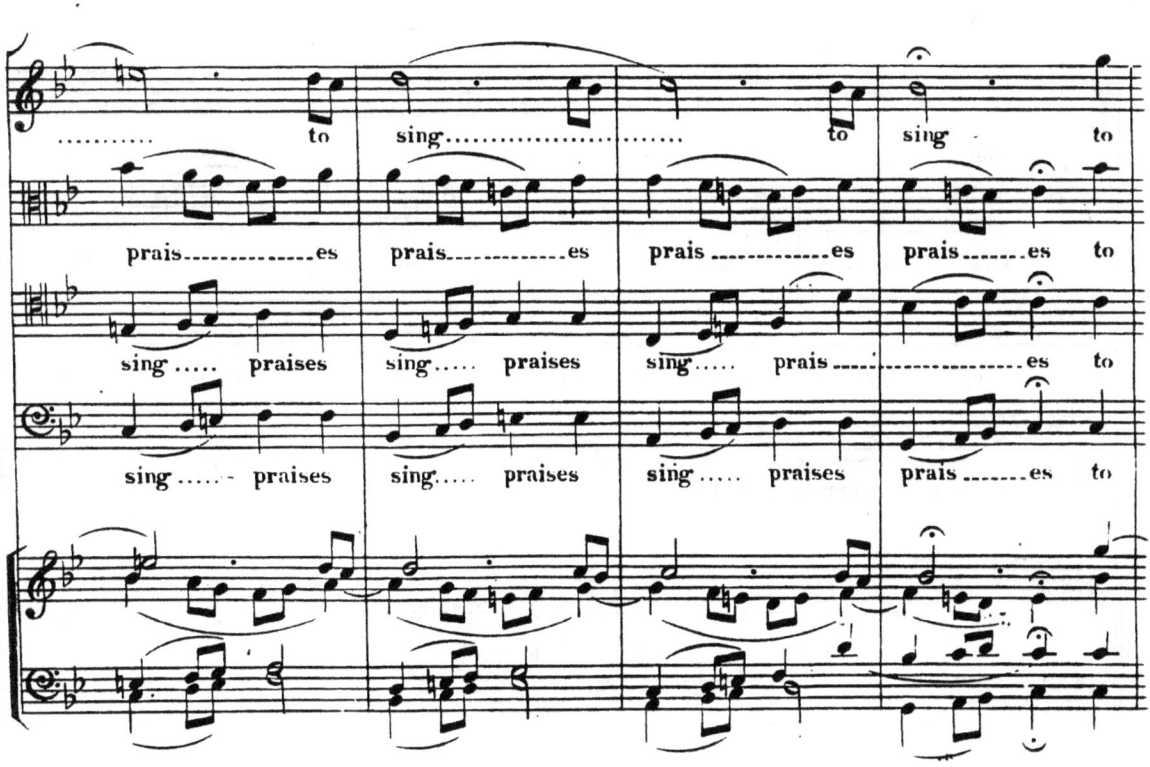

70

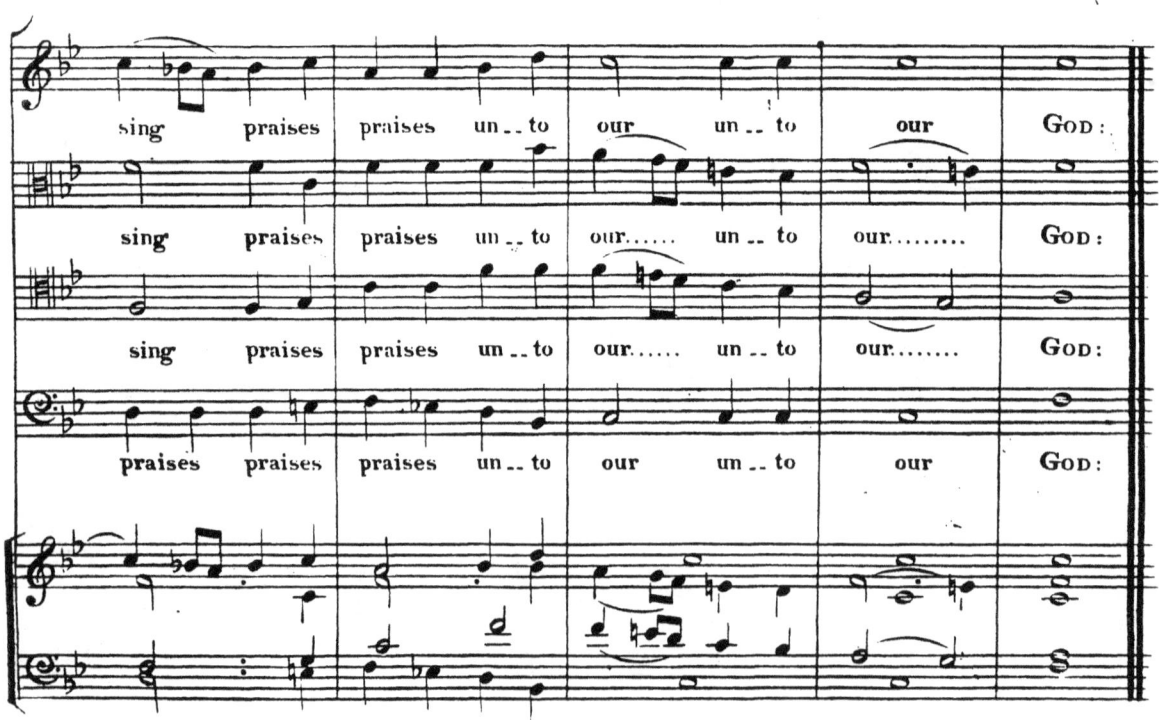

Excerpts from *Lyra Ecclesiastica*   275

71

72

Decalogue Responses.

These are two photographs of Worcester Cathedral. William Henry Havergal was made an Honorary Canon of Worcester Cathedral in 1845, and also Rector of St. Nicholas Church in Worcester. His music was composed to be sung in both large and small churches.

Excerpts from *Lyra Ecclesiastica*   279

134

Solhampton. (Recte et Retro.) L.M. Revd W. H. HAVERGAL, M.A.

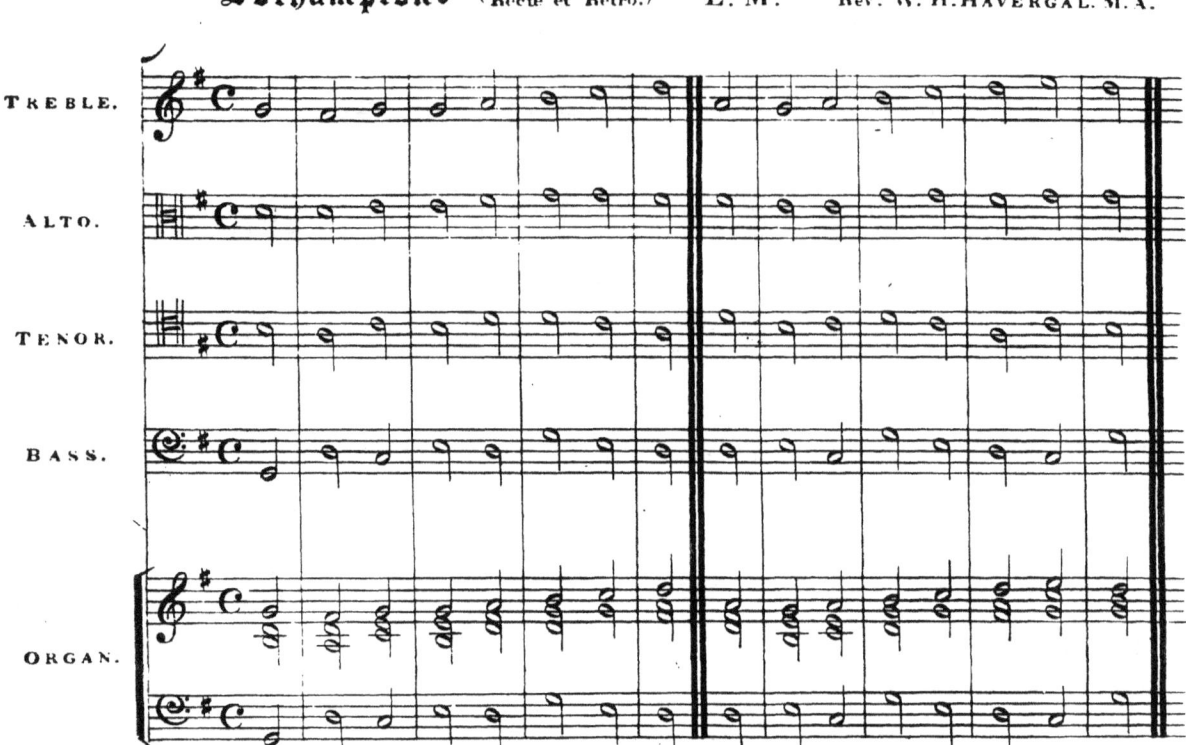

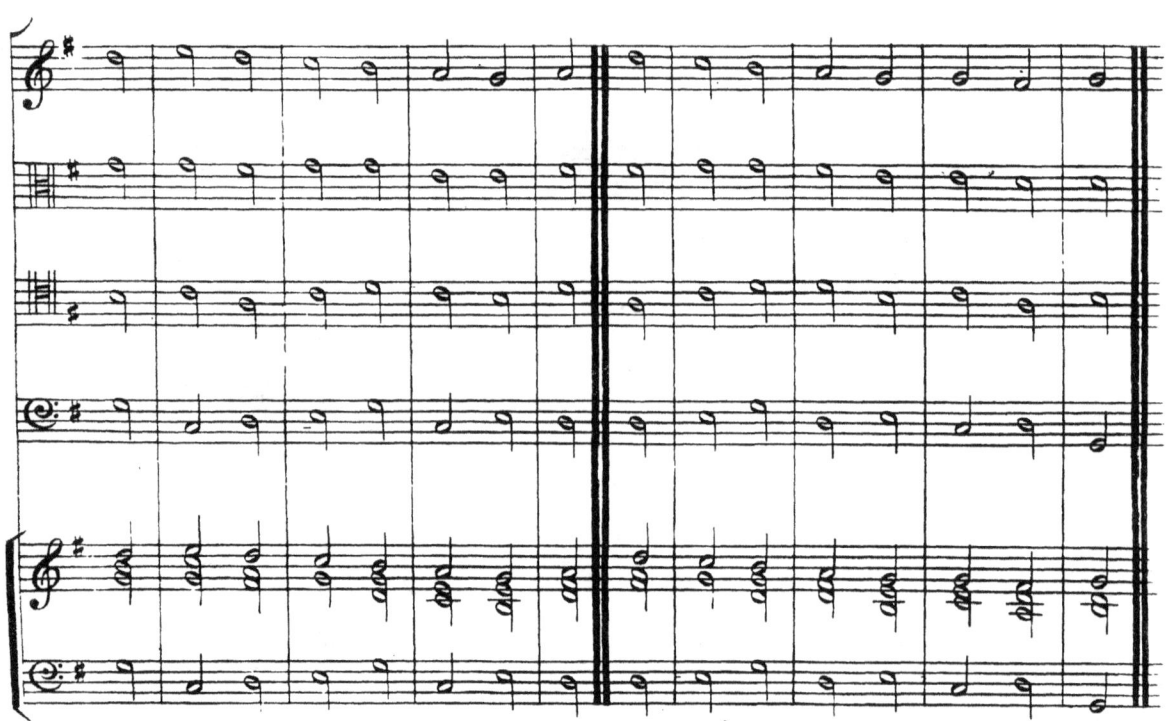

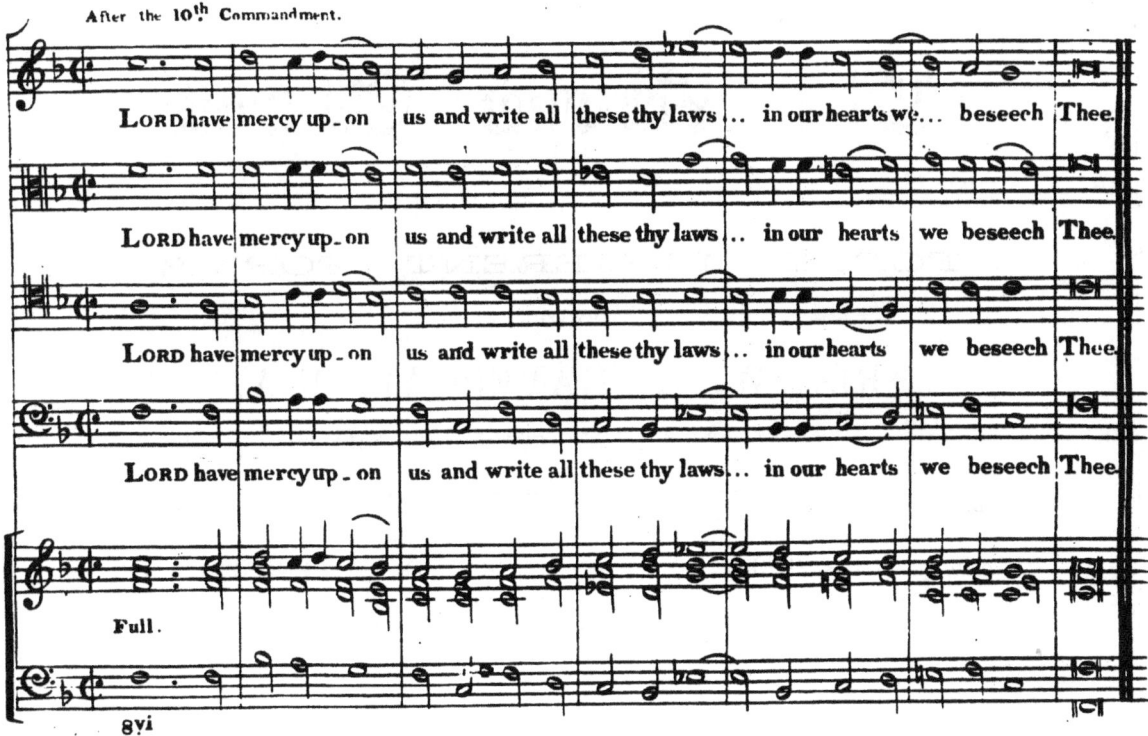

PREFATORY REMARKS.

THE "GRAND CHANT," so called, has generally been ascribed to Pelham Humphreys, first a Chorister, and then the Organist of the Chapel Royal. He died, *"regretted as a masterly genius,"* at the early age of thirty-seven, A.D. 1674.

The Chant was, probably, a juvenile composition, in the time of the celebrated Choirmaster, Captain Cook. The extreme simplicity of its melody, rather than any stateliness of harmony, seems to have gained for it the epithet *"Grand."* The harmony, indeed, as published by Dr. Boyce, is in some parts thin, and in the fifth bar faulty. Still the Chant is nobly simple, and thoroughly Anglican, which *mock* Gregorian Chants never can become. Not many years ago its use was excessive, to the fatigue of choristers and the satiety of hearers. The present method of diversifying the Chant, by using it as a Plain Song, clothed with tuneful harmonies, is no novelty, but an humble imitation of the "cunning custom" of olden times. Certain contra-puntal devices, extant in most of these specimens, selected from a larger number, are not marked, but left to the discernment of those who can appreciate them.

Like most of the Author's compositions, they are the product of invalid or travelling hours. Should they, by their aim at strict harmonic orthodoxy, be received as a quite protest against too common laxity, one hope of the Author will be accomplished. LAUS DEO.

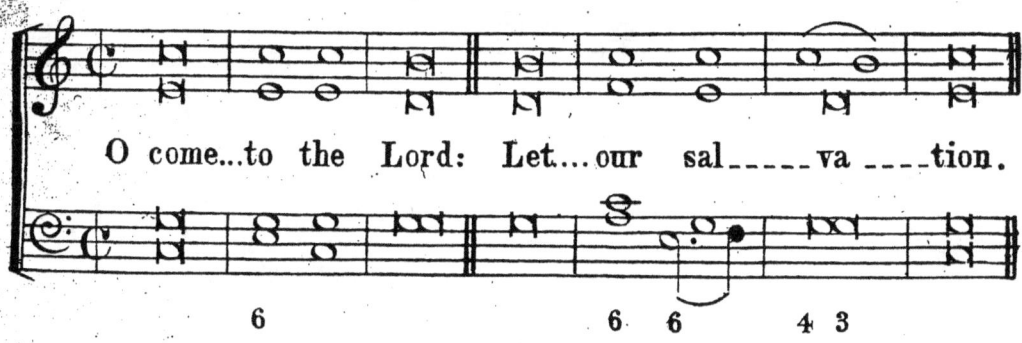

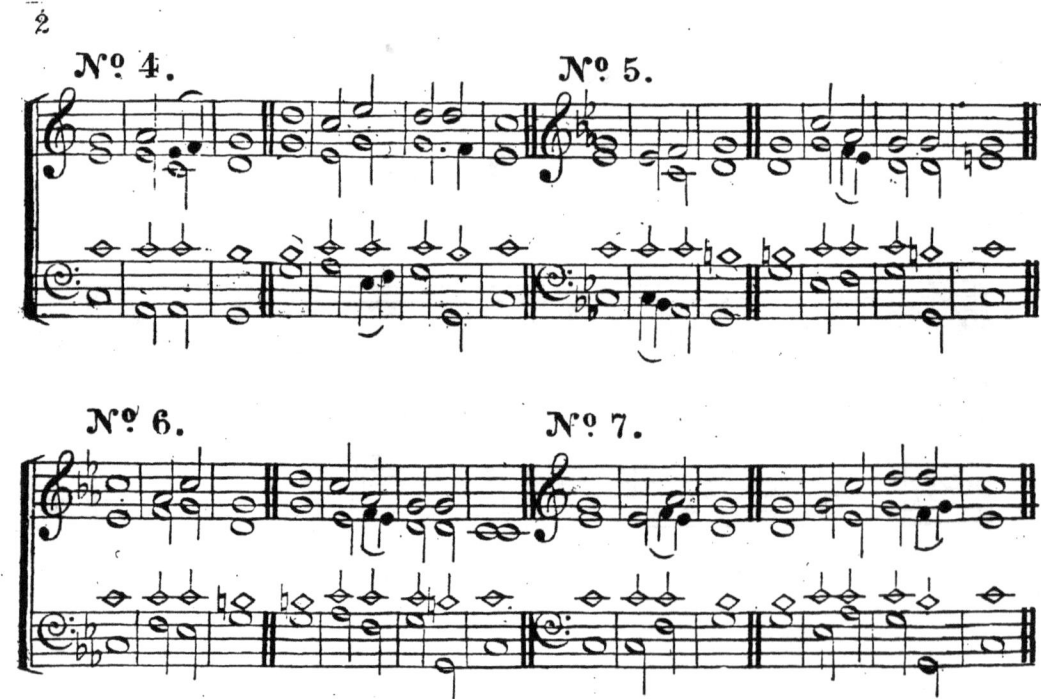

The Grand Chant in Forty Different Forms, Op. 52

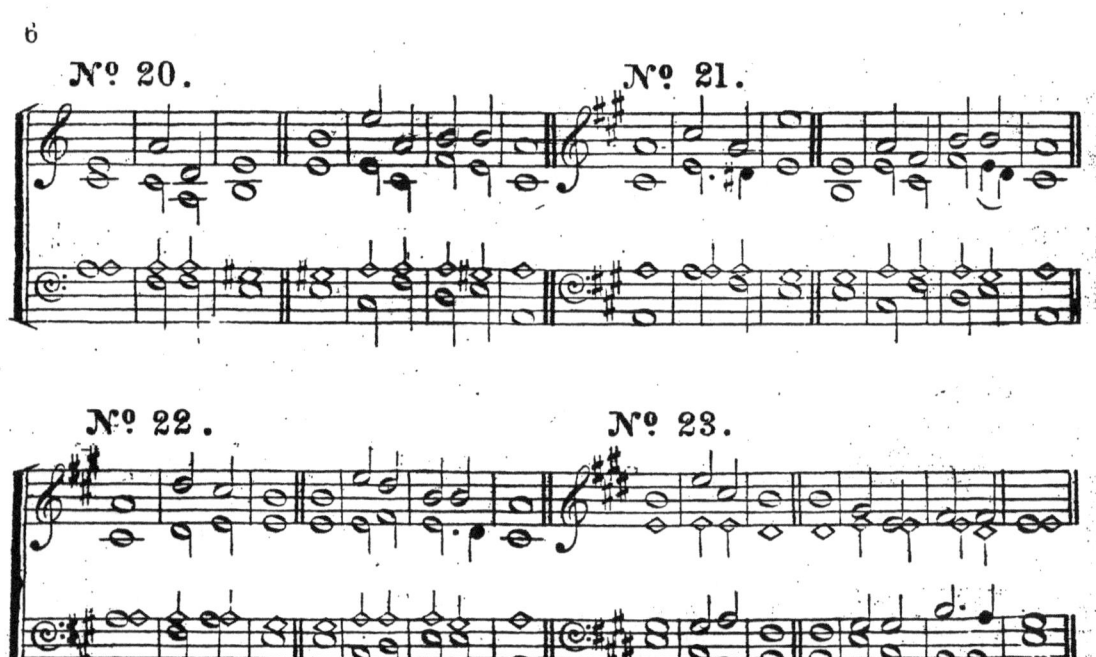

The Grand Chant in Forty Different Forms, Op. 52

N° 40.

ADDITIONAL SPECIMENS.
(More curious than useful)

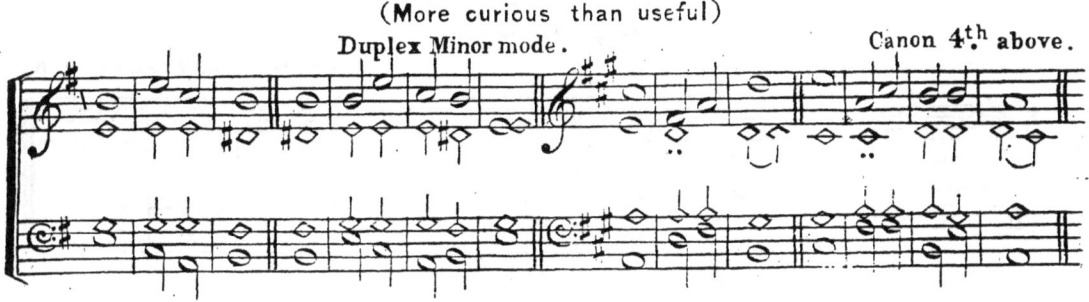

Duplex Minor mode.   Canon 4th above.

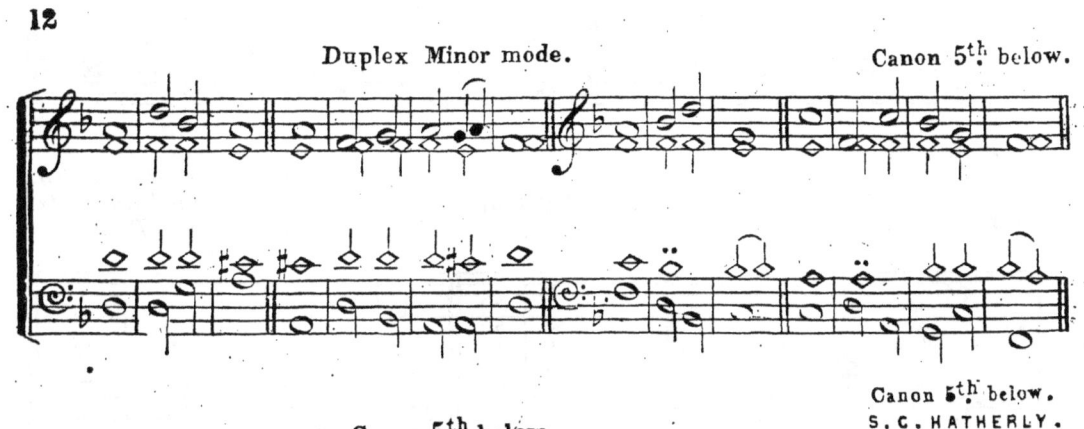

Duplex Minor mode.   Canon 5th below.

Canon 5th below.   Canon 5th below.
S. C. HATHERLY.
Mus: Bac:

This is the end of the book.

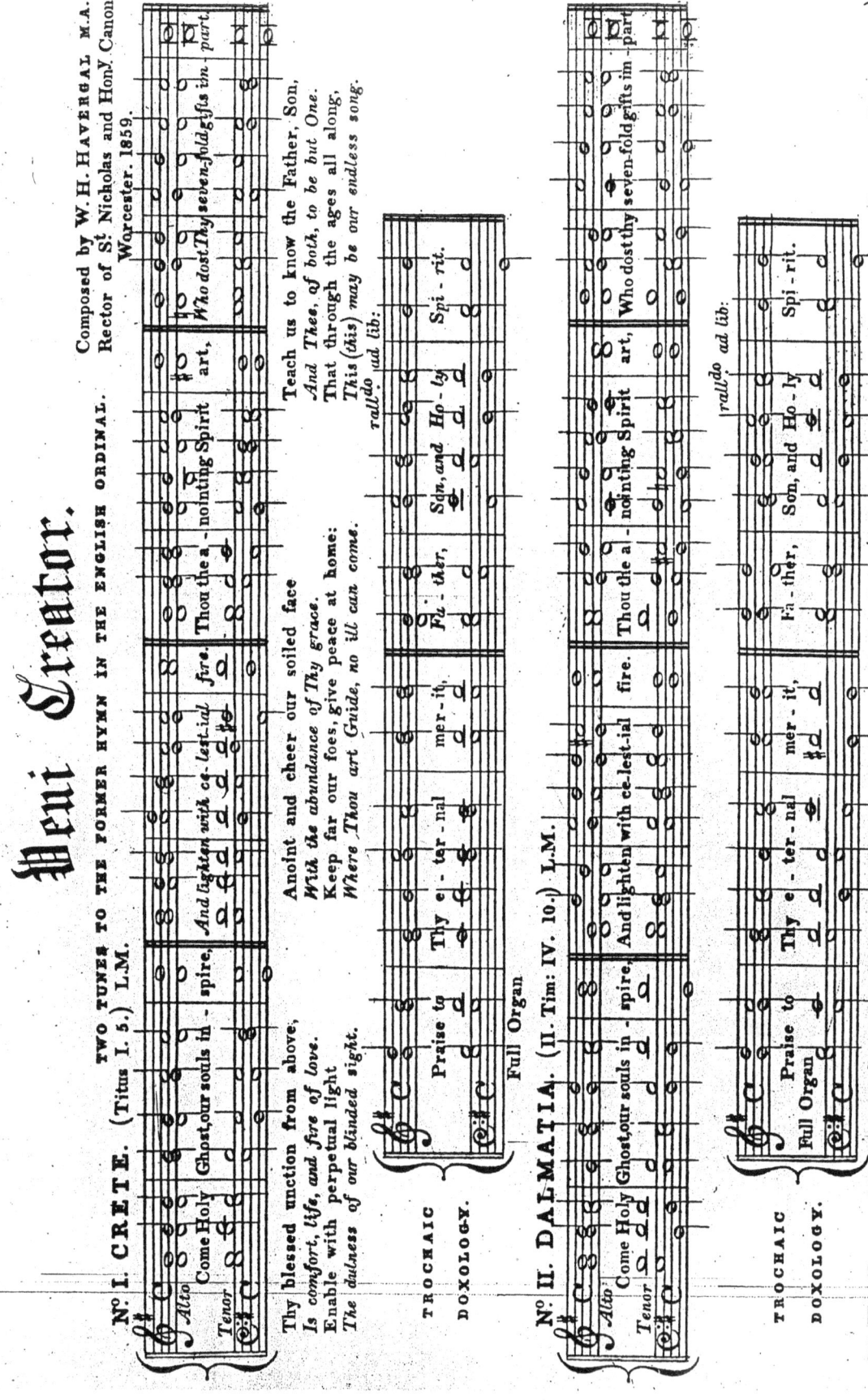

Note: This page and the next three pages (Nos. 209–212) were found among Havergal manuscripts and papers. The book or periodical in which these were published is not known.

APPENDIX.

No. 211.   ZARED.   8 5, 8 5, 7 7 7 5.   Rev. W. H. HAVERGAL.
From his 100 Tunes.

Je-sus from the skies de-scend-ing, Lies a Babe on earth!

Se-raphs o'er the man-ger bend-ing, Hail the won-drous birth!

Lo! the watch-ful shep-herds hear Sounds of joy with ho-ly fear;

Haste to gaze: then, far and near, Spread the ti-dings forth.

* *Had this second line been thus rendered—In milky country blest, the latin of Bernard would have been more literally followed, and a very abnormal mixture of urban characteristics avoided.*

FINIS.

"Non Nobis, Domine" (the first part of Psalm 115:1)

GOD SAVE THE QUEEN!
(IN MEMORIAM, DEC: 14TH 1861.)

Arranged, in the Tonic Minor,
FOR FOUR VOICES.

WORDS AND ARRANGEMENT BY W. H. HAVERGAL, M.A.
Honorary Canon of Worcester,
and Incumbent of Shareshill, Wolverhampton.

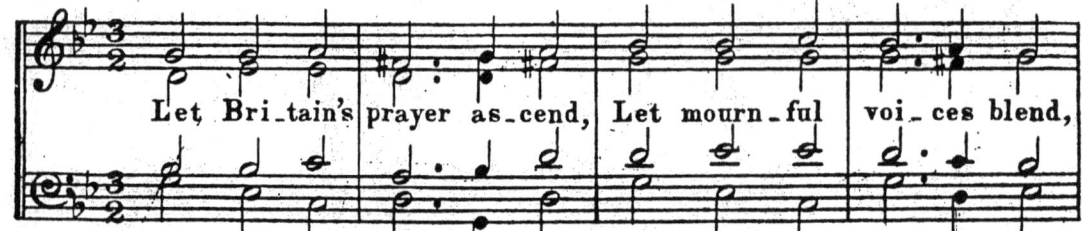

Let Britain's prayer ascend, Let mournful voices blend,

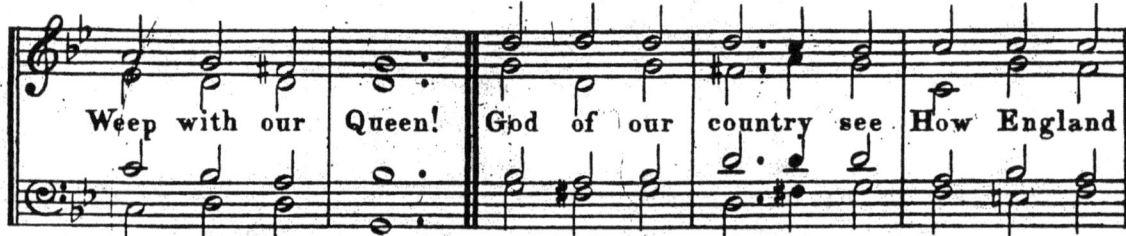

Weep with our Queen! God of our country see How England

bows the knee, How suppliants cry to Thee, God save the Queen!

In sorrow's withering hour,
When droops the smitten flower,
  Be Thy might seen:
God of the bleeding heart,
Heal Thou the bitter smart,
Thy Spirit's grace impart,
  Comfort our Queen!

Chase every cloud away,
Turn all her night to day,
  Bright but serene:
God of the widow, hear,
Dry up her burning tear,
Strong for her help appear;
  God save the Queen!

Lord, let Thy husband-arm
Be her life's heavenly charm,
  Felt, though unseen:
Long as her days extend,
Her home and throne defend,
And give a glorious end;
  God save the Queen!

N.B. The last Verse may be sung in the Major Key, according to its usual form.

God Save the Queen,

Arranged as

SOLO, DUET, AND TRIO,

With

Pianoforte Accompaniment.

Ent. at Sta. Hall

LONDON:
The Music-Publishing Company,
19 PETER'S HILL, ST. PAUL'S.

53—MUSICAL TREASURY.

GOD SAVE THE QUEEN,

ARRANGED AS A SOLO, DUET, TRIO, AND CHORUS.

[When the National Anthem is sung as a Solo only, the Symphony at the end of the Solo should be performed at the end of each succeeding verse.—When it is sung as a Solo and repeated in Chorus, it will be better to omit the Symphony between the Solo and Chorus, and perform it only at the end of the Chorus.—When it is sung precisely as here printed—namely, the first verse as a Solo, the second verse as a Duet, and the third verse as a Trio or Chorus,—the Symphonies must then be performed in the exact situations they already occupy.]

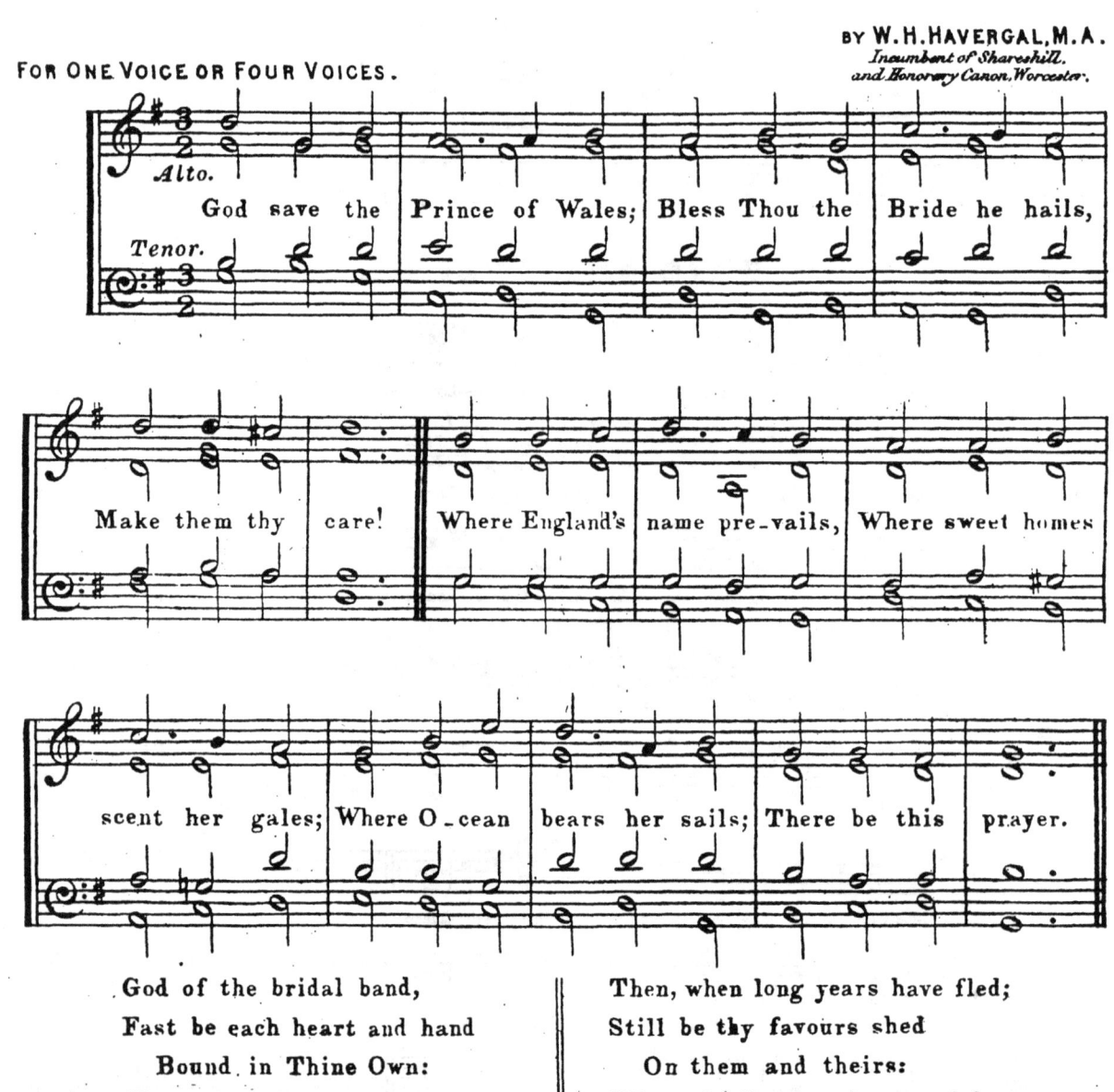

A New National Hymn,

(Especially) for March 10th 1863.

By W. H. Havergal, M.A.
Incumbent of Shareshill,
and Honorary Canon, Worcester.

For One Voice or Four Voices.

God save the Prince of Wales;
Bless Thou the Bride he hails,
Make them thy care!
Where England's name prevails,
Where sweet homes scent her gales;
Where Ocean bears her sails;
There be this prayer.

God of the bridal band,
Fast be each heart and hand
Bound in Thine Own:
Cheer them in sorrow's hour,
Spare them if troubles lower,
Gird them with truth and power
Sent from thy Throne!

Then, when long years have fled;
Still be thy favours shed
On them and theirs:
Where dwells not sin nor sigh,
Where weeps not Widow's eye,
There with our Christ on high,
Be they "joint heirs?"

PROFITS TO LANCASHIRE DISTRESS.

London, J. Shepherd, 98, Newgate Street, E.C.

"FIRESIDE MUSIC."

BY

THE REV. W. H. HAVERGAL, M.A.,

Hon. Canon of Worcester; the Editor of "Old Church Psalmody," &c.

CONTENTS:

I.
HARVEST CHORAL.

II.
THE "FIRESIDE" GOOD NIGHT.

III.
THE FIRST "FIRESIDE" ANNIVERSARY OF CHRISTMAS.

IV.
THE "FIRESIDE" GOOD MORNING.

V.
"FIRESIDE" GRACE BEFORE AND AFTER MEAT.

VI.
THE CHILD'S "FIRESIDE" MORNING HYMN.

VII.
THE "FIRESIDE" HOUR OF SORROW.

VIII.
SPRING-TIDE AND LOYALTY.

IX.
SUMMER-TIDE IS COMING.

X.
CHILDREN'S "FIRESIDE" EVENING HYMN.

XI.
THE PILGRIM'S "FIRESIDE" INVITATION.

XII.
A "FIRESIDE" HYMN OF PRAISE.

XIII.
A "FIRESIDE" INVITATION.

XIV.
A "FIRESIDE" VIEW OF SUNSET.

XV.
A "FIRESIDE" CHRISTMAS CAROL.

XVI.
CHRISTMAS CAROL.

FROM

"OUR OWN FIRESIDE."

LONDON:
WILLIAM MACINTOSH, 24, PATERNOSTER ROW, E.C.,
J. SHEPHERD, WARWICK LANE
AND
ADDISON AND LUCAS, 210, REGENT STREET.

PRICE ONE SHILLING AND SIXPENCE.

HARVEST CHORAL.

7.6.7.6. (Half Canon 5th below.)

WORDS AND MUSIC BY THE REV. W. H. HAVERGAL, A.M.,

Incumbent of Shareshill, and Hon. Canon of Worcester.

Our faithful God hath sent us
  A fruitful harvest-tide;
He summer boons hath lent us,
  And winter wants supplied.

The fields, at His ordaining,
  Stand thick with golden sheaves;
And man, full oft complaining,
  New bounty now receives.

Though Mercy largely giveth,
  Is Justice pacified?
We live through Him who liveth,
  The "Corn of Wheat" that died.

Then full be our thanksgiving,
  And clear each note of joy;
While faith and holy living
  Our earnest thoughts employ.

And, at the last Great Reaping,
  When Christ His sheaves will own,
May we, no longer weeping,
  Be garnered near His throne!

Praise we the Godhead Union,
  The Eternal Three in one:
With them may our communion
  For ever be begun.

THE FIRESIDE GOOD NIGHT.

WORDS AND MUSIC BY THE REV. W. H. HAVERGAL, A.M.,

Incumbent of Shareshill, and Honorary Canon of Worcester.

N.B. When Music for Four Voices is printed, as this is, in Short Score, to save a separate accompaniment, it is expected that persons who are accustomed to play chords with only the right hand, and an octave bass with the left, will acquire the art of transposing the lower chords to the upper part.

THE FIRST "FIRESIDE" ANNIVERSARY OF CHRISTMAS.

WORDS AND MUSIC BY THE REV. W. H. HAVERGAL, M.A.,
Incumbent of Shareshill, and Hon. Canon of Worcester.

2.
'Tis just a year ago, we say,
When night shone out as clear as day,
   And Heaven came down to earth.
How did we fear, how did we gaze,
Surrounded by the sudden blaze,
   And thrilled with sounds of mirth!

3.
Ah! see you not that angel-choir?
And hear you not that mighty lyre
   Which hushed our bleating sheep?
And, oh, that voice of sweetest awe,
Which told us all we after saw;
   Who now would silence keep?

4.
Come, shepherds, come, with prayer and song,
This night to be remembered long,
   Rejoice to celebrate.
With reedy pipe, chant forth who can
To God all glory, love to man,
   nd peace in every gate!

5.
'Tis just a year ago to-night,
From heaven came down the Prince of Light
   Our guilty world to bless:
Let Gentiles now with Israel sing
Our Saviour, Brother, Friend, and King,
   Our promised Righteousness!

"FIRESIDE" GRACE BEFORE AND AFTER MEAT.

WORDS AND MUSIC BY THE REV. W. H. HAVERGAL, M.A.,
Incumbent of Shareshill, and Hon. Canon of Worcester.

BEFORE MEAT.

Canon.—Treble and Tenor, octave below.

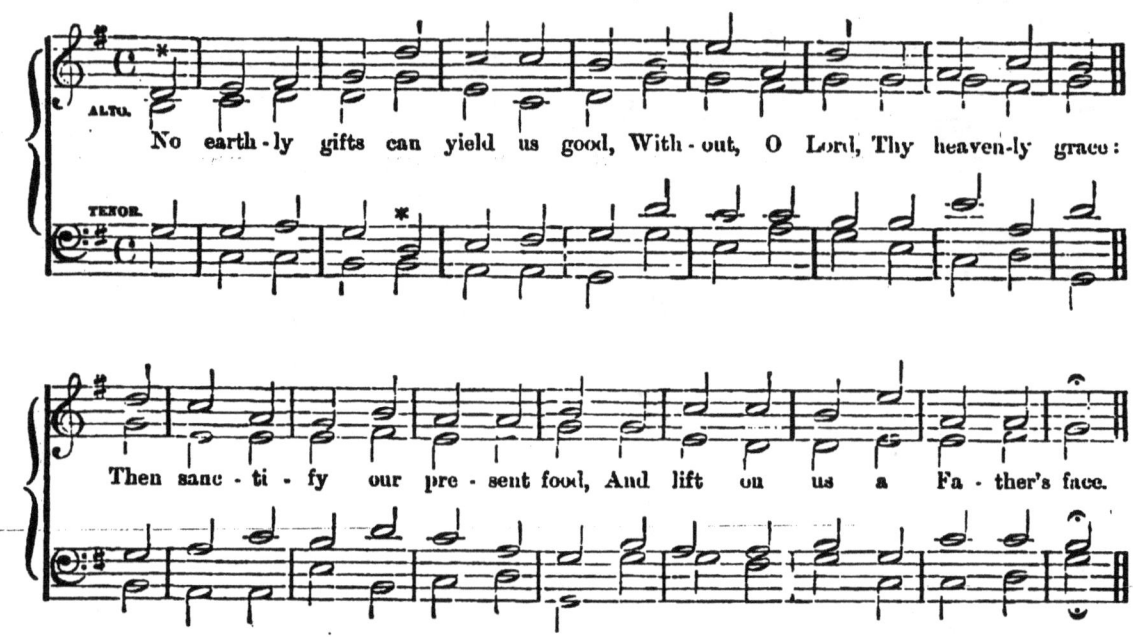

No earth-ly gifts can yield us good, With-out, O Lord, Thy heaven-ly grace:
Then sanc-ti-fy our pre-sent food, And lift on us a Fa-ther's face.

AFTER MEAT.

Canon.—Treble and Alto, fifth below.

All praise to Him who died to give The Bread by which the dy-ing live:
Our praise for all things pure shall be, When face to face Him-self we see.

THE CHILD'S "FIRESIDE" MORNING HYMN.

MUSIC BY REV. W. H. HAVERGAL, M.A.

Incumbent of Shareshill, and Hon. Canon of Worcester.

My Father, I thank Thee for sleep, For quiet and peaceable rest; I thank Thee for stooping to keep Thy little one happy and blest: Oh! how can a poor little creature repay, Thy fatherly kindness by night and by day.

VERSE 2.

My voice would be lisping Thy praise,
  My heart would repay Thee with love;
O teach me to walk in Thy ways,
  And fit me to see Thee above:
For Jesus said, "Let little children come nigh,"
And He will not despise such a young one as I.

VERSE 3.

As long as Thou sees't it right
  That here upon earth I should stay,
I pray Thee to guard me by night,
  And help me to serve Thee by day:
That when all the days of my life shall be past
I may worship Thee better in heaven at last.

Miss JANE TAYLOR.

SPRING-TIDE and LOYALTY.
Two "Fireside" Rounds.

WORDS AND MUSIC BY THE REV. W. H. HAVERGAL, M.A.,
Incumbent of Shareshill, and Hon. Canon of Worcester.

To compose a Round for 12 voices is not an easy task. The one above, as well as the more easy specimen following it, may be sung continuously, as a Sonnet or Ditty, by a single voice. If a Pianoforte be used, the usual dexterity of extemporaneous accompaniment will be required, on the harmonies of F C F in the Bass.

Her Most Gracious Majesty Queen Victoria was born May 24, 1819.

"VERIS AMŒNA DIES."

CHILDREN'S "FIRESIDE" EVENING HYMN.
A DUET.

MUSIC BY REV. W. H. HAVERGAL, M.A.,
Incumbent of Shareshill, and Hon. Canon of Worcester.

Now condescend, Almighty King, To bless this little throng; And kindly listen while we sing, Our pleasant evening song. We come to own the power Divine That watches o'er our days: For this our feeble voices join In hymns of cheerful praise.

2.
Before Thy sacred footstool, see,
  We bend in humble prayer,
A happy little family,
  To ask Thy tender care.
May we in safety sleep to-night,
  From every danger free;
Because the darkness and the light
  Are both alike to Thee.

3.
And when the rising sun displays
  His cheerful beams abroad,
Then shall our morning hymn of praise
  Declare Thy goodness, Lord.
Brothers and sisters, hand in hand,
  Our lips together move:
Then smile upon this little band,
  And join our hearts in love.

MISS JANE TAYLOR.

A "FIRESIDE" HYMN OF PRAISE.

WORDS AND MUSIC BY REV. W. H. HAVERGAL, M.A.,
Incumbent of Shareshill, and Hon. Canon of Worcester.

Praise ye the Lord! in Him rejoice: Pour forth praises like a flood:
He in his love made us his choice, And redeemed us by his blood.
Let all unite to laud his love, Men below and saints above.

2
Praise ye the Lord! whose Shepherd-hand
  Feeds and guards and guides his flock:
By him alone can we withstand
  Sorrow's storm or trouble's shock.
Let all unite to laud His love,
  Men below and saints above.

3.
Praise ye the Lord! our Brother-Friend,
  Seated on his priestly throne:
There, interceding without end,
  He will contrite suppliants own.
Let all unite to laud His love,
  Men below and saints above.

[To be sung at the end of each verse, or only at the last, *ad. lib.*]

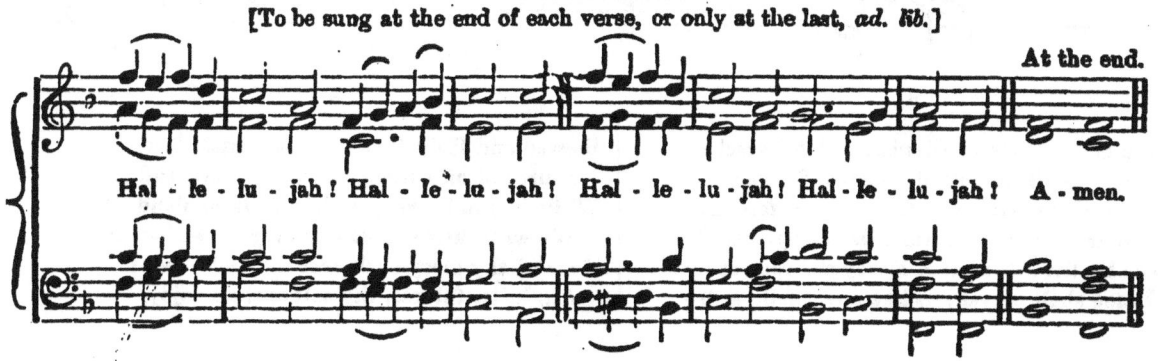

Hal-le-lu-jah! Hal-le-lu-jah! Hal-le-lu-jah! Hal-le-lu-jah! A-men.

A "FIRESIDE" INVITATION.

"That it may please Thee to succour, help, and comfort, all that are in danger, necessity and tribulation."—LITANY.

WORDS AND MUSIC BY REV. W. H. HAVERGAL, M.A.,
Incumbent of Shareshill, and Hon. Canon of Worcester.

Holy and Blessed Redeemer, we pray Thee, Succour and help us, in all time of need. Trusting in Thee and Thy promise, Oh may we always find solace and always succeed. Speak what Thou wilt, we will ever obey Thee; Honor and fear Thee in thought, word and deed.

2.
Thou art Almighty, All-wise, and All-gracious;
　Make us all humble, devoted, and true;
Clad in thine armour no foe will dare face us,
　Danger and trouble will cease to pursue.
Once let the soft arms of Mercy embrace us;
　Peace shall pervade us like sweet falling dew.

3.
Blessed and Holy Redeemer, we laud Thee,
　Source of all succour, help, comfort, and joy:
While in yon heaven bright angels applaud Thee,
　We with their echoes our tongues will employ.
None of thy glory shall ever defraud Thee;
　All, in its fulness, thy saints shall enjoy.

A "FIRESIDE" VIEW OF SUNSET.

A SACRED SONG,

WORDS AND MUSIC BY REV. W. H. HAVERGAL, M.A.,
Incumbent of Shareshill, and Hon. Canon of Worcester.

Smoothly and expressively.

How calm-ly sinks the sun Be-neath the west-ern deep, When day his gi-ant course has run, And storm is hushed to sleep.

So, like the sun would I, In tran-quil eve de-scend, And watch, with soft-ly wa-ning eye, The foot-steps of the end.

3.

But though in darkness set,
The sun seems lost awhile;
He will his shroud shake off, and yet
Arise with joyous smile.

4.

Thus, like the sun, may I
Descend to rise again,
And meet my Saviour in the sky,
With all His glorious train.

A "FIRESIDE" CHRISTMAS CAROL.

WORDS AND MUSIC BY REV. W. H. HAVERGAL, M.A.,

Incumbent of Shareshill, and Hon. Canon of Worcester.

For one or more voices.

How grand and how bright, That wonderful night, When angels to Bethlehem came, They burst forth like fires, They struck their gold lyres, And mingled their sound with the flame.

2.
The shepherds were 'mazed;
The pretty lambs gazed,
At darkness thus turned into light;
No voice was there heard,
From man, beast, or bird,
So sudden and solemn the sight.

3.
And then when the sound
Re-echoed around,
The hills and the dales all awoke;
The moon and the stars
Stopped their fiery cars,
And listened while Gabriel spoke:

4.
"I bring you (said he)
From the glorious Three,
Good tidings to gladden mankind;
The Saviour is born,
But he lies all forlorn
In a manger, as soon you will find."

5.
At mention of this,
(The source of all bliss,)
The angels sang loudly and long;
They soared to the sky,
Beyond mortal eye,
But left us the words of their song.

6.
"All *Glory to God*,"
Who laid by His
To smile on the world through his Son;
And "*Peace* be on earth,"
For this wonderful birth
Most wonderful conquests has won.

7.
And "*Good Will* to man,"
Whose days are a span,
And his thoughts all evil and wrong.
Then pray, Christians, pray;
But let Christmas Day
Have your sweetest and holiest song.

* Revised and re-arranged from the original version in 1827, entitled "The Worcestershire Christmas Carol." See Hone's "Garland of Carols."

A "FIRESIDE" CHRISTMAS CAROL.

WORDS BY REV. THOS. DAVIS, AND MUSIC BY REV. W. H. HAVERGAL, M.A.,
Incumbent of Shareshill, and Hon. Canon of Worcester.

2.
'Tis to open sweet communion
  'Twixt the earth and skies;
'Tis to bind all hearts in union,
  God an infant lies!
Gaze upon that placid brow;
And while ye admiring bow,
Holy love to cherish vow,
  Till all discord dies.

3.
O let ev'ry heart adore Him!
  Peace and love o'erflow;
Anger, hatred, sink before Him,
  To your depths below.
Be no sound beneath the sky;
Be no glance from mortal eye;
Be no thought, no feeling nigh,
  Brethren should not know.

In fcap 8vo, Illustrated, Monthly, price 6d.,

"Our Own Fireside:"

A MAGAZINE OF HOME LITERATURE
FOR THE CHRISTIAN FAMILY.

EDITED BY THE

REV. CHARLES BULLOCK,

RECTOR OF ST. NICHOLAS, WORCESTER.

WORKS BY THE REV. CHARLES BULLOCK,

Rector of St. Nicholas, Worcester; Editor of "Our Own Fireside."

Just published, price Fourpence.

INFANT BAPTISM
AND THE FATHERHOOD OF GOD.

A QUESTION WHICH THE REV. C. H. SPURGEON DECLINES TO ANSWER.

"Do you or do you not deem it right for parents to teach their children to say 'Our'—yea, My—'Father, which art in Heaven?'"

Now ready, a Cheap Edition in limp cloth, 1s. 6d., of

SIN AND ITS CURE;
Or, The Syrian Leper.

Also, in gilt cloth, pp. 280, large Type, price 2s. 6d., a New Edition of

"THE WAY HOME;"
OR,
THE GOSPEL IN THE PARABLE.
AN EARTHLY STORY WITH A HEAVENLY MEANING.

Also, Third Edition, price 1s.,

BIBLE INSPIRATION;
WHAT IT IS, AND WHAT IT IS NOT.

DR. COLENSO'S DIFFICULTIES CONSIDERED, AND OUR LORD'S TESTIMONY ENFORCED.

LONDON: WILLIAM MACINTOSH, 24, PATERNOSTER ROW.

[BENJAMIN PARDON, PRINTER,] [PATERNOSTER ROW, LONDON.

A Christmas Carol.

A "Fireside" Christmas Carol.*

Words and Music by the late Rev. Canon HAVERGAL, M.A., Editor of "Old Church Psalmody," Etc.

[THIS Carol, revised and re-arranged from the original version in 1827, entitled "The Worcestershire Christmas Carol," was contributed to the *Fireside Magazine* by the gifted author more than twenty-five years ago. We re-publish it because we are sure both the words and the tune will make it *the* favourite Christmas Carol wherever it is sung.—*The Editor of the* NEWS.]

For one or more voices.

How grand and how bright, That won-der-ful night, When an-gels to Beth-le-hem came, They burst forth like fires, They struck their gold lyres, And mingled their sound with the flame.

2.
The shepherds were 'mazed;
The pretty lambs gazed,
At darkness thus turned into light;
No voice was there heard,
From man, beast, or bird,
So sudden and solemn the sight.

3.
And then when the sound
Re-echoed around,
The hills and the dales all awoke;
The moon and the stars
Stopped their fiery cars,
And listened while Gabriel spoke:

4.
"I bring you (said he)
From the glorious Three,
Good tidings to gladden mankind;
The Saviour is born,
But he lies all forlorn
In a manger, as soon you will find."

5.
At mention of this,
(The source of all bliss,)
The angels sang loudly and long;
They soared to the sky,
Beyond mortal eye,
But left us the words of their song.

6.
"All *Glory* to God"
Who laid by His rod
To smile on the world through his Son;
And "*Peace* be on earth,"
For this wonderful birth
Most wonderful conquests has won.

7.
And "*Good Will* to man,"
Whose days are a span,
And his thoughts all evil and wrong.
Then pray, Christians, pray;
But let Christmas Day
Have your sweetest and holiest song

---

* An edition of this Carol for Church, School, and Home use—music and words—is now ready. Price, for single copies, ½d.; post free per dozen, 6d.; 100, 2s. 3d.; 250, 5s. If required, the Carol without music can be supplied, 1s. per 100. But orders should be given by the earliest post to ensure supply. Address, Mr. Charles Murray, *Home Words* Office, 7, Paternoster Square, London, E.C.

LONDON: "HOME WORDS" OFFICE, 7, PATERNOSTER SQUARE, E.C.

This Carol was first published in 1826 and was composed for the Children of Astley Sunday School.

← likely annotated in Maria's hand

BOOKS FOR THE HOME.

Now ready. Second thousand. In rich cloth bevelled, with Portrait and Illustrations, price 6s.

RECORDS OF THE LIFE OF THE REV: WM. H. HAVERGAL, M.A.

By his Daughter, JANE MIRIAM CRANE.

"'Yet speaketh!' In the memories of those
To whom he was indeed a living song.'"
Frances Ridley Havergal.

WORKS BY FRANCES RIDLEY HAVERGAL.

Second Thousand, with Portraits, 2s. 6d.

I. **SPECIMEN GLASSES FOR THE KING'S MINSTRELS.**

By the late Frances Ridley Havergal.

II. **ECHOES FROM THE WORD:** for the Christian Year.

| Advent. | Epiphany. | Easter. | Whitsuntide. |
| Christmas. | Lent. | Ascension. | Trinity. |

"Ought to be as popular as 'Keble's Christian Year.'"—*The News.*

Third thousand, leatherette gilt, with illustrations, price 3s. 6d.

III. **MY BIBLE STUDY,** for the Sundays of the Year.

A fac-simile memorial of F. R. H.
*** A printed Edition can now be had for 1s.

Fiftieth thousand, with Illustration, price 1d.

IV. **WAYSIDE CHIMES:** for the Months of the Year.

Sixtieth thousand, with Illustration, 1d.

V. **"HIM WITH WHOM WE HAVE TO DO."**

Written by F. R. H. shortly before her death for the January Number of *The Day of Days.*

MUSIC FOR FESTIVALS, ETC.

By the late FRANCES RIDLEY HAVERGAL.

I. **"O'ER THE PLAINS"**; a Christmas Carol.
Words by the Rev. W. J. VERNON, B.A.

II. **"THE GOOD OLD CHURCH OF ENGLAND."**
Words by the Rev. W. BLAKE ATKINSON.

III. **"GOD BLESS THE BOYS OF ENGLAND."**
Words by the Rev. Dr. MAGUIRE.

Price 3d. each; but quantities supplied at a great reduction on application at the Publishing Office.

LONDON: "HOME WORDS" OFFICE, 7, PATERNOSTER SQUARE, E.C.

This hand-written note on the advertisement page at the end of the published score "A 'Fireside' Christmas Carol" was likely written by Maria V. G. Havergal, though possibly another person wrote this.

THE BETHLEHEM SHEPHERD-BOY'S TALE.

A CHRISTMAS CAROL.

So happy all the day
  Had I been without play;
And such good thoughts had come o'er my mind:
  That I wondered what it meant,
  Or for why it was sent;
As I ne'er had felt aught of the kind.

  And the birds, all day long,
  Had kept trilling their song;
And the sun had gone down, Oh, so red!
  We had folded the sheep,
  And were talking of sle p,
But, somehow, we cared not for bed.

  The stars were all drest
  In their brightest and best;
And the moon shewed a streak of her gold:
  'Twas a glorious night;
  And we thought of the sight
Of which David our Father has told.

  A sound struck our ear,
  Sweet, joyous, and clear,
It seemed like a musical breeze:
  But, ere we could gaze,
  We were all in a blaze,
And found ourselves down on our knees.

  A bright one then said,
  ('Twas like life from the dead)
" Good tidings, good tidings, I bring!
  Messiah's come down;
  In your own little town,
You will find Him a Babe and a King!"

  And then the whole choir,
  Rising higher and higher,
Sang of "glory, sweet peace and good will,"
  And the sheep seemed to dance,
  And the mountains to prance,
And the stars could no longer stand still.

  Then onward we sped,
  To find out the bed
Where the Saviour in lowliness lay:
  Near Bethlehem's Inn,
  (Oh, shame on their sin!)
We found Him 'midst cattle and hay.

  But we saw the blest sight;
  'Twas our Judah's delight;
And Mary and Joseph were there:
  And soon we made known
  To all in the town,
What we heard the good angel declare.

  And now, every day,
  I sing and I pray
To the Babe, who is Saviour and all:
  May His wonderful birth
  Be known through the earth,
And cheer both the great and the small!

W. H. HAVERGAL, M.A.

THE BETHLEHEM SHEPHERD-BOY'S TALE.
A CHRISTMAS CAROL.

For one Voice or Three Voices.
Moderately Fast.

Words & Music by
W.H.F. HAVERGAL, M.A.

So happy all the day, Had I been without.... play; And such good thoughts had come o'er my mind, That I wonder'd what it meant, Or for why it was sent, As I ne'er had felt aught of the kind.

2
. And the Birds all day long,
. Had kept trilling their song;
And the sun had gone down, Oh so red!
. We had folded the sheep,
. And were talking of sleep,
But, somehow, we cared not for bed.

3
. The stars were all drest
. In their brightest and best,
And the moon shewed a streak of her gold;
. 'Twas a glorious night
. And we thought of the sight
Of which DAVID our father has told.

4
. A sound struck our ear,
. Sweet joyous and clear,
It seemed like a musical breeze;
. But ere we could gaze,
. We were all in a blaze,
And found ourselves down on our knees.

5
. A bright one then said,
. ('Twas like life from the dead,)
"Good tidings, good tidings, I bring!
. MESSIAH'S come down,
. In your own little Town,
You will find Him a Babe and a King!"

6
. And then, the whole quire,
. Rising higher and higher,
Sang of "glory, sweet peace and good will;"
. The sheep seemed to dance,
. And the mountains to prance,
And the Stars could no longer stand still.

7
. Then onward we sped,
. To find out the bed,
Where the SAVIOUR in lowliness lay;
. Near Bethlehem's Inn,
. (Oh shame on their sin!)
We found Him 'midst cattle and hay.

8
. But we saw the blest sight,
. ('Twas our Judah's delight,)
And MARY and JOSEPH were there:
. And soon we made known
. To all in the Town,
What we heard the good Angel declare.

9
. And, now, every day,
. I sing and I pray,
To the Babe, who is Saviour of all;
. May His wonderful birth,
. Be known through the earth,
And cheer both the great and the small.

Christmas Carol.

FOR ONE VOICE OR FOUR VOICES.

W. H. HAVERGAL, M.A.
*Honorary Canon of Worcester;
and Incumbent of Shareshill.*

Christians a-wake to joy and praise! Happy, Happy, Happy be our Christmas days: God is the God of truth and love: He hath sent his On-ly Son down from a-bove.

2
Hark how the holy Angels sing!
Blessing, blessing, blessing on the Infant King!
Let us repeat their noble song:
Cherubim and Seraphim the strain prolong:

3
Glory to God, our God on high!
Peace to them on earth, who are condemned to die:
Good-will to all the tribes of men:
Glory, glory, glory sing all heaven! Amen.

PROFITS TO LANCASHIRE DISTRESS.

"Mementote Vinctorum" ("A Musical Inverse Palindrome, Composed for Three Voices")

"MEMENTOTE VINCTORUM."

A Musical Inverse Palindrome, Composed for three Voices,

By the Rev.^D W. H. HAVERGAL, A.M.

The Profits will be given to the West-Bromwich Anti-Slavery Association.

The peculiarity of this Composition consists in its IDENTITY: In whatever manner it be taken, whether backwards or forwards, inverted or direct, it is the SAME. Its effect, however, may be varied by singing it, first, with the Minor third, and then with the Major.

Published (for the Composer) by JOHN SHEPHERD, 98, Newgate Street.

Price 1/3

O Jesu! Salvator! Succurre capti-vis: so-la-re oppressos: Audi nos. Audi nos.
O Jesu! Salvator! Succurre capti-vis; so-la-re oppressos: Audi nos. Audi nos.
O Jesu! Salvator! Succurre capti-vis; so-la-re oppressos: Audi nos. Audi nos.

O Jesu! Salvator! Succure captivis; solare oppressos: Audi nos. Audi nos.
O Jesus! Saviour! Help the captives; comfort the crushed (or pressed): Hear us. Hear us.

O Jesu! Salvator! Succure captivis; solare oppressos: Audi nos. Audi nos.
O Jesus! Saviour! Help the captives; comfort the crushed (or pressed): Hear us. Hear us.

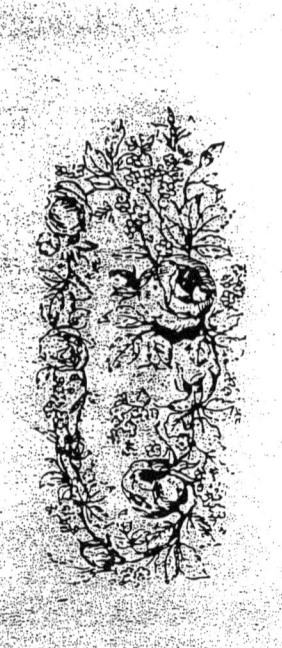

Enigma No. 23.

A MUSICAL 'MULTUM EX PARVO,' OR GAMBOLS[1] WITH THE GAMUT.

I. A LIST[2] OF OLD SONGS.

1. *Canons for Young Ladies.*

'Blooming Virgins,' 🎵 *Athalia.*

'Wise men flattering,' 🎵 *Judas Maccabeus.*

2. *The Schoolmaster's alias the Music Master's Lament.*[3]

But oh, what art can teach 🎵 ?—*Dryden's Ode.*

3. *Cotton's*[4] *subject,*[5] *and Father Matthew's answer.*[6]

What's sweeter than the 🎵 *Joseph.*

Water parted[7] from the 🎵 *Dr. Arne.*

II. A GROUND[8] FOR GRATITUDE IN RHYME.

You may be 🎵 or 🎵

Or very 🎵 in 🎵

You may be 🎵 or 🎵

With aching 🎵

Still you are 🎵

Nor with the 🎵

In earth's deep 🎵[10] yet.

W. H. H.

EDITOR'S SCHOLIA.

[1] The Viol di Gamba was formerly much used in the chapels of German princes.
[2] 'List! alias Listen;' verb. A List subst., that which is listened to, Etymol. Nov.
[3] A plaintive ditty.
[4] A celebrated bee-fancier of Ch. Ch. Oxon.
[5] The theme or text of any movement.
[6] The subordinate or corresponding phrase which follows.
[7] Specimen of 'the wisdom of the ancients' of the eighteenth century. Spring water, alias Rivers, flow from the sea !
[8] A composition of bass notes repeated to a continually varying melody.
[9] The Germans call E♭ h. Hence the celebrated Bach wrote a learned fugue on the letters of his name 🎵
[10] Whether the Author intends this for the Jewish measure of three pints, and thence a grave in which we are measured, or the modern vehicle in which we take a 'nap' while cabbed to our destination, perhaps the next century will be able to define.

Enigma No. 23 (words by W.H.H.)

The very incorrect notation (published in *Life Echoes*, London: James Nisbet & Co., 1883, pages 208–209) was likely a mistake by the music typesetter of this 19th century book. The Germans call B-natural *h*, and the typesetter was mistaken both in his sentence and his score (in the "Editor's Scolia," the item numbered 9). W.H.H. was a brilliant musician, both as a performer and as a composer, and it is hard to think that he would have missed this basic notation (B-flat A C B-natural) clearly, obviously known to so many music scholars.

This double acrostic by William Henry Havergal was published in *Life Echoes* (London: James Nisbet, 1883, page 175). See also page 1051 of Volume I of the Havergal edition. Having room on this page, this double acrostic is copied here with reference to the two palindromes on pages 1837 and 1856–1858 of Volume V of the Havergal edition.

To Miss Caroline Kingscote.

I.

K ind are thy gifts! and welcome as showers

I ⎫
   ⎬ opening spring to the delicate flowers,
N ⎭

G rowing most sweet by thy home's lovely bowers;

S o think my darlings and I.

C ould you but see their hearts in their faces,

O r witness their glee and their artless grimaces,

T would gladden thy spirit when it retraces

E ven days that smiled once and went by.

II.

ver, then, be thy lot simplicity's pleasure,
⎫
⎬ wisdom more dear than miserly treasure;
⎭
ould but the world see its own empty measure,
urely shame would soon tinge its proud cheek.
o, go, worthless world! and curb thy vain spirit
or the lofty in heart, but the lowly inherit
ehovah's best gift, the robe of Christ's merit,
ept for the childlike and meek.

1828.

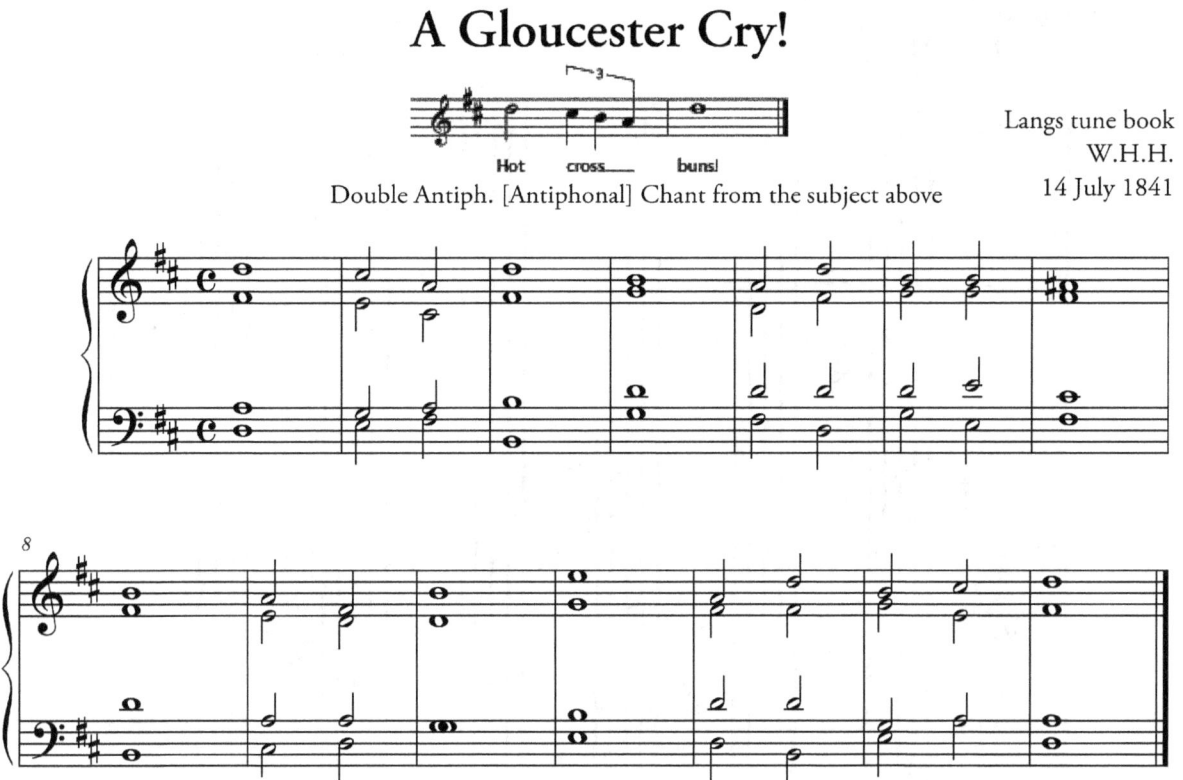

This is a manuscript of W.H.H.'s Double Canon on "A Gloucester Cry!" On the back side of the sheet he apparently gave an address to return this to him: "Please address to the S*t.* Edwards [? illegible] Hall W. Glasgow."

This is reminiscent of a detail in Haydn's last Symphony, though we do not know whether W.H.H. was aware of this. (W.H.H. likely was completely original in his use of this theme, with no awareness of Haydn's adaptation of this.) It is believed that Haydn quoted or adapted a London street song "Hot Cross Buns" in the Finale of his Symphony No. 104, "The London."

We have extant two palindrome scores by William Henry Havergal, on pages 1837 and 1856–1858 of Volume V of the Havergal edition. Palindrome scores are uncommon, very difficult to write well. Johannes Ockeghem in the 15th century wrote a number of them. There are a number of palindromes in Bach's *Musical Offering*. In the 20th century Alban Berg, Béla Bartók, and Igor Stravinsky wrote musical palindromes. Haydn's Symphony No. 47, "The Palindrome," has as its third movement a Menuetto e Trio, a "Minuetto al Roverso," in which the second part of the minuet is the same as the first part, only reversed backwards, and the Trio section is also a palindrome score.

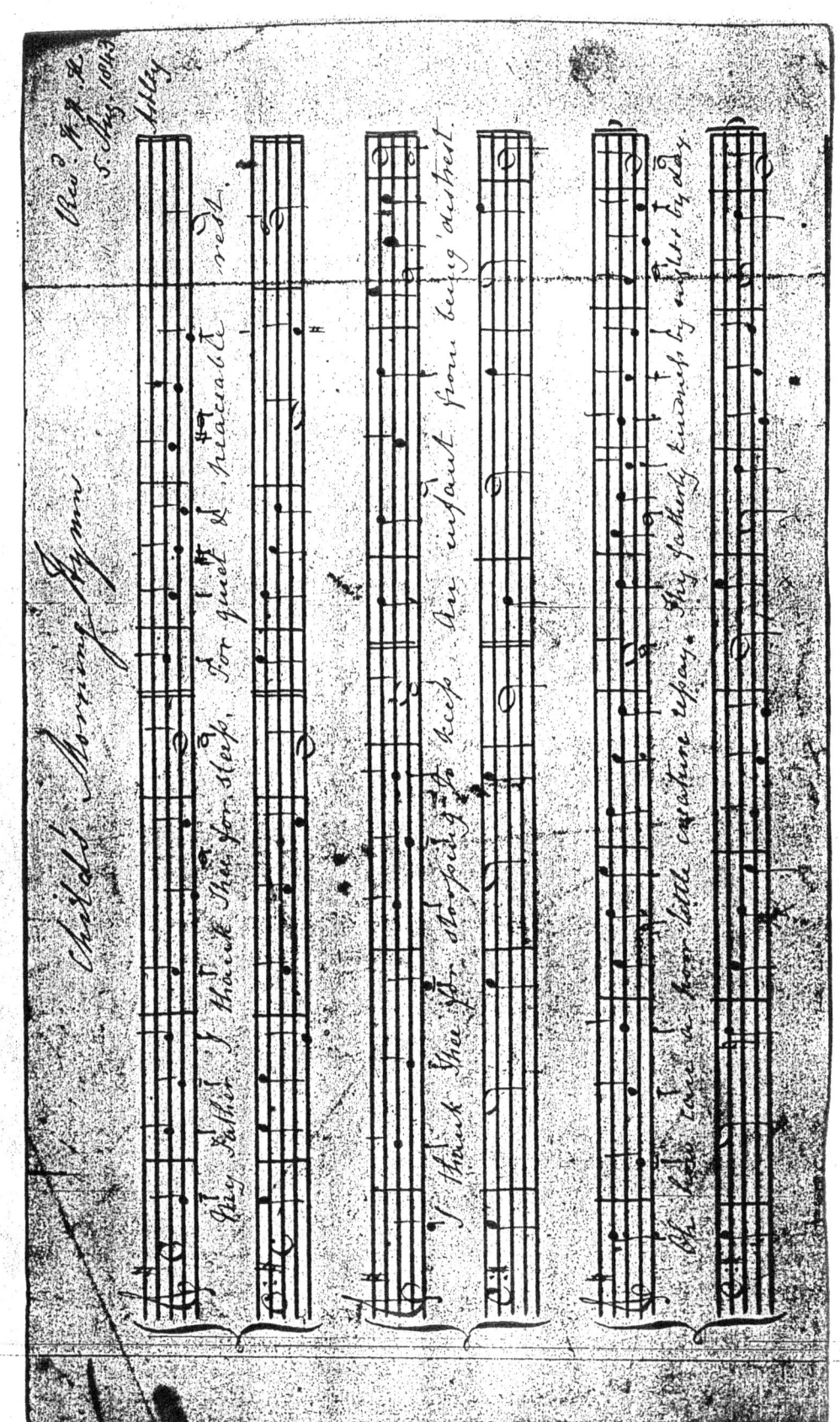

2nd Verse

Thy word doth tell me thou dost love
 my heart would repay Thee with love
O teach me to walk in thy way
 And fit me to see Thee above.

For Jesus said "Let little children come
 And forbid not, for of such is the kingdom of

3rd Verse

So long as thou dost see fit
 That here upon earth I should stay
I pray Thee to guard me by night
 That help me to serve thee by day

That when all the days of my life have been past
 May I meet Thee to praise thee in Christ.

This is another manuscript score by W.H.H. See the published score "The Child's 'Fireside' Morning Hymn" on page 1819 of Volume V of the Havergal edition. Because the words in this manuscript score are slightly different, a newly typeset text of these words is given here.

Child's Morning Hymn

Revd W.H.H.
5. Aug. 1843
Astley

2 Verse

My voice would be lisping Thy praise
   My heart would repay Thee with love.
O teach me to walk in Thy ways
   And fit me to see Thee above.
For Jesus said "Let little children come nigh ["]
And He will not despise such an infant as I.

3rd Verse

As long as Thou seest it right
   That here upon earth I should stay
I pray Thee to guard me by night
   And help me to serve Thee by day [.]
That when all the days of my life ~~have~~ shall ~~been~~ be past
I may worship Thee better in heaven at last.

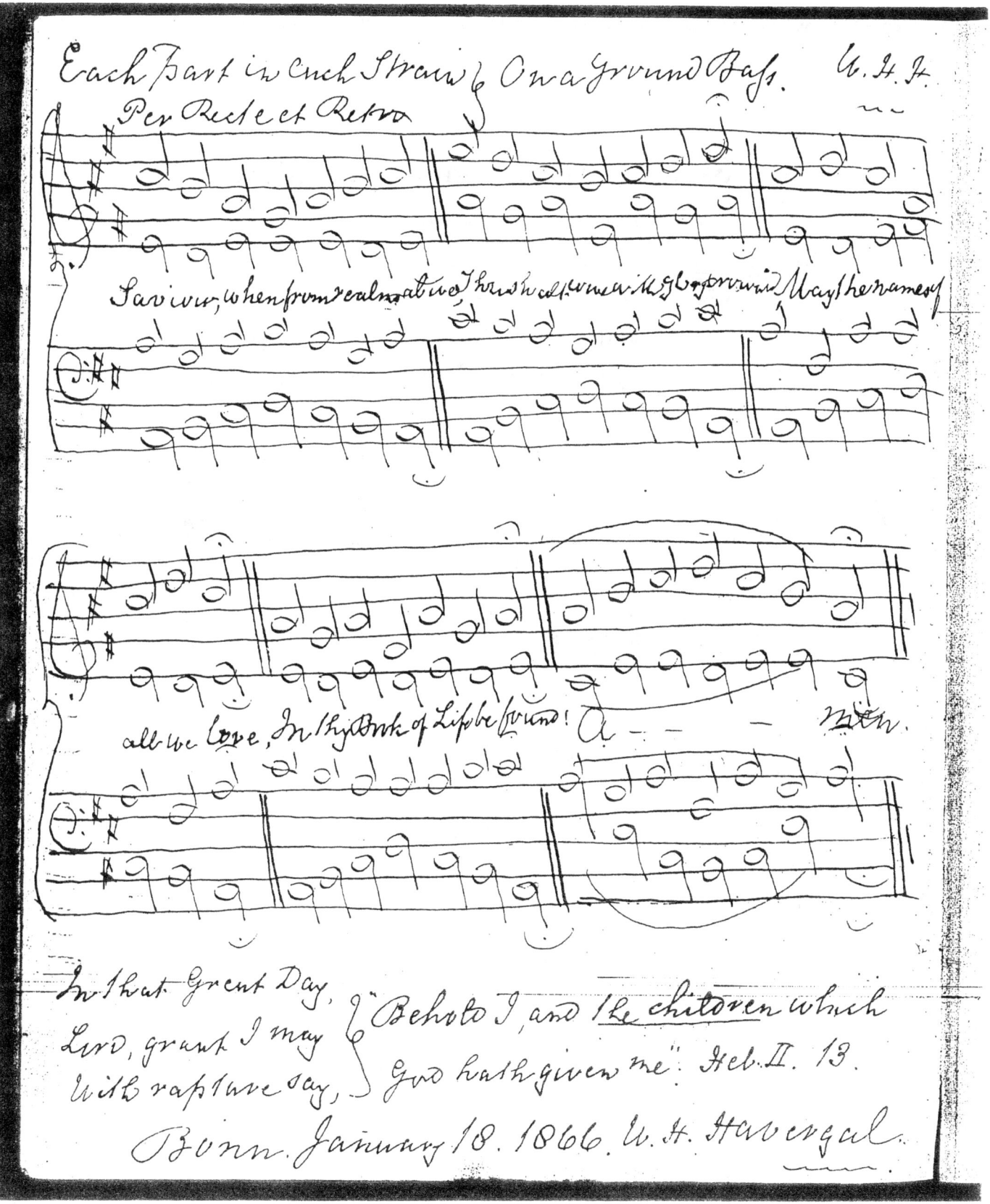

William Henry Havergal wrote this score at the end of F.R.H.'s autograph album in the 1860's.

Saviour, when from realms above

In that Great Day,
Lord, grant, I may } "Behold I, and the children which God hath given me.
With rapture say, } Hebrews 2:13.

Bonn, January 18, 1866. W. H. Havergal

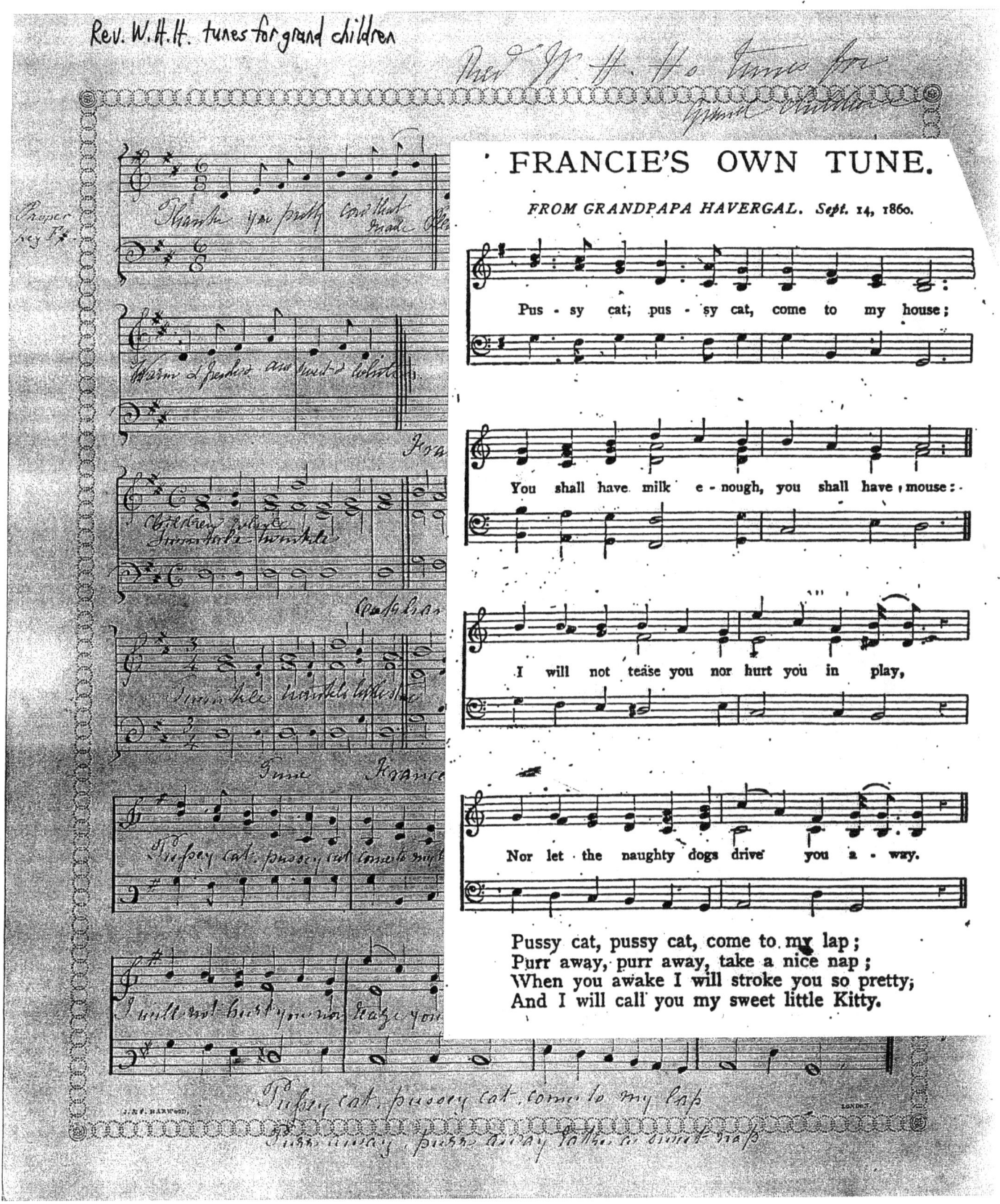

This printed score by W.H.H. was published in the fine volume *Ben Brightboots and Other True Stories, Hymns, and Music* (London: James Nisbet & Co., 1882), original book page 51, page 344 of Volume III of the Havergal edition.

Revd W.H.H. tunes for grand children

Thank you pret-ty cow that made pleasant milk to soak my bread

Ev-ery day & ev-ery night Warm & fresh and sweet & white.

Frank's tune written for him when a baby W.H.H.

Oakhampton Tune written for E.C.C. C.S.C. & J.H.C. W.H.H.

Tune Frances. Written for her at Shareshill 1861 by W.H.H.

Pus-sey cat, pussey cat come to my house. You shall have milk enough. You shall have mouse

I will not hurt you nor tease you in play, Nor shall the naughty dog drive you a-way.

Pussey cat, pussey cat, come to my lap
Purr away, purr away take a sweet nap.

These two manuscript music scores were written by William Henry Havergal on the front and back of a long piece of paper, very likely or almost certainly both the words and music by W.H.H. Both were written for his granddaughter, Frances Anna Shaw (1856–1948, the first child of Ellen Prestage Havergal Shaw, and the niece and goddaughter of Frances Ridley Havergal). Almost surely written for Francie when she was <u>very</u> young, she would have sung the second song to her brothers, William Henry Shaw (1858–1932) and Alfred Havergal Shaw (1859–1939).

Hark my mothers voice I hear Sweet that voice is to my ear
Ever soft it seems to tell Francie dear I love thee well—(begin again Hark my mothers voice

2 Didst not thou in hours of pain
　Lull this head to ease again
　With the music of thy voice
　Bid my little heart rejoice
　Hark my mothers voice I hear etc.

3 Ever gentle ever meek [mild?]
　Didst thou nurse thy little child
　Taught your [?] Francie's feet the road
　Leading on to heaven & God
　Hark my mothers voice etc.
　　　　　For Francie to sing.

Note: In an extra space below the first score (below "Hark my mother's voice I hear"), W.H.H. had started the words of his "The Worcestershire Christmas Carol," the words later crossed out and never finished: "How grand and how bright That wonderful night When angels to Bethlehem came." The words and music for this Christmas hymn are found on page 1832 of Volume V of the Havergal edition.

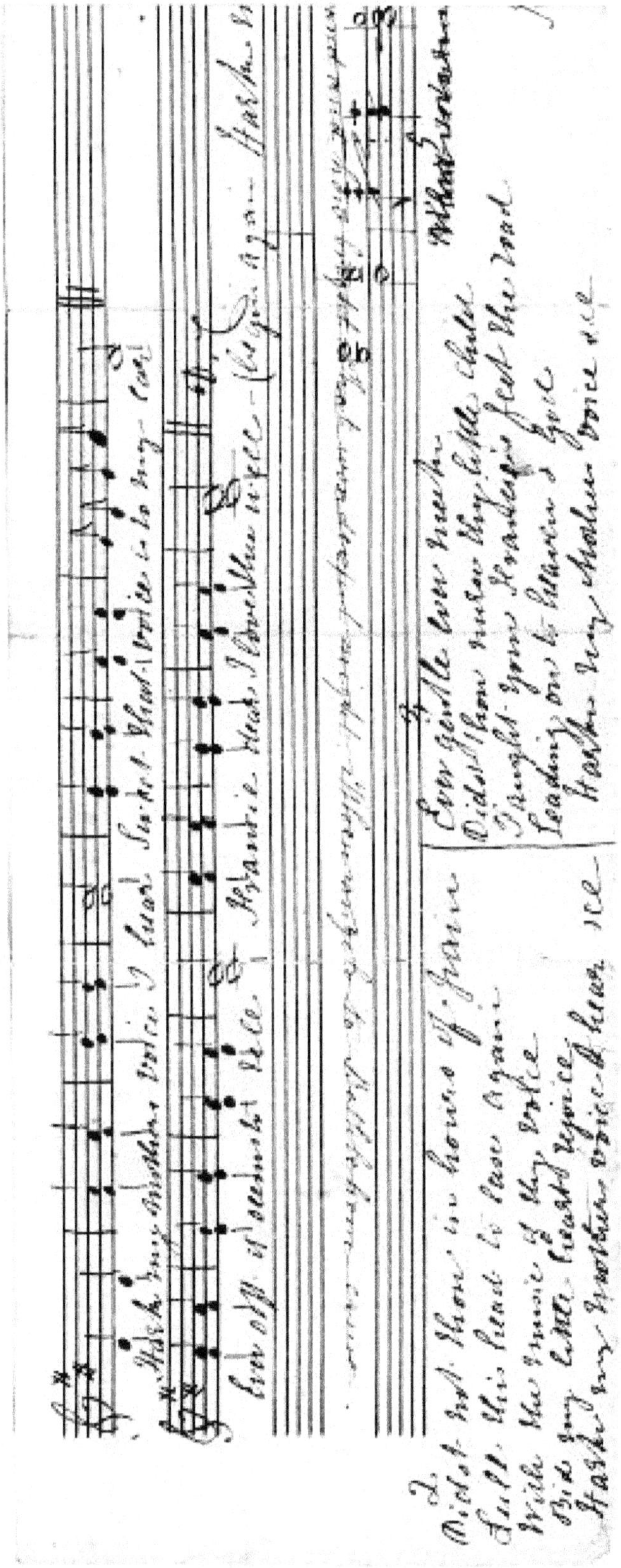

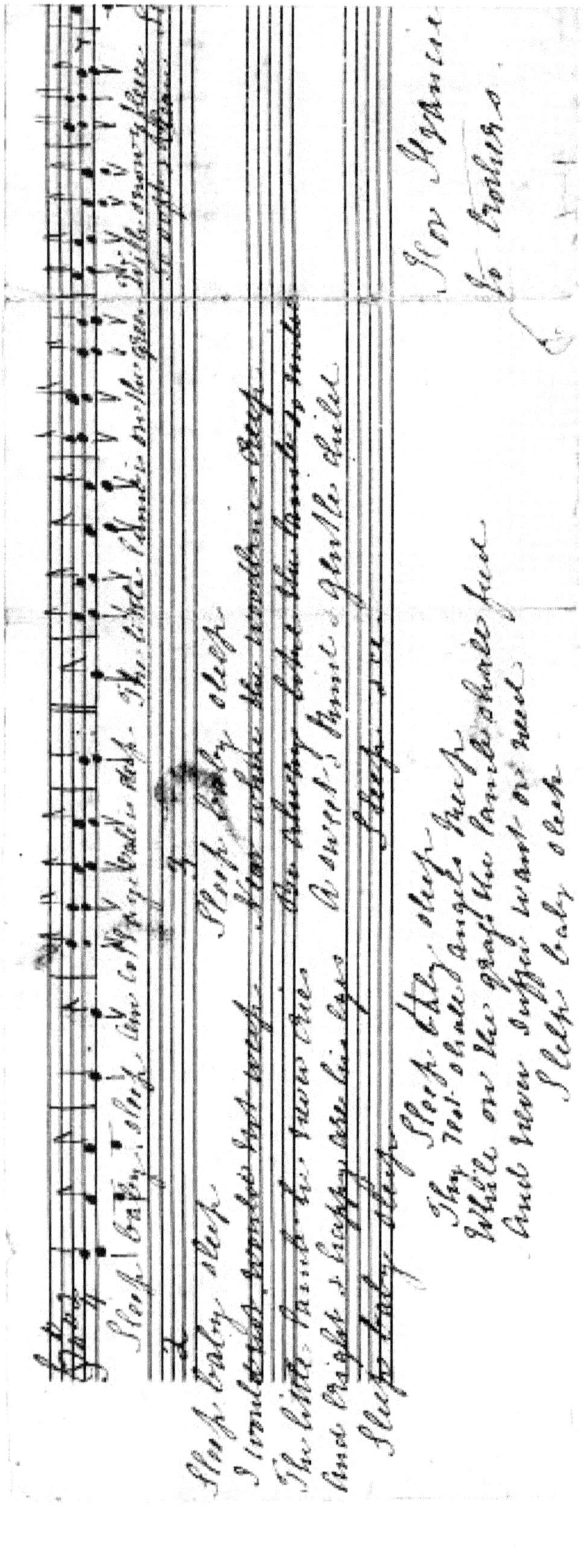

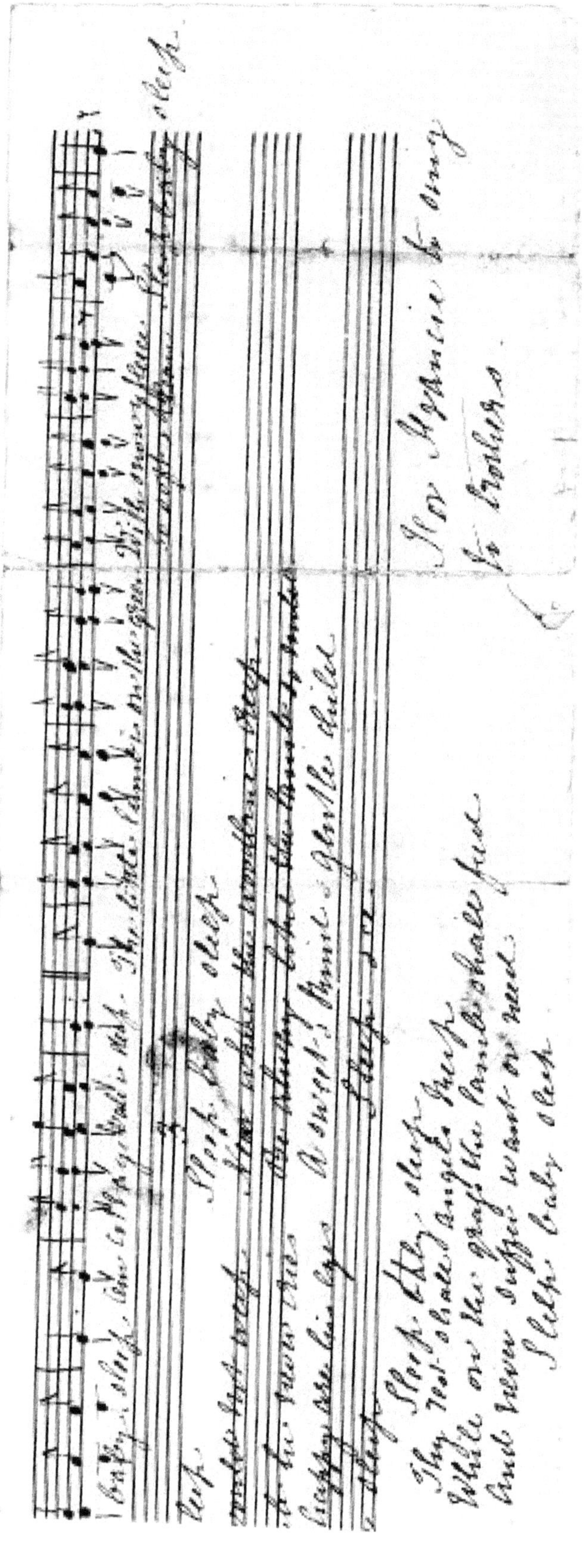

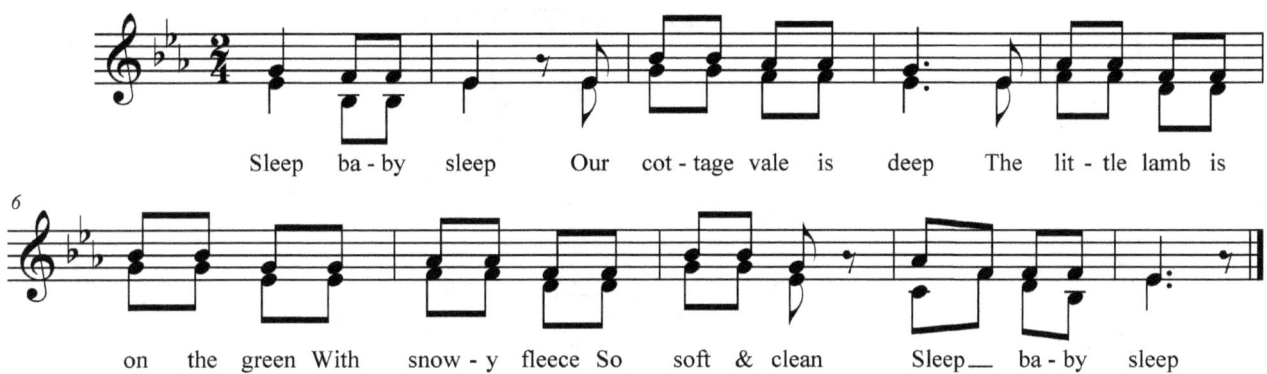

Sleep ba-by sleep Our cot-tage vale is deep The lit-tle lamb is on the green With snow-y fleece So soft & clean Sleep ba-by sleep

2 Sleep baby sleep
   I would not, would not weep
  The little lamb he never cries
  And bright & happy are his eyes
       Sleep baby sleep

3 Sleep baby sleep
   Near where the woodbines creep
  Be always like the lamb so mild
  A sweet & kind & gentle child
       Sleep etc.

4 Sleep baby sleep
   Thy rest shall angels keep
  While on the grass the lamb shall feed
  And never suffer want or need
       Sleep baby sleep   For Francie to sing to brothers.

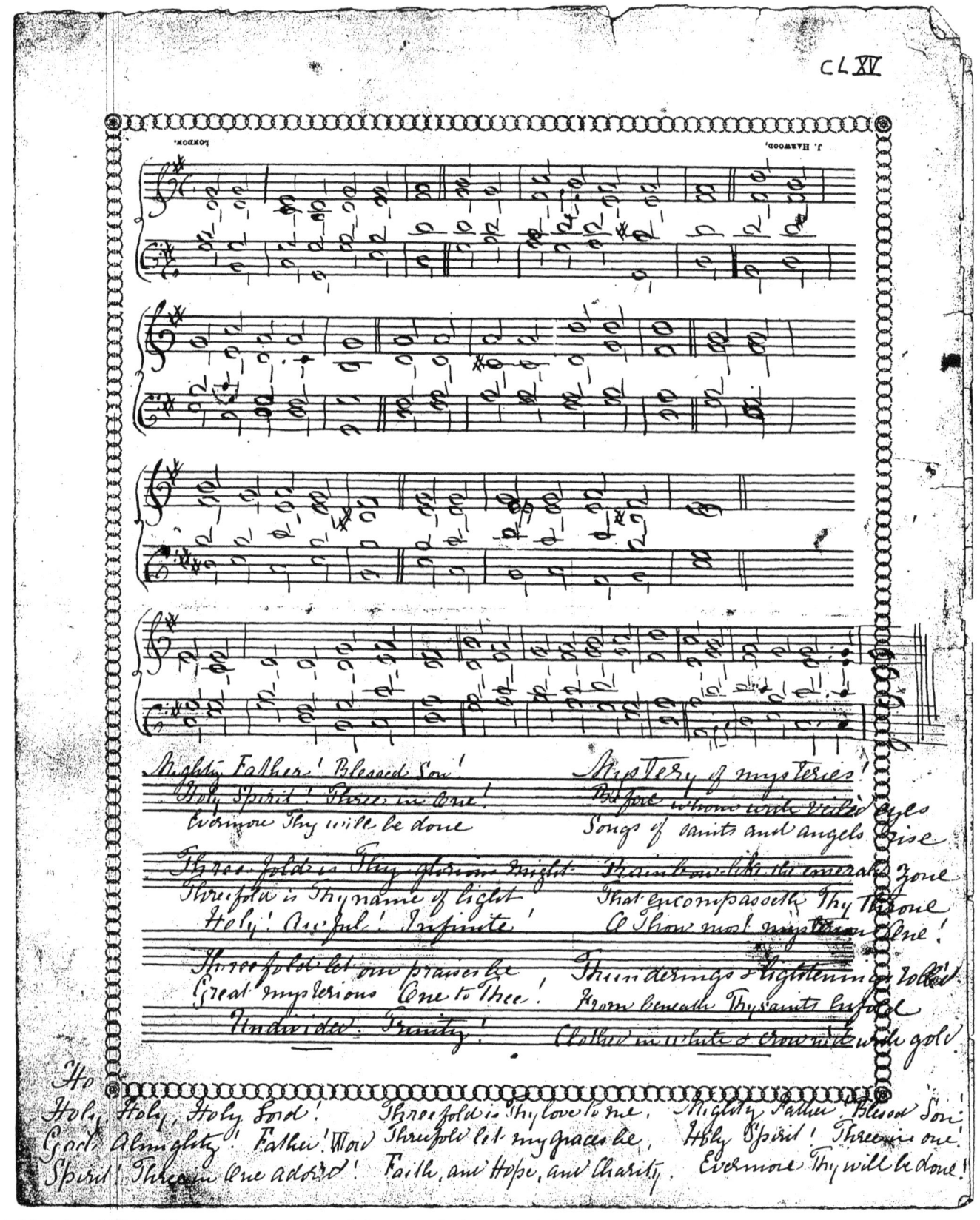

This is Number 163 in *Havergal's Psalmody and Century of Chants*, and the score for hymn number 4 in the companion *Songs of Grace and Glory*. This manuscript was the last music score composed by William Henry Havergal, composed on his last conscious day, Saturday, April 16, 1870. The text by Dr. John S. B. Monsell is symbolic of the Trinity, having three lines in each verse, three verses in each section, and three sections for one hymn. This score was posthumously named "Havergal," and his daughter Frances Ridley Havergal wrote, "The tune with its serene melody and rich harmony is itself an epitome of his musical work" (*Specimen Glasses for the King's Minstrels* by Frances Ridley Havergal, London: Home Words Publishing Office, 1881), original book pages 109–110, page 765 of Volume II of the Havergal edition.

In her article/essay entitled "Seven Clerical Hymn-Writers" (Chapter IX in the posthumously published *Specimen Glasses for the King's Minstrels*), F.R.H. presented this hymn, and at the end wrote this paragraph:[1]

> The name of the tune to this hymn—Havergal—No. 777 in "Songs of Grace and Glory," [later placed as No. 4 in *Songs of Grace and Glory*] may excite remark; but it will not be wondered that this name was chosen, when we tell that it was the last ever written by that sainted hand which now bears one of the "harps of God"—written just before the Master's voice said "Come up higher." The tune with its serene melody and rich harmony is itself an epitome of his musical work.

His oldest child Miriam (who was 19 when Frances was born, tutored her when she was two and a half, and lived 19 years after Frances died) wrote this in her biography of W.H.H.:[2]

> This Saturday [April 16, 1870] was indeed to prove my dear father's last conscious day. In a letter to a friend, written on the Monday morning, his daughter F.R.H. speaks of that day as "a very climax of peace and brightness in all respects." He twice walked out a little in front of his house, hoping to catch a young gentleman, a neighbour, to whom he thought a word in season might be useful. He also wrote his last lines, "Messiah, Redeemer!" and set them to a palindrome, and the same day he composed the beautiful tune "Havergal" to Dr. Monsell's fine Trinitarian hymn, "Mighty Father! Blessed Son!"

F.R.H. prepared this score for publication in *Songs of Grace and Glory*.

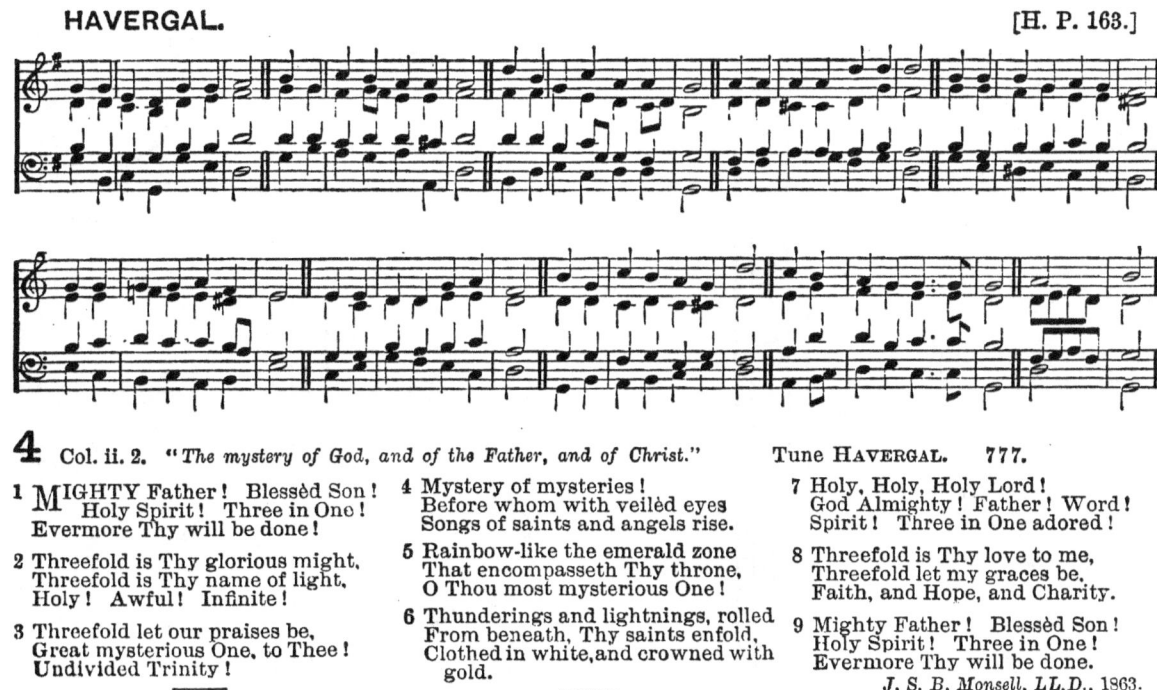

[1] *Specimen Glasses for the King's Minstrels* by Frances Ridley Havergal (London: Home Words Publishing Office, 1881), original book pages 109–110, page 765 of Volume II of the Havergal edition.

[2] *Records of the Life of the Rev. William Henry Havergal, M.A.* by his daughter Jane Miriam Crane (London: Home Words Publishing Office, 1882), original book pages 354–355, page 667 of Volume IV of the Havergal edition. Miriam also wrote this near the end of Chapter VII of the same volume (original book pages 164–165, page 625 of Volume IV):

> The last lines he composed, and which he set to a Palindrome on Easter Even, 1870, are these:—
> [She then quoted the five-line stanza, "Messiah, Redeemer."]
> Earlier in the day he had composed the beautiful tune "Havergal," No. 163 in "Havergal's Psalmody." On Easter-Day he was seized with apoplexy, and remained unconscious forty-eight hours, when he quietly passed through death into life eternal the 19th of April, 1870.

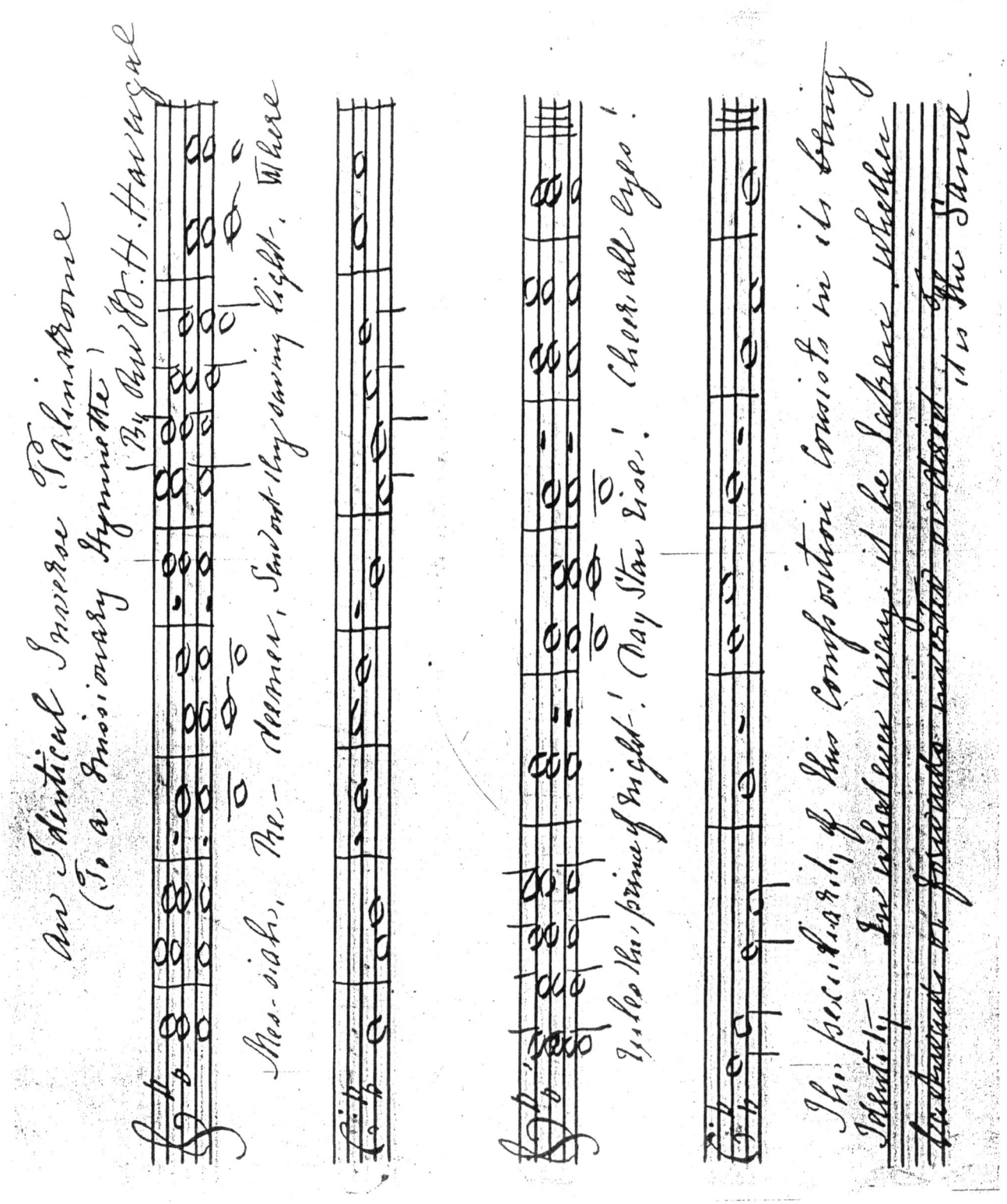

This brief stanza ("Messiah, Redeemer") was the last verse of poetry that William Henry Havergal wrote, and this palindrome score was the last music that he composed. This is newly typeset precisely as W.H.H. notated this, his last score. In the first page, the score is notated in full score; in the second page of the score, he notated the music in the four separate parts. In

Manuscript "An Identical Inverse Palindrome (to a Missionary Hymnette)" 353

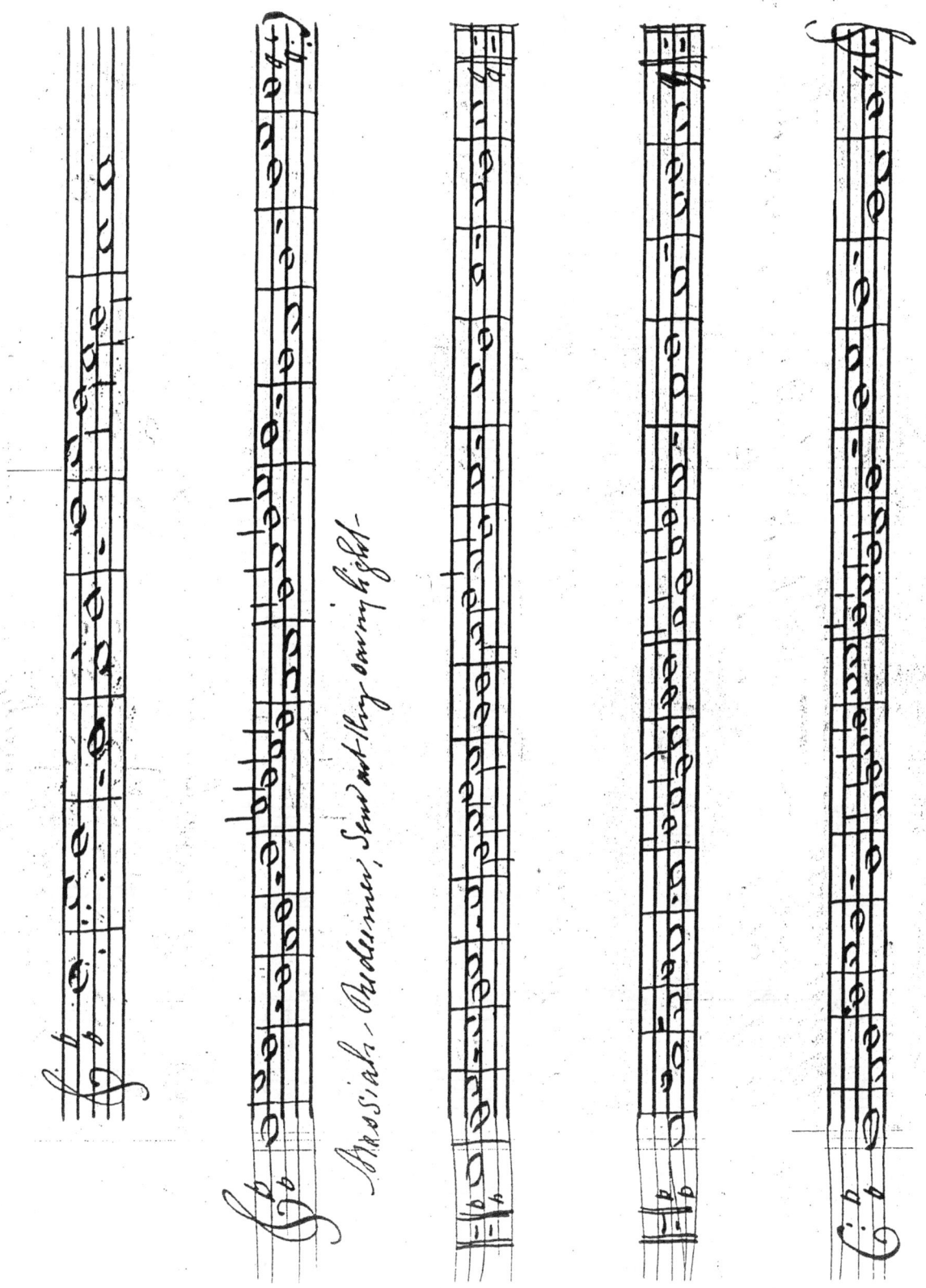

the second page, in the top treble clef, he only began but did not complete the top voice line of the four-part score (which is written in three-plus-one piano style): possibly he became distracted and later returned and re-started the top line, which is both started and completed in the second treble clef of the second page. The first page is a different score from the second

Identical Inverse Palindrome

(To a Missionary Hymnette)

By Rev W. H. Havergal

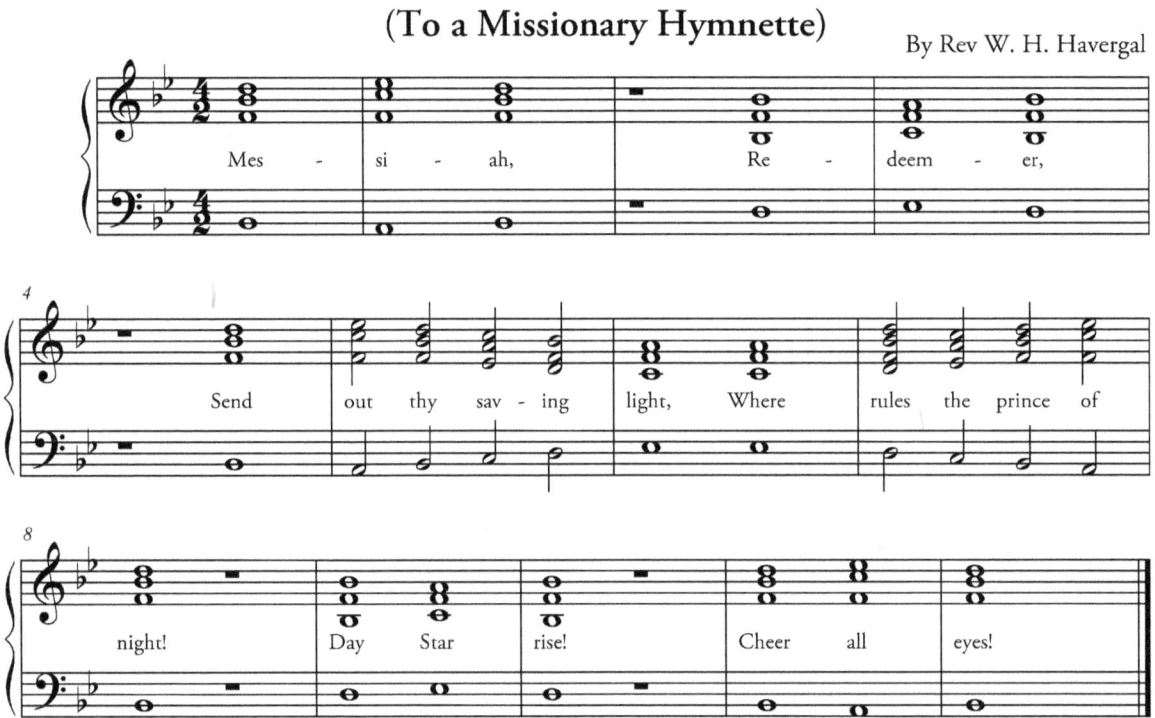

The peculiarity of this composition consists in its ~~being~~ identity [.] In whatever way it be taken, whether backwards or forwards [,] inverted or direct [,] it is the same.

page: the top and bottom voice lines are identically the same on both pages, but the music for the two inner voices of the second page was completely re-written and is different—a different score—from the two inner voices of the first page. This was written on Saturday, April 16, 1870 (the day before Easter Sunday), his last full day of consciousness in this world. His daughter Frances Ridley Havergal described that day as "a very climax of peace and brightness in all respects." He had been very ill, and was weak and not well, so that a lapse or inattention is easily understood. He rose early the next morning, became unconscious (possibly a stroke, we don't know), and never regained consciousness before he died shortly before noon on Tuesday, April 19, 1870.

This is the first page of W.H.H.'s handwritten sermon on Hebrews 13:17, preached in Worcester Cathedral September 25, 1859. Though he was so finely gifted in music, the gospel ministry was his first calling, and he preferred to write a sermon than to compose a score. The work of a pastor was his priority, and he used music to enrich his ministry and benefit his hearers, and as a personal enjoyment.

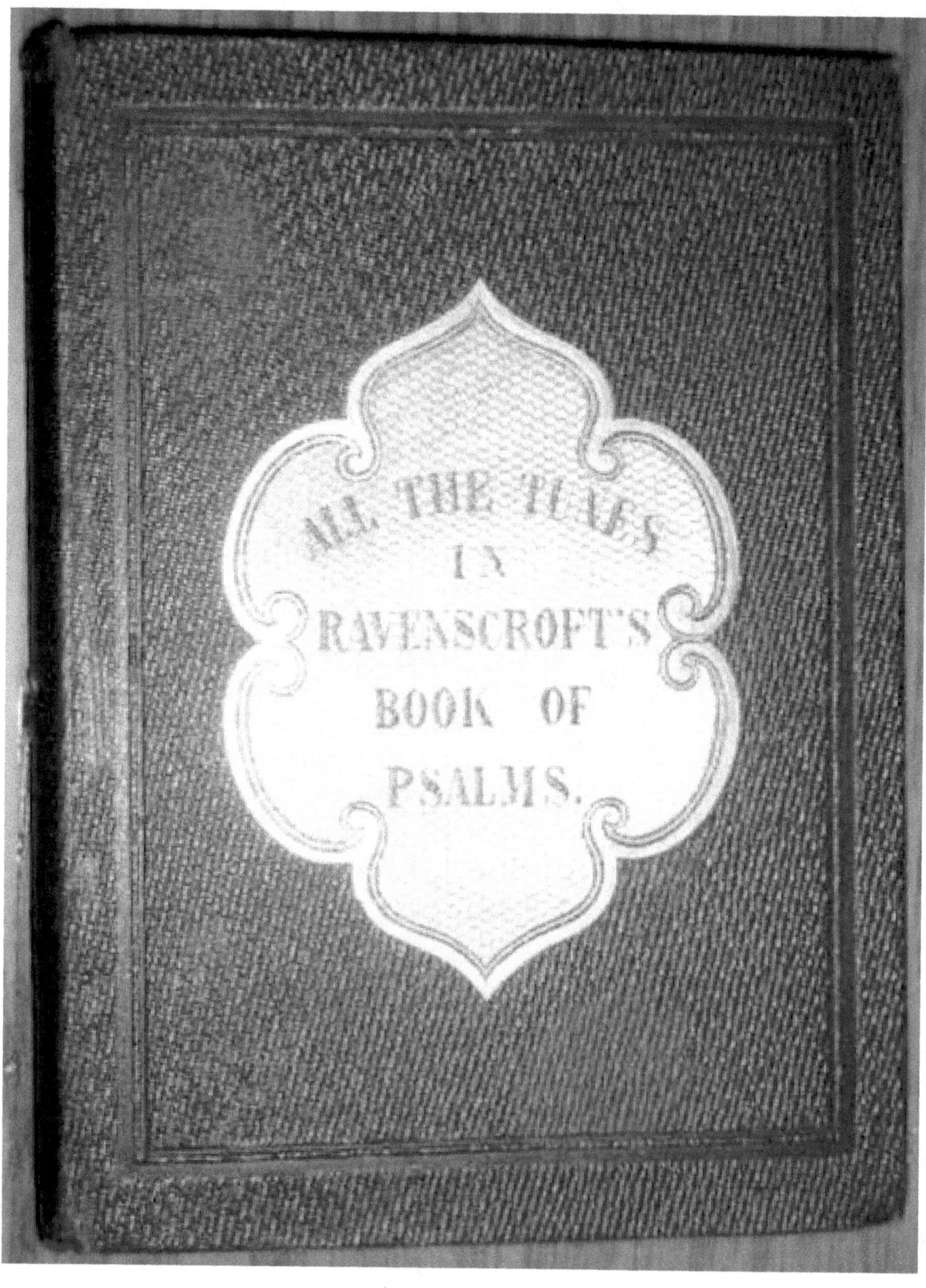

A REPRINT

OF ALL THE TUNES IN

RAVENSCROFT'S

BOOK OF PSALMS.

WITH INTRODUCTORY REMARKS.

EDITED BY THE

REV. W. H. HAVERGAL, M.A.

LONDON:
J. A. NOVELLO, 69, DEAN STREET, SOHO.

M.DCCC.XLV.

LONDON:
RICHARDS, PRINTER, ST. MARTIN'S LANE.

Note: Blank pages have not been copied here, but the correct left-page and right-page orientation is resumed with the first page of William Henry Havergal's "Introductory Remarks" (page 1869 of Volume V of the Havergal edition), matching the original book's left-page and right-page orientation from that point till the end.

THE WHOLE BOOKE OF PSALMES:

WITH THE HYMNES EVANGELICALL, AND *Songs* SPIRITVALL.

Composed into 4. parts by sundry Authors, to such severall Tunes, as have beene *and are usually sung in England, Scotland, Wales,* Germany, Italy, France, and the Nether-lands: never as yet before in one volume published.

ALSO:

1. A brief Abstract of the Prayse, Efficacie, and Vertue of the Psalmes.
2. That all Clarkes of Churches, and the Auditory, may know what Tune each proper Psalme may be sung unto.

Newly corrected and enlarged by Tho. Ravenscroft, Bachelar of Musicke.

Gloria in excelsis Deo.

Printed at London, for the *Company of Stationers,* 1621.

A contemporary of Thomas Ravenscroft, George Herbert (1593–1633) was a scholar, poet, pastor, and a very fine musician. Herbert's friend and biographer Izaak Walton (1593–1683) in his valuable memoir The Life of Mr. George Herbert *wrote that in his student years at Cambridge University, Herbert's "greatest diversion from his study, was the practice of music, in which he became a great master; and of which he would say, 'That it did relieve his drooping spirits, compose his distracted thoughts, and raised his soul so far above earth, that it gave him an earnest of the joys of heaven, before he possessed them.' " Walton also wrote this: "His chiefest recreation was Musick, in which heavenely Art he was a most excellent Master, and did himself compose many divine Hymns and Anthems, which he set and sung to his Lute or Viol; and though he was a lover of retiredness, yet his love to Musick was such, that he went usually twice every week on certain appointed days, to the Cathedral Church in Salisbury; and at his return would say that 'his time spent in Prayer, and Cathedral Musick, elevated his Soul, and was his Heaven upon Earth.' Before his return thence to Bemerton, he would usually sing and play his part, at an appointed private Musick-meeting; and, to justifie this practice, he would often say, 'Religion does not Banish mirth, but only moderates, and sets rules to it.' "—from* The Complete Angler & The Lives of Dr. Donne, Sir Henry Wotton, Mr. Richard Hooker, Mr. George Herbert, Dr. Sanderson *by Izaak Walton (London: Macmillan and Co., 1901), pages 379 and 407. This is another account of Herbert: "H. Allen, of Dantesey, was well acquainted with him [George Herbert], who has told me [John Aubrey] that he had a very good hand on the lute, and that he sett his own lyricks or sacred poems."—from* Brief Lives, chiefly of Contemporaries, set down by John Aubrey, between the Years 1669 & 1696 edited from the Author's MSS. *by Andrew Clark, Volume I (Oxford: The Clarendon Press, 1898), page 310. This portrait of Herbert is provided by the Houghton Library, Harvard University.*

Note: This was a blank page in the original book.

"THE NAMES OF THE AUTHORS

WHICH COMPOSED THE TUNES OF THE PSALMES INTO FOUR PARTS."

(WITH ADDITIONAL NOTICES BY THE PRESENT EDITOR.)

THOMAS TALLIS.
A gentleman of the Chapel Royal under Edward the Sixth, and Queen Mary. Originally of the Romish communion, but conformed to the Protestant faith in the reign of Elizabeth. Composed much of our standard Church music. Altogether a truly great musician. Died Nov. 23rd, 1585, and was buried at Greenwich.

JOHN DOULAND, Doctor of Musicke.
Born in 1562. Celebrated as a lutenist. Often called Doctor, but there is no proof of his having proceeded to that degree. Graduated B.M. together with Morley. His rare skill as a performer, enhanced his reputation as a composer. He translated the Micrologus of Andreas Ornithopareus; and published both vocal and instrumental music. Died 10th April, 1609.

THOMAS MORLEY, Bachelar of Musicke.
A pupil of Byrd. Graduated B.M. in 1588. Was a Gentleman of Queen Elizabeth's Chapel. A writer of treatises, and a composer of madrigals and other secular pieces. His ecclesiastical and devotional compositions are worthy of his age. Died about the beginning of the 17th century.

GILES FARNABY, Bachelar of Musicke.
Born at Truro. Graduated B.M. of Christ Church, Oxford, 1592. Composed canzonets for four voices, and a song in eight parts. London, 1598.

THE NAMES OF THE AUTHORS.

THOMAS TOMKINS, Bachelar of Musicke.
"Of a family which seems to have produced more musicians than any in England." A pupil of Byrd, and a Gentleman of Queen Elizabeth's Chapel. Afterwards Organist of Worcester Cathedral. Author of *numerous* Anthems mentioned in Clifford's collection. Composed and published songs in many parts; and a noble work in ten books (extant in Norwich Cathedral), "Musica Deo Sacra et Ecclesiæ Anglicanæ." Graduated B.M. of Magdalen College, Oxford, 1607. One of his sons was a prebendary of Worcester. Birth and death not certainly known.

JOHN TOMKINS, Bachelar of Musicke.
Son of the above. Organist of the old Cathedral of St. Paul, and Gentleman of the Chapel Royal. Died Sept. 27, 1638. Was reckoned "Organista sui temporis celeberrimus."

MARTIN PEIRSON, Bachelar of Musicke.
Master of the Choristers of St. Paul's, when John Tomkins was Organist. Graduated 1613. Author of sundry anthems (Clifford's Collection) and of motets or grave chamber music. Died 1650. Bequeathed £100 to the poor of Marsh, in the parish of Donnington, Isle of Ely.

WILLIAM PARSONS.
A musician of note in the early part of Elizabeth's reign, and a principal harmonist in the Brazen Nose Psalter, printed by Day in 1563.

EDMUND HOOPER.
Organist of Westminster Abbey, and Gentleman of the Chapel Royal. Author of sundry anthems. Died July 14, 1621.

GEORGE KIRBY.
A musician in the family of Sir R. Jermin; and said to be Organist to Queen Elizabeth. Published madrigals of rare excellence, in 1597.

EDWARD BLANCKS.
Composer of parts to Psalm tunes in Este's Collection, 1592-4.

RICHARD ALLISON.
Usually styled "Gent." A private and highly esteemed teacher of music in the reign of Elizabeth. Wrote for Este's volume of Psalm Tunes; and published an edition of his own arrangement of the Church Tunes in four parts, to suit a Lute also and Bass Viol. Folio, 1599.

THE NAMES OF THE AUTHORS.

JOHN FARMER.
  Published madrigals in 1599.

MICHAEL CAVENDISH.
  A musician of respectability in the middle of the reign of Elizabeth.

JOHN BENNET.
  Styled by Ravenscroft, in his "Briefe Discourse," "A gentleman admirable for all kind of composures either in arte or ayre, simple or mixt." Published in 1599 some of the best madrigals of the English school.

ROBERT PALMER.

SIMON STUBBS.

WILLIAM HARRISON.
  Musicians of good repute in the reign of Elizabeth.

JOHN MILTON.
  Born at Milton in Oxfordshire. Father of the immortal Bard. A scrivener by profession in Bread Street, London; but a very superior musician, and ranked among the first masters of his time. A madrigal of his for five voices in "The Triumphs of Oriana," published in 1601. For a composition in forty parts he was rewarded, by a Polish prince, with a gold medal and chain.

WILLIAM CRANFORD (alias CRANFIELD).
  A member of St. Paul's choir in the reign of Elizabeth, and author of excellent catches and rounds. Mentioned by Clifford as composer of an anthem supplicatory for King Charles II.

THOMAS RAVENSCROFT, Bachelar of Music.
  See introductory remarks.

  [Though the names, as given above, are the whole which Ravenscroft enumerates in his list, yet three others are mentioned in the course of the work, viz.]

WILLIAM COBBOLD.
  One of the composers in Este's volume, and one of the Madrigalists in "The Triumphs of Oriana."

THE NAMES OF THE AUTHORS.

EDWARD JOHNSON.
   B.M. of Emmanuel College, Cambridge, at the close of the sixteenth century. Author of a few anthems mentioned in the first part of Clifford's Collection. Many more in MS. in Ely Cathedral. MS. pieces of his for the Virginal in Ch. Ch. Library, Oxon. Sometimes mistaken for Robert Johnson of an earlier date, an ecclesiastic, but learned in music and notable for a more graceful arrangement than usual. Said to have been Chaplain to Anne Boleyn.

JOHN WARD.
   Madrigalist in "Oriana."

After the names of these worthies, a remark of Sir John Hawkins may fitly be quoted:—" It appears that many of the old English musicians were men of learning in other faculties, particularly in astronomy, and physic; and, what is strange, in logic."—HIST. MUS. vol. iii. p. 348.

INTRODUCTORY REMARKS.

OF Thomas Ravenscroft little is known, beyond certain brief intimations contained in his own works. From those works it appears that he was born A.D. 1592; and in due time became a chorister of St. Paul's Cathedral. He speaks of his tutor, Mr. Edmund Pearce, the master of the choristers, as "a man of singular eminence in his profession."

At the early age of fourteen, Ravenscroft took the degree of Bachelor of Music at Cambridge. Though university degrees were, in that day, taken at an earlier age than in the present day, yet was the age at which Ravenscroft graduated unusually early. He, therefore, must have been precociously clever, or intensely studious. In all probability he was both. This surmise is strengthened by the following laudatory lines addressed to him by a friend, and prefixed to his "Briefe Discourse." Of these lines the third, it will be seen, contains a punning allusion to his name.

> " Rara avis arte senex juvenis; sed rarior est, si
> Ætate est juvenis, moribus ille senex.
> Rara avis est author; (pœne est pars nominis una)
> Namque annis juvenis, moribus, arte senex.

ii   **INTRODUCTORY REMARKS.**

> Non vidit tria lustra puer, quin arte probatus,
> Vitâ laudatus, sumpsit in arte gradum.
> &c. &c.
> Arte senex, virtute senex, ætate adolescens
> I bone, rara avis es, scribe, bonis avibus."

In 1611, when only nineteen,* he was the author of " Melismata, or Musicall Phansies, fitting the Court, Citie, and Countrey Humors. To 3, 4, and 5 Voyces." In 1614 he published " A Briefe Discourse of the true (but neglected) use of Charact'ring the Degrees by their Perfection, Imperfection, and Diminution in Measurable Musicke, against the Common Practise and Custome of these Times. Examples whereof are exprest in the Harmony of 4 Voyces, concerning the Pleasure of 5 usual Recreations. 1. Hunting, 2. Hawking, 3. Dancing, 4. Drinking, 5. Enamouring." This work is dedicated " To the Right Worshipfull, most worthy grave Senators, Guardians, of Gresham Colledge, in London." As a reason for this dedication he says, I must and do acknowledge it as a singular help and benefit that I have receiv'd divers *Instructions, Resolutions,* and *Confirmations* of sundry *Points* and *Precepts* in our Art, from the *Musicke Readers* of that most famous Colledge." That this work was countenanced by the most eminent of cotemporary musicians, is evident from the panegyrical addresses prefixed to it, by John Dowland, B.M., Nathaniel Giles, B.M., Martin Peerson, B.M., and others.

In 1621 Ravenscroft published his " Whole Booke of Psalmes,

---

* If Ravenscroft were, indeed, the author of " Pammelia, or Musick's Miscellanie," and of " Deuteromelia," both 4to. London, 1609, which are sometimes attributed to him, he could not have been more than *seventeen* years of age, at the date of their publication.

INTRODUCTORY REMARKS.

&c." After this period, nothing is known of him. He probably did not live to see the second edition of his "Psalmes," in 1633.*

There is reason to conclude that he was of a good family, and possessed independent property; for in the Dedication to his "Melismata," before-mentioned, he styles himself " Mr. Thomas Ravenscroft, *Esquire*;" and one of the addresses, prefixed to his "Briefe Discourse," is thus headed, " De *ingenuo iuvene* T. R. (annos 22 nato) Musicæ studiosissimo." It, further, does not appear that he ever held any professional post in college or choir; but that he devoted himself to music as a study worthy of a christian gentleman. This latter fact is corroborated by an Epigram, addressed to him by William Austin, in the "Brief Discourse."

The arms of the family of Ravenscroft are "Argent a chevron, between three ravens' heads erased, sable."

Speaking of Ravenscroft, Sir John Hawkins says, " He was not only a good musician, but a man of considerable learning in his faculty." "A professor," remarks Dr. Burney, " not only well acquainted with the practice of his art, but who seems to have bestowed much time in the perusal of the best authors, and in meditation on the theory." To these testimonies of professional ability, higher and better things may be added. From the tenor of his remarks prefixed to his Psalm Tunes, and from the style of the "Godly Praiers" appended to them, it may be hoped that he was a truly devout man.

* In the Library of Christ Church, Oxford, there are, in manuscript, "Four Motetts or Anthems, for five voices, by Tho. Ravenscroft." The titles of them are as follows: 1. Oh let mee heare. 2. This is the day when first our Saviour bled. 3. In thee, O Lord. 4. Oh wofull ruines of Jerusalem.

iv   INTRODUCTORY REMARKS.

Account of the Booke of Psalmes.

The volume, of which this reprint contains the entire substance, was published, as both Hawkins and Burney state, *first* in 1621, and then in 1633. But the edition of 1621, from which the present reprint is taken, *may* not have been the *very first* edition: since, in the Title, it is said to be "enlarged and corrected." The fact, however, of there having been an earlier edition is, after all, dubious; because, by enlargement and correction, the Editor may have merely referred to other publications of the same or similar tunes, by former editors.

The edition of 1621, which Sir J. Hawkins seems not to have met with,* but which is possessed by the Editor of this reprint, and that of 1633, kindly lent to him by Dr. Rimbault, are in size duodecimo, and printed evidently from the same types. Though the title of the latter edition, like that of the former, professes both "correction and enlargement," yet is there not the slightest trace of either. On the contrary, the later edition contains all the errors of the former edition, and many more besides, even to an iteration of the "Errata," without any attempt to amend them, in the places where they occur. Besides the usual "Hymnes Evangelicall and Songs Spirituall," every Psalm of the Old Version† is printed in full, with a fit tune, though not a distinct or new tune, in four parts. Some tunes

---

* In proof of the scarcity of copies, full seventy years ago, Sir John Hawkins says, "Even at this day (A.D. 1776) he is deemed a happy man, in many places, who is master of a genuine copy of Ravenscroft's Psalms."—vol. iii. p. 526.

† The orthography of this version has, in this reprint, been modernized. So, also, has that of the names of the tunes. In other prominent phrases it has been retained.

INTRODUCTORY REMARKS.　　　　　　　　　　v

are repeated three, four, five, and even seven times.* The total amount of distinct tunes, including the Hymns and Songs, is ninety-eight. Of these, forty are newer tunes with names to them; the rest, with a few exceptions, are the usual "church tunes,"† which were printed, for one voice only, in the Psalters of the day. The four parts are thus disposed: on the upper division of the left-hand page is the "Cantus," or Treble; on the lower the "Tenor, or Plain Song," called, when the tune is of foreign origin, "Faburden." On the upper division of the right-hand page is the "Medius," or Counter Tenor, though evidently it is sometimes intended for a Second Treble. On the lower is the Bass. All sorts of clefs are used, from the G of the Treble, with every variety of the C, to the D of the Bass, just as the compass may require, so as *to avoid the use of leger lines.*

Names and Authorship of the Tunes.

The practice of calling tunes by the names of places, seems, in England at least, to have originated with Ravenscroft. All the newer tunes in his "Booke" are designated, except in two

---

* Cambridge, Oxford, Winchester especially, York, Chester and Martyrs, are the tunes most frequently repeated. With the exception of Martyrs, none of the so-called Scotch tunes are used more than twice.

† These tunes are not uniformly the same in all Psalters. Some were omitted and others inserted, as well as altered, by successive printers. The short metre tune which Dr. Crotch has called St. Michael's, "from the Psalter 1595," is, in that Psalter, and in one of 1588, in the key of F major; but in the Psalter of 1580, it is in D minor, having another beginning and ending. 'In a still earlier Psalter, 1575, the tune begins in F major, and ends in D minor. But, in Day's Psalter of 1565 (British Museum), commencing also in the key of F, it ends in E. In each instance, the tune is set to the 134th Psalm. In no other Psalters has the editor yet noticed the tune.

or three instances, by the names of cathedral cities or collegiate towns. " It was much about the time of the publication of this book (says Sir John Hawkins, vol. iii. p. 525) that King Charles the First was prevailed on by the clergy to attempt the establishment of the Liturgy in Scotland; and perhaps it was with a view to humour the people of that kingdom, that some of these new composed tunes were called by the names Dumferling, Dundee, and Glasgow." But in this surmise Sir John commits a singular oversight; because Charles the First did not begin his reign till 1625, and Ravenscroft published his book four years before. Besides, these very names had been given to tunes in the Scotch Psalter of 1615, printed by Andro Hart. Thomas Este, too, in his Tune Book of 1594, had used a *few* county names, but not uniformly as Hart and Ravenscroft.

Whether the tunes called English, Scotch, or Welch, in this volume, are really *national* tunes; or whether they are so called merely because the towns by which they are designated are in those countries, is not at all clear. Whether, too, the individuals who harmonized the tunes were, in any instances, the authors of them, is equally obscure. Ravenscroft himself no where says they were. He simply names those persons " who composed the tunes *into four parts*." And yet Sir John Hawkins ventures to decide that these harmonizers were the authors. His decision, it is true, accords with certain popular opinions; but, then, both the one and the other lead to sundry incongruities. York tune, for instance, is called " A Northern Tune," and St. David's " A Welch Tune." The former is universally attributed to John Milton, the father of the immortal bard, and the latter to Ravenscroft himself. But Milton

INTRODUCTORY REMARKS.

was not of Yorkshire, neither was Ravenscroft of Wales. Hence, if York Tune was really a tune of Northern origin, Milton could not have composed it: but, if he did compose it, then it cannot be a Northern tune, except only as to the name of the city by which it is distinguished. The same argument applies to St. David's, and sundry other tunes. What, also, militates against the opinion of Milton's authorship of York Tune, is the fact that Ravenscroft has given a version of the tune by Simon Stubbs, as well as by Milton. Such a circumstance could hardly have occurred, had the tune been one of Milton's composition.* With respect to the so-called "Scottish Tunes," which, like those called "Northern," are remarkably excellent, no valid proof of their local origin exists. Burns, in his "Cotter's Saturday Night," seems to regard "Dundee" as a tune of his land. But, the name alone was likely to originate the modern belief of its being a Caledonian tune. It must, however, be noted that the tune, which Burns knew as "Dundee," is not the tune which Ravenscroft calls by that name. The "Dundee" of Burns is the "Windsor or Eaton"† of Ravenscroft: while the tune which Ravenscroft calls "Dundee" is in all the Scotch Psalters denominated "French;" as though the older worthies of Scotia did not claim it for their own, but regarded it as an importation. As a proof of the very little nicety about names, among early editors, it may be stated that

---

* In the Scotch Psalter of 1615, York tune is called "The Stilt." The origin or meaning of that appellation is not known. In Scotland it is universally regarded as a national tune.

† The Editor is much indebted to Miss Gross, of Ayr, for placing this fact beyond a doubt. Throughout the entire locality of Burns, our "Windsor tune" has *always* been known as the true Scottish "Dundee."

viii INTRODUCTORY REMARKS.

the tune, to the 131st Psalm in this volume, which Ravenscroft gives as a "Low Dutch Tune," is, by Andro Hart, called an "English Tune." So "Southwell," which is commonly received as a tune of Ravenscroft's own composition, is printed without any name to the 134th Psalm, in Henrie Denham's Psalter of 1588, some years before Ravenscroft was born.

On the whole, therefore, it is plain that Ravenscroft did not concern himself with the authors of the tunes, but only with the persons who harmonized them. And, as the tunes are, in style, so much alike, with no sort of national peculiarity about them, it is but reasonable to conclude that Ravenscroft called them Scotch, or Welch, or English, either because the cities or towns, by which they are designated, were in those respective countries, or because the tunes, to which he gives a generic appellation, may have been more or less popular in their respective districts. What favours this surmise is the fact that *Northern* tunes, meaning some of the northern counties of England, are distinguished from English tunes, or tunes which are named after certain places in the more southern parts of the kingdom. In all probability, these more newly composed and locally named tunes were of no very remarkable origin; but, being collected from various sources, and, taken as found, were harmonized by erudite musicians. It may be, also, that in some instances, the harmonizer was the composer; but there is no clue to the ascertaining of those instances.

Character of the Tunes.

The tunes of newer composition, like the older tunes of the common Psalters, are extremely simple in their construction, always syllabic, and generally isochronous.* They are such as the least learned singers may sing: for, abounding with easy progressions, and having a syllable for a note, and a note for a syllable, no great skill is requisite for even their good performance. Herein the sound sense of the age was displayed. Thought was taken for "the common people." Light and ribald strains were avoided. Easy and decorous tunes were provided.

Skilfulness of the Parts.

But, though the Tenor, as the air or tune for the adult male voices of the congregation, is always plain and equal, and though the Bass, also, is generally of the easiest mould, yet the other parts are often learnedly ornate. The Cantus and the Medius, as parts reserved for the more select and skilful voices, are sometimes cleverly contrived, and frequently present very ingenious syncopations. This custom of writing ornate or learned "parts upon a plain song," was the custom of the Church long before Ravenscroft's time. It was a custom which, as any one by trial may tell, required the highest art of the composer. The application of the custom to Psalmody arose, it seems, from the desire to render unisonous singing in the congregation more agreeable to all true lovers of harmony. In an age when Psalms were sung with great energy by large masses of people, the men's voices, predominating by their power, would engross the ear, and clearly sustain the melody. The devout musician, leaving that melody to be sung with all simplicity and fulness, employed a few superior voices to encompass it with

* Of the old tunes four only are in triple time, and of the new five. The rest are all in common time.

INTRODUCTORY REMARKS.

harmony. The process was analogous to that of an architect who substantiates and ornaments a plainly built edifice, by first making good the foundation to it, and then adding a new roof embellished in becoming style: or like that of the artist in Solomon's day, who enshrined his "apples of gold in pictures of silver." As the edifice and the apples remain entire, so the plain tune continues as it was, only vocally embellished or harmoniously enshrined.

Decay of this species of Psalmody.

But Psalmody of this kind was fitted only for the age in which it originated.* It required a mass of plain Tenor voice, with a full round Bass, and a few skilful Trebles and Countertenors. Such a combination was at perfection only in Elizabeth's day. When Ravenscroft wrote, it was somewhat enfeebled. During the reign of the first Charles it grew feebler still: and, at the

---

* Respecting the origin of harmonized psalmody, our musical historians are singularly deficient. Both Hawkins and Burney state that the Church psalm-tunes were *first* harmonized in 1579, by William Damon; who, finding his first effort not well received, tried a second in 1591. As the first complete Psalter had been published in 1562, seventeen years before Damon's first attempt at harmonizing it, the interval for unisonous singing must have seemed long, indeed, to the many masters and lovers of harmony in that age. The very length of the interval might have induced our historians to suspect that it must have been filled by somewhat more than they had ascertained. But no such suspicion, it seems, occurred to them. The truth, however, can now be stated. In the year 1563, John Day, the well-known Elizabethan typographist, printed a harmonized version of psalm-tunes for the metrical translation of Sterneholde and his coadjutors. The work, which is in the library of Brazen Nose College, consists of four small octavo oblong volumes, each containing one of the four usual parts. Those parts are arranged, by sundry authors, in very masterly style. William Parsons, Richard Brimle, T. Causton, and J. Hake, are the principal harmonists. With the exception of one leaf, the

INTRODUCTORY REMARKS.

restoration of the second, it was but a ghost. The usurpation of Cromwell had starved and silenced all art in Psalmody. Hence, when things came back to something like their former state, the boys, who had sung the Cantus parts, had grown into men; but no successors for those parts had been trained. To recur, therefore, to the method of Elizabeth's day was impossible. Consequently they who wished well to Psalmody did the best which circumstances allowed. John Playford, in 1671, published a selection of the easier and more familiar Psalm Tunes, in four parts, for *men's* voices only. In that selection, the air or tune is allotted, as before, to the Tenor; above which is first a Countertenor, and then an Altus. The tunes are harmonized plainly but neatly, and were favoured with the oversight and approbation of the most learned men of the day.* But even this simpler har-

work is in excellent preservation. Certainly, it is singular that neither musical historians, nor musical antiquarians, have discovered any knowledge of the work. Both Dibdin and Dr. Cotton, in their respective catalogues of Bibles and Psalters, mention it; but, till the present year, it has been unknown as a *musical* treasure. Its discovery *as such*, is justly attributable to the editor's eldest son, one of the chaplains of Christ Church. In the early part of the last century, the Rev. Arthur Bedford, in his "Abuse of Music," mentioned *Parsons's* Psalms; but, whether by them he meant this publication of John Day, because W. Parsons was a principal contributor to it, is quite uncertain. In "The Psalm Singer's Necessary Companion, 1700," there is printed not only Playford's version of the Old 100th Psalm tune, in three parts, but, also, the version of W. Parsons in four parts, apparently from this very book of John Day.

* " Psalms and Hymns, in Solemn Music, in four parts, on the Common Tunes to Psalms in Metre, used in Parish Churches. Also six Hymns for one voice to the Organ." Folio, 1671. Mr. Hullah, in the Preface to his Psalter (the best publication of its kind, though prodigiously ponderous) omits all notice of this work. An acquaintance with the work must have disarmed him of much of that dispraise which he has so unpiteously levelled at its author. It would, at least, have checked

xii INTRODUCTORY REMARKS.

monization was too much for the popular ability: for, soon afterwards, he published another selection, for *three* voices only, assigning the air or tune to the Cantus in the G clef, and aiming at nothing beyond the veriest common-place.

In 1728, a professedly corrected edition of Ravenscroft, in larger type, edited by William Turner, was published by William Pearson; and another edition was published by J. Buckland in 1746. The "Harmonia Perfecta" of 1730, which professed to give the chief of Ravenscroft's tunes, avoided most of his syncopations, and spoiled many of his harmonies. Still it does not appear that, although the Rev. J. Cheetham and others subsequently published Psalm Tunes after the Elizabethan model, any general return was made to the earlier mode of singing psalms. The very altered circumstances of the present era render such a return neither practicable nor desirable.

him in accusing Playford of a "want of *skill*." Possibly, too, subsequent consideration will induce Mr. Hullah greatly to modify the asperity of his remarks. Certainly, a little closer investigation of facts will discover to him sundry mistakes into which he has fallen. Playford was so universally beloved, and so proverbially reckoned "an *honest* man," ("this honest old man," as Sir J. Hawkins calls him, vol. iv. p. 361) that Mr. Hullah may justly be deemed *venturous*, for tilting with sarcasm at his memory. A man, on whose death a Poet Laureate (Nahum Tate) wrote an Elegy, and which Elegy was set to music by the master genius of the age (Henry Purcell), that man might surely claim of his professional posterity all the courtesy which candour and modesty are wont to allow. Independently of the mistakes alluded to, and a multiplicity of others in the Preface, one capital point is overlooked by Mr. Hullah, viz. Playford made no innovation as to the standard *style* of psalmodic *melody!* Tunes which Mr. Hullah has published, Playford would have suppressed. Harmonies, also, are introduced in Ravenscroft's tunes, which Ravenscroft never used. Perhaps, too, a query will be pardoned;—Are Ravenscroft's syncopations, which Playford prudently omitted, *correctly* scanned by Mr. Hullah?

INTRODUCTORY REMARKS. xiii

Peculiarities of the Harmony.

The tunes, as might be expected, are harmonized according to the excellent style of their age. Though some, as Psalm 126, are characterized by a severer simplicity, yet, in general, the harmony is of the more fluent kind. It resembles that of Gibbons more than that of Tye; for though many masters were employed, the work is mainly of one school.* The great aim of all the harmonists seems to have been an easy fluency, or a certain tuneful progression of the parts. Some of those parts are so melodious that they form tunes or airs of themselves. Hence, many a Cantus will make a pleasing Psalm-tune, any may be sung as such, including the old Tenor as an original air.

But it must be confessed that, in order to secure this excellency, little sacrifices of propriety are often made. A consecutive fifth or eighth is apparently suffered to pass, if the tunefulness of the strain is thereby kept up. Instances of this sufferance will be found, at least, in Veni Creator, Psalm 1, 52, 103, 119, 124, 125, 130, 132; St. Asaph, Chester, Wolverhampton, Tallis's Canon, and Ravenscroft's version of the Old Hundredth, The Ten Commandments, A prayer against Turk and Pope, and Da Pacem. Ravenscroft's own harmonies are as remarkable as any for these liberties, though few are more tastefully arranged than his. And yet, though these defects appear to be allowed, in other cases effort to avoid them seems to be made. A minim

---

* Between Este and Ravenscroft there is considerable difference as to the general character of their style. Este is more austere both in melody and harmony. He adopts more decidedly what is called "the *pure* style," avoiding a fourth on the dominant, and using fewer syncopations than Ravenscroft. The tenor part in Este more commonly becomes the bass than in his successor's volume.

xiv INTRODUCTORY REMARKS.

is not unfrequently split into crotchets, in order that the latter of the two may just save a forbidden consecution.* This sort of escape from violation of rule is what the present age does not admit. From desire to accomplish the aim alluded to, a discord is not always speedily resolved, nor a leading note always carried upward as the ear anticipates. In fact, little things give way for the greater excellence of melodious progression.

In accordance with the style of the age, certain combinations are either studiously avoided, or commonly used. A succession of fundamental chords is a main characteristic. The Tierce de Picardie, or major third at the end of a strain in a minor key, is constantly used. Except as a passing note, the dominant seventh is hardly discoverable. True, there are two or three cases in which such seventh *appears* to be used; but on examination they may be pronounced misprints. In Psalm 1, by Thomas Morley, the fourth note of the first strain in the Cantus, C, to the word "blest," is, in both editions of the original, B flat, forming $\frac{7}{5}$ on C. But in Dr. Rimbault's copy of 1633, this B flat is altered
3
by some careful pen of many years ago to C, which, in all probability, is the true reading; because the *progression* which then occurs to the common chord of C was perfectly common; but the *progression* to B flat *on that chord* was, in Morley's day, most uncommon. It must however, be acknowledged that Turner, in 1728, did not recognize this "correction." So also, in Psalm 126, at the close of the third strain, to the word "heart," in the Cantus, is A, a dotted minim; but, in the original copies, it is

---

* See Norwich, and Martyrs, at the end of the second strain of which *caution* is evidently exercised in the bass, in order to avoid consecutive octaves.

INTRODUCTORY REMARKS.   XV

G, forming a bold flat seventh on A. It doubtless, however, is a misprint, as the close of the tune, and other parts of it, where the corrected phrase occurs, pretty clearly show. And here it may be remarked, that no errors have been corrected but such as are plainly the mistakes of the printer. The oversights of the authors have been left as they were found.

The chord of $^6_4_3$, which is hardly a century old, is not, of course, in any of the tunes. Purity of ecclesiastical style forbids its use, though so many modern composers inconsiderately introduce it. Neither is there any positive instance of the $^{6\flat}_{3\sharp}$ so common in the time of Purcell, and so abominated by Dr. Burney.

The feeble and secular sounding chord of $^6_4$ upon the accented dominant, in the major key, followed by $^5_3$ at a close, and which the old worthies used by every contrivance to avoid, is very rare indeed. An instance will be found in the Venite, in the Lord's Prayer, and in the King's Tune, with, possibly, a few others. Everywhere the more masculine combination of $^5_4$ resolved into $^5_3$ is observable. The discords of most frequent occurrence are the 7th, the 9th, $^5_4$, $^6_5$, $^4_2$, and $^9_4$. When these, or any, in fact, are used, it is always with a skill and a *fitness*, which form a striking contrast to the pedantry of those moderns, who " *stick on a discord* wherever a point will possibly hold it." Throughout the volume, consecutive fifths and eighths by *contrary* motion, and even by direct motion, when passing from one strain to another, are habitually used. So, also, is that tritonal succession of

xvi INTRODUCTORY REMARKS.

chords, (ex. gr. $_{G\ F}^{B\ C}$) now so uncommon, and so outrageously decried by Cherubini (Course of Counterpoint, vol. i. p. 16), but so frequent in the sixteenth century. In Psalm 104, the construction of the parts at "so passing in glory," is singular and hardly justifiable. It probably is a mistake; the first A in the Cantus being put for B. In Psalm 69, strain the third, are, what is rather unusual, six minor chords in succession. In some instances, the Tenor is set so high as to induce a belief that, as certainly was the case in later days, the key was not always intended for the pitch. The avoidance of leger lines, and the horror of a key in sharps, had, no doubt, much influence in determining these minor points. Psalms 124 and 137 mount up to A. The same elevation occurs, probably for the same reasons, in some of the ordinary Psalters.

In sundry instances, points of imitation between the parts are observable, and that sort of ingenious contrivance for which the age was remarkable. In Abby* Tune is an answer to a subject between the Tenor and the Bass, in the third strain; also in the fourth strain of Chichester, and in the third strain of Salisbury. The 81st Psalm, by Allison, presents skill of the same sort; to which may be added the 122nd and sundry others. In "The Song of the Three Children," by Ravenscroft, the Medius is the same as the Cantus, forming two trebles in one, till the last phrase; when, at "magnify him for ever," the Medius takes up a distinct strain, and forms a chorus of four parts. Possibly Ravenscroft, by first employing only *three* parts, intended a reference to the *three* children.

* Called, in the Scotch Psalters of Andro Hart, "Abbay."

INTRODUCTORY REMARKS. xvii

Notice of certain Tunes.

Among compositions so generally excellent, specification is almost superfluous. What tunes, of the newer sort, Ravenscroft most frequently repeated, and which may therefore be regarded as favourites with himself, have already been noticed. Of the older tunes, several must remain obsolete, unless the words of the Old Version are retained, or new words selected.

"Among the "Hymnes Evangelicall," Nunc Dimittis is remarkable, not merely for its triple measure, but for a sprightliness and buoyancy which form quite a contrast to the style of the other Hymns. It is well set by Ravenscroft, who has sobered its secular-like vivacity by clothing it with ecclesiastical harmony. The commencement of the tune, in the harmony of the subdominant of the key, will strike every student of old Church music.

The tune to the 122nd Psalm, harmonized by Farnaby, the same as in Este, and that to the 137th by Ravenscroft, though little known, are exquisitely melodious, and cleverly arranged.

Of the two versions of the Old Hundredth tune, Ravenscroft's is the more florid, but Dowland's is the better set. Both are worthy of notice; though Ravenscroft's is evidently an effort to carry out Dowland's style without copying it.

The versions of York Tune by Milton are unquestionably superior to that by Stubbs. The version in B♭* is the best and

---

* Dr. Crotch, in his copy of the tune, has assigned the modulation of this version to only the third strain. On the whole, that arrangement is an improvement. All the old versions begin the fourth strain on *mi*, the modern on *sol*.

D

xviii INTRODUCTORY REMARKS.

most original of the three. Till the present century, this tune was, in England, a universal favourite. While choirs sang it and chimes played it, nurses, says Sir J. Hawkins, hummed it as a lullaby. Next to the Old Hundredth, it was, perhaps, the most popular of all the Elizabethan tunes. But it has resigned the palm, and is now but little known. It is still, however, sung at the University Church, Oxford, to "O gentes omnes," before Latin sermons.

The fine and stately melody of the 104th Psalm has been strangely metamorphosed, in a volume of Psalm Tunes, published in 1816, by W. Cross,* B.M., Organist of Christ Church, Oxford. The tune, as it stands in all the old Psalters, is in the key of G minor, written in the counter-tenor clef. This tune, so written, has been read as though it were in the G clef, which, consequently, turns the notation into the key of F major. Thus, by the mistake of the editor, and the curiously happy construction of the original melody, an entirely new tune has been fabricated; and, yet, it is given, in the volume, as a genuine version of the Old 104th, and as such is not only sung at the University Church, but was, during Cross's time at least, a special favourite.†

Tallis's "Canon,‡ two parts in one," between the Tenor and

---

* The elaborate and learned Preface to this volume was not written by Cross. It was supplied by a well-known living member of Corpus Christi College. Cross did little else than badly arrange some tunes, and spoil the older harmonies of others. He was a good organist, but no musician.

† What makes the blunder something more than ludicrous, is the fact that the tune is said to be "Harmonized by Ravenscroft," whereas not a single part, not a single note, was penned by that master!

‡ This Canon must have been composed by Tallis long before Ravenscroft was

INTRODUCTORY REMARKS.

Cantus, is generally, and, perhaps rightly, regarded as the original of the modern Evening Hymn. This modern distortion might well excite wonder, were it not for the greater marvel of generations having lost sight of the pleasing Canon which the original quietly contained. Even Mr. Hullah does not point it out.

It may be thought singular that, in the course of the Canon, consecutive fifths should twice occur. But Tallis, in hymns of this sort, (and sundry are extant) disdains all trammel, and consults only smoothness of progression. The composition is further remarkable for being throughout in a sharp key, and the only tune to which the name of Tallis is attached.

Of all the newer tunes, those called Welch are the most singular, and the least agreeable. Bangor, St. David's, and Llandaff, contain very awkward skips, and intervals which little accord with the general character of the tunes. St. David's, however, was long ago altered, as long, at least, as Playford's day, and rendered more accordant with ordinary style. In its altered form it has been popular rather than otherwise. Canterbury and Oxford are tunes of the plainest and simplest construction; while Windsor and Wolverhampton, both harmonized by Ravenscroft, are remarkable for rythmical disruption. That disruption is most likely attributable to Ravenscroft, as it is not

---

born. It is an altered and a shortened version of the No. 8 of Tallis's Tunes, for Archbishop Parker's metrical translation of the Psalms. Whether Tallis himself ever wrote it in the shape in which Ravenscroft has printed it, cannot, perhaps, be ascertained. The original does not contain the faulty consecutives which appear in Ravenscroft's version. It was long ago suspected that Ravenscroft inserted it, for the sake of garnishing his volume with Tallis's name. As Ravenscroft has set it to "A Psalme before *Morning* Prayer," it is curious for our moderns to apply it to an "*Evening* Hymn."

found in the older Scotch version. The Prayer against Turk and Pope, though called a High Dutch Tune, is generally attributed to Luther. The words, by Robert Wisdom, Archdeacon of Ely, are little else than a translation of Luther's lines.

Concluding Remarks.

Ravenscroft's "Booke of Psalmes" was always estimated as the completest of its kind. It was justly regarded as the fount of English Psalmody. Why it ceased to be used, and why its streams dried up, is too easily accounted for. The overthrow of the Church during the grand Rebellion, confused or estranged everything belonging to it. But that "the booke" should have remained little else than a choked and covered spring for nearly two centuries, is a discredit to those who had the power to reopen it, but who spared the requisite pains.

The present reprint of "the booke," though justly due to the memory of Ravenscroft, is undertaken not so much to furnish a store of excellent tunes in suitable form for general use, as to present to musical professors, and to the Church at large, a compendium-model of genuine psalmody. What such psalmody was, as to both melody and harmony, in the most palmy days of "the divine arte," may now be seen and understood. The volume is a store-house from whence ordinary skill may derive supplies for instant use, and from the contents of which living composers may learn how to arrange any newer productions after the best models of by-gone days. For, they will do well to observe the rule which Dr. Crotch has happily elicited, viz., "new Church music, but *no new style*."

INTRODUCTORY REMARKS. xxi

In pursuance of these objects, it was deemed sufficient to reprint the volume after the present mode. By uniting the parts and bringing them into "short score," it was thought that every practised eye would readily discern their relative bearing; while the simple performance of them on a keyed instrument, will yield somewhat of their intended effect.

It is the intention of the editor, as speedily as practicable, to publish a selection of the tunes, with the Cantus and Tenor inverted or of necessity altered, to suit our present mode of singing. To such selection will be added other tunes, principally for other metres; but strictly in the same generic style of melody and harmony. The object of this selection will be to meet, at a moderate cost, the taste and wishes of those persons who very properly think that Church-music, like Church-architecture, should have a character peculiar to itself; and who, also, are of opinion that the character of Church-psalmody was truly and admirably defined in the days of Queen Elizabeth. No such exclusive selection has hitherto been printed.

In the words of Ravenscroft, "Thus I end; humbly wishing to all true Christian hearts, that sweet consolation in singing praises unto God here upon earth, as may bring us hereafter to bear a part with the choir of angels in the heavens."

W. H. H.

Henwick House, near Worcester.
    August, 1844.

The Whole Booke of Psalmes:

Hymnes Evangelicall.

A Reprint of All the Tunes in Ravenscroft's Book of Psalms with Introductory Remarks by W.H.H.

19

PSALM 21. English Tune.

John Bennet.

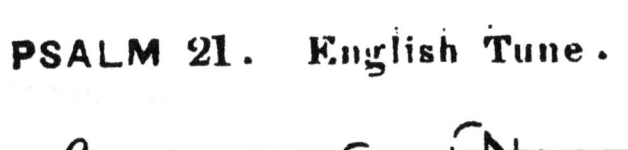

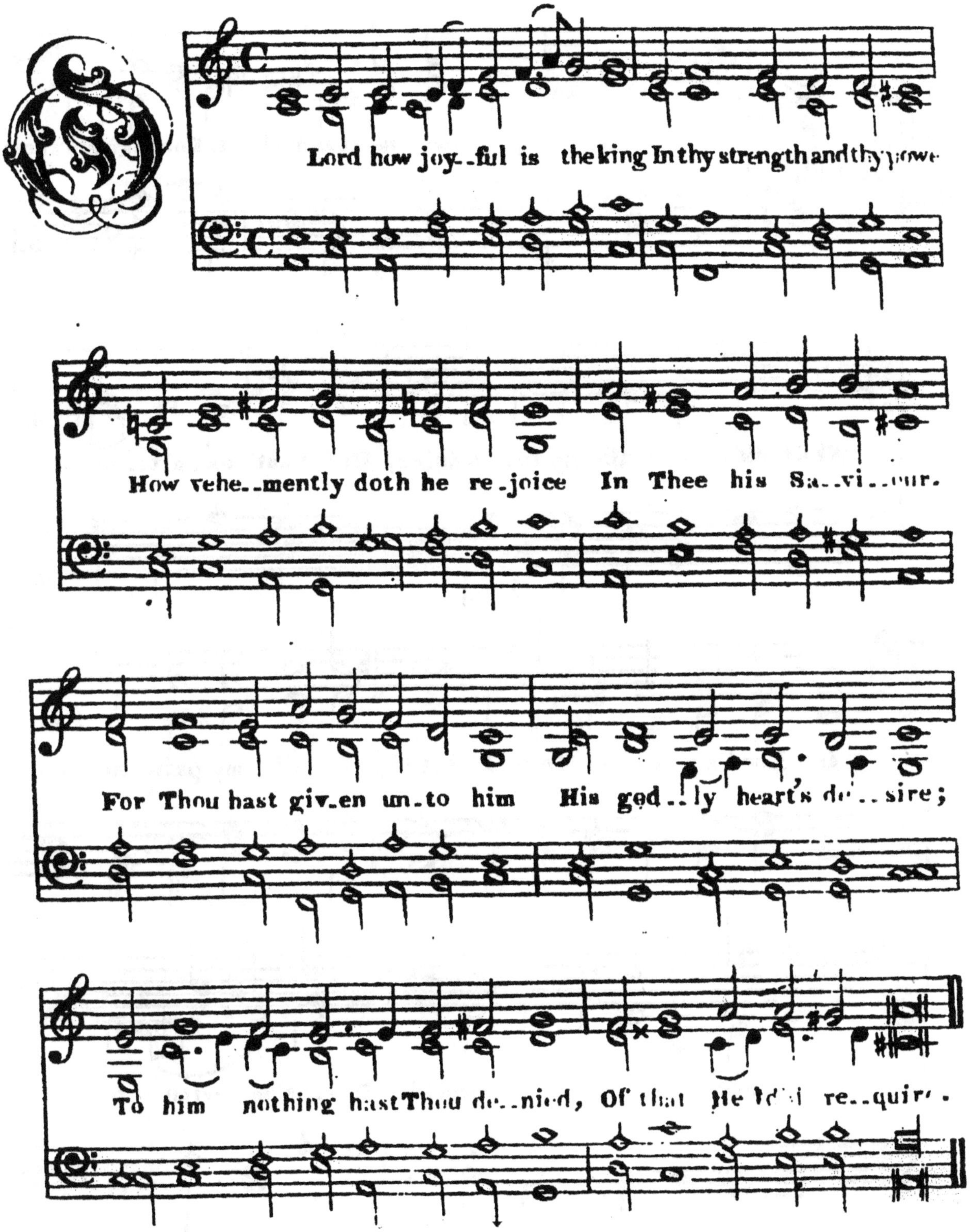

PSALM 38. English Tune.

Tho. Morley, B. of M.

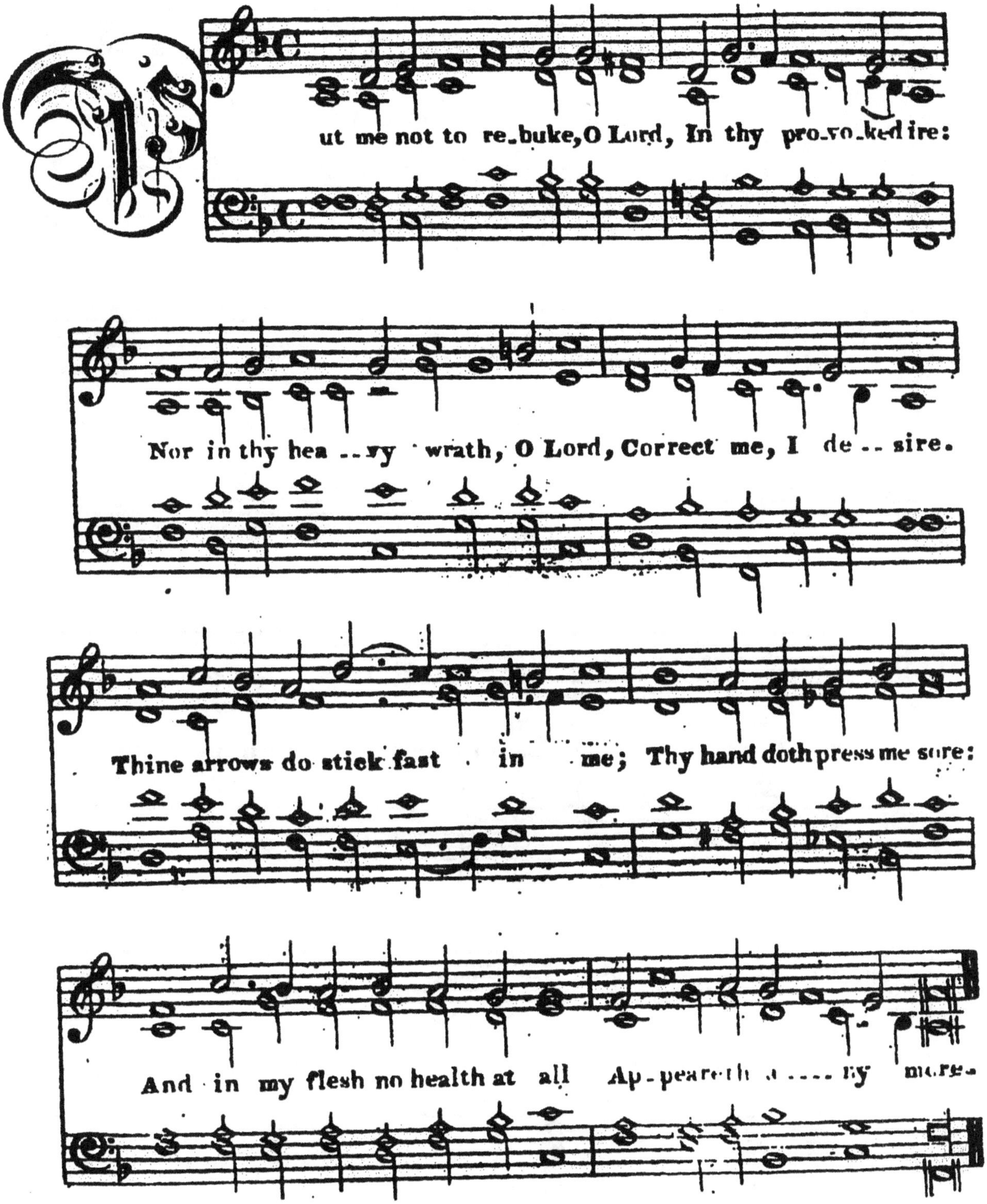

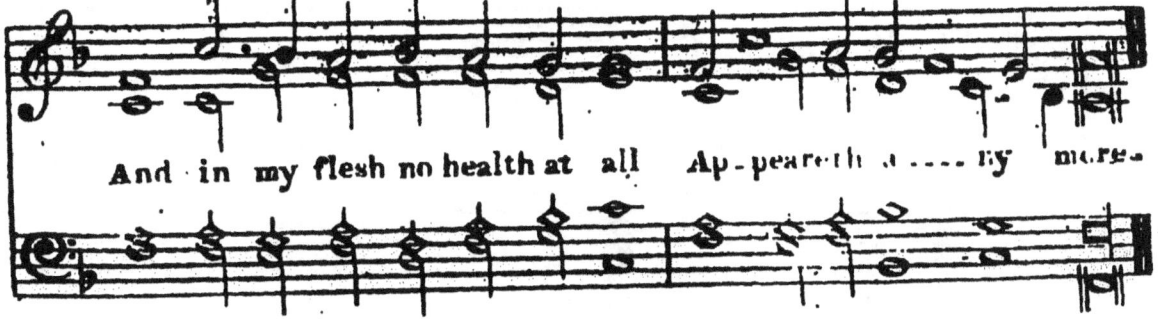

PSALM 59. English Tune.

I. Farmer.

...end aid and save me from my foes, O Lord I pray to thee:

Defend and keep me from all those, That rise and strive with me.

O Lord preserve me from those men, Whose do..ings are not good:

And set me sure and safe from them, That still thirst af..ter blood.

29

PSALM 68. English Tune.

Richard Allison.

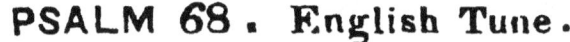

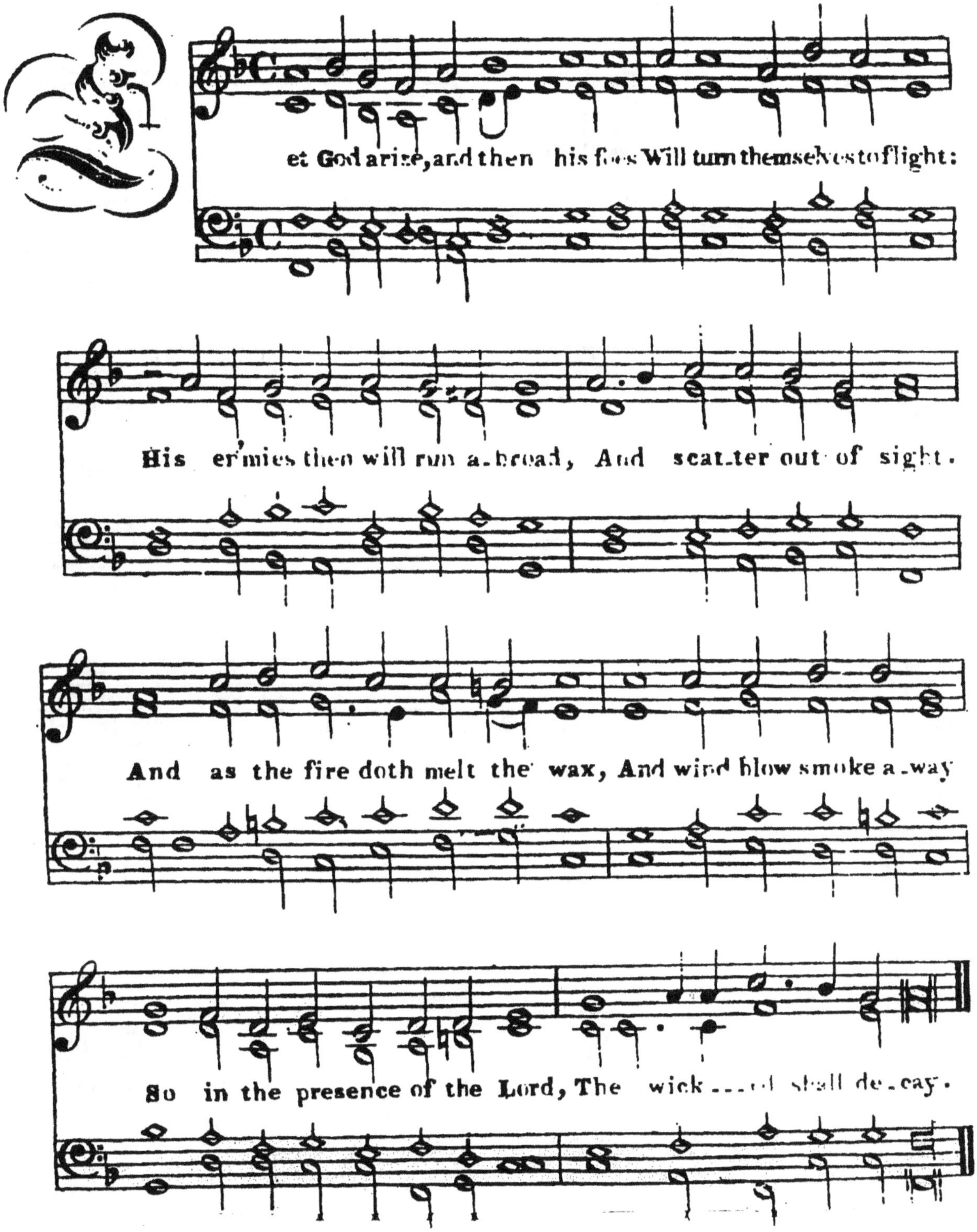

PSALM 112. High Dutch Tune.

G. Kirby.

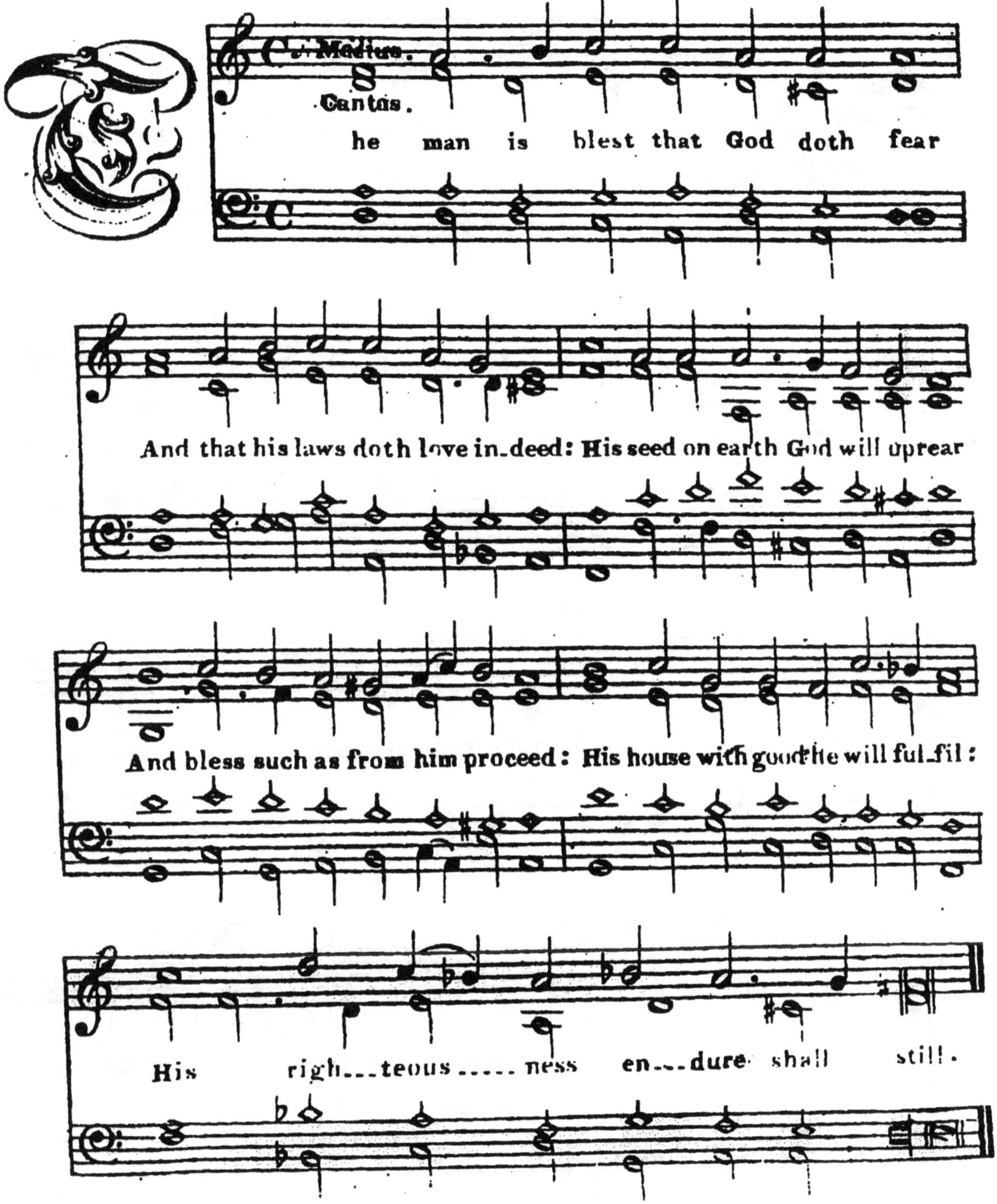

The man is blest that God doth fear
And that his laws doth love indeed: His seed on earth God will uprear
And bless such as from him proceed: His house with good he will fulfil:
His righteousness endure shall still.

A Reprint of All the Tunes in Ravenscroft's Book of Psalms with Introductory Remarks by W.H.H.

48 ANOTHER OF THE SAME. French Tune. R. Allison.

Those that do put their confidence Upon the Lord our God only;
And fly to him for his defence In all their need and mis...e...ry.

PSALM 126. French Tune. E. Johnson.

When that the Lord again his Si..on had forth brought
From bondage great and al..so ser..vi...tude ex..treme:

Tunes of Later Date.

64

DUMFERLINE. (Scotch Tune.) Ps: 89.

Tho. Tomkins, B. of M.

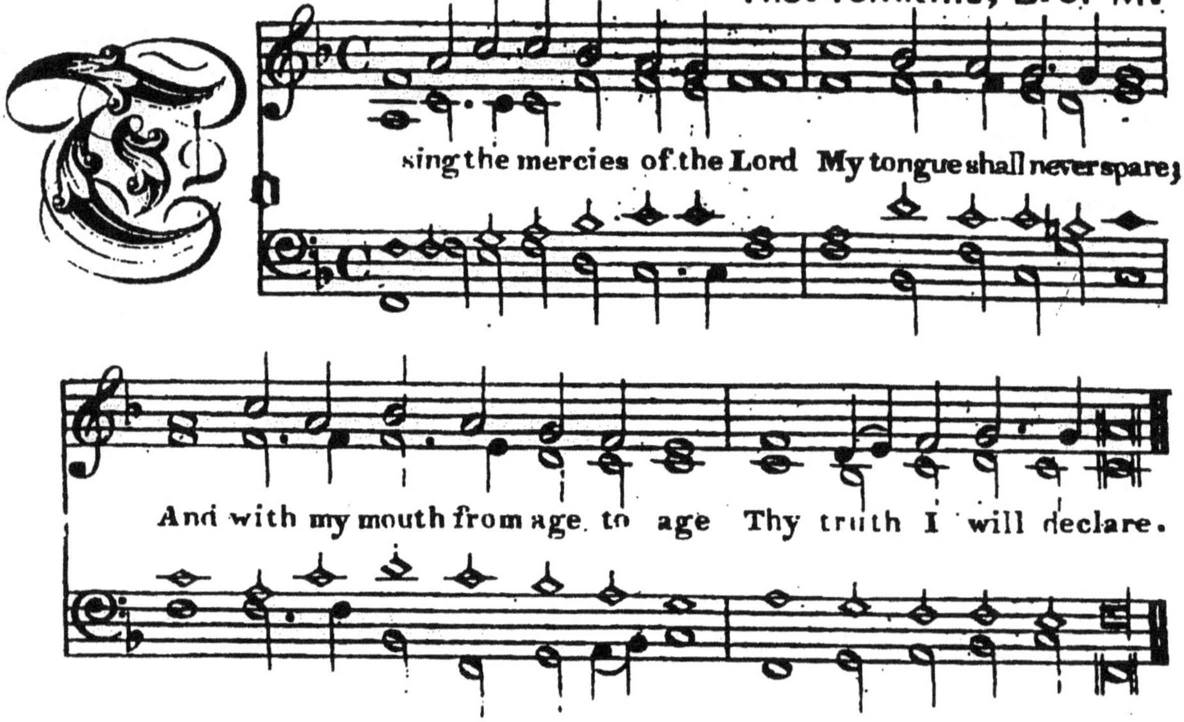

DUNDEE. (Scotch Tune.) Ps: 90.

Tho. Ravenscroft, B. of M.

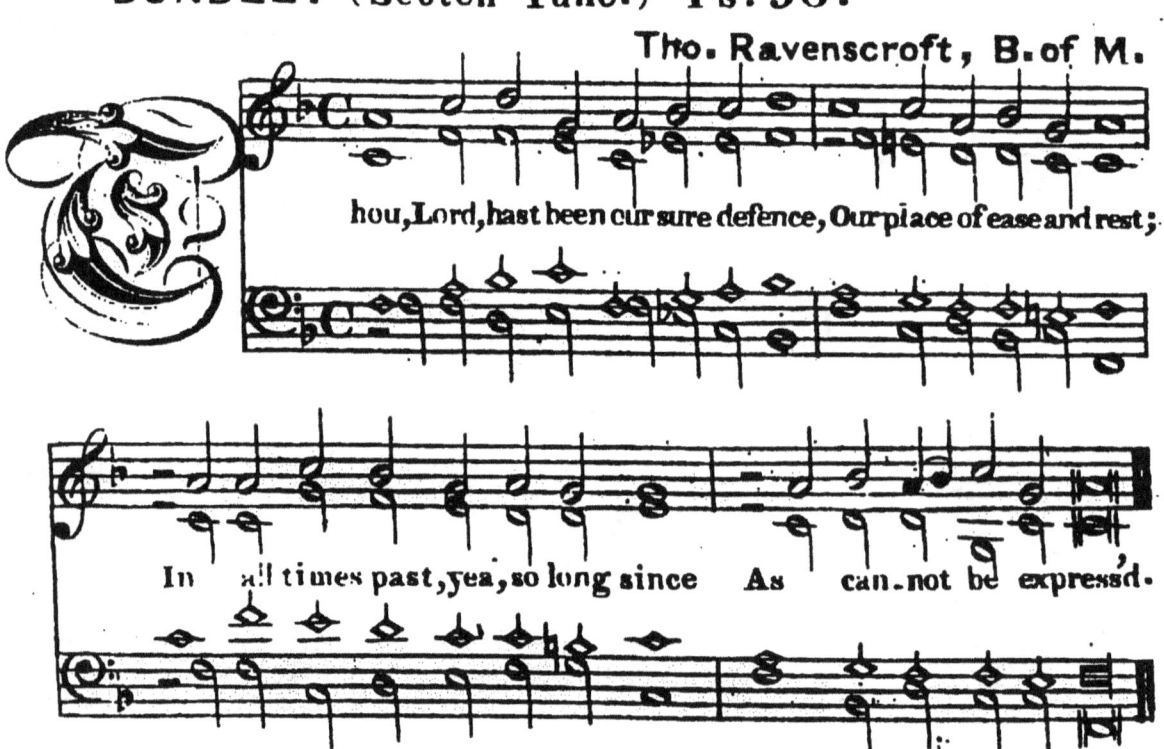

A Reprint of All the Tunes in Ravenscroft's Book of Psalms with Introductory Remarks by W.H.H.

Songs Spiritual.

80

A PSALM BEFORE MORNING PRAYER.
(CANON two in one.) — T. Tallis.

Praise the Lord, O ye Gentiles all, which hath brought you in to his light, O praise Him all people mortal, As it is most worthy and right.

82. THE CREED.

G. Kirby.

All my belief and confidence Is in the Lord of might:
The Father which all things hath made, The day and eke the night.
The heavens and the firmament, And al....so many a star;
The earth and all that is therein, Which pass man's reason far.

A Reprint of All the Tunes in Ravenscroft's Book of Psalms with Introductory Remarks by W.H.H.

Note: This was the last page of W.H.H.'s edition of Ravenscroft's Psalter.

A HISTORY OF

THE OLD HUNDREDTH

PSALM TUNE,

WITH SPECIMENS.

BY THE
REV. W. H. HAVERGAL, M. A.,
RECTOR OF ST. NICHOLAS, AND HONORARY CANON, WORCESTER.

WITH A PREFATORY NOTE

BY RT. REV. J. M. WAINWRIGHT, D. D.,
BISHOP OF NEW YORK.

NEW YORK:
MASON BROTHERS.

1854.

Entered, according to Act of Congress, in the year 1854, by

MASON BROTHERS,

In the Clerk's Office of the Southern District of New York.

STEREOTYPED BY
THOMAS B. SMITH,
216 William Street.

PRINTED BY
JOHN A. GRAY
87 Cliff St.

PREFATORY NOTE.

THERE is probably no musical composition, with the exception of the ancient Ambrosian and Gregorian tones, that has been so universally sung by worshipping assemblies, as the Old Hundredth Psalm Tune, and certainly none so familiar to the ear of Protestant communities. It has proved equally acceptable to the instructed and the uninstructed musical taste. When in any congregation, through ignorance or bad taste, it has been for a time laid aside to make way for more modern yet more feeble tunes, it has been taken up again, after the intermission, with increased interest; and as its strains have been given out by the organ, and its first tones raised by the choir or the clerk, devout affections have been roused, and voices which had been long silent have swelled the loud chorus of praise. It has been known in this country from its first settlement. It was in all probability used by the earliest Church of England missionaries in Virginia, and it was certainly one of the songs of the Puritan fathers of New England, since we find it in Ainsworth's Psalms, the book of Psalmody which they brought from Holland. It was, therefore, one of the tunes to which the wild forests in this new world were first made vocal with the praise of God. Nor was its use confined to the early European settlers; its lofty strains were taught by them to the inhabitants of the forest they found here; it was sung by the new-made converts of the missionary John Elliot, and in the various missionary settlements amongst the Indians it may yet be heard.

The history of such a composition must be a matter of interest not only to the musician, but to all who have the slightest taste for musical art, and especially to those who take delight in the service of song in the house of the Lord. Mr. Havergal has performed a most acceptable work in his curious researches. He has carefully hunted up, probably, everything that can be discovered relating to its origin, and has established its authorship as satisfactorily as can now be done. We think it will be generally conceded that William Franc must hereafter be entitled to the credit of *composing* this most remarkable of all metrical tunes. But the result of Mr. Havergal's researches is perhaps of more practical importance considered with reference to the form of the tune. This, it seems, has been greatly changed, and hence the heaviness, and almost tediousness, which sometimes attends its performance. Could its old rhythm be restored, the tune would more fully accord with the joyful character of the psalm by which it is called, and would not fail to be even more popular and useful than heretofore.

The most estimable author of this work, a clergyman of the Church of England, is well known in the United States as well as in England, for his devotion to the cause of sacred music; and no one in our day has contributed more than he has done to the revival of a taste for pure ecclesiastical melodies and harmonies. His "Old Church Psalmody," published in London, is probably the best book of the kind which has appeared since the days of Ravenscroft, and it is gradually doing its work of reform. We learn from Mr. Mason's "Musical Letters from Abroad," that Mr. Havergal's views of church music are happily illustrated in his own church. "The chanting was done," says Mr. M., "by the whole congregation, and the responding was between the occupants of the lower floor and those of the galleries; but the song was universal, men, women and children uniting harmonious voices." The tunes to which the hymns were sung, he tells us, were of "the old ecclesiastical class," in a similar rhythm to that which Mr. H. has shown to be the original of the Old Hundredth Psalm Tune, and were sung in a quick time, or "as fast as propriety would allow the enunciation of the words." We further learn from him that there were but "one or two interludes introduced in a psalm of five stanzas;" and that "these were very short, not more than about two measures, or the length of the last line of a common metre tune." That the evil custom which so extensively prevails in this country, of long interludes between the stanzas, alike foreign to the psalm and the tune, and unfavorable to devotion, should be abolished, and that the congregation should not be kept standing to be amused by the tones of the organ, or by the skill of the performer, and thus be disturbed or interrupted in their worship, is most devoutly to be desired. A passing cadence of a few chords connecting the stanzas may be useful, but more than this is rather a hinderance than a help to the religious effect of the psalmody.

Happy will it be for the Church when a more pure and devotional style of song shall be restored, and the light and powerless tunes now so often heard shall give way to those which are better adapted to awaken religious feeling, and which are more in accordance with the dignity of public worship. We most cordially commend Mr. Havergal's interesting volume on the History of the Old Hundredth Psalm Tune, as one means of promoting a reformation so much needed.

JNO. M. WAINWRIGHT.

New York, April, 1854.

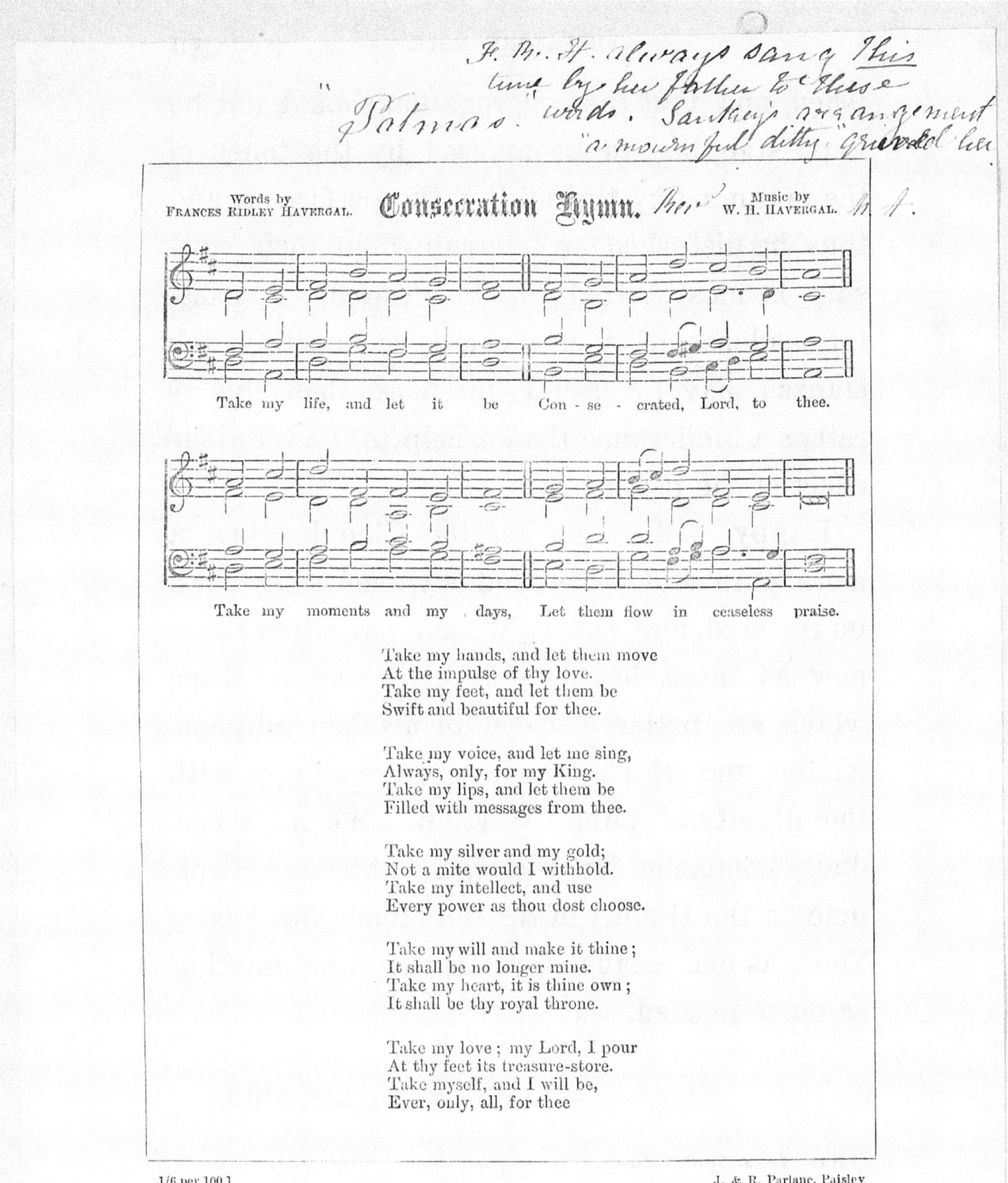

A printed copy of the Consecration Hymn by F.R.H. Her sister Maria V. G. Havergal, wrote this note at the top: "Patmos." F.R.H. always sang this tune by her father to these words. Sankey's arrangement "a mournful ditty," grieved her. *Maria also added "Rev." and "M.A." around her father's name.*

Note: This was a blank page in the original book.

THE OLD HUNDREDTH PSALM TUNE.

The Psalters of Sternhold and Hopkins were, for a long time, usually printed "with apt notes to sing withal." Some of those notes or tunes were of English origin; but the majority were brought from the Continent. The intercourse of kindred Reformers, and the return of exiled confessors, contributed to the enlargement of the little store of tunes, which sufficed, when metrical psalmody first came into use.

The number of the tunes, and the tunes themselves, were not the same in all editions of the psalter. Frequent changes were made by succeeding editors; so that, between the psalters of the early part of the reign of Queen Elizabeth, and those of the next two reigns, there is a considerable difference. The general number, however, of the tunes, which were printed, on the establishment of the Reformation, was forty. But, of the entire number, only one is now commonly known. That one is the tune to the hundredth psalm. Some of the rest, particularly " the old eighty-first, and the old hundred and thirteenth," as they were called, continued in partial use till the beginning of the present century; but modern trash has consigned them to oblivion; and the whole forty, save only this one, have (till very lately at least) ceased to be seen or heard. Happily, in almost every parish of the British Isles, this tune has continued to be known and admired.* It would be difficult, perhaps, except in Ireland, to find any parish in which it is positively unknown. Its survival, therefore, amidst the oblivion of so many excellent tunes, and its universal popularity, constitute a fair proof of its intrinsic merit, and of its genuine suitableness for divine worship.

To the devout Christian, such a tune cannot be otherwise than deeply interesting. The thought of its having been sung, for many an age, "in the great congregation," and of its having formed the solace of many a heart in the cottage or the closet, must always add a hallowed pleasure to its use. The consideration, too, that Protestant martyrs and exiled confessors have listened to its strains or joined in them, may well give an exalted and even an affecting energy, to our modulation of them.

THE NAME OF THE TUNE, as The Old Hundredth Psalm Tune, is peculiar to England. In foreign psalters, especially in the French and the Dutch, the tune is set to the hundred and thirty-fourth psalm. From the days of the Reformation to the end of the seventeenth century, it was commonly called in England The Hundredth Psalm Tune; but upon the publication of Tate and Brady's new version, its present

---

* It is also universally sung in the United States of America.

title came into use. About a century or more ago, it became the fashion to call it "SAVOY," and under that name it appears in many collections of a subsequent date. The fashion took its rise from a vague fancy respecting its Savoyard origin; but, older custom and wiser belief have given prevalence to the existing appellation. In America, an inelegant variation is made, and the tune is commonly called "Old Hundred." Why such a departure from lingual custom, and orthographic propriety should be made, does not appear.

THE TEXT OF THE TUNE, though never formally disputed, has not always been uniform. And yet, in all the older versions, the variations have been, not in the tune itself, but in *the time* of its notes. Apart from palpable misprints, the melodic progression seems to have been correctly preserved; only a somewhat altered character was given to it, according as certain notes in it were made long or short.

All the earliest copies of the tune contain a nicely-poised blending of long and short notes; but later versions present it in notes of equal length. Towards the beginning of the last century, a wanton modification of the time of the tune was made on the Continent. In 1730, John Sebastian Bach printed the tune in triple measure; but whether the conceit originated with that superlative musician, or with some one before him, is not quite clear. Since that date, several Continental editors, both Roman Catholic and Protestant, have adopted the unwarrantable modification; but no English collection of any repute contains it.

12. THE OLD HUNDREDTH PSALM TUNE.

The earliest copy of the tune, so far as is known, stands in a Genevan edition of a portion of the English Psalter, preserved as an article of rare value in the Library of St. Paul's Cathedral, London. The date of the Psalter is 1561.* The tune is therein given to Sternhold's version of the Hundredth Psalm, thus:

Psalm C.

With this earliest known copy of the tune, *all* the subsequent copies of the foreign psalters completely agree, and most of our early English psalters agree also, with the exception of a slight alteration in the last strain.†

The first edition of Sternhold's Psalter, *with notes*,

---

* The real facts of the case are thus stated by the late Rev. R. H. Barham, when Librarian of St. Paul's. "The name of Geneva is not on the Psalter which occupies the middle space in a volume, consisting of a 'Forme of Prayers, and Ministration of the Sacraments,' and 'Calvin's Catechism,' both of which have that place on their title pages, with the same date, in the same numerals (MDLXI.) The whole character of the type is the same, and I have not the slightest doubt that they were printed by 'Zacharie Durand,' whose name stands on both the last-mentioned works above the date."

† In 1561, John Day, of London, printed a Dutch Psalter, for the use of the refugees from the Low Countries. The title of the copy in the British Museum is, "Hondert Psalmen David's," octavo, London, 1561, and the "Press Mark" is "1220. c. 39." Although the first strain of the tune occurs in several psalms, the tune itself is not in the volume.

was published in 1556. It did not, however, comprise more than a third of the Psalms, nor contain either the words or the tune of the Hundredth Psalm.* It was not, however, till the year 1562 that John Day printed a complete version of Sternhold and Hopkins's Psalter, "with apt notes to sing withal." Though many authors assert the printing of this psalter, and record its title, yet others of equal repute altogether disbelieve its ever having existed. They are of opinion that it was not till 1563 that the first complete English psalter was printed. The late Mr. Lea Wilson strongly held this opinion. He possessed the only known copy of this last-named psalter, which is now in the possession of Mr. W. Pickering, the distinguished publisher. But, as Sir John Hawkins not only gives the title of the Psalter of 1562, but copies several tunes from it, there can be no reasonable doubt of its once having existed. Where his copy now is, or where, indeed, any copy is to be found, the author, after extensive and diligent search, is unable to ascertain. None of our great libraries possess it, nor does Dr. H. Cotton, in the second edition of his "List of Editions of the Bible, and the Psalms in English," give any clue to the finding of it. It is pretty certain, however, that if there was a Psalter of 1562, it did not contain the Old Hundredth Psalm tune, not only because Sir John Hawkins had seen no copy of it earlier than 1577, but because it is not to be found in Mr. Lea Wilson's copy of 1563.†

* A copy of this Psalter is preserved in the Bodleian Library.
† Singular however to say, a writer in an American periodical,

14   THE OLD HUNDREDTH PSALM TUNE.

As no complete edition of the English Psalter is known to have been printed in 1564, there can be little doubt that the first appearance of the tune in Sternhold and Hopkins's Psalter was in the edition of 1565, of which edition a beautiful copy is preserved in the British Museum. The version of the tune in that copy is precisely the same as the version in the Genevan copy belonging to St. Paul's Library.

Tracing the tune from its first known appearance, in 1561, it is next to be seen in a remarkably beautiful copy of the Genevan Psalter, printed "Par Estienne Anastase, 1562," now in possession of the author, but which appears formerly to have belonged to a Duke of Gordon. The version is again identical with its prototype, already given.

But, in the year 1563 was printed by John Day, of London, the most valuable and interesting collection of church-tunes which has hitherto come to light. It goes far to settle what may be regarded as the true English version of the tune. The work itself is in the library of Brazen Nose College,* and consists of four

("The New England Puritan," Boston, April 19, 1844,) in the course of an elaborate article upon psalmody, not only speaks with great confidence of the certainty of the Psalter of 1562, but actually gives a copy of the tune as contained in it. His copy, however, of the tune is so palpably spurious, and the tenor of his remarks so vague and unsatisfactory, that he must be considered as either having fallen into some great mistake, or as having written a convenient fable.

* This is now, perhaps, the only perfect copy in England. Dr. Rimbault is said to have sold his copy to an American library. There is an imperfect copy, or rather two of the four parts of it, in the British Museum. There are also some odd numbers of it in the Bodleian.

separate small oblong volumes. From being catalogued as a psalter, without any reference to the tunes, it escaped the notice of all our musical historians and antiquarians. For want of acquaintance with it, both Dr. Burney and Sir John Hawkins fell into many groundless surmises and positive mistakes. The discovery of the work, as a *musical* curiosity, is fairly attributable to the author's elder son, the Rev. H. E. Havergal, when, some years ago, seeking for old copies of the tune under investigation.

In this work, which was probably the first of its kind in England, and which may be called Day's Musical Psalter of 1563, the tune is printed in four parts, but,* what is rather singular, it is not ranged in its numerical position with the other psalms.† This is not only remarkable in itself, but confirmatory of the fact of the tune not being inserted in the Psalter of 1563, for, except on the surmise that the words and the tune were not at first fully established, it is difficult to account for their being placed otherwise than in numerical order, especially as the same printer was

---

* Historians mention "Parson's Psalms," but no copy of any volume bearing that designation has yet been discovered. It is, therefore, not improbable that this work of Day's was popularly known as "Parson's Psalms," because William Parsons was the chief musician of the volume, and most likely its editor.

† It may be worthy of notice that in an edition of Sternhold and Hopkins's Psalter, printed by John Crespin, in Geneva, in 1569, and now in the possession of the Rev. T. Lathbury, of Bristol, the tune and words are placed among the introductory hymns of the psalter, after the Venite, which circumstance goes to show that the long metre version of the Hundredth Psalm was not at first preferred to the common metre version, which is still found in the old psalters.

16   THE OLD HUNDREDTH PSALM TUNE.

employed for both works. In this musical psalter the melody of the tune is precisely the same as in the version of it first given, with the exception of the second and third notes of the last strain being minims instead of semibreves. That strain consequently sings thus:

Reduced, therefore, to more modern shape and notation, the tune assumes this standard form:

The tune thus slightly modified, so as to equalize the time of all its strains, seems to have been regarded by Ravenscroft as its most correct, if not its strictly original form; for after this model he printed it in 1621; and all subsequent editors of our old Church Psalters followed his decision.

The symmetry of the tune thus modelled is remarkably beautiful. Had that beauty been discerned or even suspected, it might have saved the tune itself from the violence which has been practised upon it. A few remarks may suffice for developing its peculiarities.

Among all the psalter tunes there is not one which is formed after the model of this tune. In no collection of tunes, whether foreign or domestic, has the writer of these lines ever discovered even one which resembles it in point of rhythmic structure.

Each of its four strains comprises four long and four short notes, uniformly but peculiarly disposed.

The first note of each strain, to suit a line of eight syllables, is long, the next four short, and the remaining three long.

But, the three concluding long notes of each strain seem to bear a certain symmetrical melodic relation to each other.

In the first strain, they *rise* in close succession; in the second they *fall*.

In the third and fourth strain, precisely the same alternation is kept up.

The peculiar progression of the long and short notes in each strain, may be compared to the progress of a boat when breasting a succession of billows at sea. First, poised for a moment on the top of a wave, it rapidly descends; then, steadily labors up; is poised again, and so proceeds.

THE VARIATIONS OF THE TUNE, through either the carelessness or caprice of editors, have been considerable. From the middle of the reign of Elizabeth to the date of Ravenscroft's " Booke of Psalmes," Anno Dom. 1621, sundry departures from the standard model were made. The prevailing variation was that which retained the triple succession of long notes only in the last strain: though that which made the notes of equal shortness, except the first and the last of each strain,

18   THE OLD HUNDREDTH PSALM TUNE.

was certainly very common. The following version was several times printed by John Day, before the year 1590; and became, as before intimated, a rather common version with musicians. It is next to what may be called Ravenscroft's version, in point of symmetry:

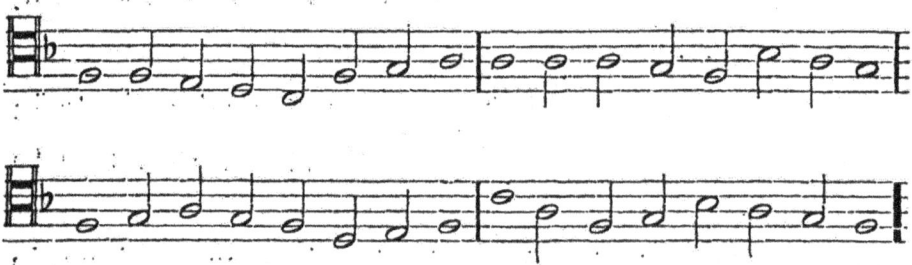

Still, the prevalent variation from the standard version was that which the American writer in the *New England Puritan* professes to give from the English psalter of 1562; and which Day printed or reprinted, apparently for the first time in 1575, both in a quarto and an octavo psalter. It is this:

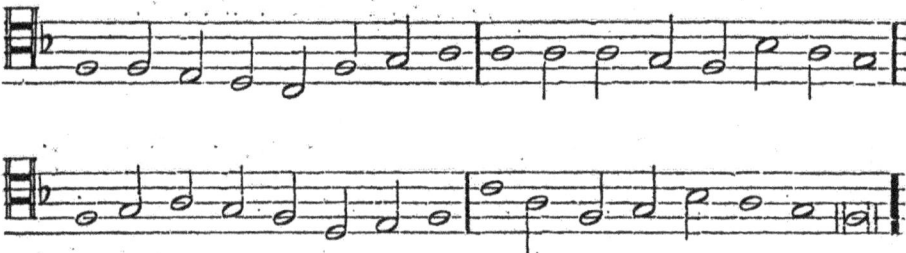

This is the version which William Damon used in 1579; and which Douland harmonized for Este's psalter in 1592, and again, as there is reason to believe, in 1611. It is found, also, in other psalters of a later date. It is adopted by Henry Ainsworth in his curious version of the Psalms, printed by Giles Thorp, at Amsterdam, in 1612. It further appears, after Ravenscroft's time, in King James' Psalter printed in 1636, by Thomas Harper, at London.

But a far greater variation, and even at an early period, was made in several psalters, by the very parties who printed the better versions. In two psalters by Day, one in 1583 and another in 1584 (Bodleian Library, and Rev. J. Metcalfe, Canterbury), the tune presents this vitiated form:

A similar corruption is printed by Windet in a psalter of 1599 (Rev. J. Metcalfe, Canterbury); and again in 1609 (Bodleian Library); and also by an anonymous printer in 1617.

From these specimens, and it would not be difficult to multiply them, it is perfectly plain that the practice of writing and printing all psalm tunes in notes of equal length, did *not* originate, as alleged by Mr. Hullah, with "honest John Playford."* In fact he did nothing half so bad as Day and Windet did, nearly a century before he printed a note. The version which

---

* " To him, as far as I can trace" (says Mr. Hullah, in the Preface to his Psalter, p. xiv.), is due *exclusively* the invention of that barbarous and monotonous manner of singing psalms,—*the making all notes of the same length.*"—How careful should living editors be of making grave charges against deceased worthies !

20   THE OLD HUNDREDTH PSALM TUNE.

he followed, and which, for distinction's sake, may be called Playford's version, as everybody afterwards followed him, is found as far back as, at least, 1588, in a psalter printed by the assigns of Richard Day, London. It is found, also, in one of 1594, quarto, London (Bodleian Library); and in another of 1595, by John Windet.

From what has been adduced, it is clear that the earlier printers or editors of our English psalters were not at all choice in selecting authentic copies of the Old Hundredth Psalm Tune. They seem to have printed, almost at random, first one version and then another. Sometimes, though not frequently, they printed even the earliest, or Genevan version; for a psalter of John Day's in 1575, and another by Henrie Denham in 1588, contain it.

The inaccuracy of many psalters is very great. The press, in some instances, can hardly be said to have been corrected. Most of the errors arise from a mere inversion of the metallic block in which the note was fixed; so that, by turning the page upside down, the true reading will appear. One common error is the dropping or elevating the note exactly a third out of place. Hence, in most cases of deviation from the true reading, it is easy to discern what was intended; for the printed note is so inconsistent with the melodic progression, and so disconnected with either the note before or the note after, that the error well nigh corrects itself.

In a small copy of Sternhold and Hopkins's Psalter, printed at Dort, in 1601, (Doucé's Collection in Bod-

THE OLD HUNDREDTH PSALM TUNE.　21

leian Library) the tune presents such a remarkable variation in the second strain, that it can hardly be regarded as an oversight. It is printed thus:

Such deviations from the original melody are not common. This specimen is unique. No printer followed it; nor was the tune in popular use affected by it. Indeed, it was not till the middle of the last century, and that in England only, that the *melody* suffered any perversion.* The Continental copies have preserved the progression of that melody with singular fidelity. The modern Parisian psalters present the tune in *triple* time, but the tune itself is otherwise unchanged. Our English singers, however, have perverted the last strain of the tune; and the perversion is so established, that editor after editor, of a certain class, has printed it, in full belief of its authenticity. As far as can be ascertained, the earliest printed copy of this perversion is found in Fox's edition of Playford's tunes in 1757. The last strain is therein given thus:

* Dr. Crotch twice or thrice published the tune with a *breve* at the end of *every* strain; but no psalter furnishes authority for the elongation.

22   THE OLD HUNDREDTH PSALM TUNE.

In this alteration of the strain there is nothing essentially wrong, or offensive to propriety. In fact, as a melodic phrase, it is as good as the original; only it is not the original. In a class of tunes, the compass of which is necessarily very limited, attention to original structure is important, otherwise the composer is injured, the identity of the tunes is destroyed, and confusion among them is produced.

In the English psalters, the tune is invariably printed in the key of F; and generally in the tenor clef. It is thus printed in the oldest copies of the German psalters, and also of the French, as may be seen in three octavo editions, printed at Lyons, in 1563, 1564, and 1587, and preserved in the Bodleian Library at Oxford. It is similarly printed in the beautifully-fresh copy of the same psalter, dated 1562, to which reference has already been made.

In the later editions of the French psalter, the tune is generally set a fourth higher, in the key of B♭, and in the counter-tenor clef. In some intermediate editions, it is in C, with the same clef. The Dutch psalters give it mostly in that key, and in that clef. If, therefore, the tune were sung as printed, the voices would be forced into an unseemly elevation. But there is ample reason for believing that the key in which a tune, in these psalters, is set, is not always a correct guide for the pitch in which it was really sung. The precentor or clerk would be supposed to have the regulation of that matter, and to settle it according to the state of the choir, the capacity of the congregation, or the time of the service.

THE OLD HUNDREDTH PSALM TUNE.

THE ORIGIN OF THE TUNE has been a topic of much dispute. Popular opinion is divided in assigning it principally to three individuals, viz., Martin Luther, Claude Goudimel, and William Franc. But, whether the tune is an original composition, or a mere adaptation, and if adapted, whether it has been derived from secular or ecclesiastical sources, has never been the subject of definite discussion. As the writer of these remarks has an hypothesis of his own to develop, a few preliminary observations may be expedient.

Metrical Psalmody was preceded, among the common people, by a sort of rude hymnology.* The doggerel-like hymns of early Protestants, both at home and abroad, were usually sung to any existing melody which could be applied to them. When the Psalms began to be used in a metrical form, those melodies were transferred to them—but then the melodies themselves were not generally sacred, but secular compositions. Many of them were "the most favorite songs of the times," or ballads, and even snatches of more vulgar strains. Others were accommodations from "such tunes as were easy to learn and play on the viol, and other instruments."

As the Reformation advanced, especially in Germany and Geneva, a better style of words was provided, and, as most of the Reformers were skilled in music, a better style of tunes followed. In Germany,† there-

---

* Some early specimens are extant among the papers of Dr. Fairfax, in the British Museum.

† "Germany was certainly furnished with innumerable psalmodists and hymnologists, long before Calvin (who was born in 1509) became

24   THE OLD HUNDREDTH PSALM TUNE.

fore, where metrical psalmody either originated, or first assumed the semblance of perfection, native musicians no doubt supplied some of the old melodies. John Huss composed a few, Luther composed more, but how many is very doubtful. John Galliculus, and probably Walther, composed others; and Rhau, a learned bookseller and musician of Wittemburgh, as well as the personal friend of Galliculus, is said to have added to their number. Melancthon, too, is mentioned as one among the early contributors to the stock of German chorals. But as it is notorious that Luther was not over-scrupulous about the adaptation of secular melodies to sacred words,* it is allowable to conjecture that his friends were also favorable to it. It, therefore, is probable that adaptation was practiced before composition was applied. If so, adaptation from well-known ecclesiastical music was quite as likely as from secular music. But there is no need to rest on probability; for it is a fact that many Gregorian phrases are traceable in Luther's own tunes, and in other Lutheran chorals; while the hymn book of the Bohemian Brethren, printed at Ulm in 1538, avowedly abounds with them.†

---

the head of a sect. He was but thirty-six when Luther died."—(Dr. Burney's Hist. of Music, vol. iii., p. 35.)

* He set a version of the Lord's Prayer to a melody which had been used for singing "*Histories in Rhyme,*" or a sort of bardic recitation of facts and circumstances. Burney and Hawkins quote other instances of adaptation, and of a more objectionable character, especially in the Roman Catholic church. If any of the German chorals come to us from this origin, time has purified them, and buried those associations.

† The only known copy of this most beautifully printed work is

But this practice of adaptation was not peculiar to the Lutheran or Germanic section of the Reformation. It was the practice also, of the French Genevan department of it. The tunes in their psalter present the same features as the German tunes, while it is historically reported that William Franc, who compiled it, was known to have availed himself of phrases from Roman chants, as well as national songs.

The ascertaining of this practice of adaptation may help the investigation of the origin of the tune in question, but as popular opinion is strongly on the side of Luther being the composer of the tune, the opinion itself must be examined.

1. The chief ground for the opinion is comparatively of modern date. It is hardly a century old; for it entirely depends on a vague report of something which Handel had been heard to say. Sir John Hawkins (Hist. Music, vol. iii., p. 447) states thus: "Mr. Handel has been many times heard to say, that the melody of our hundredth psalm, and certain other psalm tunes, were of Luther's composition." To a saying of this sort, the fame of Handel, as a musician, can impart no particular weight. Had he expressed an opinion respecting the *character* of the tune, every ear would bend in reverent attention. But, when he spoke of it only as to its *author*, he merely gave an

now in the author's possession. It formerly belonged to the celebrated Sebastian Bach, and was given by his son Emanuel to Dr. Burney, when visiting at Hamburgh. This gift is attested by the Doctor's own hand in a fly leaf of the volume; and a description of the volume itself is printed in a note at the foot of page 31 of the third volume of his History of Music.

26 THE OLD HUNDREDTH PSALM TUNE.

opinion concerning an historical fact, and placed himself on a level with other respectable witnesses. It is not stated that he ever assigned any reason for his assertion, while the circumstance of his being a German and a Lutheran, would incline him, in speaking of psalm tunes, to associate one so popular in England as was the Old Hundredth, with others which he well knew originated in his native community.

Dr. Burney, therefore, only exercised due caution when he wrote thus: "It is said to have been the opinion of Handel, that Luther himself was its author, but of this I have been able to procure no authentic proof." (Hist. Mus. vol. iii., p. 35.) Notwithstanding, however, the want of historic proof for the corroboration of Handel's opinion, and popular belief, edition after edition has, for the last century, prefixed Luther's name to the tune, or called it a German melody.

2. In opposition to the surmise of Luther being the composer of it, are the following broad facts, which, though of a negative character, go far towards a positive conclusion. (1.) The tune is not printed in any of Luther's own publications, nor in any authentic reprint of them. (2.) In none of the *old* German choral books is the name of Luther attached to the tune. (3.) In many of those books the name of *some other* composer *is* attached to the tune.* (4.) The tune was never very popular in Germany, not half so popular as

---

* Frantz assigns it to Melancthon, and Werner to Claude Gondimel. In the "Cantica Spiritualia," (Augsburg, 1845,) the tune is printed in triple time, and attributed to the San Goar *Catholic* Hymn Book of 1666.

any of the tunes which were *known* to be Luther's. (5.) No German writer, of any account, has ever contended that Luther was the composer of it. (6.) So early as 1621, Ravenscroft had not ascertained its author, but concluded that, as to its origin, it was *not* German.

In the face of these negative facts, some more positive evidence than any now extant must be adduced, ere the tune can, with any show of reason, be attributed to Luther.

3. It may be remembered that, about seven or eight years ago, newspapers and other periodicals were jubilant in announcing "an interesting and important discovery respecting the Old Hundredth Psalm Tune." It was stated that Mr. Oliphant, of the British Museum, had met with a very old book of Luther's, containing only his own tunes,* and that among them was the one which we call the Old Hundredth. This was considered as proof positive of the tune being Luther's, and, therefore, a full and satisfactory settlement of a long pending question. And such, undoubtedly, it would have been, had the facts of the case been what they were said to be. But, unfortunately for all who are interested in the question, rumor had been too hasty, and a little too busy. Mr. Oliphant had been misunderstood. His mention of a partial resemblance had been magnified into a total identity. Upon application to that gentleman, he kindly supplied a copy of the

---

* The title is "Luther (Martin) Geystliche Lieder, 8vo. Nuremberg, 1570."

28   THE OLD HUNDREDTH PSALM TUNE.

tune, which is headed, in German, "Another Spiritual Song." The following is a transcript of that copy:

Now, in the first strain of this sweet old melody, there is a resemblance* to the first strain of the Old Hundredth tune, and the fifth strain, a merely varied repetition, is almost identical with it. The first three notes, also, of the third strain of the melody, are the same as the first three of the third strain of our tune. But this is all that can be said. The metre of the two is not the same, neither is the mould of the one at all like the mould of the other.

The discovery of this old book, and the interesting melody which it contains, though, as will be shown, it is no discovery at all, furnishes, in point of fact, additional ground for believing that the Old Hundredth is *not* Luther's composition. For, as to similarity or identity of strain in phrase, it is not likely that the same composer would make that phrase or strain the leading idea in two tunes, especially as other composers have

---

* In point of fact, the strain is *identical:* for there can be no doubt, as subsequent remarks will show, that the second note of it is a misprint, A being put for B.

adopted the same idea in other once well-known tunes.

After all, the tune which was, at the time, considered a discovery, and an addition to our musical stock, is neither one nor the other. It is a well-known and commonly-printed tune, in the Lutheran church on the Continent. Hardly a German Choral Book is without it. It is ex. gr. No. 14 in Sebastian Bach's Choral Gesang Buch; No. 144 in Werner's; No. 493 in John Daniel Müller's; No. 28 in K. U. Frantz's, and page 48 in Christian Müller's. It is not printed in the Moravian Hymn Tune Book. Singular also to say, it is printed in John Day's Dutch Psalter, of 1561.

With respect, then, to Luther, it is clear that there is not only no evidence of the tune being his composition, but much to the contrary.

The claim of its authorship for Claude Goudimel is equally unsubstantial.

Goudimel was the greatest musician of his age in France. Renouncing the Roman Catholic faith, he became a Protestant; and was massacred at Lyons, at the time of the Bartholomew atrocity in Paris, in 1572. It was, say historians, his *composing* of tunes to Marot and Beza's psalms, which incensed the Roman partisans, and cost him his life.*

But, by *composing tunes* was not meant framing or composing melodies. It meant the composing or putting together, in the Latin sense of the word, certain parts to melodies already framed. This, Goudimel did;

---

* He was brutally dragged from his house, and *shamefully* treated. At length his head was cut off, and cast into the Rhone.

30 THE OLD HUNDREDTH PSALM TUNE.

for in 1565, he published, at Paris, the whole of the tunes in the Genevan Psalter, set in four parts.* But the tunes themselves had been extant, for more than twenty years; as is attested by a preface, written by Calvin himself, to one edition of the psalms, dated June 10, 1543, wherein it is said, "all the psalms, *with their music*, were printed the first time at Geneva." As there is good reason to conclude, that Goudimel became a Protestant not more than ten years before he published his parts to the Genevan tunes, it is next to impossible that he could have had any hand in the framing of the tunes themselves. Besides, Goudimel's harmonies were composed for the use of the French Protestant churches, and were never admitted into the Genevan. Hence, there is no manner of evidence to show that Goudimel was the composer of our Old Hundredth Psalm Tune, except so far as to *compose parts* to it; which was the pleasant task of many a musician in after times. The mistake has been occasioned by a wrong interpretation of the word *composed*, and is precisely of that sort which has been so commonly made with respect to the tunes in Ravenscroft's Psalter. The persons who, as he says, "*composed them, into parts*," were not the framers of the tunes, for many of those tunes were framed before the composers of the harmony to them were born.

With regard to William Franc, there is as clear evidence as can reasonably be demanded, that the tune is

---

* A copy of this work, supposed to be unique, at least in England, is in the possession of Mr. Warren, well known as an organist in London, and an editor of many publications.

his,—at least that he is its fairly reputed author. Franc himself was no great musician. His name is unknown to fame, except as connected with the tunes in the Genevan Psalter. But as his task consisted in framing simple melodies, without caring for originality or laboring at harmony, his skill might have been equal to his task.

Both Dr. Burney and Sir John Hawkins adduce ample proof, that Franc was the composer, or at least the compiler, of the melodies which were set to Marot and Beza's version of the Psalms. Both, also, state that Beza himself testified the fact, in a formal document signed with his own hand, and dated Nov. 2, 1552. They further state, that an edition of the Geneva Psalms was printed in 1564, with the name of "Guillaume Franc," as the author of the musical notes to them, and with the license of the local magistrate attesting Franc's authorship. Consequently, if Franc was the author of the tunes, as this evidence proves him to be, and if our Old Hundredth was among them, as undoubtedly it was, then, in all fairness, must Franc be regarded as the author of that tune.

Still a partisan may plead, that, although Franc may be the author of the tunes generally, it does not necessarily follow that he composed every one of them; or that, although the tune in question is now first found in the Genevan Psalter, yet, as Germany was the parent-school of psalmody, it may have been formed there, and afterwards have found its way to Geneva, without any record of the fact being extant.

32   THE OLD HUNDREDTH PSALM TUNE.

But if such pleading as this be admitted, the best evidence will cease to be respected.

It may be allowable, though hardly necessary, to add, that had Ravenscroft, in 1621, regarded the tune as of German production, he, doubtless, would have said so: for he is remarkably precise in mentioning not the personal but the national or provincial origin of the tunes in his Psalter.* But as he expressly called it "A French Tune," (i. e., printed in the French Psalter,) and as no one before him, or for more than a century after him, said otherwise, consistency requires the acceptance of his testimony. It is not unimportant, also, that Mr. Kollman, who, early in the present century, harmonized the tune in a hundred different ways, was frank enough, though a German, to avow his belief in its Genevan origin.

But though the authorship of the tune must be assigned to Franc, it is still a question how far the tune itself is an original composition.

THE HYPOTHESIS which the writer of these pages has to substantiate goes to show that the tune is rather *a fragmental compilation than an original composition.* Whether the surmise of such fact has ever occurred to any one else, or whether any attempt to illustrate it has ever been made, he has no means of ascertaining. Certainly, he never met with any allusion to it, in the course of his reading.

It has already been remarked, that *adaptation* was

---

* See the preface to the author's reprint of Ravenscroft's "Whole Booke of Psalmes." Novello, London.

the common practice of the first framers of psalm-tunes; and that their adaptations, though derived at first from secular sources, yet presently shaped themselves from ecclesiastical models. As all the reformers and musicians of their day, were perfectly familiar with the Gregorian melodies, it is natural to suppose that, in the task of mere composition, they would freely avail themselves of them. Now it is a fact, which any one may test, that, from even four of the Gregorian Hymns, in one book of "The Evening Service," edited by Mr. Vincent Novello, the whole of our old Hundredth Psalm Tune may tolerably well be made up. In pages 4, 6, 18, and 22, of the third book of that service, the several phrases of the tune are again and again repeated. The first part of the first strain of the tune will be seen in page 19 of Book I., and is quite common-place in the Gregorian Hymns.

PAGE 4. BOOK III.

Su - a - - vis Dom-i - ne.

Pau - le .. mo - res......

In page 26, as well as in page 4, of the first Book, the characteristic part of the second strain is definitely marked:

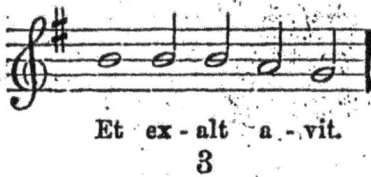

Et ex - alt - a - vit.

3 ‡ THE OLD HUNDREDTH PSALM TUNE.

In page 22 of Book III., the third strain is found, even to identity, and is, also, observable in page 4.

Chris-to ju - ben - te.. vin - cla.

The same may be said of the fourth strain compared with pages 6 and 26 of the same Book.

Mar - ti - nee ce - le - bri . plau - di - te.

So common, indeed, is the first strain, that, in even our own English psalter, it occurs three times. It commences the third psalm, and the sixty-eighth; while it forms the fifth strain of the sixty-first.* It forms, also, in triple measure, the first strain of No. 7, in Sebastian Bach's Choralgesange, and of No. 63 in Toepler's "Alte Choral Melodien," where that Number is dated 1550. In Hall's "Courte of Vertue," A.D. 1565, (Douce's Collection, Bodleian Library,) the whole of the former half of the tune is set as the former half of "A Ditie to be sung of Musicians in the Mornyng, at thyr Lord or Master's door, or els where of hymn to be heard." In a word, the use of the first strain is so common, that it would be troublesome to enumerate all the known instances.

The second strain of the tune, which also strongly

---

* Singular, also, to say, both the first and the second strain form the commencement of a rather long tune to the seventy-eighth psalm in Day's Psalter of 1563, though that Psalter, as before stated, does not contain the Old Hundredth tune itself.

resembles the mediation of the first Gregorian Tone, is found in the third psalm of our common psalters. The use of the first strain of the tune by so many composers, and even by Luther himself, in the melody before quoted, proves that the early framers of psalm tunes were accustomed to consider certain stock phrases as common property, to be employed as might best suit their purpose.

After these statements, and the almost universal belief in the Continental origin of the tune, it might seem superfluous to notice the home claim which has been set up for it. Such claim is, in itself, hardly worthy of attention; but the character and position of the individual who seriously believed it, and strenuously advocated it, almost forces a recording pen to make some remark upon it.

In consequence of Ravenscroft having prefixed the name of John Douland to the tune, as the harmonizer of it, Douland has been considered its author. The erroneous notion seems to have taken its rise from some vague remarks of Dr. Pepusch,* about the beginning of the last century. The surmise that Douland was the composer of the tune spread among the editors of the many local collections of tunes of the ensuing generation. At length the Rev. W. Bowles, Canon of Salisbury, in his interesting "History of Bremhill," (page 206, &c.,) advocated the surmise, and detailed many arguments in support of it. The process which

* Those remarks had reference to *the composition of the tune into parts*, by Douland; but the use of the word "*composition*," in its *old* sense, misled modern ears.

36   THE OLD HUNDREDTH PSALM TUNE.

the estimable poet, historian, and divine thought fit to follow, is this:—Considering that there is no authority for attributing the tune to Luther, he endeavored to prove that it is "originally English." The tune, he argues, so exactly suits the accentuation of the first verse of our hundredth psalm, old version, that it must have been composed to those words. In an old book of his own, the title of which is not given, the worthy Canon found the name of John Douland at the head of the tune. Ravenscroft, also, as he thought he had discovered, assigned it to that eminent musician. But, "after," as Mr. Bowles supposes, "Ravenscroft published the air as Douland's, he saw it in a French book of psalms, and, without sufficient examination, retracted in the index what he had advanced in the body of his work." (p. 218.) This is the sum of a rather long argument. A breath would suffice to demolish it, but the deserved repute of the pleader of it requires a little more formality in its annihilation.

It is singular that a man like Mr. Canon Bowles, should have so slurred over facts, which he was perfectly competent to investigate. He furnishes, however, another proof of what has been so often proved, that a superior mind without a special turn, is not always equal to every task. Had the poet been more of a musician, he could hardly have failed, as he has, in handling a point of musical history. A very easy glance at any of the old psalters, which must have been within his reach, would have sufficed to convince him that his argument about the accentuation of the words was but a mere cobweb, and that it was far more likely that the words were written to the tune, than that the tune was composed for the words; especially as there are many tunes of the same metre in the foreign psalters, but only this one set of words in our own *old* psalter.

The assertion that Ravenscroft "retracted in his index what he had advanced in his book," is altogether unintelligible, except as a flat mistake. In the book, Ravenscroft headed the tune thus—"French Tune, J. Douland, Doctor of Music," and, in the index, he wrote, "French Tones, Psalm 50, 100." There is no manner of retraction here, but an iteration of the same thing; for, by "French Tune or Tone," Ravenscroft expressed his belief as to the national origin of the tune itself; and, by prefixing Douland's name, told the world that he harmonized it, not that he composed it. This is sheer fact, because Ravenscroft twice printed the tune in his book, once with his own name, and once with Douland's prefixed to it, merely to indicate where parts were then set to it. Hence, according to the reverend Canon's argument, Ravenscroft is as fairly entitled to be called the author of the tune, as is Dowland himself. It is strange that *such* an oversight should have been made, especially as Sir John Hawkins had long ago, by anticipation, corrected it.

But, apart from all arguments and surmises, it is plain fact that Douland was not the author of the tune, for he was born in 1562, and the tune was printed in an English psalter, at Geneva, in 1561.

THE HARMONY which used to be set to the tune, was

38   THE OLD HUNDREDTH PSALM TUNE.

far more varied and elaborate than any which is now used. Hardly a company of singers can now be found who sing the tune, as to its harmony, in more than one way; whereas, our forefathers were accustomed to harmonize and sing it in many ways.

The date of the origin of the practice of harmonizing the simple psalm melodies, was mistaken both by Dr. Burney and Sir John Hawkins. Those historians state that the tunes in the English psalter were first harmonized by William Damon, in 1579. They made the statement in complete unconsciousness of the Brazen-Nose Psalter of 1563, which is the more remarkable, as the version of the Old Hundredth in that psalter was reprinted in subsequent manuals.

The practice in question originated in the laudable desire to make that which was good of its kind, better and more satisfactory in its results. Cultivated ears, which had been accustomed to harmony, were not likely to be satisfied with a mere air, sung at once by all sorts of voices. Masters were soon found for clothing with ornamental harmony the naked melodies of the times. The practice speedily became general in all the churches of the Reformation. France and England vied with Germany in providing harmonic embellishments for all the tunes which were usually sung. But then, that provision was made in a manner which, though differing greatly from what is now common, was admirably adapted to favor popular usage without interfering with it. For, the harmonists of the day contrived to let the people sing in unison as fully and as lustily as they pleased, and yet ornamented their singing by composing distinct parts for select voices, independent of the melody or tune, and yet beautifully agreeing with it. Hence the Old Hundredth, like other old tunes, was harmonized and sung in a totally different way to what we are accustomed to hear it.* Instead of the air or tune being sung as the uppermost part, by treble voices, and all the other parts set below it, the practice was to make it a middle part, the tenor as we call it, but "The Plain Song," as our forefathers named it. While, therefore, "the great congregation" sang the plain and simple tune, trained voices sang other parts which harmonized with it. In fact, these trained voices served as a sort of vocal accompaniment to "the plain song," especially where there was no organ or other instruments.

This sort of singing gave opportunity for considerable variety to the skilful choir, because one tune used to be harmonized in several ways, by either the same harmonist, or by other masters. It is evident, as a matter of history, that while the people sang but few tunes, the choral companies had many different accompaniments to each. Thus, if the people sang the Old Hundredth for three Sundays in succession, the choir might sing their parts in three different ways, for not only three but many ways were extant. In this man-

* The ordinary mode in which the tune is now harmonized in England, has been justly censured for its monotonous effect. According to that mode the initial and terminal note of each strain, excepting in only one instance, is set to the tonal harmony. The old masters studiously avoided such sameness. In the Appendix a specimen will be given of the mode in which the tune is harmonized after a better fashion, and as it is sung in many churches besides the author's.

40 THE OLD HUNDREDTH PSALM TUNE.

ner, a new character could be frequently given to an old tune; for nothing is more common than for old collections to furnish two or three versions of varied harmony to one tune. The ordinary prefix is, "another of the same," with the name or initials of the author. It was this composition of parts of which musicians were ambitious, and to which they were mainly anxious to attach their names. Oversight of this fact has led many an editor of collections of psalm tunes into the error of putting the name of a harmonist for that of the framer of a melody.

Of the many harmonized versions of the Old Hundredth tune, to which earlier choirs had access, none seems to have been more generally used than that of W. Parsons, first printed in Day's Psalter of 1563, at least, none seems to have been more generally selected, by succeeding editors, for republication. This is the oldest known specimen of English harmonization of the tune, and is perhaps equal to any which was produced in any other quarter and at any other date. It is thus:

THE OLD HUNDREDTH PSALM TUNE. 41

Though this method of harmonization was, for several generations, the prevailing method, yet, at an early date, what is now the present method was attempted and published. William Damon, in the year 1579, published "The Psalmes of David with notes of four parts." The work neither pleased the public, nor satisfied its author. Accordingly, some years after, in 1591, he published an improved edition, "wherein the highest part singeth the Church Tune;" but it does not seem even to have been in much repute.* A copy of the tenor and bass parts of the former edition is preserved in the British Museum, but the other two parts are lost. The two extant parts are these:

* Shortly after, in 1599, Mr. Richard Alison, a private gentleman, but a superior musician, published in a large and handsome volume,

42   THE OLD HUNDREDTH PSALM TUNE.

Another method of harmonization was occasionally adopted at a very early period. It consisted in turning some short phrase of the tune into a subject for a little fugue; and yet so ingeniously ordered as to be perfectly easy for the congregation to follow their own part. Instances of this sort of composition, which was called "In Reports,"* occur in Day's Psalter of 1563, but the author never saw a specimen of the Old Hundredth so treated. Neither is there, in Day's Psalter, "Another of the Same," as in the case of many of the tunes.

THE TIME in which the tune is now sung, furnishes an instance of alteration as remarkable as any in its entire history. Originally, and till a comparatively late period, the tune was regarded as the liveliest and most cheerful in the whole Psalter.

On the publication of Tate and Brady's New Version, the Old Hundredth Psalm Tune was singled out as a model tune "for Psalms of praise and cheerfulness." As such it is still recognized in the "Directions concerning Tunes," printed at the end of even some recent editions of that Version. But time, which changes so many things, has witnessed a strange alteration in the

---

a collection of Church Tunes, set chiefly for instruments. In this volume, also, the air or tune was the highest part; but why Mr. Alison omitted to insert the Old Hundredth Tune is as difficult to conjecture as the fact itself is singular.

* "*In Reports*" seems to have meant *a bringing back* of a musical phrase in the way of answer (from the Latin *reporto*), and so to have been another expression for *writing in fugue*, which is the following or answering of one part by another.

mode of singing this tune. Instead of being regarded as a joyous and animating melody, it is reckoned a solemn, and even a funeral strain. It consequently is no longer sung in a spirited and sprightly style, but doled forth with the utmost length of syllabic utterance. So inveterate, too, has this singular change become, that not even the extremely jubilant character of the Hundredth Psalm itself, is sufficient to awaken attention to the anomaly. Though choirs and other singers are familiar with the old title of the Psalm, "*Jubilate* Deo," and repeat its translation, "O be *joyful* in the Lord," in the Morning Service of our Church, they, nevertheless, fail to see the inconsistency of singing the tune to its metrical version, in a drawling and sleepy manner. Not even, when using either the old or new version, and repeating lines, which call on all the dwellers upon earth to rejoice in praising, lauding, and blessing Jehovah, do they perceive the incongruity; but continue to sing those lines with the same sleepy slowness as they would sing a dirge in a grave-yard. Indeed, were a company of modern singers requested to choose some very sober tune to suit some very solemn long metre hymn, the choice would inevitably fall on this liveliest of all the ancient tunes. The reason of this perversion may, perhaps, be found, now-a-days at least, in the very antiquity of the tune itself. It has become a popular notion that all old tunes must be sung in proportionably slow time. How groundless and inaccurate this notion is, there would be no great difficulty in proving at large. It is sufficient to state that in the year 1621, Thomas Ravens-

44. THE OLD HUNDREDTH PSALM TUNE.

croft, the great oracle for this species of church music, directed, "That Psalmes of Rejoycing be sung with a louder voice, and *a swift and jocund measure.*" This, no doubt, was in accordance with what had been the custom of the Elizabethan age; for, unless such custom had existed, how were our forefathers to get through twelve or sixteen verses, the usual partition of the longer psalms?*

Even Dr. Isaac Watts, who composed many of his "Imitations of the Psalms of David" to suit the measure of our fine old church tunes, remarked, about the middle of the last century, that "If the method of singing were but reformed to *a greater speed* of pronunciation, we might often enjoy the pleasure of a longer psalm, with less expense of time and breath; and our psalmody would be *more agreeable to that of the ancient churches*, more intelligible to others, and delightful to ourselves."

OF FACTS AND INCIDENTS concerning this celebrated tune, the author has no large store; what he possesses shall be detailed:

In 1620, Sir John Denham called it "*The most grave and graceful of tunes.*" By the term "grave," we must understand him to mean, what in his day it generally meant, *sober, temperate, devout.*

Such, in its structure, the tune certainly is; for.

---

* Our second Ordination Hymn contains *fifteen* verses, which were to be sung antiphonally by the bishops and the priests, with others present. Tallis's *now* well-known Tune, which was composed for it, admirably suited its antiphonal structure.

though cheerful and animated, there is nothing vehement, impetuous, or particularly stirring, in any of its strains. As to gracefulness, few tunes surpass it, especially in the easy flow of its original form. Sir John's remark may be considered a proof of the high repute of the tune, in his comparatively early day. It is the only testimony to that repute, in that day, with which the author is acquainted.

About the year 1760, Dr. William Hayes, the then Professor of Music in the University of Oxford, set instrumental accompaniments to the tune, for annual performance at the Festival of the Sons of the Clergy in St. Paul's, London,* and at the Radcliffe Infirmary and University Commemoration, in St. Mary's, Oxford. The arrangement was for two oboies, bassoon, two violins, viola and violoncello. After a prelude of twenty measures, in which the wind instruments are partially distinct in their parts from the stringed instruments, the latter conduct the ornamental accompaniment, while the former sustain the vocal parts. Compared with the fugal treatment of other tunes, by Bach and Rink, Dr. W. Hayes's accompaniments to the Old Hundredth Psalm Tune are not particularly inter-

* The Doctor always went to London to superintend the performance. His son and successor, Dr. Philip Hayes, also continued to go, to almost even the day of his death in 1797; for, while dressing in London for the occasion, on the morning of 10th March, he was seized with illness, which speedily terminated his life. He was by far the most corpulent man in England; and always booked one whole half of the inside of Bobart's coach to London. As his getting into the coach was a task of no little difficulty, a crowd of friends and gazers usually assembled to witness his departure. Since his death, his father's accompaniments to the tune have not been used.

esting or erudite. He has, too, departed from the older and better style of harmonization, in two or three instances; though at the beginning of the third strain, he has avoided a recurrence to the tonal harmony, as well as, at the close of the tune itself, any use of the $\frac{6}{4}$ before the $\frac{5}{3}$.

At the Festival of the Sons of the Clergy in 1791, Haydn was present. The singing of Jones's Unison Chant in D, and especially of the Old Hundredth, by not much less than six thousand voices, gave him, as he said, "the greatest pleasure he ever derived from the performance of music." The effect of such a number of unison trebles, with just sufficient instrumentation to support them, was, in his estimation, superlatively magnificent and altogether unparalleled. In fact, the performance of the tune in St. Paul's Cathedral is not only singularly splendid in itself, but particularly attractive to foreigners. At the Festival of 1851, the eminent, though perhaps eccentric, Berlioz, the friend of Mendelssohn, and no inconsiderable composer, was present. He wrote a somewhat spirited account of what he heard and saw. The following remarks occur in the course of it: "After a chord on the organ, the first psalm sung by this unprecedented choir, arose in gigantic unison,—

"'All people that on earth do dwell,
Sing to the Lord with cheerful voice!'

"To attempt to give you an idea of the effect, would be utterly useless. Compared in power and beauty to the most massive musical combinations that you ever heard, it is as St. Paul's at London to the church of *Ville d' Avray*, and a hundred times greater. I should add, that this Hundredth Psalm, which is in slow notes, and of a grand character, was supported by the organ (played by Mr. Goss) in superb harmonies. I was greatly surprised and pleased to learn that the melody, long attributed to Luther, is by Claude Goudimel, *Maître de Chapelle* at Lyons, in the sixteenth century. It was first printed at Geneva in 1543." This remark about Goudimel, as the composer of the tune, is not only suicidal, but illustrative of the facility with which men of science fall into historical mistakes. If Goudimel was "*Maître de Chapelle* at Lyons," it is not very likely that he would then and there compose a psalm tune for a Protestant Conventicle at Geneva. The fact is, as already shown, that Goudimel, in 1543, was a Roman Catholic in France, and far enough removed from being a Protestant in connection with Geneva.

It cannot be the least interesting fact of any, which may be told respecting the Old Hundredth, that it was the first tune ever sung at divine service, conducted by a clergyman, in New Zealand. The fact is detailed in the Missionary Visits of the Rev. S. Marsden to that country. When chaplain at Botany Bay, that eminently-devoted man sailed to New Zealand, as the pioneer of missionary exertions. His landing on the Island, for the purpose of meeting some English residents and certain native chiefs, at divine worship, is thus described by himself: "On the morning of Christmas Day, 1814, about ten o'clock, we prepared to go ashore, to publish, for the first time, the glad

48   THE OLD HUNDREDTH PSALM TUNE.

tidings of the Gospel. When we landed at Wangarva, we found Koro-koro, Duatterra, and Shunghee, dressed in regimentals, which the governor had given them, and ready with their men drawn up to be marched into the inclosure to attend divine service. The inhabitants of the town, with some women and children, and a number of chiefs, formed a circle round the whole. A very solemn silence prevailed. The sight was truly impressive. *I rose up and began the service with singing the Old Hundredth Psalm, and felt my very soul melt within me, when I viewed my congregation.* After reading the service, during which the natives stood up and sat down, as directed by the Europeans, I preached from LUKE, ii. 10."

A clerical friend, venerable in years, and well skilled in sweet sounds, says thus, in a letter to the author: "Dr. Whitaker, the Rector at Blackburn, told me that, in laying the foundation-stone of one of his ten district churches, all reared by himself, he gave out *the glorious Old Hundredth;* when it was sung by a chorus of some ten thousand Lancastrians. Now these Lancastrians, apparently by musical tradition from the days of Queen Bess, are all singers of a scientific sort; so that the chorus of ten thousand was not a mingled scream in unison, but a magnificent burst of harmony in all the four regular parts, each singer taking the part which suited his voice. I would have given a trifle to hear it."

In the year 1825, Dr. Edward Hodges, formerly of Bristol, and now, to our national loss, of New York, introduced the tune, as a tenor part, in a splendid chorus, which formed a portion of a most elaborate anthem for his Doctor's degree at Cambridge. The tune formed a stately contrast to the more quickly moving subject, which, in all the ingenuity of fugal counterpoint, was careering beneath and above it. The Doctor was heard, very characteristically, to say, that *he just wanted fifty parish-clerks* to take up the tune "lustily, and with a good courage," when the point came for beginning it in the chorus.

In a vastly more humble style, the author of this little work also introduced the tune in an anthem, to which the Gresham Prize Medal for 1841 was awarded. It is used in that anthem, (No. XI. of the Gresham Compositions,) first, as a Bass, according to Playford's version, in a verse for four voices, with a canon, two in one, formed of the different phrases of the tune; and then, according to Ravenscroft's version, as the tenor of a quartet, which, in some choirs, is sung as a Long Metre tune.

In the *Musical World* for May 20, 1836, was printed "The Hundredth Psalm, harmonized on the principles of the '*Dandy Sublime*,' and dedicated, with every appropriate feeling, to those '*profound musicians*' who consider bold progressions, and daring harmonies, in plain English, unnatural modulations, and extravagant discords, as the only tests of fine composition; by Thomas Adams."

The burlesque is very cleverly done, and displays the tact of the eminent organist, whose name is affixed to it. He deserves the thanks of every lover of propriety in the performance of psalmody. The caricature

50 THE OLD HUNDREDTH PSALM TUNE.

was well-timed, for Mr. Adams well knew that nowhere is psalmody so disgraced by the freaks and fancies of piano-forte organists, as it is in and about the metropolis.* Judging from the multitudinous manuals of psalmody which are to be met with in all the larger or more fashionable districts of London, it would also seem that those who compile them, are emulous of little else than of introducing a style of tune as much opposed to that of the Old Hundredth, as an Italian villa can be to a Gothic cathedral. But elsewhere, there are indications of high improvement, and of a well-tempered determination to carry it on. May it advance to the edification of worshippers, and to the glory of the Triune God!

In closing this brief history, the author wishes it to be distinctly understood that he lays no claim to originality in attributing the Old Hundredth Psalm Tune to Franc of Geneva. Other authors have, in a general way, attributed it to him, but none, it seems, have at-

---

* London has *long* been notorious for a bad style of psalmody, both with organists and singers, in its parish churches. Screaming charity-children, and noisy organists, were the bane of divine service to such an extent, that Bishop Porteus, at the close of the last century, made salutary efforts for correcting the evil. But, even so early as the beginning of that century, the mode of "*giving out*" a tune, as it was called, discovered the worst possible taste in the organists of the day, as a publication of Daniel Purcell (the brother of the illustrious Henry) remains to prove.[a] It seems as though the utmost pains were taken to disguise the melody by all sorts of harpsichord flourishes, and meretricious ornaments.

---

[a] "The Psalms set full for the Organ or Harpsichord, as they are played in churches and chappels, in the manner given out; as also with their interludes of great variety, by Mr. Daniel Purcell, late Organist of St. Andrew's, Holbourn."

tempted to secure the fame of it for him, by showing that it cannot, with fairness, be attributed to any one else.

From what has been adduced, it is hoped that the *vexata quæstio* as to the authorship of the tune, may now be regarded as fairly settled. There is no evidence that it originated with either Luther or Goudimel; but there is reasonable proof that it did originate with Franc.

The only claim to originality which the writer of these pages ventures to advance, is grounded on the discovery of the sources from whence Franc derived the phrases of the tune. Those phrases are so palpably Gregorian, that Franc's construction of the tune can be regarded only as a fragmentary compilation.

Considered, then, as Gregorian in its texture, the Old Hundredth Psalm Tune is indeed very old, much older than is commonly imagined. Its several strains had been sung by Christian voices not only a thousand years before Luther was born, but for centuries before the Papal system was developed.

Viewed in this light, the old tune assumes a new interest, and its antique tones vibrate with freshened impulse. May the fervor with which it used to be sung at Paul's Cross, soon after its first importation into England, be speedily revived in all our parish churches.

THE REV. W. H. HAVERGAL, M.A.
From a Bust by Robert Pauer of Creuznach in 1868.
Engraved by W. Ballingall.

This print of a bust sculpture of W.H.H. was published in his daughter Miriam's biography Records of the Life of the Rev. William Henry Havergal, M.A. *This was was made when W.H.H. was in Germany, where he went several times for his health and for help with his very poor eyesight. The photograph of the original sculpture was taken 2002.*

Note: This was another blank page in the original book.

Also note that the word "specimens" in W.H.H.'s day had a very different sense and meaning from the word at the beginning of the 21st century: W.H.H. meant by "specimen" an example set forth to be displayed and observed. Similarly Frances Ridley Havergal entitled a series of articles or essays on hymns writers "Specimen Glasses" (see pages 697–699 of Volume II of the Havergal edition). She meant not at all the less-than-pleasant association in our day of medical tests in a physician's office or a hospital, but instead (obviously understood in her day) a slender glass vase or other displaying container to hold and present a flower or flowers, and she wrote this sentence in her first "Introductory" paragraph: "Specimen-glasses are small, clear, and colourless vases, not intended to attract admiration or attention, but only to serve the purpose of presenting choice single specimens of roses or other flowers." Thus William Henry Havergal meant by "specimens" examples to be displayed and observed.

SPECIMENS

OF THE

OLD HUNDREDTH PSALM TUNE.

I.

PSALM C. From the Brazenose Copy of DAY's "Musical Psalter." 1563.
W. PARSONS.

II.

A DITTIE, to be svng of Musiciens in the Mornyng, at theyr Lord or Master's chamber-door, or elswhere, of him to be heard. From HALL's "Courte of Vertue." 1565.

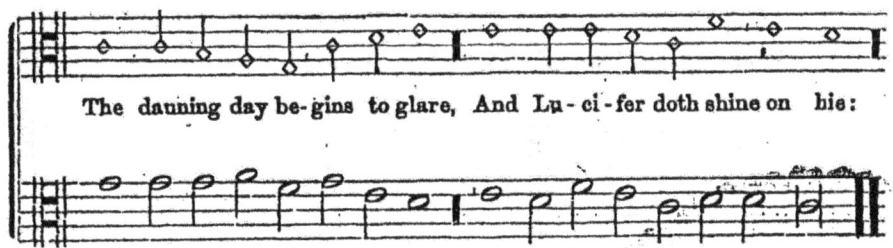

The dauning day be-gins to glare, And Lu-ci-fer doth shine on hie:

And saith that Phebus doth prepare To shew himself im-me-diate-ly.

54   THE OLD HUNDREDTH PSALM TUNE.

III.

The two extant parts of WILLIAM DAMAN's Version. 1579.

IV.

PSALM CXXXIV. CLAUDE GOUDIMEL. Printed at Paris, by ADRIAN LE ROY. 1565. Also in a German Psalter (Bodleian Library), printed at Herborn. 1595.

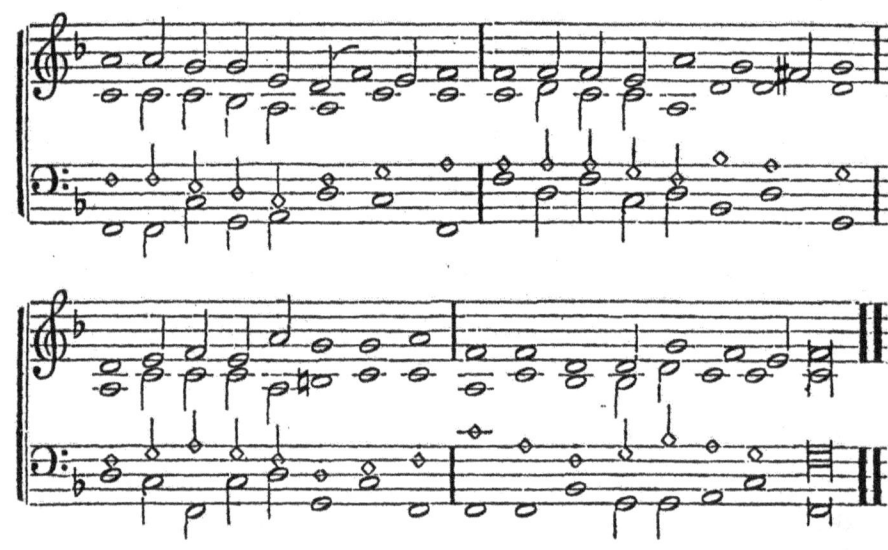

V.

From ESTE's "Psalter." 1592. "J. DOULAND, B. of Musicke."

THE OLD HUNDREDTH PSALM TUNE.

VI.

From RAVENSCROFT's "Psalter." 1621. 100TH Ps. "J. DOULAND, Doct. of M."

VII.

From the same. A PSALM BEFORE EVENING PRAYER. "THOS. RAVENSCROFT, B. of M."

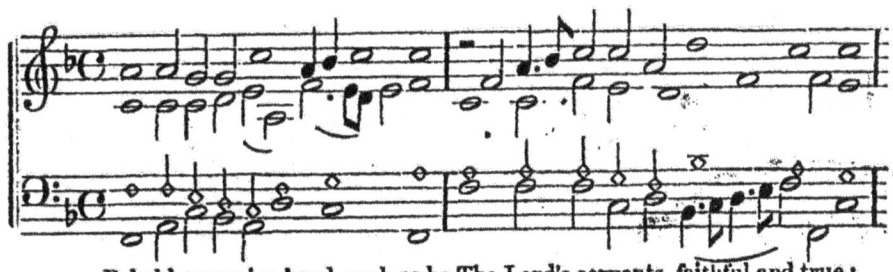

Behold, now give heed, such as be The Lord's servants, faithful and true:

56   THE OLD HUNDREDTH PSALM TUNE.

Come, praise the Lord, every degree, With such songs as to Him are due.

VIII.

PSALM CXXXIV. From French Psalter. Geneva: 1627. Leyden: 1635.
CLAUDE LE JEUNE.

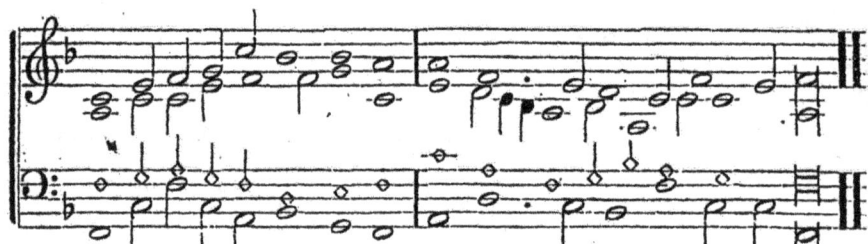

IX.

From the Scotch Psalter. Printed at Edinburgh, by ANDRO HART, 1635.

THE OLD HUNDREDTH PSALM TUNE. 57

X.

PSALM C. From a MS. in Christ Church Library. Oxford. WM. LAWES. 1640.

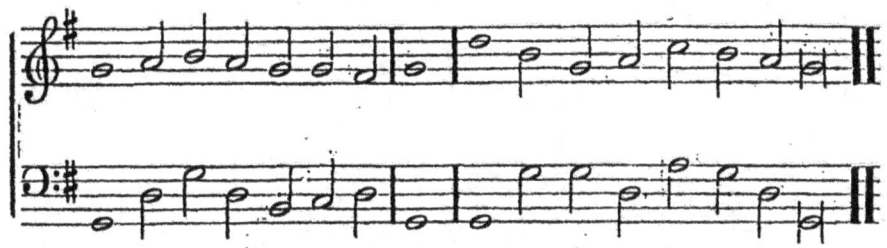

XI.

PSALM C. From PLAYFORD's "Psalms and Hymns in Solemn Music." Folio. 1671.

58 THE OLD HUNDREDTH PSALM TUNE.

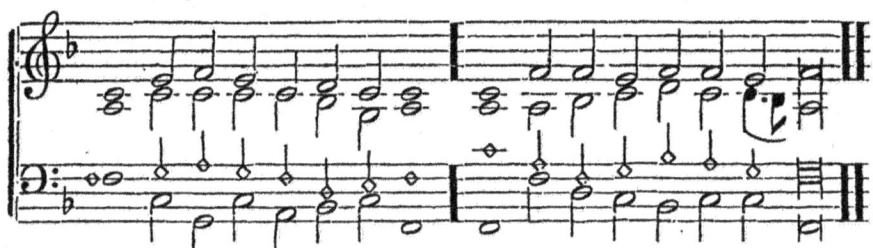

XII.

PSALM C. From PLAYFORD's "Whole Book of Psalms," composed in three parts. 1680.

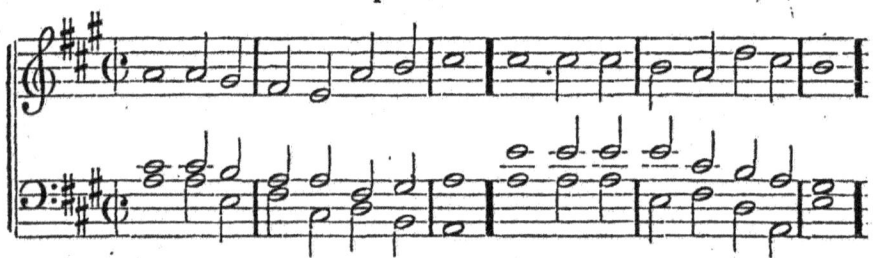

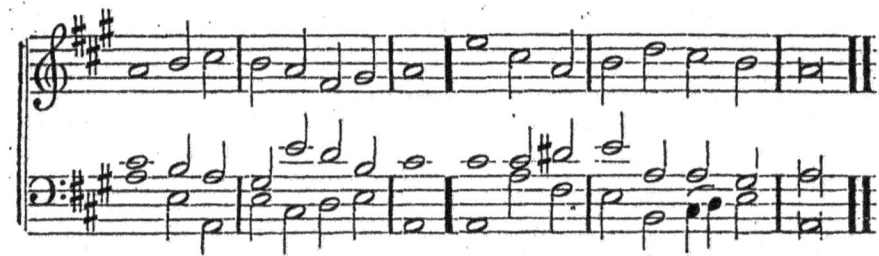

XIII.

PSALM CXXXIV. From a German Psalter, "David's Jewels."
CHRISTIAN MÜLLER. 1703.

THE OLD HUNDREDTH PSALM TUNE. 59

XIV.

PSALM C.   DANIEL PURCELL, circ.: 1700.

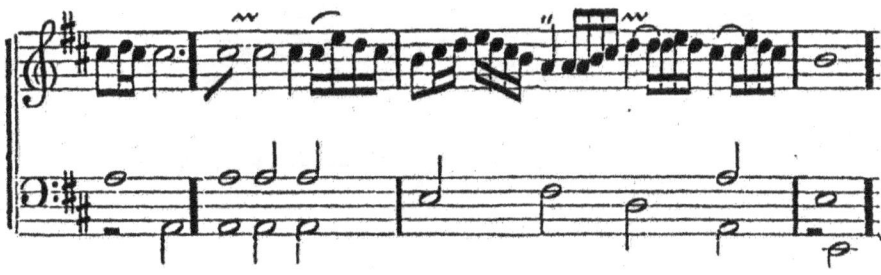

60   THE OLD HUNDREDTH PSALM TUNE.

THE OLD HUNDREDTH PSALM TUNE. 61

XV.

PSALM C. From the Supplement to the new Version. 1710.

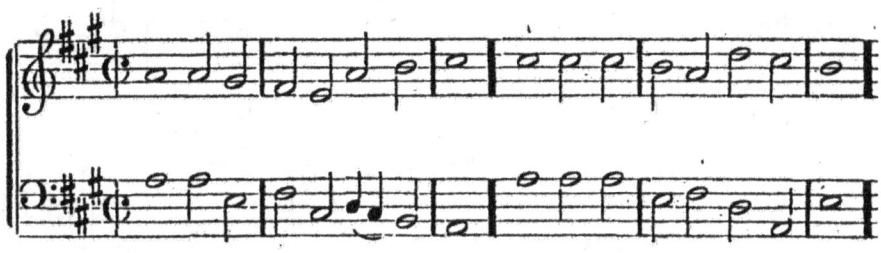

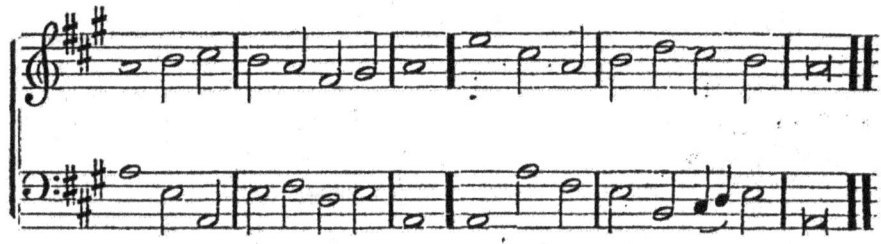

62   THE OLD HUNDREDTH PSALM TUNE.

XVI.

Psalm C. From "The Harmonious Companion." By B. Smith and P. Prelluer. 1720.

XVII.

Psalm cxxxiv. From John Sebastian Bach's "Choral Gesang Buch." 1730.

THE OLD HUNDREDTH PSALM TUNE. 63

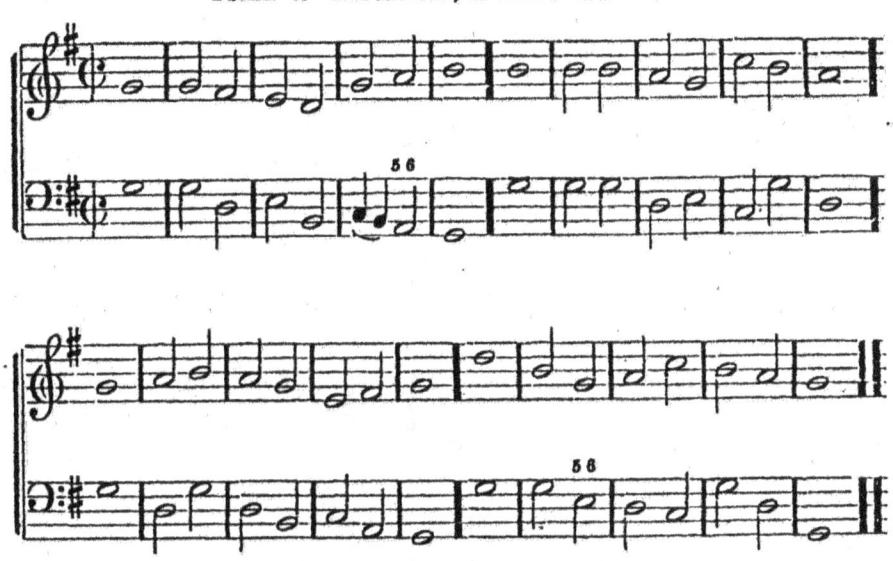

XVIII.

PSALM C. Mr. AVISON, of Newcastle. 1740.

XIX.

PSALM CXXXIV. VON MÜLLER. Circ. 1740. From Dr. BURNEY's "Mus. Extracts," VII. The same as in JOHN DANIEL MULLER's "Choral Book." 1754. British Museum.

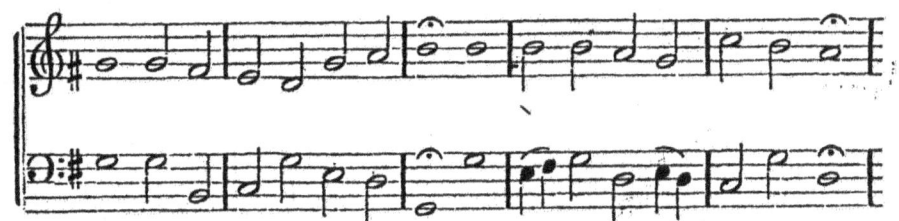

64   THE OLD HUNDREDTH PSALM TUNE.

XX.

PSALM C.   Rev. JOHN CHETHAM (Yorkshire).   Circ. 1740.

XXI.

PSALM CXXXIV.   From an edition of the Genevan Psalter.   London.   1757.

THE OLD HUNDREDTH PSALM TUNE. 65

XXII.

PSALM C. From Mr. MATTHEW WILKINS' "Book of Psalmody." Great Milton, Oxon. 1775.

XXIII.

The Hundredth Psalm, from examples and directions for a hundred different harmonies, by A. F. Kollman, organist of Her Majesty's German Chapel, at St. James. Circiter, 1802.

SYNCOPATION.

XXIV.

Psalm c. "Collection of Old Psalm Tunes." Dr. Crotch. 1803.

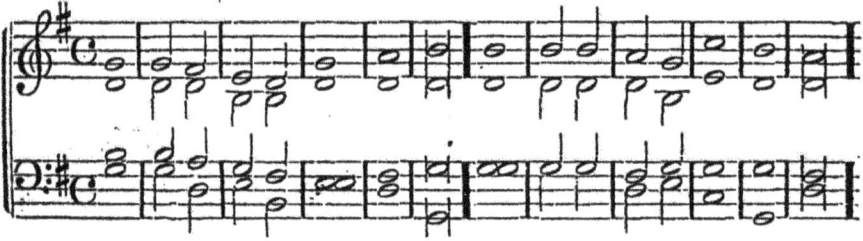

THE OLD HUNDREDTH PSALM TUNE.

XXV.

PSALM C. From J. GOTTLOB WERNER's Choral Book. Leipzig. 1815.

68 THE OLD HUNDREDTH PSALM TUNE.

XXVI.

PSALM C. Harmonized on the principles of the "Dandy Sublime."
THOMAS ADAMS. 1836.

THE OLD HUNDREDTH PSALM TUNE. 69

XXVII.

Quartett in Gresham Prize Anthem, by Rev'd. W. H. Havergal. 1843.

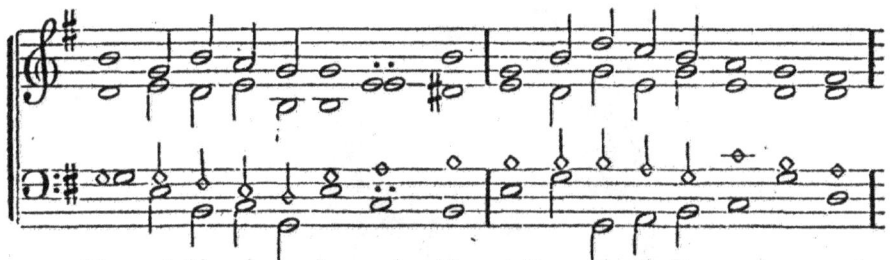

Sing unto him, sing psalms un-to him; talk ye of all his wondrous works.

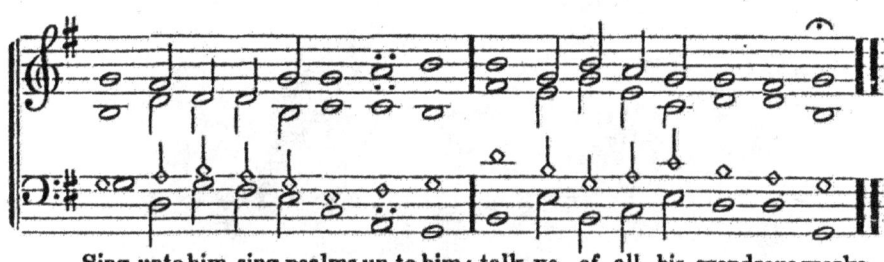

Sing unto him, sing psalms un-to him; talk ye of all his wondrous works.

XXVIII.

From "Old Church Psalmody." 1847.

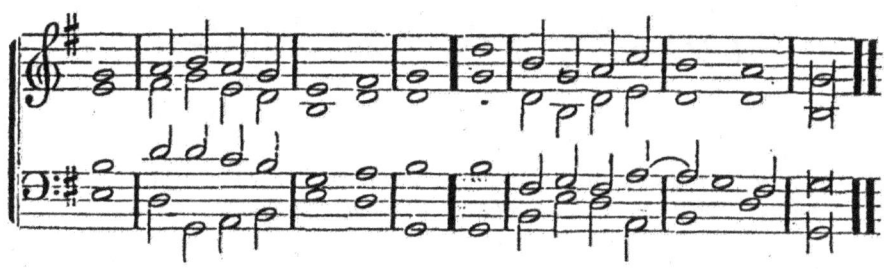

From a Painting by S. Cole.

Engraved by R. & E. Taylor.

This portrait of W.H.H., the frontispiece of Records of the Life of the Rev. William Henry Havergal, M.A. *by his eldest child, Miriam Crane, was based on an oil painting by Solomon Cole in 1845. He had his 52nd birthday on January 18, 1845. See also page 1984.*

Note: This was another blank page in the original book.

REMARKS ON THE SPECIMENS.

Numbers 1, 4, 5, 6, 7, 8, 9. In these seven specimens the musical observer has an opportunity of comparing the skill and the tact of some of the great masters of harmony in the earlier days of Psalmody. A comparison between Numbers 1 and 4, the earliest English and the earliest French version, will furnish some curious coincidences. It is singular that Parsons and Goudimel should have struck on so many points in common, as it can hardly be supposed that Goudimel was acquainted with Parsons's composition. The F penultimate in the second strain of Number 1 was most likely sung sharp, as in Goudimel's version. This, however, is a point open to debate.

No. 5. This version of Dowland's was popular up to the last days of such singing in England. The simplicity and easy flow of its parts rendered it acceptable to our parish choirs.

No. 6. Dowland adopted this version of the melody probably in compliance with the wishes of the Editor and his friend, Thomas Ravenscroft. While the varied style attests his command of ideas, the more artful texture of the parts shows his skill as a harmonist.

No. 7. In this version Ravenscroft seems to have

72 REMARKS ON THE SPECIMENS.

taken Dowland as his master, as it contains palpable imitations of his style. Spite of faulty consecutives in the third strain, the parts, particularly the Bass, are elegantly melodic.

No. 8. This version, only barred in modern fashion, is given by Dr. Burney in his History of Music. It proves what was commonly asserted, that Claude le Jeune was a great master of harmony. It differs from every other specimen in the rich and masculine turn given to the end of the first strain. In Dr. Burney's Musical Extracts, belonging to the British Museum, there is an abbreviated version of this tune, the time being reduced to one half of its original measure. By whom this abbreviation was made, whether by Claude le Jeune himself, Dr. Burney, or any other professor, does not appear. Claude le Jeune composed another set of three parts to the tune, and published them at Paris in 1608. They are at once so ornate, and yet so loosely put together, that the present writer has never been able to score them in an intelligible manner.

No. 9. The first strain of this setting bears a strong resemblance to the first strain of Number 4. The second strain, however, contains a feature which distinguishes it from all its fellows, viz., a modulation, by contrary motion, into the scale of the minor seventh, a transition common in old music, and especially notable in Orlando Gibbons's service in F.

No. 12. Playford intended the middle part of this setting to be sung by either treble or tenor voices.

The unprepared seventh in the fourth strain, is one of Playford's oversights.

No. 13. The punctuation of this version is as unaccountable as it is unique.

No. 14. The absurdity and ill taste of this specimen of "Giving out," as it was called, will strike every person who has not been previously acquainted with the vitiated practices of the English organ school, a century and a half ago, when the evil seeds which had been sown on the restoration of the second Charles had attained their full blossom. The malpractices of that age had not ceased at even the beginning of the present century. The custom of interluding a flourish at the end of every strain in a tune, is still rife on the Continent, and is not quite extinct in our metropolis.

No. 16. The book from which this is taken had a wide circulation. The arrangement of the parts to the tune, is made out of the second specimen from Playford, No. 13.

No. 20. The reverend composer of this version, was as an oracle for psalmody in Yorkshire. This volume of tunes reached eleven or twelve editions. The author has not met with any earlier edition than the fifth; neither has he been successful in obtaining any biographical information respecting Mr. Cheetham, whose fame is not yet extinct in his native county. His version of the Old Hundredth is truly respectable, and his introduction of a minor third on the dominant in the last strain, savors of "sweet antiquity," and shows a master-hand. No other specimen contains a similar instance.

No. 22. Mr. M. Wilkins was a worthy man and a respectable musician. He taught many choirs in the

74   REMARKS ON THE SPECIMENS.

neighborhood of Great Milton, and usually printed his own books at home. This version of the tune is a mere abbreviation of Dowland's, in Ravenscroft's volume. The author, when very young, often heard it sung by the Milton choir at the beginning of the present century. It is the only specimen of such singing which he remembers ever to have heard. The fall of the treble voice to an octave in the beginning of the second strain, and the rustic *pomposity* with which it was achieved, made an indelible impression on his mind.

THE END.

Frances Ridley Havergal, in a letter to her sister Ellen Prestage Shaw, dated October 3, 1857, wrote this:[1]

> I left Papa marvellously better; he is going to Gräfrath by very easy stages. He was so delighted with a piano, sat down and played a few minutes, and then seemed quite overpowered, it was so touching.
>
> He is so beautiful in illness or trouble, people don't half know him who have not seen him at such times; talk about sweet memoirs, etc., no memoir that ever was written would be good enough for him!

[1] *Letters by the Late Frances Ridley Havergal* edited by Maria Vernon Graham Havergal (London: James Nisbet & Co., 1885), original book page 19, page 151 of Volume IV of the Havergal editon.

The next seven pages have facsimile copies of original printed sheets, announcing sermons with hymns, church services on behalf of the Church Missionary Society. Of the 36 hymns printed (words only) in 12 announcements sheets that were found, 32 were written by W.H.H., and 4 were written by others.

W.H.H. was an early, heartful, and very important advocate for the Church Missionary Society, the foreign missionary organization for the Church of England. He donated much of his money to the C.M.S., and travelled to other churches to present their work to congregations, making many aware and encouraging donations and support for the missionaries.

This was the first page of W.H.H.'s sermon on Acts 14:27, written in his handwriting. "Stourport, for C.M.S. June 22, 1856. M." For decades W.H.H. was very involved in making many aware of the work of the Church Missionary Society, donating significant money himself and preaching in many churches to raise support—both by prayer and by money—to send and support missionaries to foreign lands. The work of bringing the truth of Christ to people in distant, dark lands was very dear and important to him. He worked more on music when his physical health prevented him from pastoral work.

Church Missionary Society.

ON SUNDAY MORNING, THE 28th OF SEPTEMBER, 1828,

A SERMON, *(collected with—)*

ON BEHALF OF THE ABOVE SOCIETY, *Mr Corker's Psalm*

WILL BE PREACHED IN

THE PARISH CHURCH OF ASTLEY, £17. 13. /

BY

THE REV. JOHN CAWOOD, A. M.

SERVICE WILL COMMENCE AT ELEVEN O'CLOCK.

HYMN I.

" And he said unto them, that the Son of Man is Lord also of the sabbath." Luke, 6.

Hallelujah! Lord, our voices
Rise in choral strains to Thee:
Son of Man, Thy Church rejoices
In her weekly jubilee!

Hallelujah! mercy beaming
Lights the path that leads to God:
Herald-lips divinely teeming
Publish blessings bought with blood.

Hallelujah! praise ascending,
Shall our faith-wing'd breathings stay?
Lord, before Thine altar bending
Let the Heathen hail Thy day!

HYMN II.

Christians, haste! The morn is breaking;
Darkness wheels his downward flight;
But, your polished armour taking,
Stand!—nor quit the waning fight.
Great Redeemer,
Guard us with Thy shield of light!

Onward, Christians, onward pressing
Triumph in the Crucified!
Endless honor, rest and blessing,
Wait you at His radiant side.
Cease not, cease not,
Till you see Him glorified!

— W. H. H.

HYMN III.

[Left margin, handwritten:] Sept. 20. Acts. 14. 15 "To turn them from the power of Satan unto God."

Hallelujah! Saviour hear us!
  Downward send Thy quickening Dove:
May His silver pinions bear us
  To the realms of rest and love!

HYMN II.

"A light to lighten the Gentiles." — Luke, ii.

Widely 'midst the slumbering nations,
  Darkness holds his despot-sway:
Cruel in his habitations,
  Ruthless o'er his prostrate prey.
    Star of Bethlehem,
    Rise, and beam in conquering day!

Bound and sightless, scourged and dying,
  Millions throng the gaping tomb;
While the Oppressor mocks their sighing,
  Reckless of the fiery doom.
    Light of Israel,
    Burst the bands of Gentile gloom!

Where, oh where, is that effulgence
  Beaming erst from Juda's fane?
Idols fell;—and Rome's indulgence
  Trembled, when it shone again.
    Source of wisdom,
    Spread Thy rays o'er every main!

Light of Light, our sole defender!
  Rise with healing on Thy wing;
Rise, in all Thy soothing splendour;
  Rise, and earth with joy shall ring!
    Israel's Glory,
    Gentiles call Thee Lord and King!

HYMN III.

"And men shall be blessed in Him: all nations shall call Him blessed."—Psalm, 72.

Shout, O Earth!—from silence waking
  Tune with joy thy varied tongue:
Shout! as when from chaos breaking
  Sweetly flowed thy natal song.
Shout! for thy Creator's love
Sends Redemption from above.

Downward, from His star-paved dwelling,
  Comes the incarnate Son of God:
Countless voices thrilling, swelling,
  Tell the triumphs of His blood.
Shout! He comes thy tribes to bless,
With His spotless righteousness.

See His glowing hand uplifted!
  Clustering bounties drop around:
Rebels e'en are richly gifted;
  Pardon, peace, and joy abound.
Shout, O Earth! and let thy song
Ring the vaulted heavens along!

Call Him blessed! on thy mountains,
  In thy wilds, and cited plains:
Call Him blessed!—where thy fountains
  Speak in softly murmuring strains.
Let thy captives, let thy kings,
Join thy lyre of thousand strings!

Blessed Lord, and Lord of blessing!
  Pour Thy quickening gifts abroad:
Raptured tongues Thy love confessing
  Shall extol the living God.
Blessed, Blessed, Blessed Lord!
Heaven shall chant no other word!

W. H. H.

Collection for the Sermon — 16. 6. 6.
Captn. Boys — 2. 2. 0.
A friend Chaps Key — 2. 13. 0.
£21. 1. 6

ON SUNDAY MORNING, THE 26th OF SEPTEMBER, 1830,

A Sermon,

ON BEHALF OF THE CHURCH MISSIONARY SOCIETY,

WILL BE PREACHED IN

THE PARISH CHURCH AT ASTLEY;

BY *Johnson Buckle L.B.*

THE REV. W. H. HAVERGAL, A.M.

HYMN I.

"*The sabbath was made for man.*" Mark II. 27.

Inhabitants of earth,
Hail, hail the day of rest!
Ye saints, who boast a higher birth,
Hail it with raptured breast!

The Sun of Righteousness
Uplifts His healing face;
And Joy and Peace unite to bless
The suppliants of His grace.

The voice of saving truth
Strikes on these hallowed walls:
Here Wisdom cries to age and youth,
And patient Mercy calls.

But lo! 'midst deathly gloom,

HYMN II.

Send Thy Spirit, Lord, or never
Will they hail Thy glorious light.
Rise, Redeemer,
Rise, and claim them as Thy right!

Draw us to Thee:—draw each nation,
With Thy love's mysterious cord:
So the world, in adoration,
Shall obey Thy sovereign word.
Wondrous Sufferer,
We will own no other Lord!

W. H. H.

HYMN III.

"*And let the whole earth be filled with his glory. Amen, and Amen.*" Psalm LXXII. 19.

Brighter than meridian splendor,
Beams Messiah's spotless fame:

But lo! 'midst deathly gloom,
  The untaught heathen lies;
And trusts, though sinking to the tomb,
  In refuges of lies.

No sabbath cheers his eye,
  No gospel thrills his ear;
No hope of life beyond the sky
  Dispels his horrid fear.

Then ye, who love the Lord,
  In prayer lift up your voice:
Bestow on heathen tribes His word,
  And bid the world rejoice!

W. H. H.

HYMN II.

"And I, if I be lifted up from the earth, will draw all men unto me." John XII. 32.

Why, Emmanuel, wast Thou lifted
  On the tree of infamy?
Was it that we might be gifted
  With thy life-bought liberty?
    This, O Saviour,
  Draws the sinner's heart to Thee.

Now enthroned above all blessing,
  Bid the gods of earth retreat:
Bid mankind, Thy name confessing,
  Come to Thee with holy feet.
    Let the heathen
  Soon Thy might and mercy greet.

Sure, no arm, but Thine, can sever
  Chains which bind their souls in night;

Beams Messiah's spotless fame:
Him we laud, our firm defender:
Him let every tongue proclaim.
  He is precious;
  He is gracious;
He for ever is the same.

Crowned with honor, might and glory,
  See Him high in majesty!
These He won (Oh thrilling story)
  By His manhood's agony.
    Now adore Him;
    Bow before Him;
Own His just supremacy.

Where, 'neath papal witchcraft sleeping,
  Victim-souls heed not His blood;
Where, in distant darkness weeping,
  Captives dread the oppressor's rod;
    Where the Pagan
    Chops his Dagon
There shall reign the incarnate God.

Lord of glory! Source of favor!
  Bid Thy heralds take their stand:
Let Thy name's reviving savor
  Wake each dark and drowsy land.
    Saviour, hear us;
    Speak and cheer us,
When we lift the suppliant hand.

Thou art all! and all adore Thee,
  Where they hymn one ceaseless song:
Soon shall earth, subdued before Thee,
  Peal Thy name her tribes among.
    Sons of glory,
    Chant the story;
  And your deep Amen prolong!

W. H. H.

MARY NICHOLSON, PRINTER, BRIDGE STREET, STOURPORT.

ON SUNDAY MORNING, THE 25th OF SEPTEMBER, 1831,

A Sermon,

ON BEHALF OF THE ABOVE SOCIETY,

WILL BE PREACHED IN THE PARISH CHURCH AT ASTLEY,

BY

THE REV. G. PINHORN, A.B.

(OF ROCK.)

HYMN I.

"The Dayspring from on high hath visited us, To give light to them that sit in darkness, and in the shadow of death." Luke I. 78, 79.

No dawn of holy light,
No day of sacred rest,
E'er breaks upon the heathen's sight,
To soothe his troubled breast.

But lo! with healing ray,
The Dayspring meets our eye:
And christians, on their Master's day,
Rejoice to feel Him nigh.

To Him let praise be given,
The noblest, sweetest, best;
For He has brought us light from heaven,
And hope of endless rest.

Lord, let Thy saving light,
Thy day of glorious rest,
Soon chase from earth the irksome night,
And soothe each wearied breast!

HYMN II.

"Be still, and know that I am God: I will be exalted among the heathen, I will be exalted in the earth." Psalm XLVI. 10.

In vain the gods of earth and air
Arouse for deadly fight;
In vain their night-sprung hosts prepare
To crush the Sons of light.

Stand, christians, stand, with crest and cross,
Your Master's Godhead own:
Your spoils then shall feel no loss,
Though worlds be overthrown.

HYMN III.

"And it shall come to pass in the last days, that — — he shall judge among the nations, and shall rebuke many people: and they shall beat their swords into plough-shares, and their spears into pruning-hooks: nation shall not lift up sword against nation, neither shall they learn war any more". Isaiah II. 2, 4.

Art Thou, Lord, Lord, rebuking nations?
Hast thou bared Thy glittering sword?
War, and death's dread devastations,—
Are they marching at Thy word?
Shield us, Saviour,
With Thy favour,
When Thy vials are outpoured!

If Thy judgments now are waking,
Let not Thy compassions sleep
But, while earthly thrones are shaking,
Firm and free Thy kingdom keep.
Jesu, hear us,
Be Thou near us,
When the storm shall round us sweep!

Courage, saints, your fears assuaging,
Chant a bold and blissful strain!
Holy seers, of peace presaging,
But us hail Messiah's reign.

To crush the Sons of light.

In vain their weapons fast and far
Are hurled, with furious arm:
The God of gods will rule the war,
And shield His church from harm.

Then, warrior saints, "Be still! Be still!"
Why dread the vaunted fray?
Your Captain's love and might and skill,
Shall nobly win the day.

In heathen climes, ten thousand tongues
Shall chant the conqueror's fame;
And emulate angelic songs,
In honour of His name.

The monster-gods, who hold the earth
In darkness and dismay,
Shall hear your shout of sacred mirth,
And, vanquished, quit their prey.

Bid us hail Messiah's reign.
Strife, sedition,
Superstitions,
Then no votaries shall gain.

Warrior-hosts, no longer mustering,
Cease the gleaming lance to wield;
Now they watch the fruitage clustering;
Thus shall suffices
Change to gladness,
When Messiah is revealed.

Prince of peace, let every nation
Soon Thy Spirit's empire own;
Bow the world in supplication:
Bring the heathen to Thy throne!
Earth possessing
Boundless blessing,
Then shall honor Thee alone!

Divine Service will commence at Eleven o'Clock.

Mary Nicholson, Printer, Bridge Street, Stourport.

CHURCH MISSIONARY SOCIETY.

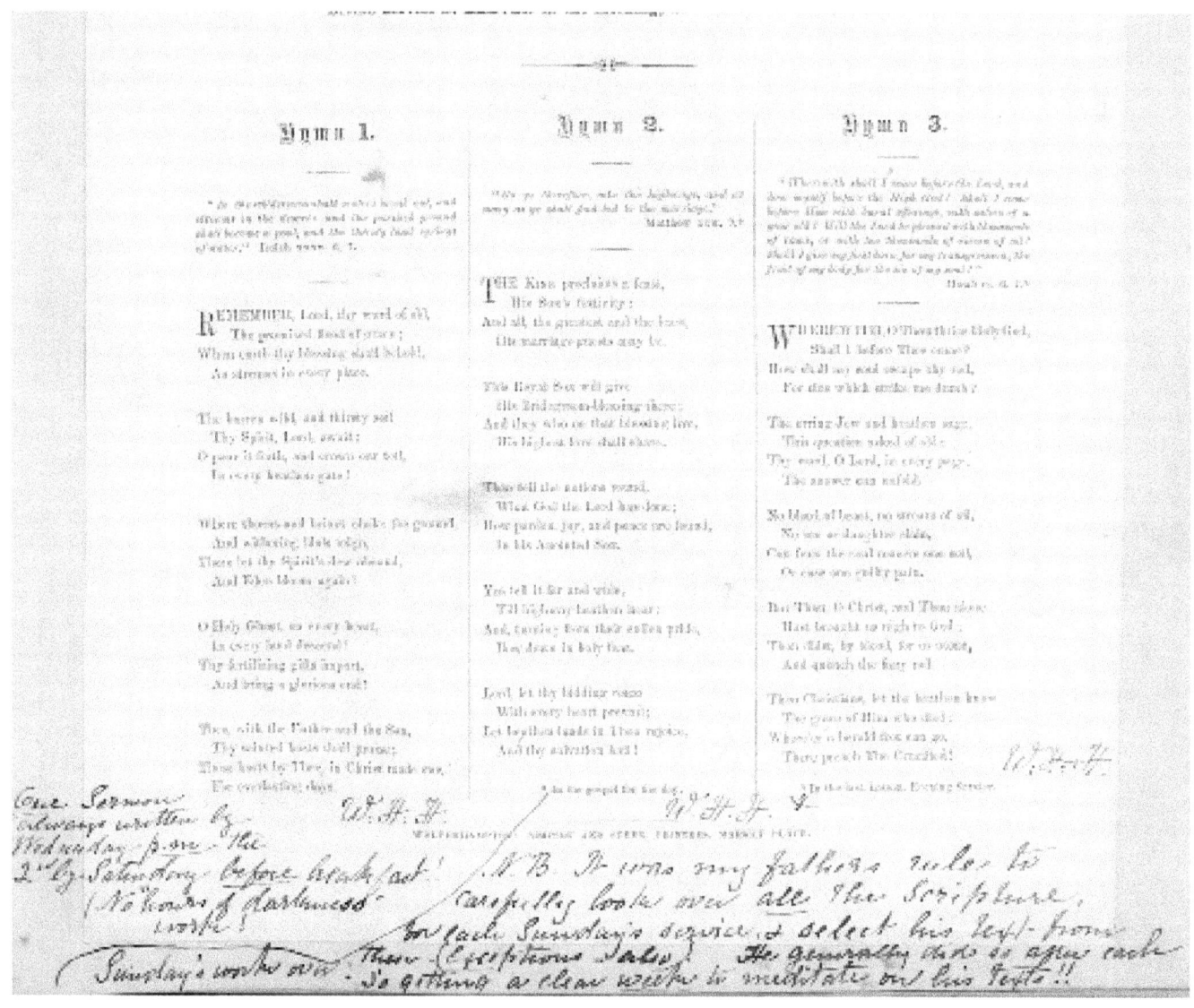

This is the bottom half of an announcement sheet dated October 21, 1860. The handwritten notes at the bottom were likely Maria V. G. Havergal's handwriting:

<u>One</u> Sermon always written by Wednesday <u>p.m.</u> – the 2nd by Saturday <u>before</u> breakfast. ! (No "hours of darkness" work! N.B. It was my fathers rule to carefully look over <u>all</u> the Scripture, for each Sunday's service, & select his text from these. (Exceptions – also). He generally did so after each Sunday's work over. So getting a clean <u>week</u> to meditate on his texts ! !

TWENTY-ONE MISSIONARY HYMNS BY WILLIAM HENRY HAVERGAL

These 21 poems by William Henry Havergal, found in research on F.R.H., are missionary hymns that were found on printed announcement sheets of meetings on behalf of, for support of, the Church Missionary Society: the earliest announcement sheet found was printed for the meeting of Sunday, September 24, 1826, and the latest sheet was printed for the meeting of Sunday, October 21, 1860. These announcement sheets were placed in a Photograph Album which Maria Vernon Graham Havergal gave (with items of F.R.H. and also other items of W.H.H.) to the Church Missionary Society in 1886, the year before she died. These missionary hymns by W.H.H. were printed in full, to be sung in the meeting, with a Sermon, to raise awareness and support for C.M.S. missionaries in distant lands. At the top of a few of the printed announcement sheets, details of the amounts of money raised for the C.M.S. were written by hand. W.H.H. was a true advocate for foreign missions, travelling to many churches to raise awareness and support—money and prayer—for missionaries bringing the truth of Christ to foreign lands.

This is the list of the hymns, each with the date of the meeting when it was to be sung. The announcement sheets each had three hymns printed, a few of the hymns by others, most by W.H.H. Hymns written by others, and repetition of the same hymns by W.H.H. printed for other announcement sheets, are not given in this list.

1. "Soon the trumpet of salvation Loudly, sweetly shall be blown" September 24, 1826 . . . 2094
2. "Heralds of the Lord of glory!" September 23, 1827 2094
3. "Hallelujah! Lord, our voices" September 28, 1828, first of three hymns printed on the announcement sheet for that day 2094
4. "Widely 'midst the slumbering nations" September 28, 1828, second of three hymns printed on the announcement sheet for that day 2095
5. "Shout, O Earth!—from silence waking" September 28, 1828, third of three hymns printed on the announcement sheet for that day 2095
6. "Inhabitants of earth, Hail, hail the day of rest!" September 26, 1830, first of three hymns printed on the announcement sheet for that day 2096
7. "Why, Emmanuel, wast Thou lifted On the tree of infamy?" September 26, 1830, second of three hymns printed on the announcement sheet for that day 2096
8. "Brighter than meridian splendor" September 26, 1830, third of three hymns printed on the announcement sheet for that day 2096–2097
9. "No dawn of holy light" September 25, 1831, first of three hymns printed on the announcement sheet for that day 2097
10. "In vain the gods of earth and air Arouse for deadly fight" September 25, 1831 . . . 2097
11. "Isaiah 2:4." (first line: "Art Thou, Lord, rebuking nations?") September 25, 1831 . . 2098
12. "Astley Wake" (first line: "Our festal morn is come!") September 28, 1834 2098
13. "Arm of the Lord, awake!" September 28, 1834 2099
14. "Redemption." (first line: "Redemption! Oh the thrilling word!") September 25, 1836 . . 2099
15. "The Light of Life" (first line: "In doubt and dread dismay") September 24, 1837 . . 2099–2100
16. "Our Isle in darkness lay, Remote from Judah's light" September 22, 1839 . . . 2100
17. "In vain the heathen bows, To gods of wood and stone" September 22, 1839 . . . 2100–2101
18. "The God of love, with bounteous hand" September 27, 1840 2101
19. "Missionary Hymn" (first line: "Remember, Lord, thy word of old") October 21, 1860 . . 2101
20. "The King proclaims a feast" October 21, 1860 2102
21. "Wherewith, O Thou thrice Holy God, Shall I before Thee come?" October 21, 1860 . . 2102

"Soon the Trumpet of Salvation."

Soon the trumpet of salvation
    Loudly, sweetly shall be blown;
And each kindred tongue and nation,
    Shall the thrilling mandate own.

Myriads, verging on perdition,
    Roused by its persuasive sound,
Shall with ardour and contrition,
    Come from earth's remotest bound.

Then the wounded and the fainting,
    Then the tortured idol-slave,
Then the captive exile panting,
    And the borderers of the grave:

All shall haste and come believing
    To the refuge of the cross;
And, the Saviour's grace receiving,
    Joyous count all else but loss.

Great Immanuel! send thy spirit!
    Let the gospel trump be blown;
May the Heathen know thy merit,
    May they bow before thy throne!

"Heralds of the Lord of Glory."

"Say (Tell it out) among the Heathen that the Lord reigneth."—Psalm 96:10.

Heralds of the Lord of glory!
    Lift your voices, lift them high;
Tell the Gospel's wondrous story,
    Tell it fully, faithfully:
Tell the Heathen, 'midst their woe,
Jesus reigns, above, below!

Where the Tempter rules with terror,
    Where obscene his idols stand;
Where the deathful night of error
    Broods malignant o'er the land:
Heralds! there your message tell,
Jesus reigns o'er Death and Hell!

Haste the day, the bright, the glorious!
    When the sad, and sin-bound slave
High shall laud, in pealing chorus
    Him who reigns, and reigns to save.
Tempter, tremble! Idols, fall!
Jesus reigns, the Lord of all!

Christians! send to joyless regions
    Heralds of the glad'ning word;
Let them, voiced like trumpet-legions,
    Preach the kingdom of the Lord:
Tell the Heathen—Jesus died!
Reigns He now, though crucified!

Saviour! let thy quick'ning Spirit
    Touch each herald-lip with fire:
Nations then shall own thy merit,
    Hearts shall glow with thy desire,
Earth in jubilee shall sing—
"*Jesus reigns*"—th' eternal King!

Hymn.

" And He said unto them, that the Son of Man is Lord also of the Sabbath."—Luke 6:5.

Hallelujah! Lord, our voices
    Rise in choral strains to Thee:
Son of Man, Thy Church rejoices
    In her weekly jubilee!

Hallelujah! mercy beaming
    Lights the path that leads to God:
Herald-lips divinely teeming
    Publish blessings bought with blood.

Hallelujah! praise ascending,
    Shall our faith-winged breathings stay?
Lord, before Thine altar bending,
    Let the heathen hail Thy day!

Hallelujah! Saviour, hear us!
    Downward send Thy quickening Dove:
May His silver pinions bear us
    To the realms of rest and love!

"Widely 'midst the slumbering nations."

"A light to lighten the Gentiles."—Luke 2:32.

Widely 'midst the slumbering nations,
    Darkness holds his despot-sway;
Cruel in his habitations,
    Ruthless o'er his prostrate prey.
        Star of Bethlehem,
    Rise, and beam in conquering day!

Bound and sightless, scourged and dying,
    Millions throng the gaping tomb;
While the Oppressor mocks their sighing,
    Reckless of the fiery doom.
        Light of Israel,
    Burst the bands of Gentile gloom!

Where, oh where, is that effulgence
    Beaming erst from Juda's fane?
Idols fell;—and Rome's indulgence
    Trembled, when it shone again.
        Source of wisdom,
    Spread Thy rays o'er every main!

Light of Light, our sole defender!
    Rise with healing on Thy wing;
Rise, in all Thy soothing splendour;
    Rise, and earth with joy shall ring!
        Israel's Glory,
    Gentiles call Thee Lord and King!

Christians, haste! The morn is breaking;
    Darkness wheels his downward flight;
But, your polished armour taking,
    Stand!—nor quit the waning fight.
        Great Redeemer,
    Guard us with Thy shield of light!

Onward, Christians, onward pressing,
    Triumph in the Crucified!
Endless honor, rest, and blessing,
    Wait you at His radiant side.
        Cease not, cease not,
    Till you see Him glorified!

"Shout, O Earth! from Silence Waking."

"And men shall be blessed in Him: all nations shall call Him blessed."—Psalm 72:17.

Shout, O earth! from silence waking,
    Tune with joy thy varied tongue;
Shout! as when, from chaos breaking,
    Sweetly flowed thy natal song:
Shout! for thy Creator's love
Sends redemption from above.

Downward, from His star-paved dwelling,
    Comes the incarnate Son of God;
Countless voices thrilling, swelling,
    Tell the triumphs of His blood:
Shout! He comes thy tribes to bless
With His spotless righteousness.

See His glowing hand uplifted!
    Clustering bounties drop around;
Rebels e'en are richly gifted,
    Pardon, peace, and joy abound!
Shout, O earth! and let thy song
Ring the vaulted heavens along.

Call Him blessèd! on thy mountains,
    In thy wilds and citied plains;
Call Him blessèd! where thy fountains
    Speak in softly murmuring strains.
Let thy captives, let thy kings
Join thy lyre of thousand strings.

Blessèd Lord, and Lord of blessing!
    Pour Thy quickening gifts abroad:
Raptured tongues, Thy love confessing,
    Shall extol the living God.
Blessèd, Blessèd, Blessèd Lord!
Heaven shall chant no other word.

"Inhabitants of Earth, Hail, Hail the Day of Rest!"

"The sabbath was made for man."—Mark 2:27.

Inhabitants of earth,
  Hail, hail the day of rest!
Ye saints, who boast a higher birth,
  Hail it with raptured breast!

The Sun of Righteousness
  Uplifts His healing face;
And Joy and Peace unite to bless
  The suppliants of His grace.

The voice of saving truth
  Strikes on these hallowed walls:
Here Wisdom cries to age and youth,
  And patient Mercy calls.

But lo! 'midst deathly gloom,
  The untaught heathen lies;
And trusts, though sinking to the tomb,
  In refuges of lies.

No sabbath cheers his eye,
  No gospel thrills his ear;
No hope of life beyond the sky
  Dispels his horrid fear.

Then ye, who love the Lord,
  In prayer lift up your voice:
Bestow on heathen tribes His word,
  And bid the world rejoice!

"Why, Emmanuel, Wast Thou Lifted?"

"And I, if I be lifted up from the earth, will draw all men unto me."—John 12:32.

Why, Emmanuel, wast Thou lifted
  On the tree of infamy?
Was it that we might be gifted
  With thy life-bought liberty?
    This, O Saviour,
    Draws the sinner's heart to Thee.

Now enthroned above all blessing,
  Bid the gods of earth retreat:
Bid mankind, Thy name confessing,
  Come to Thee with holy feet.
    Let the heathen
    Soon Thy might and mercy greet.

Sure, no arm, but Thine, can sever
  Chains which bind their souls in night;
Send Thy Spirit, Lord, or never
  Will they hail Thy glorious light.
    Rise, Redeemer,
    Rise, and claim them as Thy right!

Draw us to Thee:—draw each nation,
  With Thy love's mysterious cord;
So the world, in adoration,
  Shall obey Thy sovereign word.
    Wondrous Sufferer,
    We will own no other Lord!

"Brighter than Meridian Splendour."

"And let the whole earth be filled with his glory. Amen, and Amen."—Psalm 72:19.

Brighter than meridian splendor,
  Beams Messiah's spotless fame:
Him we hail, our firm defender;
  Him let every tongue proclaim.
    He is precious;
    He is gracious;
    He for ever is the same.

Crowned with honor, might and glory,
  See Him high in majesty!
These He won (Oh thrilling story)
  By His manhood's agony.
    Now adore Him;
    Bow before Him;
    Own His just supremacy.

Where, 'neath papal witchcraft sleeping,
  Victim-souls heed not His blood;
Where, in distant darkness weeping,
  Captives dread the oppressor's rod;

　　　　Where the Pagan
　　　　　Clasps his Dagon;
　　　There shall reign the incarnate God.

　　Lord of glory! Source of favour!
　　　　Bid Thy heralds take their stand:
　　Let Thy name's reviving savour
　　　　Wake each dark and drowsy land.
　　　　　Saviour, hear us;
　　　　　Speak and cheer us,
　　　When we lift the supplant hand.

　　Thou art all! and all adore Thee,
　　　　Where they hymn one ceaseless song:
　　Soon shall earth, subdued before Thee,
　　　　Peal Thy name her tribes among.
　　　　　Sons of glory,
　　　　　Chant the story;
　　　And your deep Amen prolong![1]

"No Dawn of Holy Light."

"The Dayspring from on high hath visited us, to give light to them that sit in darkness, and in the shadow of death."—Luke 1:78, 79.
"To turn them from darkness to light, and from the power of Satan unto God."—Acts 26:18.
"I am the light of the world."—John 8:11.

　　　　No dawn of holy light,
　　　　No day of sacred rest,
　　　E'er breaks upon the heathen's sight,
　　　　To soothe his troubled breast.

　　　　But lo! with healing ray,
　　　The Dayspring meets our eye:
　　　And Christians, on their Master's day,
　　　　Rejoice to feel Him nigh.

　　　　To Him let praise be given,
　　　　The noblest, sweetest, best;
　　　For He has brought us light from heaven,
　　　　And hope of endless rest.

　　　Lord, let Thy saving light,
　　　　Thy day of glorious rest,
　　Soon chase from earth the toilsome night
　　　　And soothe each wearied breast!

"In Vain the Gods of Earth and Air."

"Be still, and know that I am God: I will be exalted among the heathen, I will be exalted in the earth."—Psalm 46:10.

　　　In vain the gods of earth and air
　　　　Arouse for deadly fight:
　　　In vain their night-sprung hosts prepare
　　　　To crush the Sons of light.

　　　In vain their weapons fast and far
　　　　Are hurled, with furious arm:
　　　The God of gods will rule the war.
　　　　And shield His church from harm.

　　　Then, warrior saints, "Be still! Be still!"
　　　　Why dread the vaunted fray?
　　　Your Captain's love and might and skill,
　　　　Shall nobly win the day.

　　　In heathen climes, ten thousand tongues
　　　　Shall chant the Conqueror's fame;
　　　And emulate angelic songs,
　　　　In honor of His name.

　　　The monster-gods, who hold the earth
　　　　In darkness and dismay,
　　　Shall hear your shout of sacred mirth,
　　　　And, vanquished, quit their prey.

　　　Stand, Christians, stand, with crest and cross,
　　　　Your Master's Godhead own:
　　　Your spirits then shall feel no loss,
　　　　Though worlds be overthrown.

---

[1] At the end of these previous three hymns, in the bottom right corner of the sheet, Maria V. G. Havergal wrote this note: "F.R.H. called these 'splendid'!" See pages 2088–2089 of Volume V of the Havergal edition.

Isaiah 2:4.

"And it shall come to pass in the last days, that . . . he shall judge among the nations, and shall rebuke many people: and they shall beat their swords into plough-shares, and their spears into pruning-hooks: nation shall not lift up sword against nation; neither shall they learn war any more."
—Isaiah 2:2-4.

> Art Thou, Lord, rebuking nations?
>   Hast Thou bared Thy glittering sword?
> War, commotions, tribulations,
>   Are they marching at Thy word?
>   Shield us, Saviour,
>   With Thy favour,
>   When Thy vials are outpoured!
>
> If Thy judgments now are waking,
>   Let not Thy compassion sleep;
> But, while earthly powers are shaking,
>   Firm and free Thy kingdom keep.
>   Jesu, hear us,
>   Be Thou near us,
>   When the storm shall round us sweep!
>
> Courage, saints, your fears assuaging,
>   Chant a bold and blissful strain!
> Holy seers, of peace presaging,
>   Bid us hail Messiah's reign.
>   Strife, sedition,
>   Superstition,
>   Then no votaries shall gain.
>
> Warrior hosts, no longer mustering,
>   Cease the gleaming lance to wield:
> Now they watch the fruitage clustering,
>   Now they crop the sunny field.
>   Thus shall sadness
>   Change to gladness
>   When Messiah is revealed.
>
> Prince of Peace, let every nation
>   Soon Thy Spirit's empire own;
> Bow the world in supplication,
>   Bring the heathen to Thy throne!
>   Earth possessing,
>   Boundless blessing
>   Then shall honour Thee alone!   1831.

Astley Wake.

"Many persons require to be informed, and others to be reminded, that a parish Wake is properly a Religious Festival. It was originally the Feast of the Dedication of the Parish Church; and was kept by watching, or waking, unto prayer and praise, during the whole of the preceding night, till sunrise." Jane Miriam (Havergal) Crane, in her biography *Records of the Life of the Rev. William Henry Havergal, M.A.* (page 135 of the original book, page 603 of Volume IV of the Havergal edition).

"Blow up the trumpet in the new moon, in the time appointed, on our solemn feast-day."—Psalm 81:3.

> Our festal morn is come,
>   And, Lord, we come to Thee;
> Thy house shall be our joyful home,
>   Thy name our melody.
>
> "These temples of Thy grace,
>   How beautiful they stand!
> The honours of our native place,
>   And bulwarks of our land." [1]
>
> Our fathers built this fane, [2]
>   And watched the livelong night:
> They sleep in death; but we remain
>   To hail a purer light.
>
> Then blow the trumpet, blow:
>   The psalm, the psaltery take:
> Let every heart with praise o'erflow,
>   And every lip awake.
>
> Sound, sound that sweetest strain,
>   The gospel-jubilee,
> Till, bursting from their idol-chain,
>   The heathen shall be free.
>
> Thus let us keep the feast,
>   Thus wake to righteousness:
> And teach the world, from sin released,
>   The Lord our God to bless.

"In the Jewish Church, notice was given of feasts, jubilees, &c. by sound of trumpet. We have now our religious feast-days. On these and all other solemn occasions, let the evangelical trumpet give a sound of victory over death, of liberty from sin, of joy and rejoicing in Chirst Jesus our Saviour."—Bishop Horne.

[1] The second verse is quoted from Dr. Watts.   [2] fane: temple

"Arm of the Lord, awake!"

"Awake, awake, put on strength, O arm of the Lord; awake, as in the ancient days, in the generations of old. Art thou not it that hath cut Rahab, and wounded the dragon?"
—Isaiah 51:9.

ARM of the Lord, awake!
Seize thy bright sword and take
   Strength for the fight:
Smite, smite the dragon's [1] head,
Rome's mystic harlot-bed [2]
False gods and Mahommed,
   —Offspring of night. [3]

O Saviour, Son of Man!
Art Thou not He who can
   Conquer and bless?
Soon let thy truth o'erthrow
Idols and every foe;
Soon let the whole earth know
   Thy righteousness.

Thou art the mighty God,
And thine avenging rod
   Reddens with ire:
But, Jesu, stay thine hand,
Spare, spare, thy little band,
Blood-bought, in every land,
   Baptized with fire!

Then when the fight is won,
And every toil is done,
   Rest on thy throne!
All thy victorious throng,
Marching the heavens along,
Shall, in one ceaseless song,
   Praise Thee alone!

[1] Revelation 12:9. [2] Rev. 17:5. [3] Rev. 9:1–12.

Redemption.

"Who gave himself a ransom for all, to be testified in due time."—I Timothy 2:6.

REDEMPTION! Oh the thrilling word!
   It tells of joy in woe;
Of more than prophets saw or heard,
   Of all that *we* can know.

Redemption! God's great charity
   To man imprisoned long;
The world's reprieve; the sinner's plea;
   And heaven's eternal song.

Redemption! but—its countless cost!
   It cost the blood of Him
Who spread the heavens, and rules the host
   Of flaming Seraphim.

Redemption! be its joy proclaimed
   By men of every tongue,
Where Christ has never yet been named,
   Where Satan's power is strong.

REDEEMER, Thou who diedst *for all!*
   Let all Thy love adore:
Let Jew and Heathen join to call
   Thee—*Lord* for evermore!

The Light of Life.

"In Him was life; and the life was the light of men."
—John 1:4.

IN doubt and dread dismay,
'Midst Superstition's gloom;
The heathen grope their way,
And joyless reach the tomb:
   No holy light,
   No balmy ray
   Of Gospel-day
Has blessed their sight.

Then, Star of Life, arise!
And on thy healing wing,
With blood of sacrifice,
Thy great salvation bring:
 Let heathen lands
 Thy brightness see:
 Oh set them free
 From cruel bands.

With searching beam explore
The dark strongholds of sin:
And on the prisoners pour
Transforming light within.
 Bright morning Star!
 Unveil thy face,
 And shed thy grace,
 In realms afar.

O Jesu, Light of Life!
Arouse the world from sleep;
Send holy love in place of strife,
And joy to those who weep.
 Great King of Kings!
 Thy Spirit give!
 Let Gentiles live,
 Beneath thy wings.

"Our Isle in Darkness Lay."

"The people that walked in darkness have seen a great light: they that dwell in the land of the shadow of death, upon them hath the light shined."—Isaiah 9:2.

Our Isle in darkness lay,
 Remote from Judah's light;
No beam of truth, no holy ray,
 Dispelled the Druid-night:

Till o'er the barrier-sea,
 Came messengers of good:
They brought the lamp of life, that we
 Might hope through Jesu's blood.

But, still the heathen lie
 In deep and loathsome gloom;
Fast bound in deadliest misery,
 And sightless of their doom.

Then up, ye favoured race,
 Lift high the beacon-flame,—
The cross of Christ, His boundless grace,
 His healing cheering name!

Send, send to lands of death,
 That torch of living light;
And fan its blaze with prayerful breath,
 The Spirit's inward might.

Rejoice we in that light,
 The glory of our land;
And be our works and armour bright,
 Till Christ on earth shall stand.

"In Vain the Heathen Bows."

"Neither is there salvation in any other; for there is none other name under heaven given among men, whereby we must be saved."—Acts 4:12.

In vain the heathen bows,
 To gods of wood and stone;
No cruel rites or vows
 Can e'er for sin atone.
  No name but one,
  Jehovah gave,
  With power to save,
  Beneath the sun.

That name! our hope below;
 That name! the theme above:
Nor men nor angels know
 Aught greater, than its love.
  Thy power to save,
  Blest Nazarene!
  Is sung and seen
  Beyond the grave.

All hail Immanuel!
 O'er earth uplift thy face;
Let Satan's captives tell
 The triumphs of thy grace.
  Where idols reign,
  Let prayer abound,
  And faith be found,
  Through thy great name!

No name but Thine shall be
Earth's solace and her song;
When heavenly minstrelsy
Shall dwell her tribes among:
    When saved by Thee,
    No more to weep,
    Thy church shall keep
    Her Jubilee.

O God of Love! thy Spirit grant
To turn to plenty heathen want:
May Jew and Pagan, Bond and Free,
Soon share our feast and joy in Thee!

"The God of Love, with Bounteous Hand."

"Then he said unto them, go your way, eat the fat and drink the sweet, and send portions unto them for whom nothing is provided."—Nehemiah 8:10.

The God of love, with bounteous hand,
Has scattered mercy o'er our land;
To us unsparingly are given
The means of grace, the hope of heaven.

For us an ample board is spread
Of wine and milk and living bread;
And pastors watch our souls to guide
In knowledge of the Crucified.

But millions die for lack of food,
For lack of knowing Jesu's blood:
Then, while we feast, let generous hands
Send portions meet to distant lands.

The fainting heathen perish fast;
And present time speeds on to past:
O haste we then to holiest deed,
And from our store supply their need!

Missionary Hymn.

"In the wilderness shall waters break out, and streams in the desert: and the parched ground shall become a pool, and the thirsty land springs of water."—Isaiah 35:6, 7.

Remember, Lord, Thy word of old,
    The promised flood of grace;
When earth Thy blessing shall behold,
    As streams in every place.

The barren wild and thirsty soil
    Thy Spirit, Lord, await;
Oh, pour it forth, and crown our toil
    In every heathen gate!

Where thorns and briers choke the ground,
    And withering idols reign,
There let Thy Spirit's dew abound,
    And Eden bloom again.

O Holy Ghost! on every heart,
    In every land descend!
Thy fertilizing gifts impart,
    And bring a glorious end.

Thee, with the Father and the Son,
    Thy sainted hosts shall praise;
Those hosts by Thee in Christ made one,
    For everlasting days.

"The King Proclaims a Feast."

"Go ye therefore, into the highways, and as many as ye shall find bid to the marriage."—Matthew 22:9.*

THE King proclaims a feast,
    His Son's festivity:
And all, the greatest and the least,
    His marriage-guests may be.

This Royal Son will give
    His Bridegroom-blessing there;
And they who on that blessing live,
    His highest love shall share.

Then tell the nations round,
    What God the Lord has done;
How pardon, joy, and peace are found,
    In his Anointed Son.

Yea tell it far and wide,
    Till highway-heathen hear;
And, turning from their sullen pride,
    Bow down in holy fear.

Lord, let thy bidding voice
    With every heart prevail;
Let heathen-lands in Thee rejoice,
    And thy salvation hail!

* In the gospel for the day.

"Wherewith, O Thou Thrice Holy God."

"Wherewith shall I come before the Lord, and bow myself before the High God! Shall I come before Him with burnt offerings, with calves of a year old! Will the Lord be pleased with thousands of rams, or with ten thousands of rivers of oil? Shall I give my first born for my transgression, the fruit of my body for the sin of my soul?"—Micah 6:7.*

WHEREWITH, O Thou thrice Holy God,
    Shall I before Thee come?
How shall my soul escape thy rod,
    For sins which strike me dumb?

The erring Jew and heathen sage,
    This question asked of old:
Thy word, O Lord, in every page,
    The answer can unfold.

No blood of beast, no stream of oil,
    No son or daughter slain,
Can from the soul remove one soil,
    Or ease one guilty pain.

But Thou, O Christ, and Thou alone
    Hast brought us nigh to God;
Thou didst, by blood, for us atone,
    And quench the fiery rod.

Then Christians, let the heathen know
    The grace of Him who died:
Where'er a herald foot can go,
    There preach The Crucified!

* In the first Lesson, Evening Service.

These are two pages from W.H.H.'s bound volume of sermons he preached, from March 31, 1816 to January 3, 1869. This bound volume has 160 pages in his handwriting, recording the place, date, and Scripture text for each sermon. At the end, one of his children wrote this entry: "My father's last Sermon was preached at Pyrmont Waldeck [in Germany] (C.C.C.S.) Sept 12 1869, text 'The Lord Jesus Christ be with thy spirit.' 2 Timothy IV.22."

In her biography *Records of the Life of the Rev. William Henry Havergal, M.A.*, Jane Miriam Crane quoted this hymn that he wrote for the wedding of his daughter Ellen Prestage Havergal to Giles Shaw:[1]

> My father composed a hymn to be sung when the guests were in their places at the wedding breakfast, and as such a musical grace was a novelty, a copy is given.

NUPTIAL GRACE.

For G.S. and E.P.H.

February 5, 1856.

> *"Holy Matrimony — instituted of God in the time of man's innocency, signifying unto us the mystical union that is betwixt Christ and his Church; which holy estate Christ adorned and beautified with his presence, and first miracle that He wrought, in Cana of Galilee."*

O Thou, whose presence beautified
    Poor Cana's nuptial board,
By Thee let ours be sanctified,
    And Thou shalt be adored.

Thyself to us, ourselves to Thee
    In mystic union join;
And grant us greater things to see
    Than water turned to wine.

Thy glory show, our faith make strong,
    Like rivers be our peace:
And seat us where Thy Marriage Song
    Shall never, *never* cease!

To Him who wove the marriage tie,
    In Eden's thornless bower,
To Him, the Christ of God Most High,
    Be glory, praise, and power!

This grace was sung to a tune then called St. Nicholas, but named Eden in Havergal's Psalmody, No. 38.

EDEN. [H. P. 38.]

This is the score composed by William Henry Havergal, sung to the words "Nuptial Grace," sung on the morning of his daughter Ellen's wedding. This score is found in *Havergal's Psalmody and Century of Chants* and also in Hymn No. 68 in *Songs of Grace and Glory*, given on pages 188 and 584 of Volume V of the Havergal editon.

---

[1] *Records of the Life of the Rev. William Henry Havergal, M.A.* by his daughter Jane Miriam Crane (London: Home Words Publishing Office, 1882), original book pages 211–213, pages 635–636 of Volume IV of the Havergal edition. The quotation before the hymn is taken from the Book of Common Prayer. The score "Eden" in *Havergal's Psalmody and Century of Chants* is found on page 188 of Volume V, and also in Hymn No. 68 in *Songs of Grace and Glory* on page 584 of Volume V.

Here, at the end of the scores by W.H.H. (only a portion, he composed far more music than is given in this selection in Volume V), and before the start of the art songs with words by F.R.H. set to music by other composers (begun on page 2189 of Volume V of the Havergal edition), this text by F.R.H. set to music by W.H.H. is given next. See also hymn number 1093 in *Songs of Grace and Glory*, on page 982 of Volume V.

Frances wrote the words on December 23, 1873 (entitled "For New Year's Day, 1874," 20 stanzas, of which this score gives the first stanza), and W.H.H. had died in 1870; thus, we know that this score by him was posthumously adapted to this poem. We do know that he composed the score "Baca" specifically for Frances' hymn "I gave My life for thee" (see hymn number 633 in *Songs of Grace and Glory*, on page 801 of Volume V of the Havergal edition). See also pages 2416–2418 of Volume V.

This four-page letter was written by Rev. R. Jarratt to W.H.H. (and was placed by Maria V. G. Havergal in her Photograph Album given to the Church Missionary Society in 1886). See also pages 1430 and 1434.

> Wellington Somerset
> June 19th 1826.
>
> My dear Sir,
>
> As you have requested by my son Samuel that I would write to you to say about some benefaction to our Church Missionary Society, I send you the following account. But first, I must inform you that my son Samuel reached Wellington to our surprise on Friday afternoon in safety & William on the following day. William appears to me as well as I expected, & I would pray to God, in submission to his will, that his strength may be restored & his life prolonged. [This was only the first page of the letter. See page 1430 for the next two pages. Below the original letter, Maria V. G. Havergal wrote this next note:]

A most striking <u>fact</u> in <u>1826</u> given in the above from the <u>Rev R. Jarratt</u> to my father W.H.H. A <u>poor</u> woman bringing first £ 14..0..0 – her own day labour being 7 <u>s</u> per day! In the parcel of money was a ragged slip of paper "This money is for the mishnery (sic) "look unto Me and be ye saved all ye eands of the earth." In six months she again brought £ 20 and again £ 6—from a small annuity left her. Shall not this <u>be told</u> " for a memorial of her?"

This is a photograph of William Henry Havergal, obviously cut out from the complete photograph, placed in a Photograph Album which Maria Vernon Graham Havergal gave to the Church Missionary Society in 1886. Maria wrote "1869" next to the photograph, with flowers and leaves placed on the page around the photograph of W.H.H., and to the right of him was placed the quotation from Isaiah 52:7, "How beautiful upon the mountains are the feet of him that bringeth good tidings, that publisheth peace."

This is the single-verse poem written by his youngest child, Frances Ridely Havergal:

Tis fully known to One, by us yet dimly seen,
    The blessing thou hast been,
Yet speaks the silent love of many a mourning
    The blessing that thou art;   [heart,
While traced on coming years in faith & hope
    A blessing thou shalt be;   [we see,
Then here in holy labour, there in holier rest,
    Blessing, thou shalt be blest.
              For Papa's birthday
              Jan 18. /59

But If I had not taken the money, she would have given it, I have no doubt, to some other [S.M. ? illegible]. With the last money I had a scrap of paper with the following words written.
 "I gave you many thanks the first-was 14
 "the next was 20 this es [is ?] 6 all together 40 pounds
 "pleas to send it safe   I gave you many thinks [thanks ?]
 "for your trouble pleas to lit [let] me know where i come
 "the right time for you to sen it away."

Rev. W. H. Havergal   Astley   Stourport   Worcester

I have not mentioned these donations at the meetings in this place, not wishing out of regard to the feelings of my Friend, who wishes to remain secret. I write in haste to save this post.
 With kind regards to Mrs. Havergal, in w^h [which ?] my C^hn [Children ?] join
     I remain dear Sir, your's sc [sincerely ?] R Jarratt

This is the final page of the letter from Rev. R. Jarratt to W.H.H. See pages 1428 and 1430.

HOLY PRAISE OFFERED BY MEANS OF HOLY MUSIC:
AND
THE UNION OF SACRIFICE AND SONG.

TWO SERMONS,

PREACHED IN

THE CHURCH OF THE HOLY TRINITY,

STRATFORD-ON-AVON,

IN AID OF THE FUNDS OF THE CHURCH CHOIR,

ON

SUNDAY, 11th JUNE, 1843,

BY

THE REV. W. H. HAVERGAL, M.A.

Late Rector of Astley, in the County of Worcester,

THE PROFITS WILL BE APPROPRIATED TO THE FUND FOR WHICH THE SERMONS WERE PREACHED.

STRATFORD-ON-AVON,

PRINTED AND PUBLISHED BY

R. LAPWORTH,

1843.

TO

THE REV. JOHN CLAYTON, M.A.

The Vicar;

TO

THE REV. S. H. PARKER, B.A.

The Curate,

OF STRATFORD-ON-AVON;

AND TO

THE CONGREGATION AND CHOIR

OF

THE PARISH CHURCH IN THAT TOWN;

These Sermons,

PUBLISHED AT THEIR EARNEST AND UNANIMOUS REQUEST,

ARE FAITHFULLY

AND

AFFECTIONATELY INSCRIBED,

BY

THE AUTHOR.

Henwick House, near Worcester,
July 1843.

MORNING SERMON.

2 Chronicles 5:13.

"It came even to pass, as the trumpeters and singers were as one, to make one sound to be heard in praising and thanking the LORD; and when they lifted up their voice with the trumpets and cymbals and instruments of music, and praised the LORD saying, For he is good; for his mercy endureth for ever: that then the house was filled with a cloud, even the house of the LORD."

THE church of the Living God has its musical history. The principal events in that history are the Passage of the Red Sea, the Dedication of the Temple, and the Nativity at Bethlehem. Each of these events is eminently interesting; but each has a character peculiar to itself. To the second of them your attention is now invited. May He guide and bless that attention, who gave to the Temple of Solomon all its glory, and who marked the music of its Dedication with such tokens of approval as have never since been seen.

The text, as to its narrative, is clear and comprehensive. Solomon at the Dedication of his Temple exhibited at once an essential and most interesting part of its future services. He appointed a large and goodly company of singers, and players on instruments, to thank and praise the GOD of all goodness and mercy. When voices and instruments uniting had attained their zenith of energy and sweetness, then the LORD of heaven came down, and filled the house with the glory of his presence. So overpowering was the splendour of this manifestation, that the ministering priests were necessitated to retire from their station, and desist from their service. "The priests could not stand to minister by reason of the cloud: for the glory of the LORD had filled the house of God." (ver. 14.)

Hence we may remark,

I. *That holy praise is an important part of divine worship.*

To *pray* to Almighty God is a duty which, so to speak, we owe to ourselves. To *praise* Him is a duty which we owe to his ineffable majesty. In prayer we seek for the relief of our own necessities. In praise we acknowledge and adore the divine perfections. By prayer we set forth our poverty and dependence. By praise we magnify the riches of the Saviour's love, and extol the independence of his almighty power. Assuredly, therefore, if prayer be a self-interested duty; praise should be our thankful delight.

A moment's glance at our position as favoured sinners will suffice to show the propriety of holy praise forming a prominent part of divine worship. All the incentives to praise which existed, when Solomon was King of Israel, exist, at this present, in a far higher degree, seeing that Jesus is exalted at the right hand of God to be a Prince and a Saviour to his church. Solomon, as the greatest of natural philosophers, (1 Kings 4:33) had, doubtless, a vast and comprehensive perception of the goodness of GOD in creation. As a man of surpassing knowledge, he must have been minutely acquainted with the history of his people, their redemption from Egypt, their rescue from subsequent oppressions, and their unparalleled privileges. And, as to the mercies which had been shewn to his father's house, and to himself especially, his impressions must have been vividly fresh and tenderly deep. Well, therefore, did it become him to station a choir in his magnificent Temple to praise and thank the LORD, and to say "For He is good; for his mercy endureth for ever!" And, surely, if GOD would not have his Jewish Church come before Him in a sorrowful and dejected attitude, how much more may his Christian Temple ring with the notes of praise, and the accents of thanksgiving! The goodness of GOD in creation is not less conspicuous than it was in the days of Solomon. The heavens are not less gorgeously arched, nor the earth less beautifully garnished now than then: neither are summer and winter, seedtime and harvest less sure than heretofore. While these things remain as they were, how far more wonderfully are other things developed! Things which prophets and righteous man in vain desired to see and hear, are unveiled and declared to us, with a plainness and force which make insensibility as guilty as it is inexcusable. Shadows are become realities, and types have issued in facts. Promises and predictions have received a glorious accomplishment; and life and immortality are brought to light by the advent of the Beloved Son of God.

Mindful of these things, the martyred compilers of our incomparable Liturgy have blended praise with prayer, in a manner as beautiful as it is consistent. As soon as the burthened heart has confessed its sin, and listened to the joyous announcement of absolution through faith in the merits of the One Great Mediator, the voice of the ministering priest gathers strength and says, "O Lord, open Thou our lips;" while congregated saints hasten to respond, "And our mouth shall shew forth *thy praise*." Then follow Psalm and Song with a plenitude and fitness which the calmest judgments must admire, and the warmest affections will readily welcome. And who is there, among the members of our church, who comes to the house of prayer, and forgets that it also is a house of praise? No one, surely, but that individual who forgets to pray. Only let the sinner feel his sin, and penitently confess it, and whose lip will then be more ready to praise Him who died to pardon it? They who find that they have much to supplicate, will soon discover that they have much, also for which to offer praise. Like Solomon, so also the humblest christian (who as a christian is greater than Solomon), will call to mind the wonderful works of his Creator. He will say "When I consider the heavens, the work of thy fingers, the moon and the stars, which thou hast ordained; what is man, that thou art mindful of him? and the son of man that thou visitest him?" (Psalm 8:3, 4.) And, then, as the unworthiest, in his own estimation of all God's *creatures*, he will praise Him for his *goodness*. But speedily, and as the ground of all his thoughts, he will think of his Father's "inestimable love in the redemption of the world, by our Lord Jesus Christ:" and then, as a ransomed *sinner*, he will arouse both heart and lip to praise Him for his *mercy*. Mercy, indeed, is the great object of the penitent sinner's adoration. He vividly sees that infinite as is the divine goodness, and boundless as its treasures are, he has no reason to expect that one particle thereof will ever descend on him, but through the mercy of God in Christ Jesus. Full well does he know that, unless Mercy and Truth had met together in Calvary, no message of reconciliation could have blessed a rebel world. While, therefore, he prays, "Shew us thy mercy; and grant us thy salvation," he "magnifies the Lord, and rejoices in God his Saviour, because He hath remembered his mercy and truth towards" Jew and Gentile. So also, as the christian worshipper walks up to the house of his God, and thinks of the mercies which have followed him all his days, or met him within the last few hours of the week, he joyfully says, "My *praise* shall be of Thee in the great congregation." It, consequently, is a delight to him to find that it is not yet become obsolete for "singers and players on instruments" "to make one sound to be heard in praising and thanking the Lord; and to say, For He is good, for his mercy endureth for ever." Hence the lively christian cordially assents to our proposition, That holy praise is an important part of divine worship.

Advancing from this proposition we present another: viz.

II. *That, in offering holy praise, instrumental music may very fitly accompany singing voices.*

The instruments of music mentioned in the text, were, it is probable, some of the many which had been provided by David as the Royal Psalmist and Sweet Singer of Israel. To those instruments frequent allusion is made in sacred history, after the first mention of them in 1 Chronicles 16:42. They are there denominated "musical instruments of God," but more literally "instruments of the song of God." Hence in the Vulgate, or Latin translation, they are called "instruments of music for singing unto God;" (omnia musicorum organa *ad canendum Deo*) meaning without much question, that they were instruments for accompanying the voices of those who sang praises unto God. Now, though these instruments are called "the instruments of David," and are repeatedly said to have been furnished by him, we are not to conjecture that he appointed the use of them in the Sanctuary without any divine warrant, at the mere dictum of his kingly pleasure, or for the gratification of a refined taste. Were we left in doubt upon this point, the opponents of instrumental music might be a little more brave than they sometimes venture to be. But the wisdom of the Great Head of the Church has taken good care to certify us that these very instruments were ordained of God. David, indeed, prepared them; but it was Jehovah who both directed them to be prepared, and then sanctioned their use in his service. The proof of these statements is found in 2 Chronicles 29:25, 26. It is there said that Hezekiah "set the Levites in the house of the Lord with cymbals, with psalteries, and with harps, according to the commandment of David, and of Gad the king's seer, and Nathan the prophet: for so was *the commandment of the Lord* by his prophets."

The use, then, of musical instrumentation in the services of the church is an ordinance of God. But, says the rather sullen objector, "It was an ordinance of the Jewish church, and, therefore, was abrogated with that church. There is no mention of its use, nor warrant for its adoption in the New Testament, nor was it practised in the primitive church." All this is very plausible; but it is not strictly consistent either with truth, or with itself. Let us briefly examine the complex objection. Instrumental music was not an ordinance of the Jewish church in the same sense in which other things were ordinances. It is not of the same class of ordinances as sacrificial rites, and typical ceremonies; but ranks with such institutions as reading and expounding the word of God, and singing his praises; all of which are more or less prior to the Jewish church, and respecting which no one presumes to say that they were abrogated with that church. Instrumental music was a devotional adjunct, and not a typical appointment. Besides, there is no injunction respecting it in the Law of Moses. Consequently, if we have the same affections as the spiritually minded Hebrews, we may reasonably enough make use of the same devotional helps: and if Moses did not injoin instrumental music, it cannot be said that Christ Jesus annulled it. If it be granted that in the New Testament no recognition of instrumental music occurs, nor any command for its adoption is recorded, it certainly may be pleaded that not a single word is written against it, neither is the slightest intimation given that it is inconsistent with christianity or displeasing to Christ. On the contrary, the beloved one of the disciples, and the last of the apostles, was commissioned to give us some anticipation of the nature of heavenly worship, by allusions to instrumental music. "I heard (says St. John the Divine) the voice of harpers harping with their harps." (Revelation 14:2.) If then, the services of the true sanctuary admit of "harpers harping with their harps," it is very hard to suppose that the use of musical instruments is ineligible or unbecoming in the church below.

To object to instrumental music on the ground of our not reading of it in the New Testament, is scarcely more reasonable than to object to the building of a church, a chapel, or a schoolroom, because the Apostles made no mention of such good works. To argue, too, that primitive congregations did not call in the aid of musical instruments, is in effect to argue that they failed to do what they had no facility for doing. They were a new and an oppressed community. They, consequently, were intent upon the plain essentials, and not upon the embellished adjuncts of divine worship. They were poor, too, and persecuted. Musical instruments were cumbersome as well as costly. Such instruments could not easily be taken to a crowded upper chamber, or to a darksome cavern, or to the lone locality of a martyr's tomb; especially when the sound of them would be a signal for an assault, or a clue to a discovery.

But apart from objections;[1]—be it the concern of British christians to make a legitimate use of that noble instrument, which, happily, is more common in our churches than heretofore. The organ, as a concentration of many instruments is well adapted to accompany and sustain the voices of either a choir or a congregation, or of both united. To the legitimate[2]

---

[1] Years ago, it was a favourite and frequent objection against the use of instrumental music in the house of God, that such music originated in the infidel family of Cain. Jubal, the descendant of Cain, "was the father of all such as handle the harp and organ." (Genesis 4:21.) But this objection employed as an argument proves rather more than is convenient: for, by parity of reasoning, dwellers in tents, and keepers of cattle, and workers in brass and iron would fall under puritanical prohibition; inasmuch as the father of all such dwellers, keepers and artificers, were the brethren of Jubal, and alike the descendants of Cain. Besides, Jubal's being called "the *father* of all such as handle the harp and organ," no more proves that instrumental music *originated* with him, than Jubal's being denominated "the father of such as have cattle" proves that he was the *first* person who tended a flock. "Abel was a keeper of sheep" centuries before Jubal lived.

[2] A church organ is *legitimately* used when the style of performance on it accords with the genius of the instrument itself and with the character of the edifice in which it is heard. A church organ ought not to be debased into Piano Forte, or forced to such an imitation of *stringed* instruments as ill accords with its very construction. What is called fingering and execution may well be exchanged for that steady, stately, seraphic style of performance, which alone befits the architecture of our churches, and the servant of Almighty God. Such style the older masters carefully studied, and excellently practised. They would have been shocked at hearing the crashing discords, the flighty chromaticisms, and the wanton or sickly prophesies of many a modern organist. The music of the theatre, the concert-room, or the parade is an abomination when brought to the organ of the house of God.

use of an organ may be attributed the continuance of our national style of church music. While the Roman church, by admitting modern orchestral accompaniments, has deviated into Operatic levities, our own church, by adhering to the grave and solemn tones of the organ, has pretty generally maintained, in her larger choirs at least, the original dignity, and high devotion of her holy music. The character of that music is eminently vocal. A simple organ accompaniment, while it requires no mean skill, allows that character to remain. But where elaborate instrumentation takes the place of more simple accompaniment, attention is divided, and devotion lowered. Experience, at least, proves such to be the fact. Mere pleasure may follow from splendid or elegant instrumentation; but, is the spirit of piety thereby quickened, or does it swell the current of that feeling which is essential to genuine worship? Possibly not. And here let me caution my hearers against confounding things which materially differ, but which difference, unhappily, is not always discerned, and, certainly, not always maintained. Sacred music, as it is called, is not necessarily *ecclesiastical* music. Much, indeed, that passes for *sacred* music is utterly unfit for the church.[1] What may be suitable for an Oratorio may be out of character in divine service; and what may be allowable for the chamber may be very inappropriate for the church. In the one we may legitimately indulge a refined though hallowed taste; but in the other we are bound to cultivate the best affections of the heart. The topic, however, is, in its bearings, too extensive for an occasion like the present: yet it is clear, that our church community stands very much in need of a little wholesome admonition respecting it.

Recurring more directly to our present proposition, suffice it to add, that when a congregation has the advantage of a superior organ, that congregation is not to regard the organ as a substitute for their singing, but as an auxiliary to it. He who is silent because the organ sounds, is an indolent and, therefore, an irreverent worshipper. I can well understand how the rich tones of an organ, as they float full and deep through the aisles of a venerable fabric, may thrill the very soul of the devout worshipper, and for a moment choke his aiding voice, but, then, the momentary pause will be followed by a more ardent effort to join the praises of the Saviour whom he loves. If, dear brethren, you have a better organ than you had, see that your vocal efforts bear a corresponding improvement. Grudge not to take a little pains, not merely when at church, but in your families at home. It is worth a churchman's best while to do all he can to make the public worship of God an admiration to others and a comfort to himself. At the Dedication of the Temple, the people were not wholly silent; but, at a proper season, joined the stated singers in their sublime chorus of praise. "And when all the children of Israel (it is said) saw how the fire came down, and the glory of the LORD upon the house, they bowed themselves with their faces to the ground, upon the pavement, and worshipped and praised the Lord, saying, For he is good; for his mercy endureth for ever." (2 Chronicles 7:3.)

In primitive times such was the ardour of congregational praise, that St. Augustine said "The voices flowed in at my ears, truth was distilled in my heart, and the affection of piety overflowed in sweet tears of joy." And such, at one period, was the full-toned and magnificent character of the Psalmody of our own church, that organs have, as it were, been drowned and pavements shaken, by the voices of assembled worshippers.[2] God grant that the increased union of instrumental with vocal music, in this congregation, may largely increase his praise and your comfort.

Consecutively our next remark is

III. *That in offering holy praise, the union of vocal and instrumental music, if accompanied with the gracious affections of the heart, is peculiarly pleasing to God.*

We arrive at this conclusion from the fact which, with great precision, is stated in the text. For the Dedication of the Temple there had been a goodly series of preparatory services. There had been the stately procession, the multitudinous sacrifice, and the joyful elevation of the ark to its resting place. Still, no token of the divine presence was vouchsafed. As soon, however, as the white-linened choir struck up their chorus of praise, and instruments and voices were as one, then "*even*" then, it is emphatically said, "the glory of the LORD filled the house." Such honour did God put upon the religious union of instruments and voices.

In a musical point of view the text, though interesting, is not explanatory, as to the long pending question about ancient harmony. Whether the Hebrew minstrels knew and practised that combination of sounds which we call harmony or

---

[1] Many of HANDEL's (sacred) Oratorio Songs are of this description. Either the music of them is too secular, or the words not sufficiently hallowed. Neutrality in either language or music does not befit the worship of God. Hence the unseemliness of such selections as "Angels ever bright and fair," "From mighty kings," and "O lovely peace," for some extra singers on charitable occasions, on a Lord's Day. Across the Channel they descend to even such *things* as "Angels of Life," and "The Last Man," and that in a metropolitan cathedral. The church should have a style of music all her own. That style is developed in the compositions of the Elizabethan worthies, and their successors prior to the day of Oliver Cromwell.

[2] Master Thomas MACE, in his quaint and good tempered book entitled "Music's Monument," describes the singing of Psalms at York Minster, in the year 1644, as "the most remarkable and excellent of any known or remembered, and infinitely beyond all verbal expression or conceiving." "The organ, I say, when the Psalm was set before the sermon, being let out in all its fulness of stops, together with the quire, begun the Psalm. But when that vast concording unity of the whole congregational chorus came, as I may say, thundering in, even so it made the very ground shake under us. Oh the unutterable ravishing soul's delight!"

counterpoint, the text, dispassionately construed, can hardly be said to decide. We are, indeed, told that "the trumpeters and singers were *as one*, to make *one sound* to be heard in praising and thanking the Lord;" but, whether by that "*one* sound" we are to understand sweet and perfect accordance in unisons and octaves, or rich and faultless harmony, with component chords, I will not venture to decide.

Jehovah, in testifying his approbation of the union of instruments and voices, may have designed us to learn a great moral lesson. *Everything is to be devoted to his praise.* He is Lord of all,—of all things as well as of all beings. He is the God of creation,—inanimate as well as animate. All creation, then, is to praise Him. Now that self-same Spirit which said, "Let everything *that hath breath* praise the LORD;" said also, "Let the *fields* rejoice, and all that is therein. Then shall *the trees of the wood* sing out." Consequently when we bring to the house of God, or set up in it, musical instruments made of the produce of the field and the wood, we honour Him as *the Lord of creation*: and when we sing to Him, with our own voices, we honour Him as *the Lord of redemption*. Thus the union of instrumental with vocal music perfects our praise, so far, at least, as the external act is concerned: for God, as the God of *all* harmony, beholds his animate creatures forming *musical* harmony by means of his inanimate creatures, at once for his own honour and glory.

That the eternal God, who has thronged the place of his presence with beings who have never been unlovely or impure, should delight in the praises of sinners afar off from his throne, is not only a mystery which we must always adore, but an act of condescension which we never can adequately admire. Marvellous, indeed, is it that He should permit Himself to be addressed as the God "who inhabiteth the praises of Israel;" (Psalm 22:3.) as One who taketh such delight in the songs of his people that their praise, rather than the temple in which it is offered, should be considered as his pavilion. But, let it never be forgotten that, pleasing as external acts may be when reverently performed for the honour and praise of Almighty God, they, nevertheless, carry with them no inherent excellency. The most splendid celebration of divine song is odious discord if unaccompanied with the breathings of a renewed heart. The gentlest sigh of a contrite spirit will penetrate the ear of our Divine Mediator, while the loudest chorus without faith and godliness will fail to reach it. When we sing elsewhere for our intellectual pleasure, or rational refreshment, we do not indeed assume the attitude of worshippers, though we should never forget that we are christians:[1] but, when we come to the house of God, we stand in a very different position. Every performer and every singer, and every auditor, too, is in the presence of God. While the one plays or sings for God, the other is to hear for God. If the professional man comes as a mere professional man to take his part, he is little better than a heathen. And if an auditor comes as a mere auditor *to be amused*, in what does he differ from a sacrilegious intruder? Brethren, if we would praise God acceptably, whether in the congregation or the choir, we must praise Him from the heart.

Should there be any among you who, through natural infirmity or defective habit, are unable to take part in congregational singing, or who enter but little into the hallowed pleasure of having in their church a superior organ and an efficient choir, let me kindly admonish them not to undervalue what others can enjoy. We are not all moulded alike as to capacity, taste, or sentiment; but we all have a common interest in common praise as well as in common prayer. Let, then, such individuals as are now alluded to, turn their infirmities or deficiencies to a good account, by making them stimulants for the exercise of good will, and, if they have ability, of generous contribution, for the comfort and edification of their fellow worshippers.

And should there, also, be any who feel real interest in the hallowed proceedings of this high and holy day, and yet are oppressed with sorrow, sickness, or any other adversity, and, therefore, cannot elicit their interest; let them be cheered by the thought that the offering of acceptable praise is not restricted to the medium of vocal or instrumental music, or any other single mode. That God who said, "Whoso offereth me praise glorifieth me;" and who "out of the mouth of babes and sucklings, hath perfected praise," will not assuredly disregard the less vocal or even the totally silent offerings of his aged or afflicted servants. The melody of a sanctified heart can ascend to heaven, even through the barrier of a sorrow-closed lip.

And now, christian friends, need I marshal arguments for storming your purse? Need I even *ask* you to contribute towards the cost which has been incurred for the better accommodation of your very commendable choir, in aiding the congregation to thank and praise the Lord? *Need* I ask you? Not, indeed, if you reckon holy praise an important branch of divine worship. Not, indeed, if you deem instrumental music a becoming adjunct to singing voices. Not, indeed, if you are intent on making that adjunct a means of grace which brought into Solomon's Temple not only the hope but a sight of the divine glory. Not, indeed if you venerate all that the Bible sanctions and the church loves. Not, indeed, if looking beyond the vanities of life, and this vale of tears, you are living and even

---

[1] Meetings for the practice of church music, in preparation for church service, require judicious management, especially where the singers are not confined to one sex. Secularity and levity are too apt to intrude. They who practise for holy service should be careful to observe a devout and reverent demeanour. The attendance of the clerical precentor, or parochial minister, cannot be otherwise than salutary, as well as encouraging. Cases are extant where a prayer, short and fervent, precedes the singers' practice.

dying daily, as the servants of the Triune God, and are exercising a "good hope through grace," that you shall one day enter a Temple which is greater than Solomon's, and join a song which shall know no end.

EVENING SERMON.

2 Chronicles 29:27.

"And when the burnt offering began, the song of the LORD began also."

KING Hezekiah, as a man of God, was zealous for the house of God. In the very first month of the first year of his reign, he did to the Temple at Jerusalem, what has recently been done to this church. He cleansed, repaired, and beautified it. On a set day, he assembled his princes and people; and "went up into the house of the LORD." And there, while some Priests and Levites offered burnt offerings and sin offerings, other Priests and Levites sounded musical instruments; and "the singers sang."

Those instruments had originally been prepared by King David "at the commandment of the LORD." Their use had become obsolete; at least in the Temple-service. If they had at all been used, it was in the abominable idolatries of Baal. But now the good Hezekiah restored their use in the worship of his God. On the great day of assembling in the renovated Temple, he either so arranged, or so restored, the parts of the service, that, as soon as the burnt offering began to blaze, the beautiful "song of the LORD" struck up.

In dependence, then, on the grace of the Eternal Spirit, let us turn our thoughts to that *union of sacrifice and song*, which the text describes, which union was and is, and, in one respect, ever will be, the grand peculiarity of that worship which alone is acceptable to the Trinity in Unity.

It is purposed, through God's assistance, to consider,

I. *The union of sacrifice and song, under the Jewish Dispensation.*

Song is older than sacrifice; inasmuch as holiness preceded sin. At the immaculate creation of the world, "the morning stars sang together, and the sons of God shouted for joy." It is likely that Adam, supreme in the paradise of Eden, would sing of the *goodness* of his Creator, while as yet the *mercy* of a Redeemer was needless and unknown. The interval between the commission of the first sin, and the revelation of the only Saviour, must have been as songless as it was dreadful. But, as soon as "the seed of the woman" was announced, it was time for "the song of the LORD" to begin. As to when it really did begin, curiosity must be content to wait, till we know even as we are known: for, from the creation of the world to the time of Jubal, no allusion is made to music. It is, however, intimated that as early as even his day, instrumental music, which usually follows vocal music, was perfectly common. For ages onward, all allusion to both the one and the other is dropped; 'till Laban complained of not having been allowed to send Jacob away, "with mirth, and with tabret and harp." But it is not 'till the passage of the Red Sea, that we read of any musical performance of a distinctly sacred character. As to *that* performance, it is more than probable that it was only one of many which preceded it. The Hebrews must have been accustomed to choral music, to be able to sing and play such a Song as the Song of Moses, at short notice, and *antiphonally*[1] too; for Moses and the men formed one choir, and Miriam and the women formed another. Subsequent incidents, such as their

---

[1] Simplicity, no doubt, united with energy and expression, was the characteristic of this performance. Whether or not it was the *first* instance of *antiphonal* performance, it unquestionably shews that antiphony, or singing responsively in turns, by two separate companies, is older than the establishment of the Jewish polity. That it was continued all through the existence of that polity is clear, from the arrangements of David, (1 Chronicles 25:8.) and the renewal of them by Nehemiah. (Nehemiah 12:24.) A very earnest advocate for antiphonal singing may refer not only to the vision of Isaiah, (Isaiah 6:3.) for a celestial recognition of the practice; but to the very first song of all, coeval with creation itself, "when the morning stars sang together, (as one choir) and the sons of God shouted for joy," as another choir. Certain it is that it became, at a very early period, the practice of the christian church. Antioch, where church choirs were first regularly formed, as well as where believers were first called christians, is generally reputed as the birth place of christian antiphony. Hence the error of regarding the antiphonal singing of our cathedrals as "a relique of popery."

See Hooker's *Eccles. Pol.* Book v, ch. 39, (2.)

singing before the golden calf, shew that they were habituated to mingle song with sacrifice. Upon the establishment of the Tabernacle-service, arrangements for musical worship, and the blowing of trumpets, were systematically made. But it was reserved for David, as the sweet singer of Israel, to enlarge and prepare for perfection, the Psalmody of his national church. Then, indeed, "the song of the LORD" abounded; and the courts of the Sanctuary rang with gracious mirth.

We need only allude to the number and excellency of the instruments made by Solomon, for they were made on the eve of degenerate days. (2 Chronicles 9:11.) "There were none such seen before in the land of Judah." After short lived revivals, sacrifice gradually ceased, and holy song ceased with it. Hezekiah at length arose, a further-reformer in Judah. He restored the offering of burnt sacrifice, and the performance of divine song. When he kindled the altar, he awoke the choir. As before intimated, he, most likely, followed the arrangement which David, as God's inspired servant, had defined. "When the burnt offering began, the song of the LORD began also, with the trumpets and with the instruments ordained by David, King of Israel."[1] And, verily, in this scene, there must have been much to affect and elevate the heart of the pious Hebrew. When he saw the sacrificial victim, he was reminded at once of the pardon of his sin, and of the joyous peace which passeth all understanding. When, also, the sound of the song ascended with the smoke of the sacrifice, it intimated to him not only that without shedding of blood there is no remission, but that without acceptable sacrifice there can be no acceptable thanksgiving. It obscurely told him a truth which, in later days, has clearly been told to us, that the atonement of the One Great Mediator is both the only basis of spiritual praise, and the grand subject of that praise. It taught him, too, the momentous difference between the most imposing ceremonies, and the renewed affections of the heart. Hence said David, "I will praise the name of God with a song, and will magnify him with thanksgiving. This, also, shall please the Lord better than an ox or bullock that hath horns and hoofs." (Psalm 69:30, 31.)

The perfection of Hebrew worship was the union of sacrifice and song with corresponding devoutness of soul. Doubtless this union will, at the last great day, be found to have existed among many a "seven thousand in Israel." God will shew that He had a people formed for his praise, amidst the scantiness of revelation, and the imperfections of ritual worship.

After the harp of Judah had hung, for many a long year, on the willows of Babylon, the burnt offering and "the song of the LORD" were renewed, under Ezra and Nehemiah. The provision which was made for the choir, in the second Temple, is rather minutely recorded. The singers were privileged persons; as much so as the ministers of the sanctuary. "It shall not be lawful (said the King of Persia) to impose toll, tribute, or custom, upon them." (Ezra 7:24.) "It was the King's commandment concerning them, that a certain portion should be for the singers, due for every day." (Nehemiah 11:23.) Their services were continued, amidst sundry interruptions, 'till that age in which Simeon and Anna waited daily in the Temple, for the coming of the Redemption of Israel. And when the lowly Redeemer did come, He himself attended the Temple-service, and gazed on the type of his own sacrifice, and listened to the song, which, though little suspected by those who were singing it, was indeed composed for his own praise. Messiah was the true burden of that song, inasmuch as He was the antitype of every sacrifice. But, when He with incarnate eyes beheld the burnt offering, the time was come for its flame to expire; but *not* for "the song of the LORD" to cease. That song is continued to this day; and eternity is not destined to witness its end. It will be everlasting, and yet ever new.

And here, before we proceed to the second part of our subject, two remarks may, from the character of the times and our present opportunity, be appropriately introduced. 1st. It has become the fashion, in what is called the musical world, to decry the ancient Hebrew music. Even persons of education have ventured to say that "The music of the Temple must have been insufferably coarse; and had Mozart heard it, he would have been horrified and shocked."

They who assert such things forget or conceal certain facts, before which their "great swelling words" shrink into native insignificance. They forget that they cannot define what Hebrew music really was. They overlook the fact that the Hebrew music school was on a scale both as to numbers, training, and stipend, which no church in christendom ever had the heart to attempt. They do not bear in mind that Hebrew trumpets were of silver, and that Jewish harps and other instruments were of the choicest manufacture. They, also, quite overlook one omnipotent consideration,—*The days of Hebrew music were days of divine inspiration.* He who inspired mechanics to construct the Sanctuary was, at least very likely to inspire musicians to sing and play in it.[2] That such inspiration was extant is more

---

[1] "And even in thy daily sacrifices each morning and evening, I find a heavenly mirth; music, if not so loud, yet no less sweet and delicate: no fewer than twelve Levites might be standing on the stage, every day, singing a divine ditty over thy sacrifice; psalteries, not fewer than two, nor more than six; pipes, not fewer than two, nor more than twelve; trumpets, two at the least, and but one cymbal: (Maimonides) so proportioned by the masters of thy choir; as those that meant to take the heart by the ear."
Bishop Hall's Soliloquies, lxxvi.

[2] "KIRCHER supposes that the Hebrew musicians were inspired with the knowledge of vocal and instrumental music, and that their performance was equal to their skill. He doubts not but that there were many, especially in the time of King SOLOMON, who were skilled in divine music; for that the most

than probable. What instrument in modern days can produce such effects as the harp of even the youthful David? Or what military band ever awed an opponent army, and gave a decisive turn to the battle, like that company of sacred musicians whom Jehoshophat led into the field? (2 Chronicles 20:21, 22.) Verily, in spite of semi-infidel surmises, there must have been something wonderfully touching, or strikingly beautiful, or overwhelmingly grand, in the music of the Hebrew church. How the holy and all-wise God testified his approbation of it, we heard in this morning's discourse.

Europe is now gazing on Palestine; and the Jews are in the eye of the world. But it is remarkable that God has constantly set his ancient people not only before the eye, but in the *ear* of the world. The voices of the seed of Abraham have always attracted attention.[3] For sundry generations of late, a Jew or Jewess has stood in the very first rank of European singers.[4] And, if Jewish voices be so splendid in the days of their degradation, what may they not have been in the time of their glory? and what may they not yet be on their coming restoration? (Romans 11:12, 15.) Jerusalem may yet hold the empire of song; and exhibit a model of christian music to Christ's holy catholic church.

2nd. The other remark proposed for introduction is this: We are too apt to regard the service of the Hebrew church as a dark, dull, and irksome service. We think of the dying victim, the fuming altar, and the sprinkled blood; and picture to ourselves a scene of humiliation, tedium, and cold formality. But far different was the real state of things. The service of the Temple though a mingled service was singularly cheerful. Enough has been said of its singing and instrumentation to show that it was far more spirited and lively than anything we are accustomed to witness. "The song of the LORD," under various modifications of historic recital, prophetic declaration, and devotional breathing, was kept up, day and night, in the Sanctuary, even when no sacrificial offerings were going on. (Psalm 134:1.) Thus by far the greater part of the Temple service was of a very exalted and joyous character;—a fit emblem of the worship of that "Tabernacle which God hath pitched and not man." For, as in heaven so on earth, while God will have his redeemed ones mindful of their sins, He designs them to be thankful for his mercies. This will of God was largely in the mind of our Reformers, when they modeled our invaluable Liturgy. Hence *we* have a cheerful service, and yet such an one as becomes a company of "miserable sinners."

Our next relative topic is,

II. *The union of sacrifice and song under the Christian Dispensation.*

That dispensation began with a song, but in anticipation of a sacrifice. "Glory to God in the highest," sang the angelic choir, because "a Saviour" from *sin* was announced. That beloved Saviour habitually kept his sacrifice in view: and though his disciples could but little understand it, yet did He soothe and cheer them with considerations drawn from the mysterious consequences of it. On the night of his betrayal, He virtually abolished that grand sacramental type of his own sacrifice,—the Passover. He ate of it for the last time; and then instituted and ordained another sacramental service significative of his death. This service he closed by singing a hymn. Whether that hymn was the great Hillel, *i.e.* the Passover selection of Psalms from the hundred-and-thirteenth to the hundred-and-eighteenth inclusive, or another hymn properly so called, may admit of question; seeing the Passover was abolished when it was sung, and the Lord's Supper established in its stead. Be the fact as it may, our church has followed this very first model of eucharistic service, and put in the lips of her communicants a noble and glorious song,[5] just before they rise up to go away.

Subsequently to our Lord's crucifixion and ascension, when the Spirit had been poured out from on high, somewhat of the worthiness of his sacrifice began to be seen and felt. Hearts exulted with the love of Christ, and tongues were eloquent in rehearsing the wonders and virtues of his death. That death was, in fact, the all comprehensive event which was to be told to a ruined and a wretched world; and from which that world was to take up a new song, and gather new hopes and joys.

---

excellent music was fittest for the wisest of mortals, and that of the Hebrews must have been more efficacious in exciting the affections, than that of the Greeks, or of later times."
Sir J. Hawkins's *Hist. Mus.* Vol. 1, p. 258.

[3] The Babylonians were compelled to admire the singing of their Jewish captives. (Psalm 137:3.) The Romans, who besieged Jerusalem, are described as little less than enchanted with "the music which they heard played, many a night, upon the high walls of the city, with hautboy, clarion, and dulcimer. I never," says one of them, "heard any music like the music of the Jews. Why, when they came to join the battle, their trumpets sounded so gloriously that we wondered how it was possible for them to be driven back. And, then, when their gates were closed, and they sent out to beg their dead, they would play such solemn awful notes of lamentation, that our plunderers stood still to listen, and their warriors were delivered to them, with their mail on, just as they had fallen."
Lockhart's *Valerius in loco.*

[4] There was so much ambiguity respecting the parentage of the wonderful MADAM MARA, that, among other surmises, she was suspected of being by birth a Jewess. MRS. BLAND captivated all ears by the sweetness of her singing. Some fifty years ago, all London was going to the Jewish Synagogue to hear LEONI chant. In earlier life, BRAHAM surpassed his competitors of every nation, with as much ease to himself as, perhaps, envy to them. And now, on all great occasions, and for all the most important bass songs, whether delicate, difficult, or scientific, who does not look to HENRY PHILLIPS?

[5] The Gloria in Excelsis of our Communion Service is better sung than said. It can easily be so versicled as to be used with a chant. TALLIS is the only composer in BOYCE's Cathedral Music, who has set it for singing.

Because Jesus was bound, the prisoner was to be loosed. Because He was smitten, the ailing were to be healed. Because He wept, the sorrowful were to rejoice. Because He cried with a loud and grievous cry, the tongue of the dumb was to speak the language of praise. In a word, because Jesus died, the church is to live. Consequently, be the lot or state of individuals what it may, they are to bring the burthen of their griefs and woes to the Lamb of God. On Him they are, with the hand of faith, to cast the weary load; and, then, with the song of praise to laud and magnify his holy name. The first christians could say, "Believing we rejoice with joy unspeakable and full of glory." Through their faith in the crucifixion, the dungeon was turned into a choir, the rack into a psaltery, and the stake into a music staff. And, verily, from the time that believers began to say each one for himself, "God forbid that I should glory, save in the cross of our Lord Jesus Christ," there never have been wanting a succession of faithful souls to sing the song of their crucified Lord. "Thou art the King of glory, O Christ! When thou hadst overcome the sharpness of death, Thou didst open the kingdom of heaven to all believers!" This joyous confession has yielded corresponding consolation to christians in all climes, and under all circumstances. It has animated them in perplexing life, and cheered them in the dark valley of death. And what, indeed, but the atoning death of the Lord can give energy to "the song of the LORD"? That man must be very angelic or very antichristian who thinks he can offer welcome praise, without holy faith in the sacrifice of Christ. Angels may sing of the Lord's *goodness*, but if man come to sing of his *mercy*, it must be on ground upon which angels may gaze, but on which they cannot stand. The shade of the cross is the area for human rejoicing. There the contrite sinner may kneel; and while repentance fills his eye with a tear, faith may charge his lip with a song. Sorrow may be as the softening dew which falls upon that area, but joy is the bright atmosphere which surrounds it.

Right happy should we deem ourselves at being the members of a church, in the services of which, the sacrifice of Christ is most unequivocally made the basis of all prayer and praise. Whether we ask any petition, or offer any thanksgiving, we are taught to look for acceptance only through the merits and mediation of our Lord and Saviour Jesus Christ. So true is it that, when our Reformers cast away the crucifix, they the more joyfully embraced the *doctrine* of the cross. It is remarkable, too, that in the very arrangement of "The Daily Service" of our church, it may almost be said that,—when the burnt offering begins, the song of the Lord begins also: for scarcely is our sin acknowledged, and the sacrifice of prayer kindled into a flame, when the Minister says, "Praise ye the Lord"; and presently a Psalm succeeds. And, Oh, blessed be the God of our fathers, for restoring to us "the song of the LORD" in its scriptural purity, and in our own mother tongue! Our Liturgy is clean swept of the idolatrous or deceitfully dangerous compositions with which it was once defiled. We retain "the Song *of* the blessed Virgin Mary, in English," because she uttered that song under the inspiration of the Holy Ghost; and because in it she *magnified* her Saviour and our Saviour, her God and our God. But we have no hymn *to* the Virgin, no "Audi, Mater," no chanted invocation to the queen of heaven, no musical worshipping of angels, no lauding of wafers;—nothing that is offensive to a holy and jealous God, who cannot give his glory to another.

Assuredly it cannot be out of place or season to say, Let Protestant musicians be on their guard against the wiliness of the Romish church, in linking beautiful music to idolatrous or equivocal words. The thin gauze of the Latin tongue is not of sufficient texture to shield their consciences from guilt, or their conduct from the charge of inconsistency. Let the most beautiful music go for naught, if it cannot be separated from language and sentiments which endanger souls, and insult the God of heaven.[1]

On an occasion, too, such as the present, it may be far from inappropriate to offer a remark or two upon topics inseparable from the use of an organ in the house of God. The petulant controversy about such use, though, as you know, here and there kept up, is happily on the decline. Truth has prevailed, pretty generally, at least, in England. But religious good sense will be requisite to maintain the conquest. If our church-organs are used for mere display, or for something like congregational amusement, they will merit the sharp rebuke which,

---

[1] Cathedralists and Members of large choirs will do well to be a little more circumspect than hitherto has been common. Mischief is being done by admitting the compositions of *modern* Romanists, under the specious garb of adaptations as anthems and other choral forms. Those compositions are utterly opposed to the genius and style of our own church music. They are essentially Operatic: for with the almost compulsory exception of here a phrase and there a modulation, they very little differ from the Operas of the very same authors. Truly it is appalling, and to our older worthies it would have been little short of maddening, to hear our choirs singing the harlot strains of a Roman Opera-Mass; while the noble organ is debased to "a chest of viols," and made to imitate all the levities and puerilities of a fantastical accompaniment. As an illustration of these remarks, it is sufficient to name generically one very *popular* anthem, "*Plead thou my cause.*" It is an adaptation from a Kyrie Eleeson of MOZART, and worthy of him as an Opera writer, but not as an *ecclesiastical* composer. "*Pretty*" it certainly is; but its prettiness is its fault, being as much out of place, in the house of God, as a Corinthian screen in a gothic cathedral, or the taudry dress of a Madonna in front of marble sculpturings. The evils of admitting such music into our cathedrals are great and various. Good taste is gradually vitiated; perception of proprieties is dulled; familiarity with incongruous style is increased; and the line of demarcation between the church and the world is in the way to be obliterated. Besides, such musical adaptations prepare the public ear for the decoy performances at Papal chapels. Romanists themselves fail not to boast of our borrowings, but take good care not to borrow in return. A LUTHERAN tune cannot be tolerated in a Popish service.

in the second part of the Homily "Of the place and time of Prayer," is passed upon the instrumental music of our churches just before the Reformation.[1] The use of an organ is to aid devotional singing, not to overpower or seduce it. Hence an organist should be a devout person, ever vigilant to adapt the powers of the instrument, and the style of playing it, to the varying circumstances of divine worship. Skill is not more requisite than discretion in using a tune, adapting a symphony or playing a voluntary.[2] As to what, generally speaking, should be the style of parish-church music, there is no difficulty in determining. The difficulty lies in bringing persons of musical feeling, but not of musical knowledge, to consent to that determination. They have been accustomed to tunes in a most faulty style, and, consequently, cannot soon be induced to like such as are legitimate and good.[3] Common, indeed, is it, to hear psalms and hymns sung in our churches, to tunes of really illiterate origin, and vulgar construction. Some of those tunes are song-like, march-like, ballad-like, while others are of such a nondescript character as to be like nothing but their own unecclesiastical selves. And yet, if an intelligent and right minded organist selects such a tune as Luther and our forefathers liked, it is called dull, prosy, and intolerable. The main cause of this evil has been the want of competent oversight, especially during the past and present generation. Our parish-church music has been suffered, like our parish-church architecture of a somewhat earlier period, to become debased. We blame the churchwarden for the one, and the parish-clerk for the other; but, in candour, we must come a little nearer to the reading-desk and pulpit, to find the blame of both. The remedy is one, as well in architecture as in music, viz. to go back to older models. But in using the older tunes we must bear in mind this fact;—they are in their very structure adapted for large congregations, for masses of voice. Hence, if all who can sing *will* sing, the fine old melodies and rich harmonies of the sixteenth and seventeenth centuries will no longer appear dull and over grave. Only let them be sung not drawlingly but with becoming vivacity,[4] and we shall presently determine on their incomparable superiority for devotional purposes. In a word, we must be content to let the world have its *pretty* tunes, while the church holds fast the *good*: for it is fitting and highly proper that there should be a marked difference between the music of the church, and of the world. "Religious harmony" (said one who well understood its nature) "must be moving, but noble withal; grave, solemn, seraphic; fit for a martyr to play, and an angel to hear." (Jeremy Collier.)

There remains a consideration of a somewhat more practical cast. It is desirable to have in our churches, not only good music, but grateful hearts and ready voices. An organ and a choir of singers are not to be regarded as substitutes for the voices of the congregation. It will, however, readily be conceded that occasionally, and as extra service may demand, the organ and the choir alone may praise the Lord "*skilfully*," for such was a common practice in the Jewish church, under the inspiration of the Holy Ghost. (Psalm 33:3.) Nor is it an ill thing for us to be reminded that, although the Majesty of heaven will mercifully listen to the poorest praises of the simplest heart, yet the best that human skill can offer is far too mean for the worthiness of his great and glorious name. Still in our customary worship, while the organ and the choir make suitable harmony, and both lead and sustain it, the mingled voices of the congregation should follow, and give that noble fulness which nothing else can give. To transfer the work of praise wholly to the lips of other persons, can never be consistent, unless we transfer

---

[1] An objection against the reformed church-service is represented as being uttered by one woman, in conversation with another. "Alas, gossip, what shall we now do at church, since all the goodly sights, we were wont to have, are gone; since we cannot hear the like piping, singing, chanting, and playing upon the organs, that we could before?" Upon which the preacher interposes, and says, "But, dearly beloved, we ought greatly to rejoice, and give God thanks that our churches are delivered out of all those things which displeased God so sore, and filthily defiled his holy house, and his place of prayer."

[2] It is not discreet to choose for a psalm or hymn of many verses, a tune in triple time with sundry divisions of the accented part of each bar; nor a tune in any time, in which lines or half lines are repeated. Too many Organists violate all propriety and unity by the style of their interludes, or symphonics, between each verse. To such Organists, the last note of the tune is but a starting post for running into all the fripperies or whinings of some light and chromatic Opera music. Hence, between the style of the tune and the style of the symphony, there is the widest possible diversity.

Few things shew the *good* Organist more than *good keeping* in all he plays. His symphonics will never divert the thoughts, nor his voluntaries, after a solemn service, dispel all serious feelings.

[3] Till the beginning of the last century, the excellent tunes of the Elizabethan age as published by Ravenscroft and afterwards by Playford, were universally used. Even new tunes were composed after their model. It is curious and painful to see how, about a century ago, tunes of lighter but less simple character began to be introduced. Many a locality had its wiseacre in concocting and publishing new, wretchedly *new*, "Psalm and Hymn tunes." Volume after volume sprung up; and though they speedily withered, yet each left some evil roots or cast some noxious seeds. Still, many of the good old tunes survived; as may be seen in such publications as are kept for curiosities. But, of late years, these remnants of better psalmody have nearly all disappeared. "The Old Hundredth Psalm Tune" is, perhaps, the *only* Elizabethan tune which is now commonly known. "*Bedford*," "*Hackney* or *St. Mary's*," "*St. Ann's*," and all the tunes in triple time of more solid structure, though generally considered as old tunes, are of a date long subsequent to the age of Elizabeth. The tunes of her age were uniformly simple and easy, yet sober and chaste. They were, also, *syllabic*, having a note for a syllable and a syllable for a note; without repetitions, and mostly in common time. Probably some of these tunes, if not all, with their original harmonies, will, ere long, be published.

[4] It is a great mistake to suppose that because a tune is old it should be sung or played very slowly. The old tunes were always sung, in older days, rather briskly. Hence ten or twelve verses were not thought too long. The Old Hundredth, now esteemed so solemn, was formerly the specimen of a lively and most cheerful tune, as all the older Prayer Books testify.

See "*Directions about the Tunes*," etc.

our benefits also. Devout and thankful individuals who from long, and, perhaps, faulty disusage, think that they cannot themselves sing, will yet discover such an interest in the singing of others, as will virtually make it their own. But, when persons, who can sing blithely enough in their homes, are habitually silent in the house of God, there must be something wrong in either their frame of mind, or their estimate of the duties and privileges of a christian worshipper. Besides, to be able to sing, and yet to refrain from singing, in even "an humble and lowly voice," is as unwelcome a sign of mere half-churchmanship, as not joining in the responses. In all the old editions of our metrical psalms, it is stated that they were set forth "to be sung of *all* the people *together*." So well had this hint been taken even before it was so given, that christians of the Reformation were noted for singing in crowds, even six thousand together at Paul's Cross,[1] the version newly made by STERNHOLD of some of the Psalms of David. No singing can be dull, when the voice of a congregation is "as the sound of mighty waters." Nor can it be more the duty than the interest of a congregation, to help forward the blessed "song of the LORD."

> "For this our *truest interest* is
> Glad hymn of praise to sing."
> (Psalm 135:3. *New Ver.*)

The Hebrews were of old exhorted to join their choir; and christians are bidden to abound "in psalms and hymns and spiritual songs;" singing, at the same time, with grace in their hearts, and understanding what they sing. As, therefore, advancement in holy comfort is one great end of such singing, they who use it best and most, as a means of grace, will proportionably find it an auxiliary to the hope of glory.

It remains for us to contemplate,

III. *The union of song with sacrifice, retrospectively considered in the world to come.*

---

[1] In a letter from Bishop JEWEL to PETER MARTYR, dated London, March 5th, 1560, that admirable prelate says, "Religion is now somewhat more established than it was. The people are everywhere inclined to the better part. The practice of joining in church music has very much conduced to this. For as soon as they had once commenced singing in public, in only one little church (*a*) in London, immediately not only the churches in the neighbourhood, but even the towns far distant, began to vie with each other in the same practice. You may now sometimes see at Paul's Cross, after the service, six thousand persons, old and young, of both sexes, all singing together and praising God. This sadly annoys the Mass-priests and the devil: for they perceive that by these means the sacred discourses sink more deeply into the minds of men, and that their kingdom is weakened and shaken at almost every note."

Zurich Letters, p. 71.

(*a.*) St. Antholin's, where, in September, 1559, the new morning prayer began, the bell ringing at *five* o'clock (!!!) when a psalm was sung by all the congregation together.

"The souls of the faithful," as our Burial Service testifies, "after they are delivered from the burden of the flesh are with Christ in joy and felicity." Their bodies, meanwhile, though sentenced to dust, are sleeping in peace. In the morning of the last day, they shall awake in the glorified likeness of their Redeemer; and "they shall awake *in tune*." They shall awake with mighty and instant capacity to begin the song which will be already prepared for them: for thus saith the prophet, "Thy dead men shall live, together with my dead body shall they arise. *Awake* and *sing*, ye that dwell in dust." (Isaiah 26:19.) But though ready to begin their immortal song, they will hear a voice which, while it singles them from the countless crowd, will remind them of the sacrifice by which they were saved. "Our God," says the Psalmist, "shall come. He shall call to the heavens from above, and to the earth, that He may judge his people. Gather my saints together unto me, those that have made a covenant with me *by sacrifice*." (Psalm 50:3–5.) And then, when the Judge shall bid his good and faithful servants enter into *the joy* of their Lord, a song shall commence at which the very heavens shall be astonished, and the angelic hosts delighted. But that song will still be "the song of the LORD," "great, wonderful and holy:" and it will still be a song of sacrifice; for it will be "the song of the Lamb." "Thou wast slain," will say the sanctified choir, "and hast redeemed us to God *by thy blood*, out of every kindred, and tongue, and people."

Startling as it may seem to us, when wrapt in comfortable meditation, it nevertheless is plainly true, that *in heaven there will be a constant remembrance of former sin*. But it will not be such a remembrance as there is, or ought to be, on earth. It will be a remembrance not of sin to be repented of, but of sin abundantly pardoned. The saints of God will never forget their sins. David will remember his adultery, and Peter his denial. Else, how will they adore the Lamb as slain for them, and as having *washed* them from their *sins* in his own blood? But, by an arrangement, as admirable as it is mysterious, "all tears will be wiped from all faces," and every fresh recollection of sin will be followed by a flood of joy, and a burst of song. "Unto Him that loved us, and washed us *from our sins* in his own blood; and hath made us kings and priests unto God and his Father; to Him be glory and dominion, for ever and ever." (Revelation 1:5, 6.)

Such will be the song of those, who placed *all* their hope of salvation in the sacrifice of Christ. May we hear it; may we join it! But, bear in mind the solemn fact;—they alone will hear it, they alone will join it, who begin it now. In the exercise of godly sorrow, we must seek the Saviour's mercy, and sing of it too. Our song, however, must not be confined to the lip; it must spring from the heart, and be echoed in every part of the life. Unutterably sad will it be, should the case be found otherwise with us. If "the song of the LORD" shall have dwelt on our lip, and not have found its way to our heart, we never shall find our way to heaven. In vain will it prove, at the great assize, to say "Lord, Lord, have we not prophesied in thy name?" have we not *sung* in thy name? You know what the answer will be. God in infinite mercy grant that it may not be addressed to us!

But, there will be another peculiarity in "the song of the LORD" in heaven. On earth we are accustomed to sing, "Hallelujah, Amen!" In heaven they say "Amen, Hallelujah!" Of this fact we are certified throughout the Apocalypse. (Revelation 19:4.) But, as to the reason of this inversion, nothing is told us. If, however, we may indulge an humble surmise, the reason, possibly, is this:—The angelic choir are in some way, mysterious to us, affected by the Incarnation of Christ. They perpetually celebrate its wonders. Let us suppose that, at every fresh inspiration, they pause. With their mighty intellect, they grasp, at a glance, the whole history of Redemption. They behold the deep and affecting mystery of the cross. They survey the infinite love of Him who hung upon it. They see the amazing wisdom of God's dealings with man. They trace the intricacies of his providence, and understand the chastisements of his church. And then, approving, admiring and adoring, the entire scheme of grandeur and of grace, they say of it, "Amen!" and quickly their everlasting "Hallelujah" ascends before the throne of the Lamb.

Brethren, think of these things: and if your hearts and lives are in good tune, you will love the melody of a good work. You will, for Christ's sake, generously remember the fund for the liquidation of certain costs, connected with the accommodation of those, who stand in this "holy and beautiful house," to bless and praise the LORD. You will see in your voluntary choir, not merely a goodly company of those who freely offer their services to the Lord, but a lively representation of that better choir which fills heaven with rapture. In your organ, also, you will see a type of what the church below should be, and of what it is above; viz. a wonderful combination of little and great, feeble and strong to make up one harmonious hymn to Christ. You will, also, learn what is better than the best earthly music, for your death-pillow,—the love of that Name which angels and archangels, cherubim and seraphim incessantly admire and adore. And if in the interim you meet with "trouble, sorrow, need, sickness or any other adversity," "you shall have a song, as in the night, when a holy solemnity is kept; and gladness of heart, as when one goeth with a pipe to come into the mountain of the Lord, to the Mighty One of Israel." (Isaiah 30:29.)

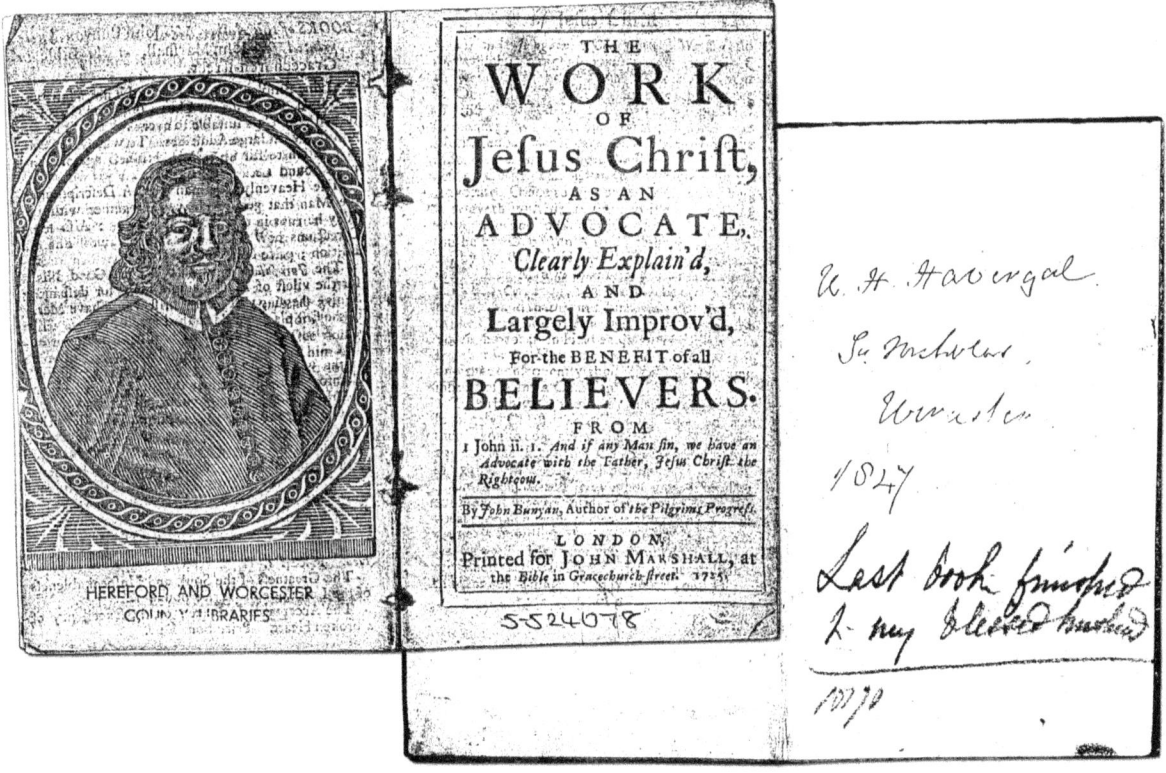

On the inside of the book, near the front cover, William Henry Havergal wrote: W. H. Havergal St. Nicholas Worcester 1847. Below that, his widow Caroline Ann Havergal wrote: Last book finished by my blessed husband 1870.

Elisha and the Minstrel:

A Sermon,

PREACHED ON THE MORNING OF THURSDAY,
NOVEMBER 29, 1849

AT THE

Opening of a New Organ,

IN THE

PARISH CHURCH OF ST. MICHAEL, BATH,

BY THE

Rev. W. H. Havergal, M.A.,

RECTOR OF ST. NICHOLAS', WORCESTER,
AND HONORARY CANON OF THE CATHEDRAL IN THAT CITY.

PUBLISHED BY REQUEST.

London:
HATCHARD & SON, PICCADILLY.
MDCCCXLIX.

WITH THE ACCUMULATED FRIENDSHIP OF MORE THAN THIRTY YEARS,

This Sermon

IS AFFECTIONATELY INSCRIBED TO

THE REV. JOHN EAST, M.A.,

THE RECTOR OF THE PARISH IN WHICH IT WAS PREACHED,

BY

THE AUTHOR.

THE PROFITS ARISING FROM THE SALE OF THIS DISCOURSE ARE TO BE GIVEN TO THE FUND FOR ERECTING THE NEW ORGAN IN ST. MICHAEL'S CHURCH, BATH.

Elisha and the Minstrel:

A Sermon.

2 Kings 3:15.

"But now bring me a minstrel. And it came to pass, when the minstrel played, that the hand of the Lord came upon him."

THESE words are part of a very remarkable narrative. The king of Israel and the king of Judah, in company with the king of Edom, marched, in hostile array, against the king of Moab. The three confederate kings, in order to come upon their adversary unawares, took a circuitous course, through a wilderness. After a march of seven days, the combined armies halted, in consequence of the want of water. In their fearful extremity, the sovereigns held a council. Jehoshaphat, the king of Judah, very properly inquired whether any prophet of the Lord were present. On learning that Elisha had, unknown to them, accompanied the army, they reverently went to him. The good prophet rather warmly reproached Jehoram, king of Israel, with the idolatries of his family: indeed, he boldly told him, that unless a better man than himself, meaning Jehoshaphat, had been with him, he would not so much as look at him. But, though more than a little ruffled, the holy prophet forgat neither his humanity nor his religion. Recollecting himself, he called for the soothing influence of music, that he might thereby be the sooner fitted for receiving from God such communications as would benefit the fainting troops. In the language of the text, he said, "But now bring me a minstrel." Instantly it is added, "And it came to pass, when the minstrel played, that the hand of the Lord came upon him." The result was, that Elisha foretold the preservation of the perishing host by a supernatural supply of water.

Now, apart from other considerations, and with an eye to the special object of this morning's service, what is the plain truth which the text sets before us? Is it not that a man of God, at that time the most eminent saint on earth, sought, by means of holy music, a revival of holy feelings and spiritual affections? Such is the fact. If, then, God was found of the prophet, and the prophet was found of God, through the use of devout music, can we be wrong in concluding that such music, in a Christian church, is favourable to all the devotional exercises of that church? Answering that question in the affirmative, it will be the object of the present discourse to illustrate the affirmation in such manner as, by God's sanctifying grace, may edify and profit all who hear it. The introduction of a few historic and correlative remarks will, it is thought, be justifiable and expedient on an occasion like the present. Above all things, however, may that "hand" which came upon Elisha come on us, and so touch and tune our hearts that all our minstrelsy in the church on earth may fit us for the songs of "the church of the firstborn in heaven"!

I. With the fact before us of Elisha's calling for a minstrel to soothe his mind, and to prepare his soul for the inspiration of the Holy Spirit, it is meet that we should be correctly informed respecting the minstrel and the nature of his performance.

The Jewish minstrel, as our best students think, was not merely "a player on instruments" (Psalm 87:7), but a singer also,—one who accompanied his voice with the tones of a lyre, or of some instrument of that sort. Hence it has been suggested, that the minstrel, whom Elisha wished to be called, was not a rhapsodist or strolling bard, but a Levite skilled in the music of the temple, both vocal and instrumental, as arranged by David, according to the commandment of his God.

Such a minstrel (and such alone would the good Jehoshaphat seek), well knowing the character of Elisha and the purpose for which he desired his performance, would not fail to adapt his selection of both words and strains to the occasion for which he was employed. To suppose the contrary would be the imagining of things hardly credible. Assuming, then, the performance of the minstrel to be both hallowed and *suitable*, we may, thus early, suggest to every church minstrel the propriety of studying to adapt his performance, whether vocal or instrumental, to the varying circumstances before him. The times and seasons of our church, and the diverse character of the words selected for singing, should induce him to study *suitableness*,[1] and that sort of adaptation which the intelligent discern and the devout approve.

II. When Elisha said, "Bring me a minstrel," he said nothing which excited surprise. The minstrel was soon brought, for the case was well understood. The reason was, the Jews were,

---

[1] Too many organists still play most *unsuitable* interludes between the verses of a psalm or hymn. Such interludes prove the bane of *good* singing. They elongate the service, divert attention, and engender ill taste. Happily, it is becoming common to omit them altogether.

in a remarkable degree, a musical people. Indeed they seem always to have been such; while the spirit of song, which once beautified their temple, has certainly lingered among them in all their judicial dispersions. By their exquisite quality of voice, Jehovah, for the last half-century, has been setting them in the ear,[1] and so before the eye, of a vain world, which is too willing to forget His purposes respecting them. In the days of their tenure of Palestine, it was a prevailing belief among them that music had a mysterious power over the soul, and that it prepared the mind for prophetic inspiration. Hence, as Bishop Lowth[2] and Dr. Gray[3] assert, it is a well-authenticated fact, that the Jewish prophets were familiar with musical instrumentation as well as vocal strains. In the ordinary modes of prophesying, they were accustomed to compose their odes, hymns, and other poetical effusions, to the sound of some sweet instrument, either touched by themselves or more commonly played upon by an attendant symphonist.[4] Elisha, therefore, acted in accordance with ordinary usage. He desired the spirit of power and of prophecy. He consequently called for a minstrel. The minstrel came, and the Divine Spirit condescendingly followed.

III. Much might, from this circumstance, be said of *the natural fitness of music* to bring the minds of men into certain moods. It is, however, sufficient for us to recollect that the God of our souls and of our salvation prescribed the use of music, instrumental as well as vocal, for his church, and that not a whisper of the revocation of that prescription was ever heard. Before the establishment of the Jewish ritual, music was a religious exercise;[5] and, long after the establishment of that ritual, the Spirit of God devised means for the larger introduction of both vocal and instrumental music into the services of the sanctuary. It is expressly asserted that David, " at the command of God," prepared an abundance of musical instruments and a numerous company of singers. The selfsame Spirit, too, inspired him to compose divine songs, and, according to the title of some Psalms and the "Selah" of others, even to direct the manner in which they should be sung and the instruments with which the singing should be accompanied. As we are sure also that such music as Elisha invited was agreeable to "the mind of the Spirit," for, otherwise, the Spirit would not have followed it; and as we further know that the Eternal Spirit is unchangeable, and that human hearts are precisely what they were; is there any reason why the same blessing should not attend the same means? The question gathers strength from the fact of holy music being not a typical but a moral ordinance. It formed no item in the Jewish ritual, as delivered by Moses: not a word is said in that ritual about music or singing as a part of divine worship, for the blowing of trumpets by the priests was a signal for worship, rather than an act of worship. Holy music, therefore, does not rank with sacrificial observances, which ceased to be requisite when the One Great Sacrifice was offered, but with such spiritual institutions as the offering of prayer and the reading of Holy Scripture.

IV. Objections to the use of instrumental music, in public worship, have often been made, but never substantiated. The New Testament is, in vain, appealed to for the support of objections; and early ecclesiastical history is summoned for the same purpose, but not really with any better success.

The main argument of the Church of Scotland, against the use of instrumental music in public worship, is this,—That, as instrumental music was employed, not in any synagogue, but only in the tabernacle and the temple, and there *only* at the time of offering sacrifice, such music was plainly ceremonial; and, being such, was abolished, when Christ, "the true temple," came down from heaven.[6] Now, this argument, if such it may be called, has two capital defects;—it assumes that to be a fact, which is not a fact, and then proves a little too much.

Instrumental music was no more ceremonial, because it accompanied a sacrifice, than was vocal music, which, also, began when a sacrifice began. There is no intimation to be found of such music, either separate or united, being typical only; while, as we have already heard, no music at all, as a part of Divine worship, was recognised in that exposition of the

---

[1] Older readers will recollect the names of Billington and Leoni Lee; while those of Braham, Henry Phillips, and Mdlle. Rachel, are still familiar. The present idol of our oratorial orchestras—Felix Mendelssohn—was, by family, *a Jew*. Bishop Lavington, when a canon of Worcester, preaching there, September 8, 1725, at the anniversary of the three choirs, said thus: "The Jews have a tradition of extraordinary music at their future conversion, when, on the restoration of Jerusalem, '*all her streets shall say, Hallelujah!*'" But "*we* have a more sure word of prophecy" in the Revelation of St. John, where *music and singing* are the constant attendants on the increase of Christ's kingdom. At the *fall*, also, of *Anti-Christianism*, contemporary with the Jews' conversion, those, who had gotten the victory over "*the Beast*," are represented with the "*harps of God*," and singing "*the song of Moses, and the song of the Lamb*." The *Lamb*, the legislator of the New Testament, has *his song*, as well as Moses.

[2] Prælectiones Poet. P. 18.
[3] Key. P. 357.
[4] Ezekiel's remark in chap. 33, ver. 32 is thought to be an allusion to it.
[5] The singing of Israel at the Red Sea is proof that the people, under even the depressing power of captivity, had attained a high degree of skill in the practice of choral antiphonal music.

[6] See "A Treatise on the Use of Organs, etc.: by the Rev. J. Begg, Glasgow, 1808;" in which the strength and *weakness* of the Scotch Church is plainly shown. The *right* of that church to decline the use of instrumental music is not likely to be denied; but to argue against its *lawfulness* in any church is somewhat of an infringement upon a neighbour's *liberty*. Singular enough, since the prevalent introduction of the piano-forte, many pious Scotch families sing their morning or evening psalm to that instrument; though *not* on the Lord's-day! This is one among other symptoms of an abatement in the severity of early prejudice.

typical services of the Jews which was made by Moses. Besides, if the argument proves anything, it proves what its advocates do not approve,—the abolition of music altogether, *vocal* as well as instrumental, in the house of God. It must do this, because, at the offering of a sacrifice, while the instrumentalists played, *the singers sang*. Whether or not the Jewish worshippers abstained from playing and singing, in a synagogue, or used both only on sacrificial occasions, is of little consequence, as they are not topics of divine authenticity. Whereas, we are divinely certified that the Hebrew believers did use holy music for holy purposes, in other places than the temple.[1] Our text is proof of that.

It is remarkable that, while the New Testament in no way discountenances the use of instrumental music, in congregational worship, it does indirectly sanction it. Not only do the apocalyptic harpings, whether past historical, millennial, or celestial, favour the views of those who contend for the use of such music; but, the very text which, on the other side, is adduced as the strongest plea against it, will, upon examination, be found the weakest. The expression, "singing and *making melody in* your *heart* to the Lord," instead of disfavouring instrumental music, actually makes, in the original Greek, such allusion to it as is altogether favourable to its use. The Greek word which is translated, "making melody," means *playing on an instrument*, or *singing with an instrument*; and, as every scholar knows, "*in* your heart" may just as properly be rendered "*with* your heart."[2] Thus, the entire phrase may literally stand in this way, "*instrumentizing*, or *psalming, with* your heart (or heartily) unto the Lord." Such a choice of words would hardly have been made, if the Holy Ghost had intended christian believers to forget and forego the use of instrumental music in their hallowed assemblies.

Nothing but *the abuse* of such music can furnish any plea against it. Wherever that abuse occurs, or is likely to occur, let vigilance and vigorous discipline be applied. This is what the early fathers did; and our own reformers followed their example. Surrounded by a heathen population, madly bent on the music of the theatre, some christian fathers interdicted the use of instruments in church-singing: while others, more remote from danger, encouraged it.[3] Because, too, of grievous perversions in the time of Edward the Sixth, honest Latimer boldly put down, for a season, both singing and playing in the cathedral of my own diocese. By one vote alone, among our reformers, and that given by proxy, were church-organs allowed to remain. Godly minds were reasonably offended at the lengthened interludes, and the wanton or over-curious performances of organists or choirs.[4] Allusions to these grievances will be found in the second part of the "Homily of the place and time of Prayer;" and in that part of the Preface to our Book of Common Prayer, which is intitled "Concerning the Service of the Church."

Happily, by God's blessing on the wisdom, piety, and moderation of our holy reformers, things took a better turn. A foundation was laid, though not without godly jealousy, for that grave, decent, and devotional style of church music which has long marked the English choir. But the jealousy of other days must not be suffered to sleep in the present day. The performance of good music is not, alas, always associated with the practice of true piety. Our clergy, therefore, will do well always to exercise that power over the musical part of the service, which the Church most unequivocally lodges with them. At the same time, we must be prepared to bear with the infirmities of tender minds. It can be no marvel that such minds are sensitive at any change or addition in the musical part of the congregational worship, however good in itself, seeing that attention to church music has sometimes been a stepping-stone to church apostacy.[5] While, however, we bear with such likely sensitiveness, we must not permit it to become unreasonable. We must shew that we know how to discriminate between the

---

[1] There was *instrumental* music *outside* the tabernacle, when David carried up the Ark to it (Psalm 24, etc.); and a *psalm* was sung on closing the doors in the evening, and on opening them in the morning (see Bishop Patrick on Psalm 134 and 135.) Other occasions, on which instrumental music was used, apart from all *typical* reference, are too obvious to require mention.

A fellow of Balliol college, in the 17th century, turned the table of *this* notion of *type* against the opponents of instrumental music in his day. He contended that David, as a musical king, was a type of a musical Messiah; and that the many instruments made by the one were intimations of the abundance which should be used during the reign of the other.

[2] "Be filled *with* the Spirit" is the same form of expression. That the Apostle could *not* mean any *silent* melody *within* the heart, as opposed to audible sounds by the lips, is evident from his wishing christians to speak to and admonish one another by *the act of singing*.

[3] St. Basil, Hom. in Psalm 1; Clemens Alexadrinus, Pœdag., Lib. ii. c. 4; St. Augustine in various works; St. Cypr. Epist. ad Donatum, "Prolectat aures religiosa *mulcedo*."

[4] Profane liberties, such as descanting all sorts of lewd ballads on the plain song, became so gross and enormous, that the Pope and the Council of Trent were obliged to interfere. Romanist writers rather freely admit the horrible fact. Some of our own choristers and singing-men are not altogether innocent on such score.

[5] The gradation has been somewhat thus: the antique (without distinguishing between the true and the false) is venerable. The Gregorian music is very antique, and therefore very venerable. But the Church of Rome alone retains and practises it; and so that Church is worthy of every musical man's veneration. Another step or two completes the fatal plunge.

The *talk* of younger aspirants about Gregory and Tallis is sometimes painfully amusing; while the attempts, in certain quarters, to foster Gregorianism, are based neither upon truth nor common sense. The practice, also, of organists and editors calling certain modified versions "Gregorian chants," is as delusive in itself as it is contemptible in the estimation of Romanists. Who would exhibit a jeweller's trinket as a specimen of *native* Californian gold?—or describe a fleece of wool by shewing a piece of broadcloth?

safe and the unsafe,—between what is good as well as lawful, and what *is*, certainly in these unsettling days, *not* expedient. In a word, we may hold fast to the fact, which, in spite of efforts to wrest it from us, is still a fact, that our ecclesiastical authorities never contemplated what is called "*full cathedral service*" being the order for *parish* churches.[1]

V. As a mechanical combination of instruments, an organ is admirably adapted to supply the place of Hebrew minstrels. At an early period organs, such as they were, found admission into the Christian church. The precise date, however, of their admission is so conflictingly stated by historians that no certain conclusion can be formed. With the exception of a vague quotation by the Venerable Bede, we meet with nothing on the subject before the year 650. Other writers carry it on to the year 820.[2] But, it is tolerably certain that, although St. Dunstan, as he is called, was the great patron of organs in the tenth century, their use in the cathedrals and larger churches of England was not common till just before the blessed Reformation. Indeed, it is not two centuries ago since lutenists, or minstrels, were as much in office as organists now are.

The advance of skill, and the increase of facilities, have brought organs into almost all our parochial churches. And now that an organ of larger contents and better quality than before is erected within your own elegant and beautiful church, the friend of your beloved pastor may well congratulate you. He, I am sure, has not, in its erection, sought to provide his flock with either attraction or amusement; but rather to put the choral part of divine service under such auxiliary guidance as will help you, with increased freshness and exhilaration, to laud and praise that holy Saviour to whom alone all song is due.

VI. Henceforth, then, because of your greater facilities for singing the praises of the Lamb, you will be under greater responsibilities to promote such singing, either by studying to join in it, or, if that be impracticable, by listening, *with all your heart*, to the singing of others.

If, in the same hallowed temper, as Elisha said, "Bring me a minstrel," you have said, "Build us an organ," you may reasonably expect that the God of Elisha will visit you, not indeed with the spirit of prophecy, but with the spirit of grace and edification. You may expect your God to bless the use of that organ, for your greater composure of mind, sanctity of spirit, and fervency of affection, as often as you come up to worship Him within these inviting walls. Remember, also, that what Elisha sought, in the use of a minstrel, was nothing less than the inspiration of the Holy Spirit. For that selfsame Spirit we are to seek, not only in every act of our lives, but in the worship of God especially. We are admonished to "walk in the Spirit," and to abound in "the fruits of the Spirit," as daily parts of our christian calling: but, when we apply ourselves to the direct worship of the Triune God, then is it that we most need the hand of the Lord to come upon us. "God is a Spirit; and they that worship him (whether with prayer or praise) must worship him in spirit and in truth." Consonant with these words of our Lord, the words of his apostle may now, in a modified sense, be understood and applied, "I will sing with the Spirit," and "I will pray with the Spirit:" not that we by them mean to express any expectation of being so inspired, or wrought into such a rapture, as was common in the pentecostal age, when members of the church were enabled to stand forth and pray or sing extemporaneously, in a marvellously lofty, edifying, and hallowing manner. No. This is not our expectation: but we are bound to seek the grace and power of the Spirit, to kindle in us warm and steady affections; that the melody of the heart may find its tuneful outlet by the lips, and that what we sing with our lips may, by a becoming reaction, edify our hearts,

Taught by our Scriptural Church to learn true doctrine from Holy Scripture alone, and to pray for the cleansing of our hearts by the inspiration of the Holy Spirit, we, surely, after the example of Elisha, may seek for the grace of that Spirit by the same means as he sought it. "It came to pass, when the minstrel *played*, the hand of the Lord came upon him." This, undoubtedly, certifies us that there is in holy music a power which the Spirit of God can use for the loftiest purposes. Christians are too prone to give way to the policy of Satan in underrating the true value, and in lowering the real dignity, of genuine music. They regard it chiefly as sensuous, and therefore capable of acting only on the animal feelings. With this low view of a divinely elevating medium, we cannot wonder that they meet, with timidity and suspicion, any excitation of which they may be sensible, from the power of musical sounds, in a church or a cathedral. But, all such reluctance to avail themselves of a scripturally legitimate means of calming, elevating, or hallowing their minds, is like giving up a large space of vantage ground to the wily god of this world. So long as he, by music, can exhilarate the votaries of folly, and keep the children of God in fear of being cheered by it, so long will he be gaining a certain advantage over them. If, however, he, by "*pretty* tunes,"

---

[1] See a Sermon by Dr. Thomas Bisse, Chancellor of Hereford, in the cathedral of that city, at the anniversary of the three choirs, Sept. 7, 1720. That learned divine and sound churchman was of opinion, that "*saying*" is *fitter* than "*singing*" for our liturgical service in parish churches. Chanting of the prayers, as it is called, is based, he argues, on *necessity*, in large and resonant buildings, and not on any supposed inherent fitness.

[2] See the History of Music, by Dr. Burney, and that by Sir J. Hawkins, in loco. An ancient organ, at Munich, was a sort of monster bagpipe, being formed of an elephant's hide and twelve bored box trees!

can call up all sorts of passions in his dupes and devotees, do let us, in the use of good and hallowed tunes,[1] be willing for the hand of the Lord to come upon us!

The reasonable expectation of this blessed result from holy music was, most likely, the ground of that ancient custom which Queen Elisabeth recognised, when she sanctioned the singing of a hymn, or such like song, at *the beginning*, as well as at the end, of common prayer. Universal custom, also, (and it is still sedulously observed in our universities) has recognised the same ground, in the singing of a psalm or hymn, always *before* the homily or sermon. In our cathedrals, soft and sweet playing has, of late years, been substituted for singing then; because, it would seem, much has been previously sung. In either case, the principle is, and the expectation ought to be, the same. Our Reformers, however, went much beyond many among us, in approaching the mark which the text sets before us. They encouraged singing, not only before sermon, but after it. We are wont to think that singing is apt to diminish the impression of a sermon, but they thought it would deepen it. This difference arises from our giving way to that lax and low view (unintentional, I can believe) to which allusion has been made. How one of our Reformers, yea, that one to whom we are as much indebted as to any, expressed himself on this topic, you shall hear, by an extract of a letter of Bishop Jewel to Peter Martyr, dated London, March 5, 1560.

Religion is now somewhat more established than it was. The people are everywhere exceedingly inclined to the better part. The practice of joining in church music has very much conduced to this. For, as soon as they had once commenced singing in public, in only one little church[2] in London, immediately not only the churches in the neighbourhood, but even the towns far distant, began to vie with each other in the same practice. You may now sometimes see at Paul's Cross, *after the service*, six thousand persons, old and young, both sexes, singing together and praising God. This sadly annoys the mass-priests and the Devil. For they perceive that by these means the sacred discourses sink more deeply into the minds of men, and that their kingdom is weakened and shaken at almost every note. (Zurich Letters, Parker Soc., p. 71.)

Now discourses cannot sink deeply into the minds of men, unless the hand of the Lord come upon them. Bishop Jewel was of opinion that that hand did come upon hearers, in his day, by means "of joining in church music." Here, therefore, as churchmen, you have authority, and, as christians, encouragement.[3] May it, then, be that henceforward your increased attention to the pleasant duty of vocal and instrumental praise shall witness the coming of the hand of the Lord upon you, at once for your more perfect perception of divine truth, and for your greater consolation in it.

VII. But, when we speak thus of singing, and of the Holy Spirit, let our thoughts firmly apprehend him who is "worthy" of every song, and by whom alone we receive the Spirit—the Holy Lamb, the Lord Jesus, "who taketh away the sin of the world." He is the grand object of all adoration and all praise. To Him Elisha, as one in "the goodly fellowship of the prophets," "gave witness." Never should it be out of mind with us, that our sins cost his sorrows, and that by those sorrows we have songs. But for his crying, with a loud and lamentable voice, "It is finished," no sound of minstrel-song would ever have been heard in our world. Unless the Eternal Father had heard that voice, "lamentation, and mourning, and woe," would have been the doleful melodies of unredeemed mankind. Because, also, after his atoning death and glorious resurrection, he ascended up on high and received gifts for men, we may hope for the grace of the Holy Ghost to come upon us, in the exercise of that minstrelsy with which we are invited to come into his presence.

VIII. Nor should we ever cease to recollect that, as there is "the *prayer* of faith," so also must there be the *song* of faith. No petition can ascend to heaven "without faith" in the One Great Mediator; and no praise can glorify God but such as is offered in the name of his beloved Son. Elisha, we may be assured, did not look for the coming of the hand of the Lord upon him *merely* by the agency of minstrel-music: doubtless the fingers and lips of the minstrel were not more intently employed than was the heart of the prophet,—while the one was performing, the other was seeking, desiring, believing. Thus, in all our offerings of holy song, there must be the conformable affections of the heart,—that spirit-sung melody, which, wafted on the breath of faith, mounts to the ear of God. While that song is progressing, the soul is to be communing with its Saviour, or glancing with ethereal rapidity at eternal realities, or grasping some precious truth, vividly seen and intensely felt. It is not, perhaps, too much to assert, that some of the most thrilling emotions of which the sanctified heart is capable are experienced during the singing of a psalm or hymn in the great congregation. Apart from some merely tender or touching associations, what more elevating or affecting consideration

---

[1] The progress of the restoration of *good* tunes to our parish churches is slow, but, seemingly, sure. Wherever the *old* tunes of the Church, or new ones *like* them, are introduced, congregational singing flourishes. A revised and an enlarged edition of "Old Church Psalmody," by the Author, is in the press, printed and published by J. Hart, 109, Hatton Garden, London.

[2] St. Antholin's; where the people used to assemble, at five o'clock, every morning.

[3] The beautiful hymns in our Ordination Service are hymns to the Spirit and *for* the Spirit.

can be presented to those who join in singing than this?—"I am now engaged," each helper of the song may say, "in that work which occupies my departed fellows, my holy kindred, above;—in that which shall be the delight of the whole earth, in its millennial age;[1]—in that which shall be the business and the bliss of the elect of God to all eternity!" Oh! may the hand of the Lord come upon us more frequently than ever for the production of these blessed effects! Such desire is necessary; because singing without spiritual-mindedness, or any musical service without vital religion, will but insult the Saviour and cheat the soul.

IX. Let me not wind up this discourse without reminding you that the sight and sound of your new organ should freshen your attention to a great moral truth. *Our God is a God of order, harmony, and love.* He has made *everything* in his church subservient to *something*; while the well-arranged and well-ordered whole is subservient to himself. From this order follows harmony. He loves his saints, and they are to love one another.

Now, an organ is a fair type of such arrangement. It is composed of various materials, of sundry parts, of many kinds of pipes, some large and some small, some loud and some soft; and yet, though everything in it is dependent on something, the whole is fitly joined together, and capable, at the touch of a master-hand, of yielding goodly harmony. Let it not, then, be deemed inopportune to say, that your parish, your church congregation, your individual souls, should henceforth be more and more like your new organ. "Seek peace, and ensue it." Let every man, in that station of life in which it hath pleased God to call him, strive for moral harmony and spiritual brotherhood. Let him who is placed in an humble station, like some tiny, and obscure pipe, be *content*; and him who stands on a greater scale, in the front of society, be *useful*: and let all "love as brethren." So, also in what is the core and vitality, the very essentiality of the moral organ,—*the church congregation,*—let the same principle be carried out. Assembling under one roof, where "one Lord, one faith, one baptism" is acknowledged, there let every worshipper, like Elisha, when calling for a minstrel, desire to forget all rufflings and perturbations, seeking only the spirit of love, "peace, unity, and concord." Such spiritual harmony is always grateful to the ear of Him who heareth not as man heareth. Nowhere, too, is it more grateful than when practised around his own table, where, "with angels and archangels and all the company of heaven, we laud and magnify his glorious Name."

And, what shall we say to the man of the world who loves music, but who does not love religion;—who, perchance, likes both sacred and ecclesiastical music, but does not like to be told that he may, almost with rapture, hear or perform such music, and yet "lose his own soul"? We pity that person, whether male or female, who is in this case, because there is something winning, something sympathetic, in even the love of music. But it is grievous, even to anguish, to think that such individuals are loving that which will not only not last them long, but which must be exchanged for something appallingly opposite. They dream of being musical for ever, and frivolously fancy that they shall hear the songs of heaven: but it is a fearful dream, and a terrific fancy. Unless the hand of the Lord come upon them *now*, and create in them a new heart and a new spirit, they will never become jubilant minstrels in the choirs above, but wailing fiends in the dungeons below. No tuneful sound will ever be heard by them there; but their own voice, and every other voice around them, will be, more truly than was fantastically said in another instance, the horrid "*concentration of a thousand screams.*" "There shall be weeping, and wailing, and gnashing of teeth." God grant to all, who hear this note of warning, "repentance unto life."

X. And, now, "beloved in the Lord," is there need of exhortation to elicit your generous contributions? I trust not. Christian generosity should never require "the enticing words of man's wisdom" to call it forth. It should be as free to give, as your new organ is to speak. A touch on that is enough: a word with you should be sufficient. And it will be sufficient with all, who see in the minutest parts of the enlightened worship of the Saviour a dignity and an importance, which surpass all earthly splendours. When that sight strikes the mental eye, it will be even joy to the heart to forward whatever sets forth the honour or the praise of the only Redeemer. Your help is this day asked, not only for the bringing of minstrel-power into your church, but for furnishing seats for little scholars, who, it is presumed, will soon learn to follow its sounds, and swell your congregational songs. The singing of children in a church is always interesting. Something of the sort once pleased the ear of him whom, though not seen, you love. Their little voices will be heard in the Lord's house long after ours are silent in the dust. Themselves also will remember the opening, on this day, of your organ, when our memories have left us, or we have left the world. These thoughts should touch us. Especially should we be touched by the music of that Name, which "is as ointment poured forth." It will cheer us by day, and give us "songs in the night." It will prepare us, too, for a song which is prepared for us, when all earthly scenes are ended, and when the hand of the Lord shall so come upon us that we shall sing and not be weary, and shout everlastingly to the Lamb, and yet not be faint. Amen and Amen.

---

[1] "Perhaps the singing and music at the sanctuary were mentioned, as external expressions of that joy and praise, *which would most abound in the church,* after the coming of the Messiah." Scott, on Psalm 87:7.

www.ingramcontent.com/pod-product-compliance
Lightning Source LLC
Chambersburg PA
CBHW081919180426
43200CB00032B/2855